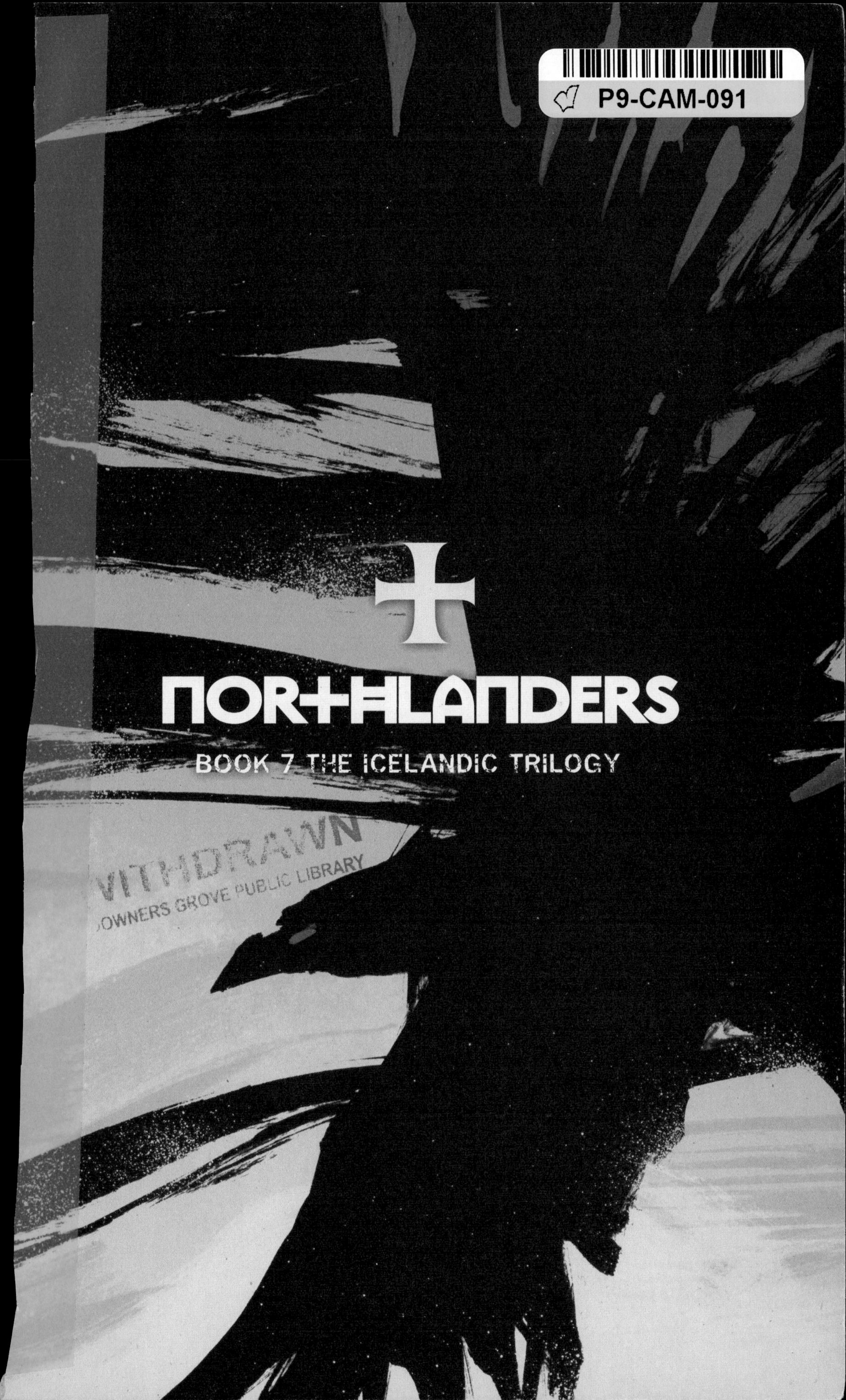
NORTHLANDERS
BOOK 7 THE ICELANDIC TRILOGY

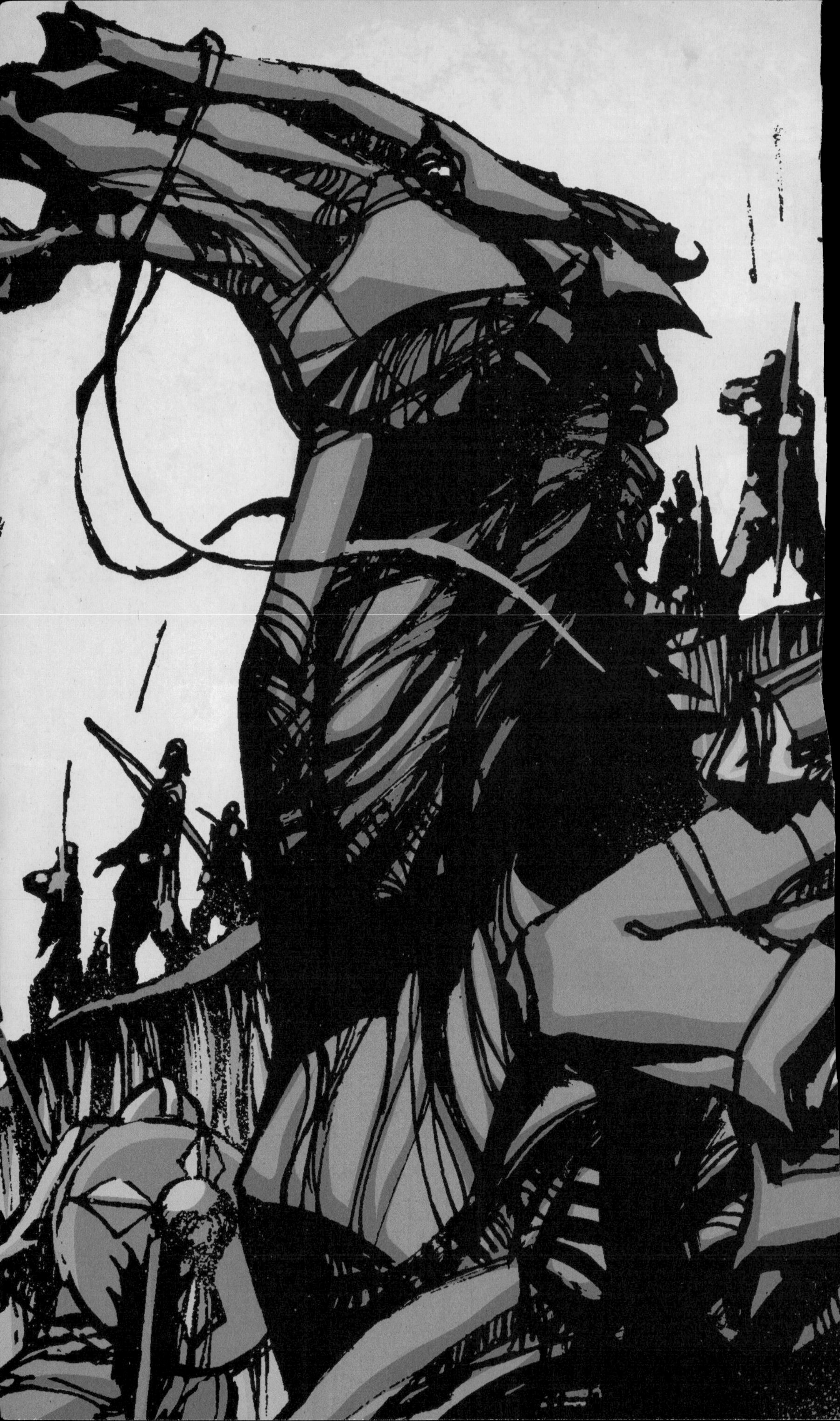

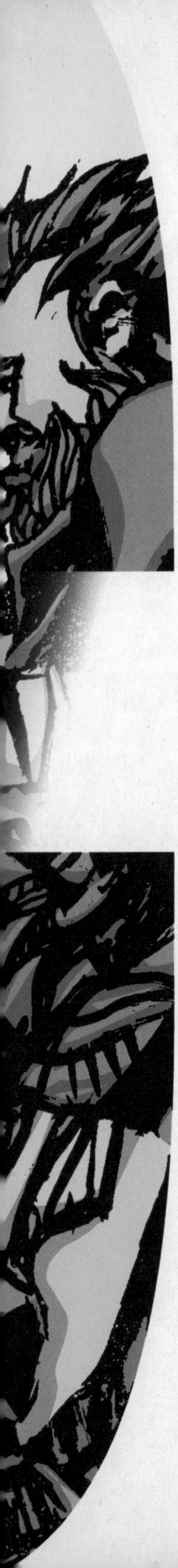

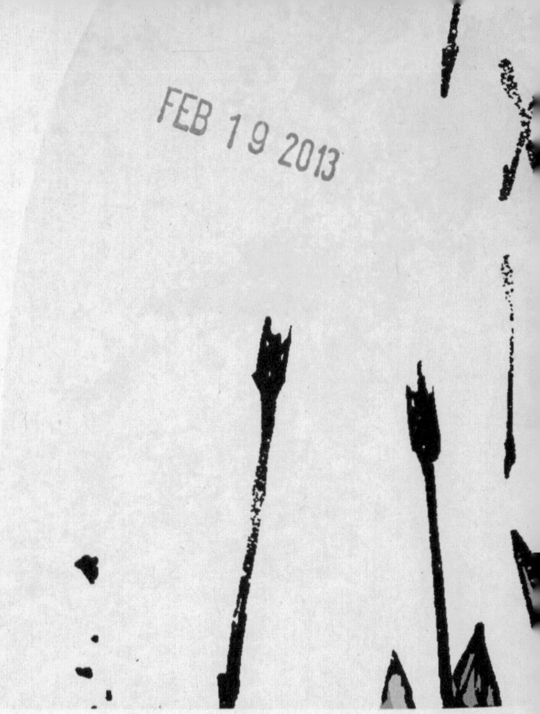

NORTHLANDERS

BOOK 7 THE ICELANDIC TRILOGY

Brian Wood Writer

Paul Azaceta
Artist – "SETTLEMENT 871," "SECURITY 880" & "SLAVERY 886"

Declan Shalvey
Artist – "CONVERSION 999," "CHRISTIANITY 999" & "COMMERCE 1000"

Danijel Zezelj
Artist – "WAR 1260," "WEALTH 1260" & "WAYGONE 1260"

Dave McCaig Colorist

Travis Lanham Letterer

Cover art and original series covers by
Massimo Carnevale

Cover design by Brian Wood

Northlanders created by
Brian Wood

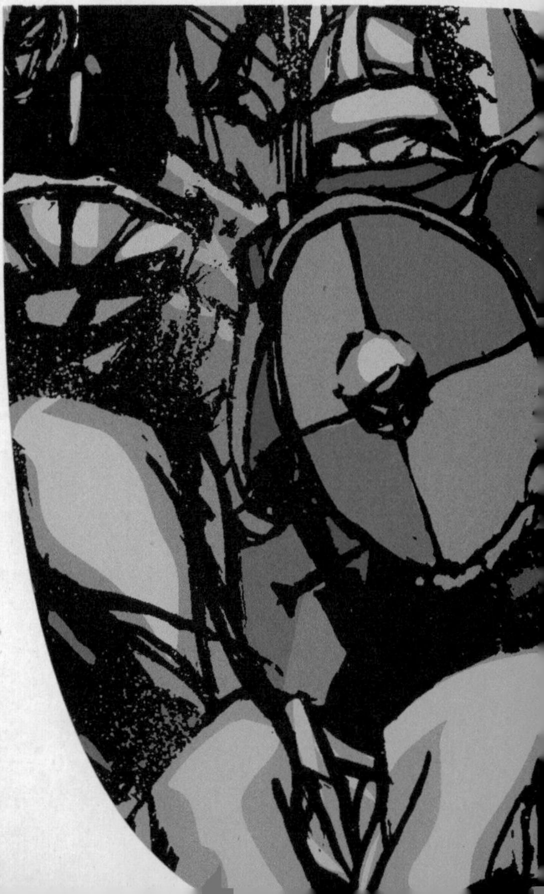

Mark Doyle Editor – Original Series **Rowena Yow** Editor.
Robbin Brosterman Design Director – Books

Karen Berger Senior VP – Executive Editor, Vertigo **Bob Harras** VP – Editor-in-Chief

Diane Nelson President **Dan DiDio** and **Jim Lee** Co-Publishers **Geoff Johns** Chief Creative Officer
John Rood Executive VP – Sales, Marketing and Business Development **Amy Genkins** Senior VP – Business and Legal Affairs
Nairi Gardiner Senior VP – Finance **Jeff Boison** VP – Publishing Operations **Mark Chiarello** VP – Art Direction and Design
John Cunningham VP – Marketing **Terri Cunningham** VP – Talent Relations and Services
Alison Gill Senior VP – Manufacturing and Operations **Hank Kanalz** Senior VP – Digital
Jay Kogan VP – Business and Legal Affairs, Publishing **Jack Mahan** VP – Business Affairs, Talent
Nick Napolitano VP – Manufacturing Administration **Sue Pohja** VP – Book Sales
Courtney Simmons Senior VP – Publicity **Bob Wayne** Senior VP – Sales

NORTHLANDERS VOLUME 7: THE ICELANDIC TRILOGY

DC Comics, 1700 Broadway, New York, NY 10019. A Warner Bros. Entertainment Company.
Printed in the USA. 11/23/12. First Printing. ISBN: 978-1-4012-3691-5

Library of Congress Cataloging-in-Publication Data

Wood, Brian, 1972-
Northlanders. Volume 7, The icelandic trilogy / Brian Wood, Paul Azaceta, Declan Shalvey, Danijel Zezelj.
p. cm.
"Originally published in single magazine form in Northlanders 42-50."
ISBN 978-1-4012-3691-5 (alk. paper)
1. Vikings--Comic books, strips, etc. 2. Graphic novels. I. Azaceta, Paul. II. Shalvey, Declan. III. Zezelj, Danijel. IV. Title. V. Title: Icelandic trilogy.
PN6727.W59N678 2012
741.5'973--dc23

Part One Settlement 871

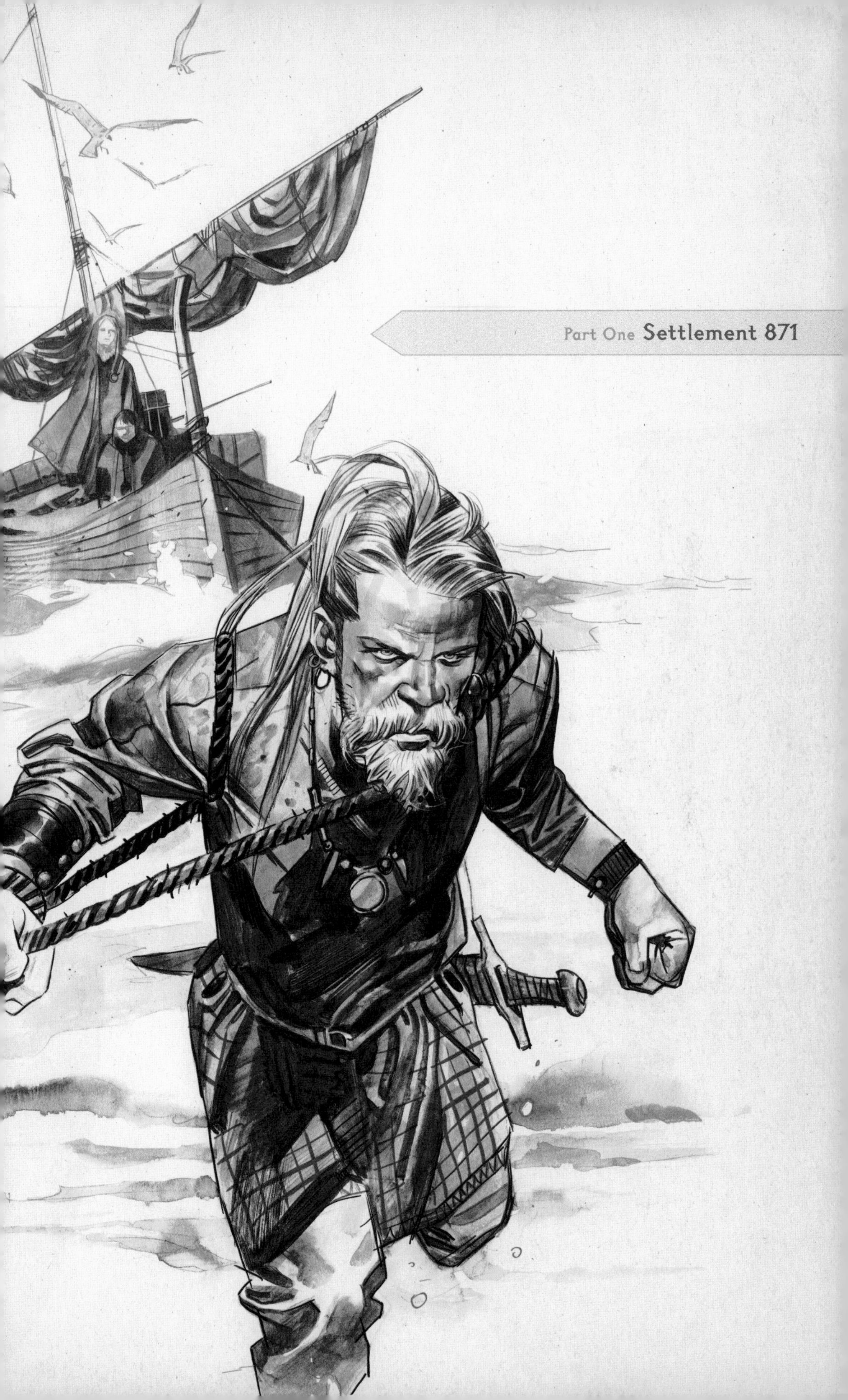

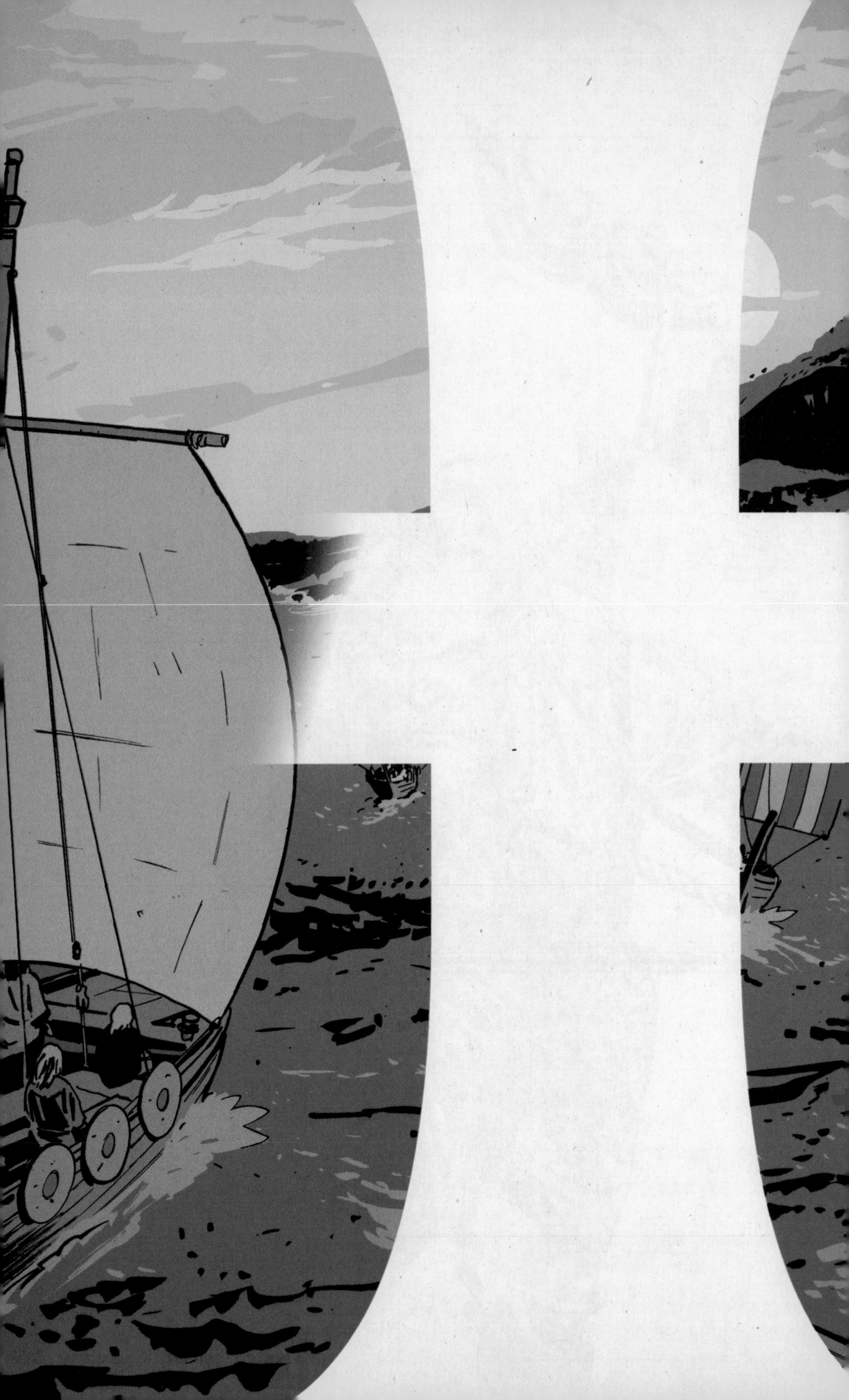

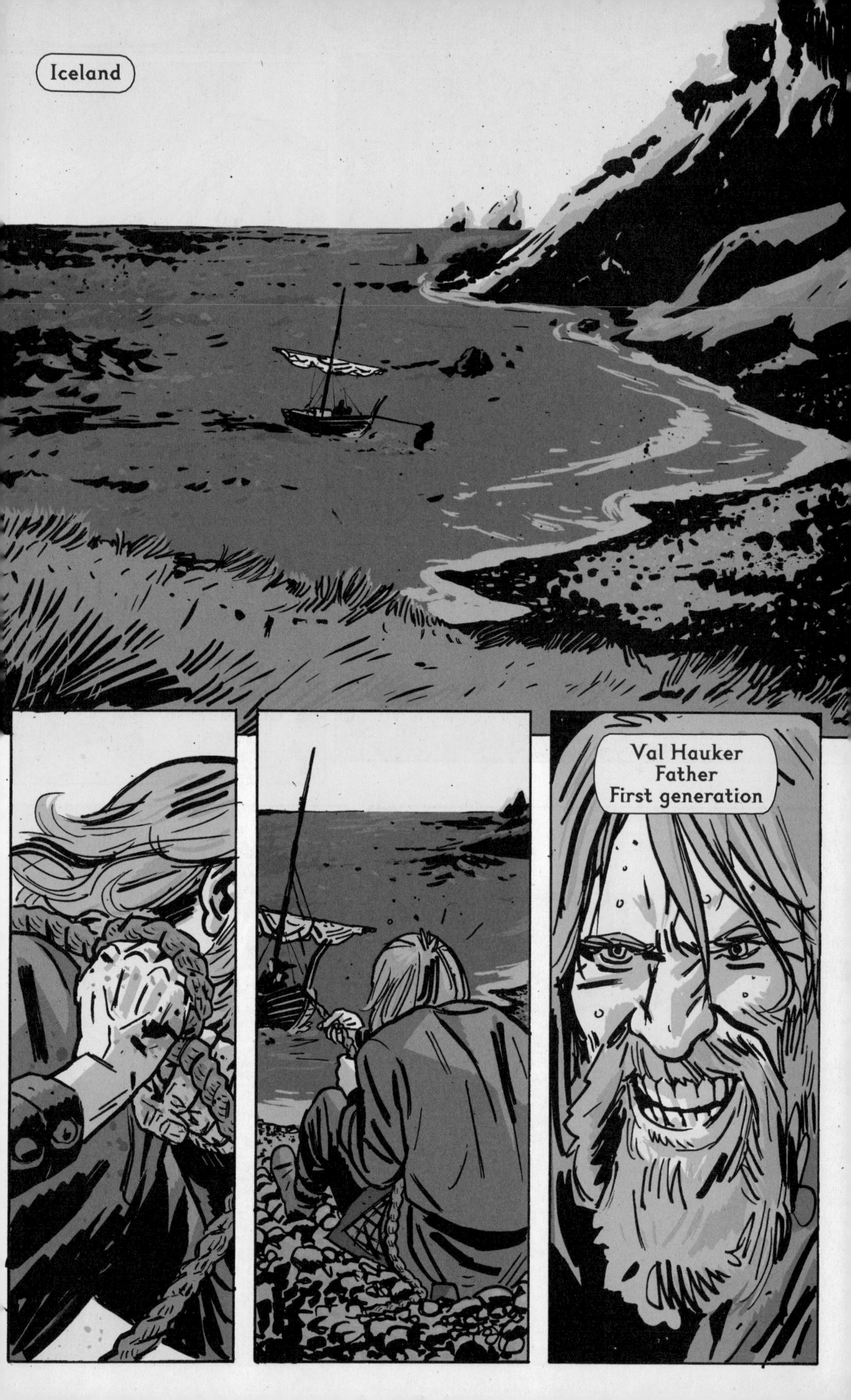
Iceland
Val Hauker
Father
First generation

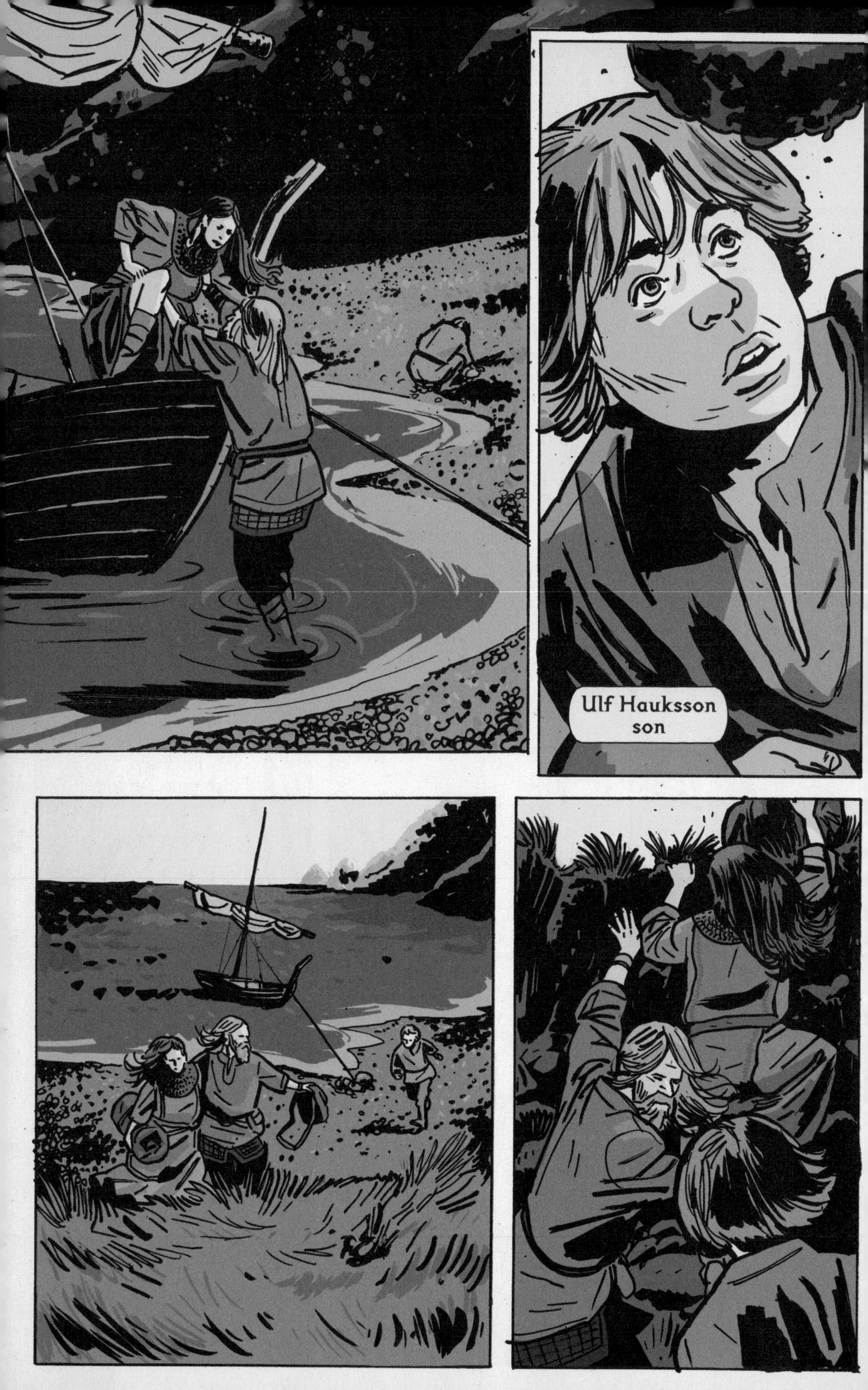
Ulf Hauksson son

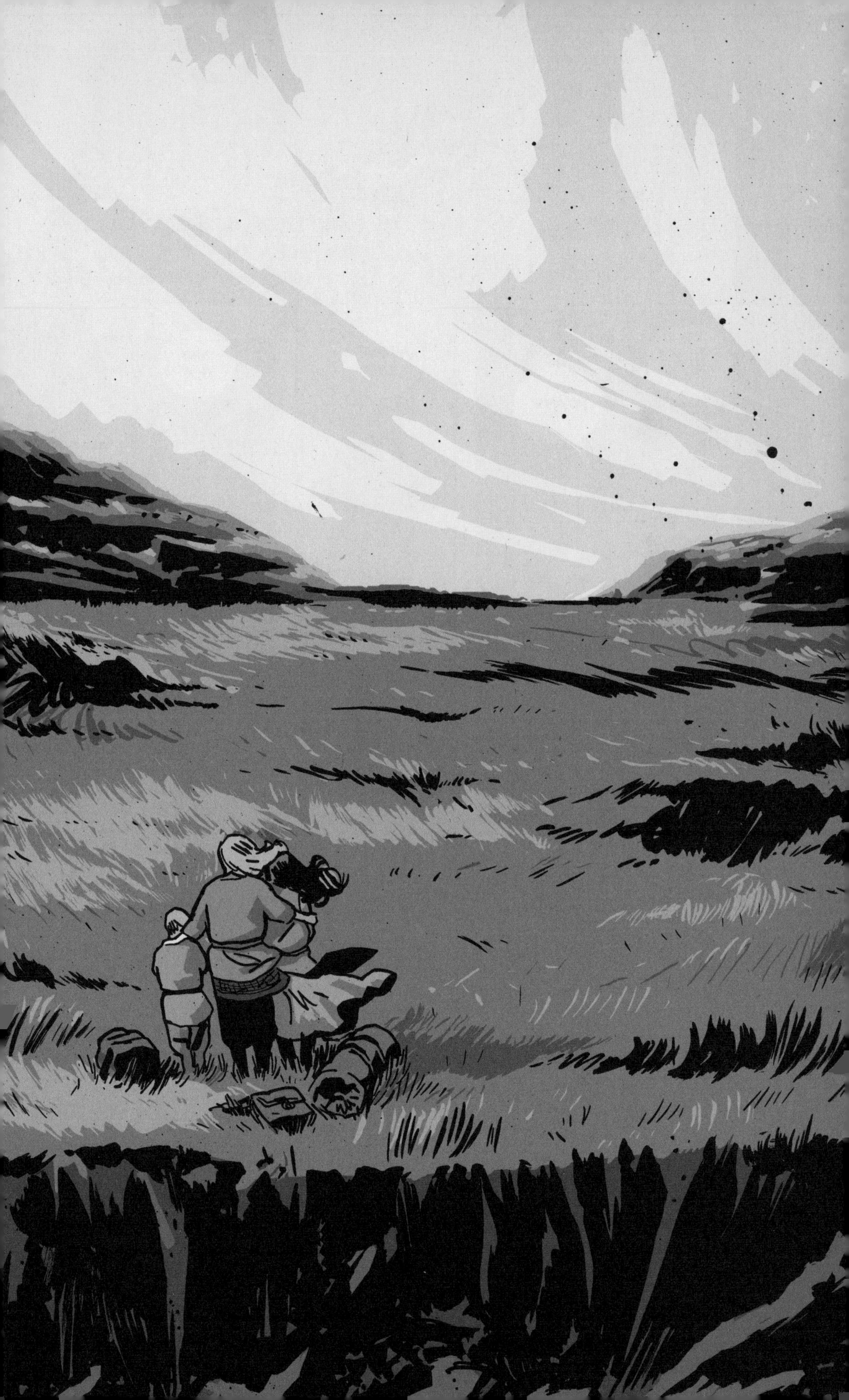

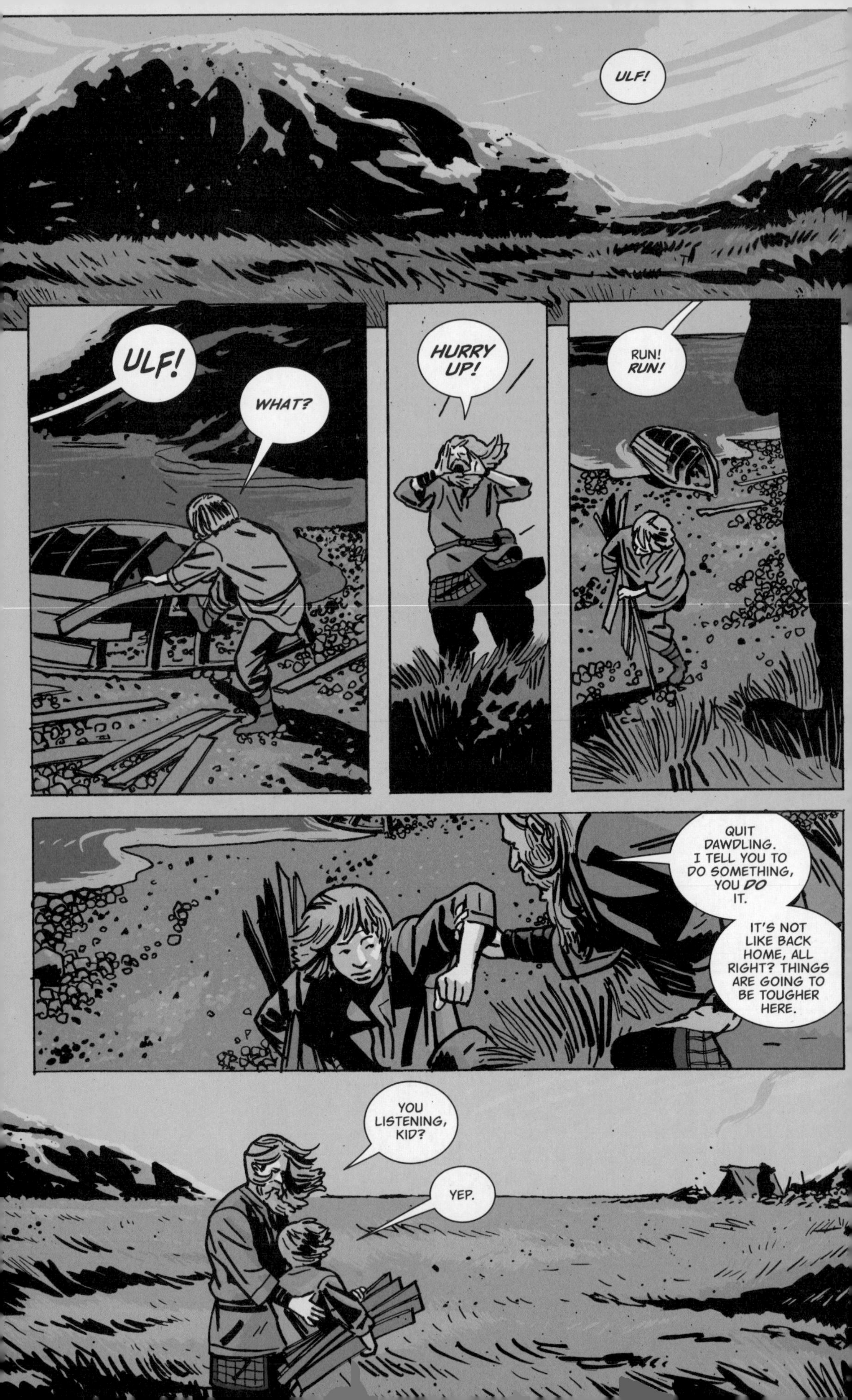
ULF!
ULF!
WHAT?
HURRY UP!
RUN! RUN!
QUIT DAWDLING. I TELL YOU TO DO SOMETHING, YOU DO IT.
IT'S NOT LIKE BACK HOME, ALL RIGHT? THINGS ARE GOING TO BE TOUGHER HERE.
YOU LISTENING, KID?
YEP.

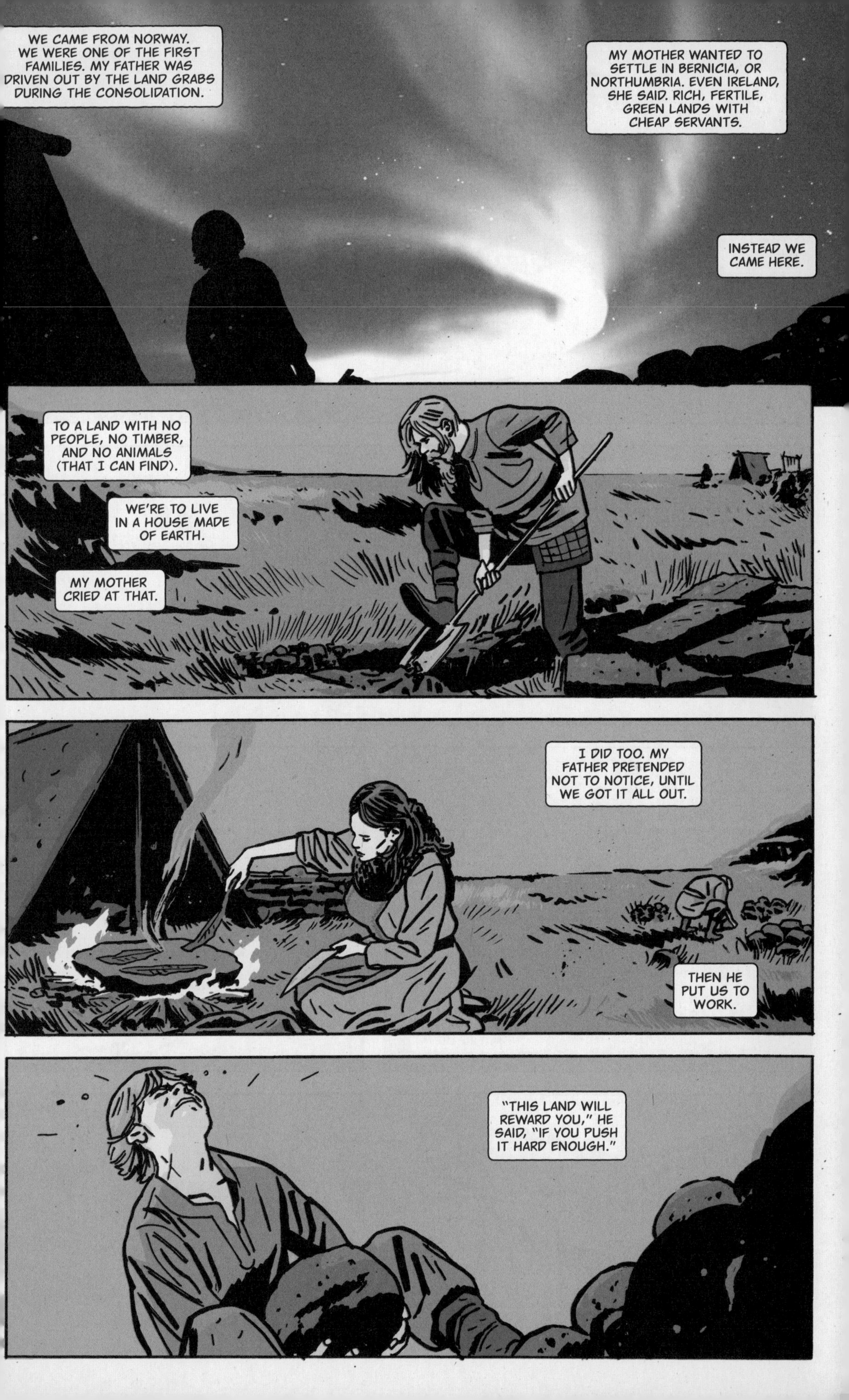
WE CAME FROM NORWAY. WE WERE ONE OF THE FIRST FAMILIES. MY FATHER WAS DRIVEN OUT BY THE LAND GRABS DURING THE CONSOLIDATION.
MY MOTHER WANTED TO SETTLE IN BERNICIA, OR NORTHUMBRIA. EVEN IRELAND, SHE SAID. RICH, FERTILE, GREEN LANDS WITH CHEAP SERVANTS.
INSTEAD WE CAME HERE.
TO A LAND WITH NO PEOPLE, NO TIMBER, AND NO ANIMALS (THAT I CAN FIND).
WE'RE TO LIVE IN A HOUSE MADE OF EARTH.
MY MOTHER CRIED AT THAT.
I DID TOO. MY FATHER PRETENDED NOT TO NOTICE, UNTIL WE GOT IT ALL OUT.
THEN HE PUT US TO WORK.
"THIS LAND WILL REWARD YOU," HE SAID, "IF YOU PUSH IT HARD ENOUGH."

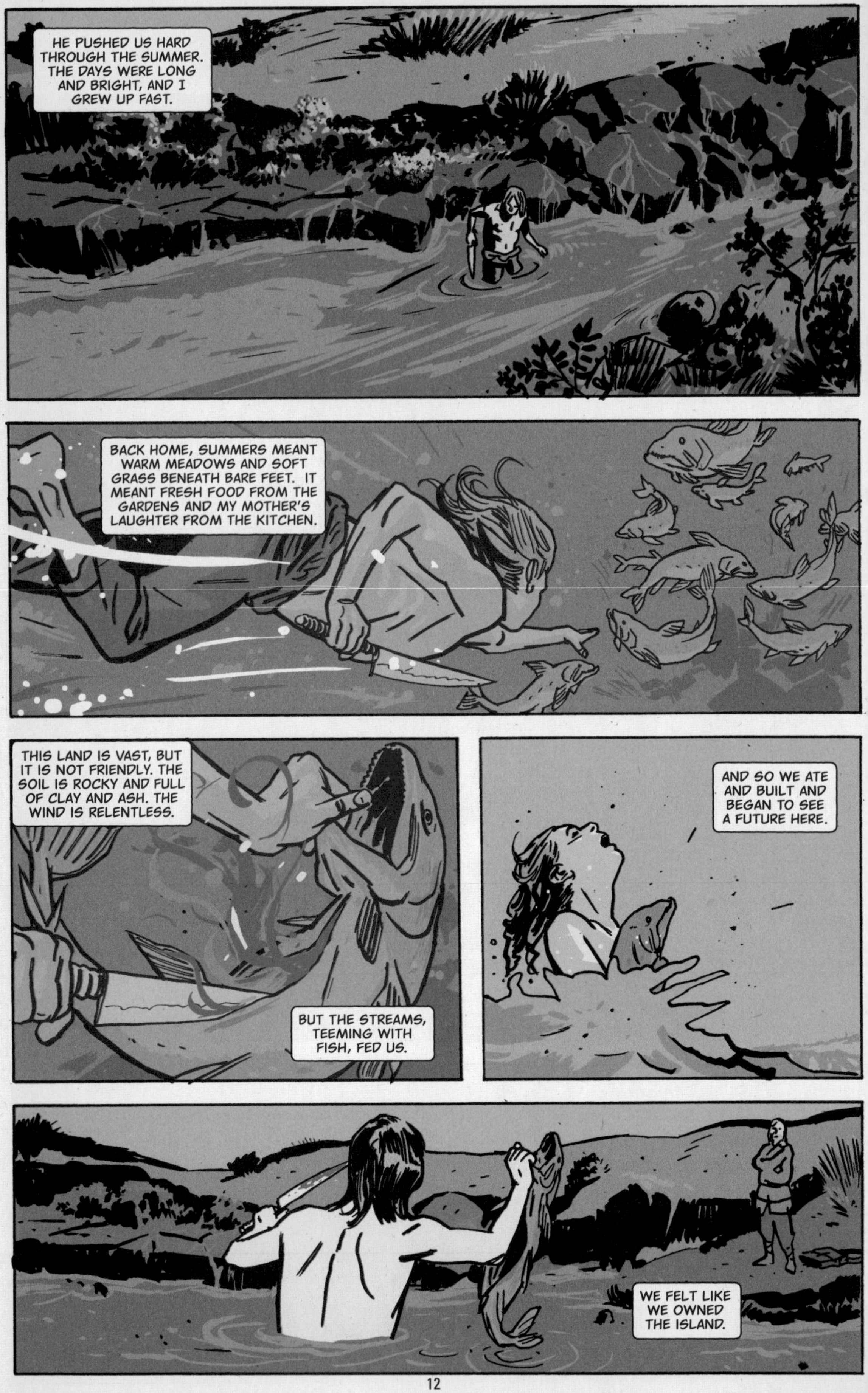
HE PUSHED US HARD THROUGH THE SUMMER. THE DAYS WERE LONG AND BRIGHT, AND I GREW UP FAST.
BACK HOME, SUMMERS MEANT WARM MEADOWS AND SOFT GRASS BENEATH BARE FEET. IT MEANT FRESH FOOD FROM THE GARDENS AND MY MOTHER'S LAUGHTER FROM THE KITCHEN.
THIS LAND IS VAST, BUT IT IS NOT FRIENDLY. THE SOIL IS ROCKY AND FULL OF CLAY AND ASH. THE WIND IS RELENTLESS.
BUT THE STREAMS, TEEMING WITH FISH, FED US.
AND SO WE ATE AND BUILT AND BEGAN TO SEE A FUTURE HERE.
WE FELT LIKE WE OWNED THE ISLAND.

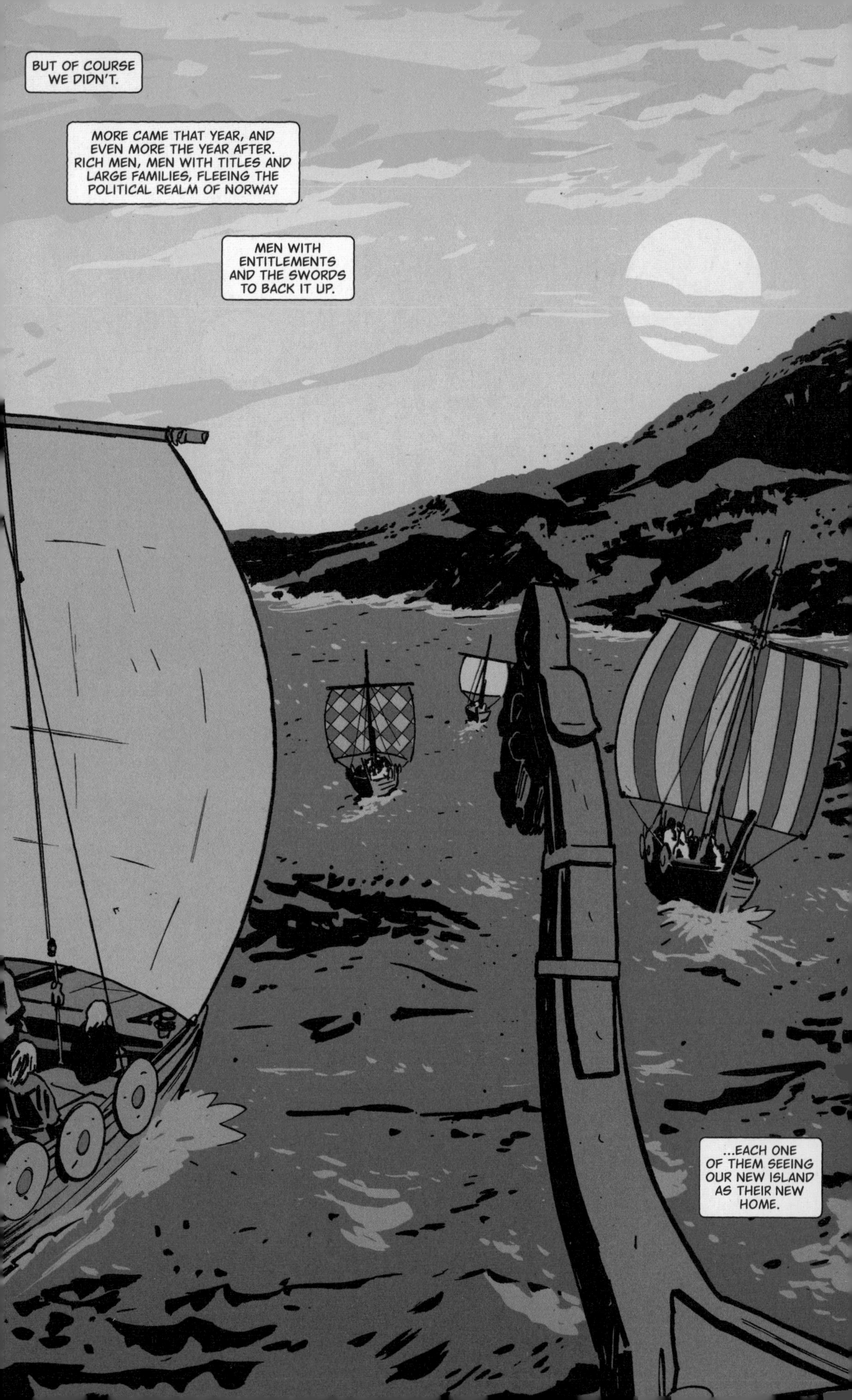
BUT OF COURSE WE DIDN'T.
MORE CAME THAT YEAR, AND EVEN MORE THE YEAR AFTER. RICH MEN, MEN WITH TITLES AND LARGE FAMILIES, FLEEING THE POLITICAL REALM OF NORWAY
MEN WITH ENTITLEMENTS AND THE SWORDS TO BACK IT UP.
...EACH ONE OF THEM SEEING OUR NEW ISLAND AS THEIR NEW HOME.

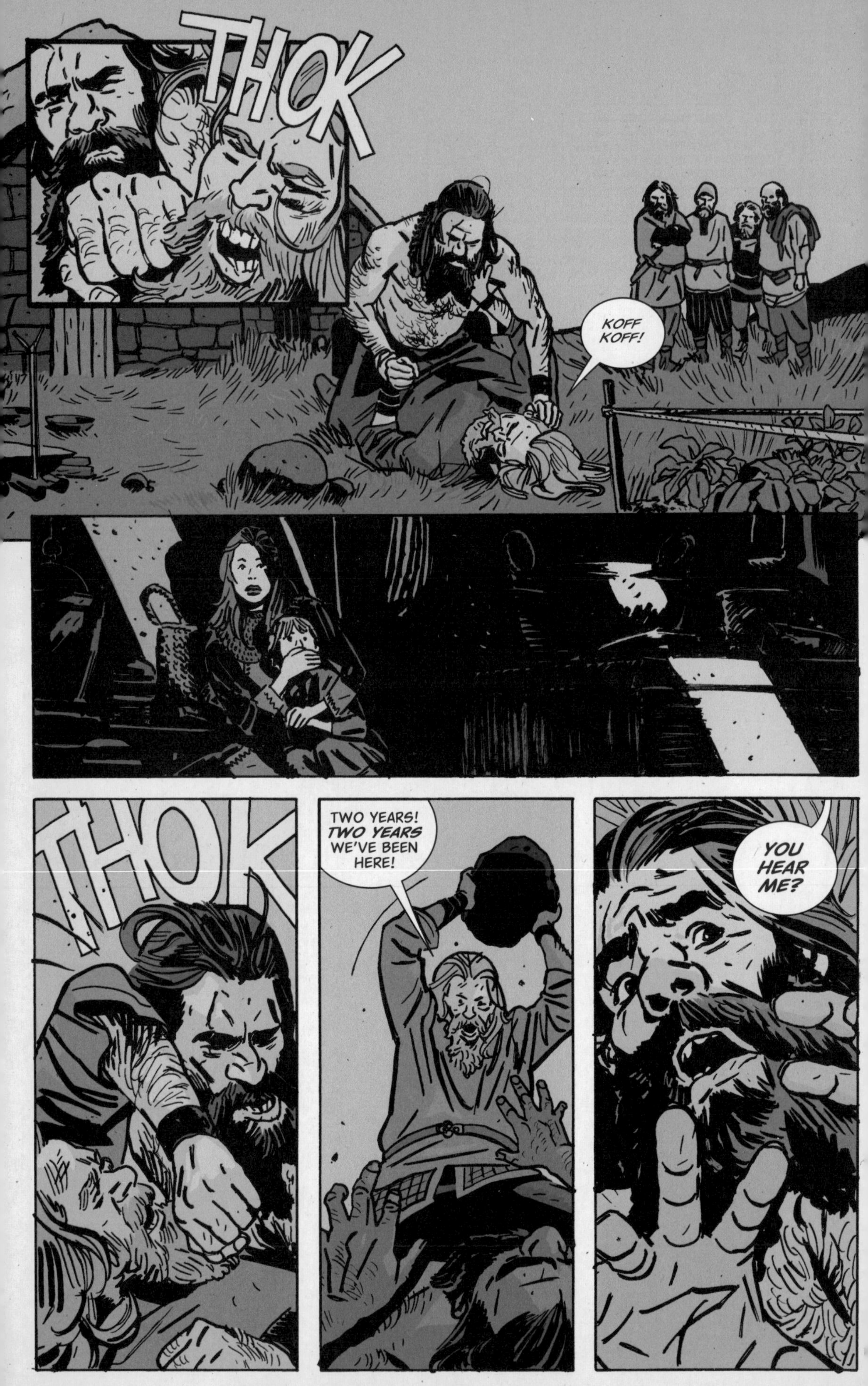
THOK
KOFF KOFF!
THOK
TWO YEARS! *TWO YEARS* WE'VE BEEN HERE!
YOU HEAR ME?

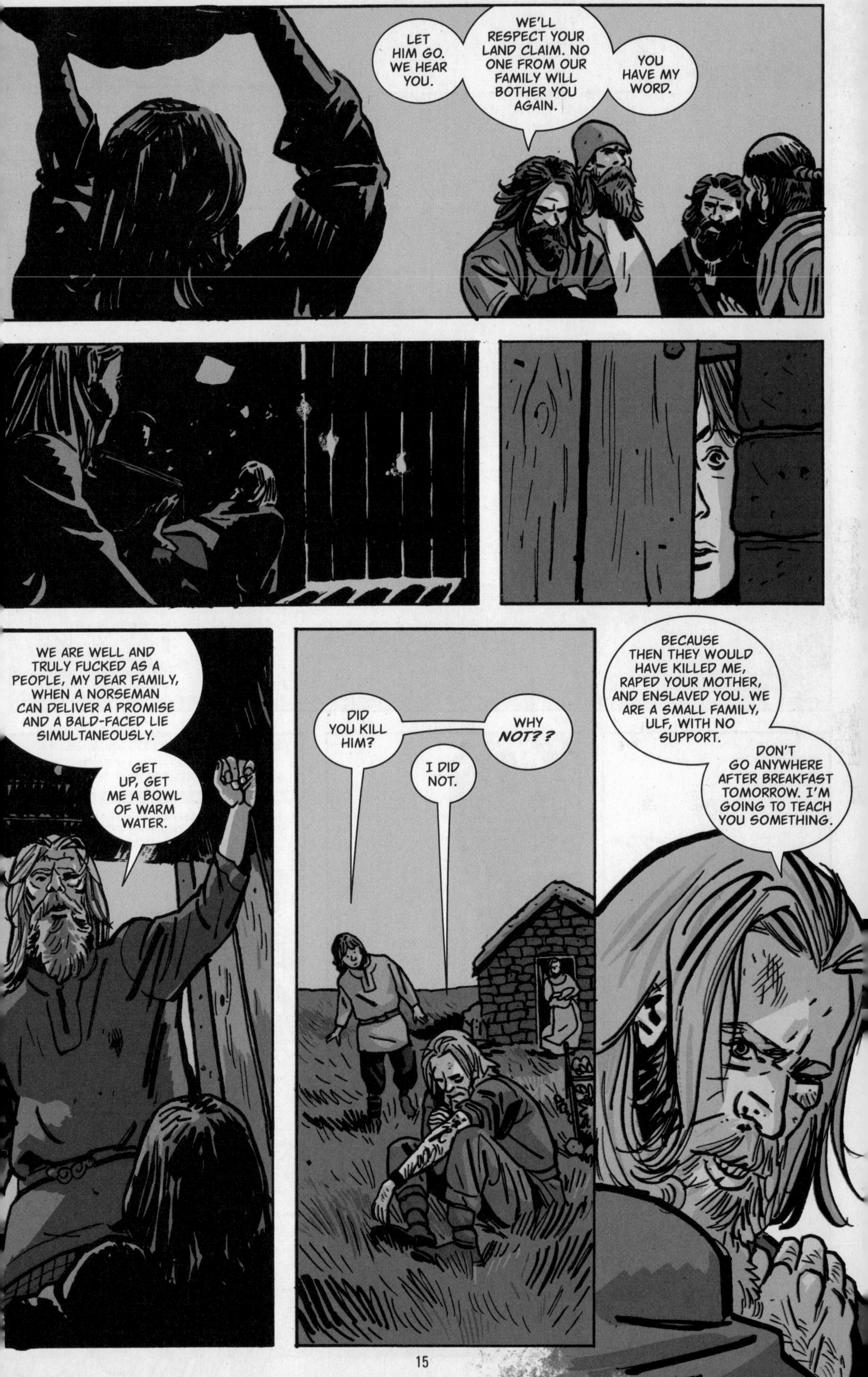
LET HIM GO. WE HEAR YOU.
WE'LL RESPECT YOUR LAND CLAIM. NO ONE FROM OUR FAMILY WILL BOTHER YOU AGAIN.
YOU HAVE MY WORD.
WE ARE WELL AND TRULY FUCKED AS A PEOPLE, MY DEAR FAMILY, WHEN A NORSEMAN CAN DELIVER A PROMISE AND A BALD-FACED LIE SIMULTANEOUSLY.
GET UP, GET ME A BOWL OF WARM WATER.
DID YOU KILL HIM?
I DID NOT.
WHY *NOT??*
BECAUSE THEN THEY WOULD HAVE KILLED ME, RAPED YOUR MOTHER, AND ENSLAVED YOU. WE ARE A SMALL FAMILY, ULF, WITH NO SUPPORT.
DON'T GO ANYWHERE AFTER BREAKFAST TOMORROW. I'M GOING TO TEACH YOU SOMETHING.

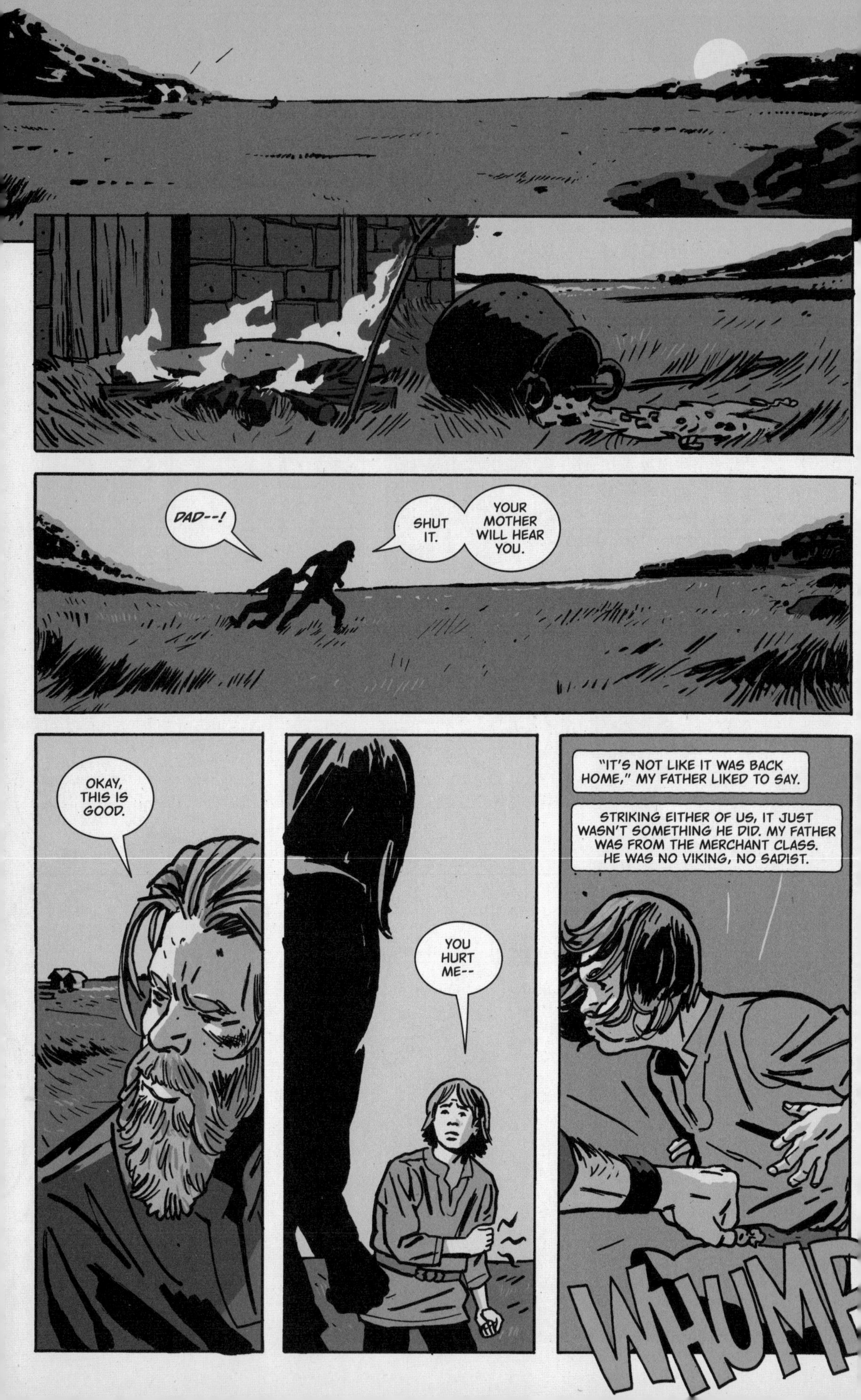
DAD--!
SHUT IT.
YOUR MOTHER WILL HEAR YOU.
OKAY, THIS IS GOOD.
YOU HURT ME--
"IT'S NOT LIKE IT WAS BACK HOME," MY FATHER LIKED TO SAY.
STRIKING EITHER OF US, IT JUST WASN'T SOMETHING HE DID. MY FATHER WAS FROM THE MERCHANT CLASS. HE WAS NO VIKING, NO SADIST.
WHUMP

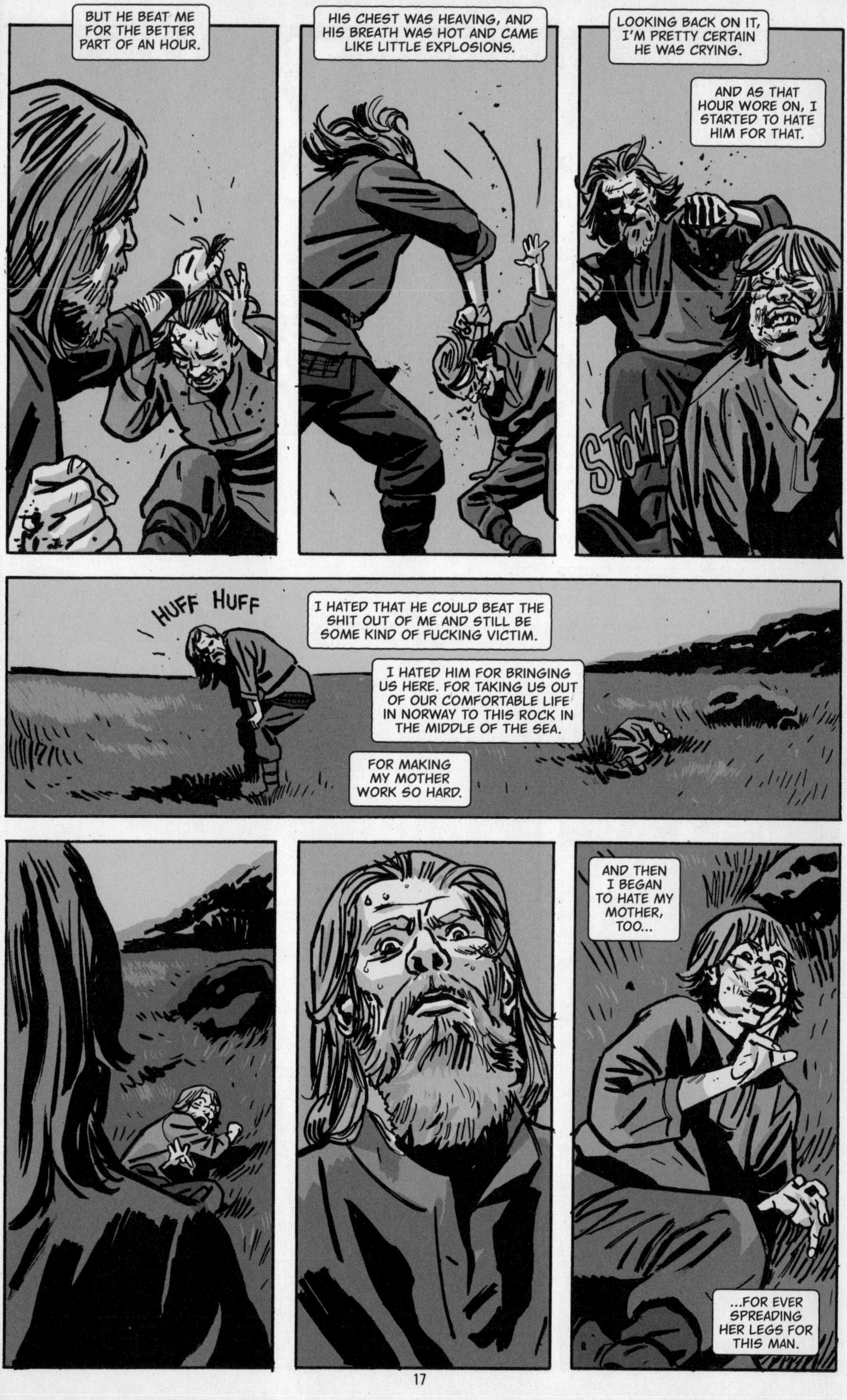
BUT HE BEAT ME FOR THE BETTER PART OF AN HOUR.
HIS CHEST WAS HEAVING, AND HIS BREATH WAS HOT AND CAME LIKE LITTLE EXPLOSIONS.
LOOKING BACK ON IT, I'M PRETTY CERTAIN HE WAS CRYING.
AND AS THAT HOUR WORE ON, I STARTED TO HATE HIM FOR THAT.
STOMP
HUFF HUFF
I HATED THAT HE COULD BEAT THE SHIT OUT OF ME AND STILL BE SOME KIND OF FUCKING VICTIM.
I HATED HIM FOR BRINGING US HERE. FOR TAKING US OUT OF OUR COMFORTABLE LIFE IN NORWAY TO THIS ROCK IN THE MIDDLE OF THE SEA.
FOR MAKING MY MOTHER WORK SO HARD.
AND THEN I BEGAN TO HATE MY MOTHER, TOO...
...FOR EVER SPREADING HER LEGS FOR THIS MAN.

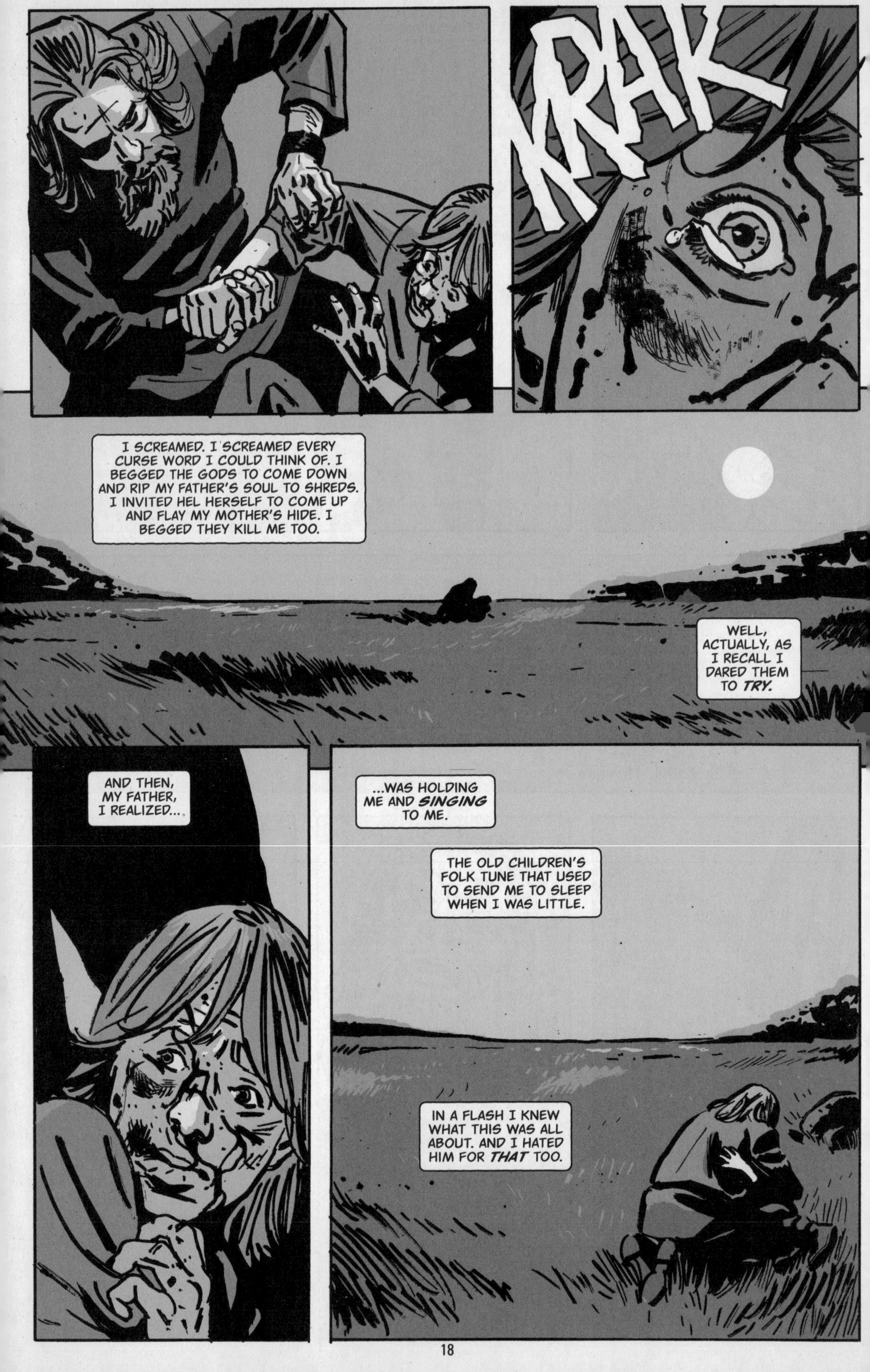
KRAK
I SCREAMED. I SCREAMED EVERY CURSE WORD I COULD THINK OF. I BEGGED THE GODS TO COME DOWN AND RIP MY FATHER'S SOUL TO SHREDS. I INVITED HEL HERSELF TO COME UP AND FLAY MY MOTHER'S HIDE. I BEGGED THEY KILL ME TOO.
WELL, ACTUALLY, AS I RECALL I DARED THEM TO *TRY*.
AND THEN, MY FATHER, I REALIZED...
...WAS HOLDING ME AND *SINGING* TO ME.
THE OLD CHILDREN'S FOLK TUNE THAT USED TO SEND ME TO SLEEP WHEN I WAS LITTLE.
IN A FLASH I KNEW WHAT THIS WAS ALL ABOUT. AND I HATED HIM FOR *THAT* TOO.

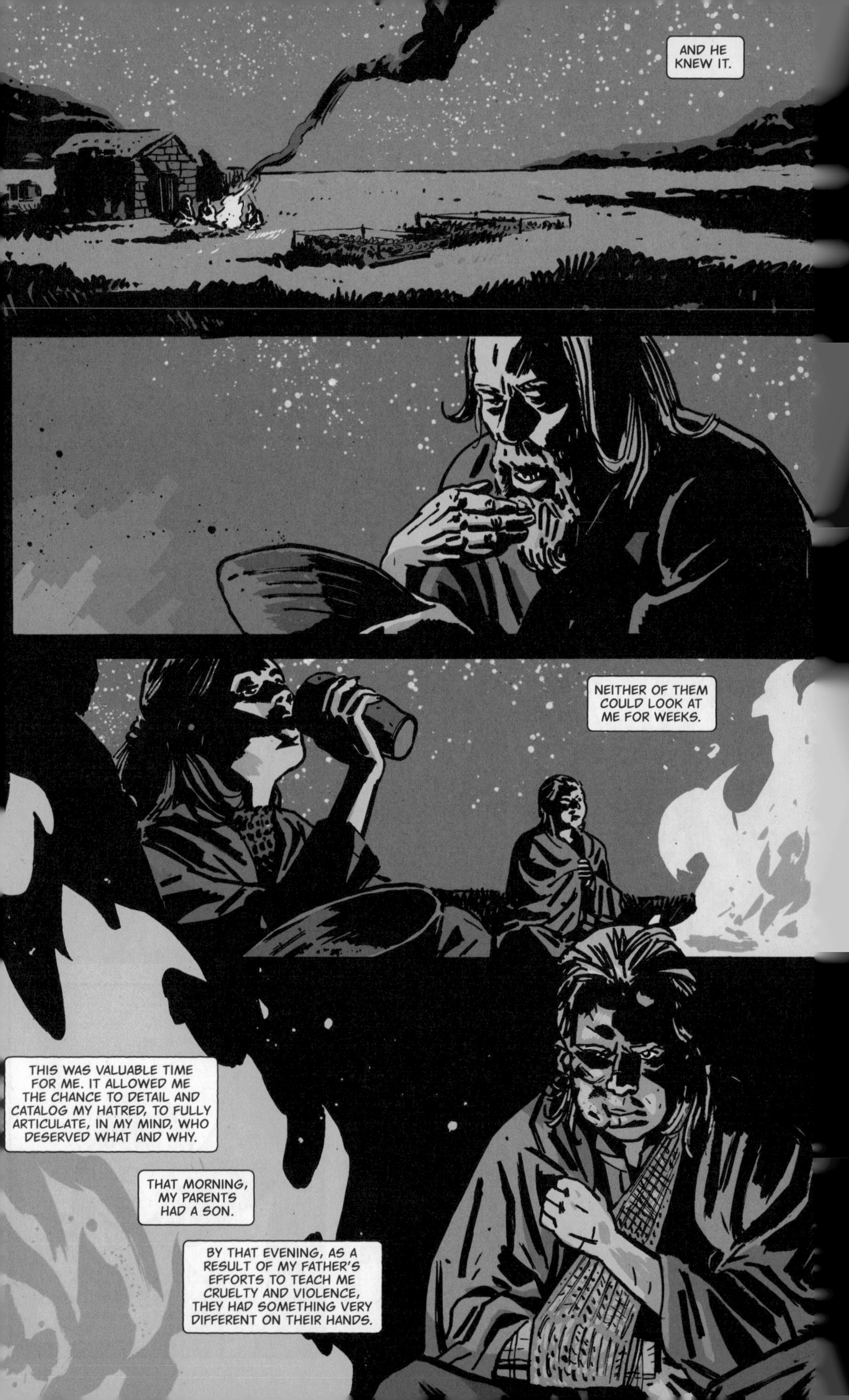
AND HE KNEW IT.
NEITHER OF THEM COULD LOOK AT ME FOR WEEKS.
THIS WAS VALUABLE TIME FOR ME. IT ALLOWED ME THE CHANCE TO DETAIL AND CATALOG MY HATRED, TO FULLY ARTICULATE, IN MY MIND, WHO DESERVED WHAT AND WHY.
THAT MORNING, MY PARENTS HAD A SON.
BY THAT EVENING, AS A RESULT OF MY FATHER'S EFFORTS TO TEACH ME CRUELTY AND VIOLENCE, THEY HAD SOMETHING VERY DIFFERENT ON THEIR HANDS.

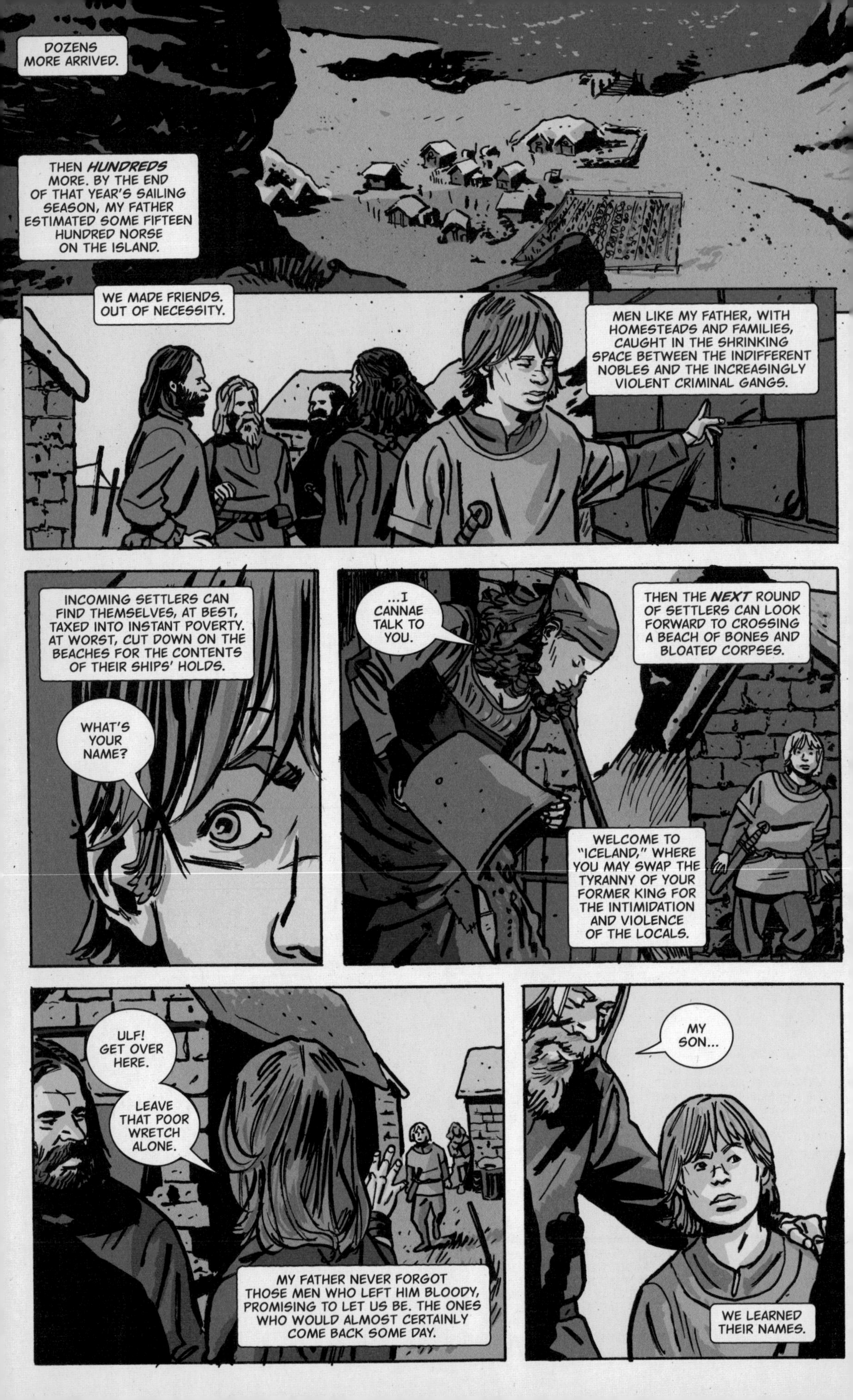
DOZENS MORE ARRIVED.
THEN *HUNDREDS* MORE. BY THE END OF THAT YEAR'S SAILING SEASON, MY FATHER ESTIMATED SOME FIFTEEN HUNDRED NORSE ON THE ISLAND.
WE MADE FRIENDS. OUT OF NECESSITY.
MEN LIKE MY FATHER, WITH HOMESTEADS AND FAMILIES, CAUGHT IN THE SHRINKING SPACE BETWEEN THE INDIFFERENT NOBLES AND THE INCREASINGLY VIOLENT CRIMINAL GANGS.
INCOMING SETTLERS CAN FIND THEMSELVES, AT BEST, TAXED INTO INSTANT POVERTY. AT WORST, CUT DOWN ON THE BEACHES FOR THE CONTENTS OF THEIR SHIPS' HOLDS.
WHAT'S YOUR NAME?
...I CANNAE TALK TO YOU.
THEN THE *NEXT* ROUND OF SETTLERS CAN LOOK FORWARD TO CROSSING A BEACH OF BONES AND BLOATED CORPSES.
WELCOME TO "ICELAND," WHERE YOU MAY SWAP THE TYRANNY OF YOUR FORMER KING FOR THE INTIMIDATION AND VIOLENCE OF THE LOCALS.
ULF! GET OVER HERE.
LEAVE THAT POOR WRETCH ALONE.
MY FATHER NEVER FORGOT THOSE MEN WHO LEFT HIM BLOODY, PROMISING TO LET US BE. THE ONES WHO WOULD ALMOST CERTAINLY COME BACK SOME DAY.
MY SON...
WE LEARNED THEIR NAMES.

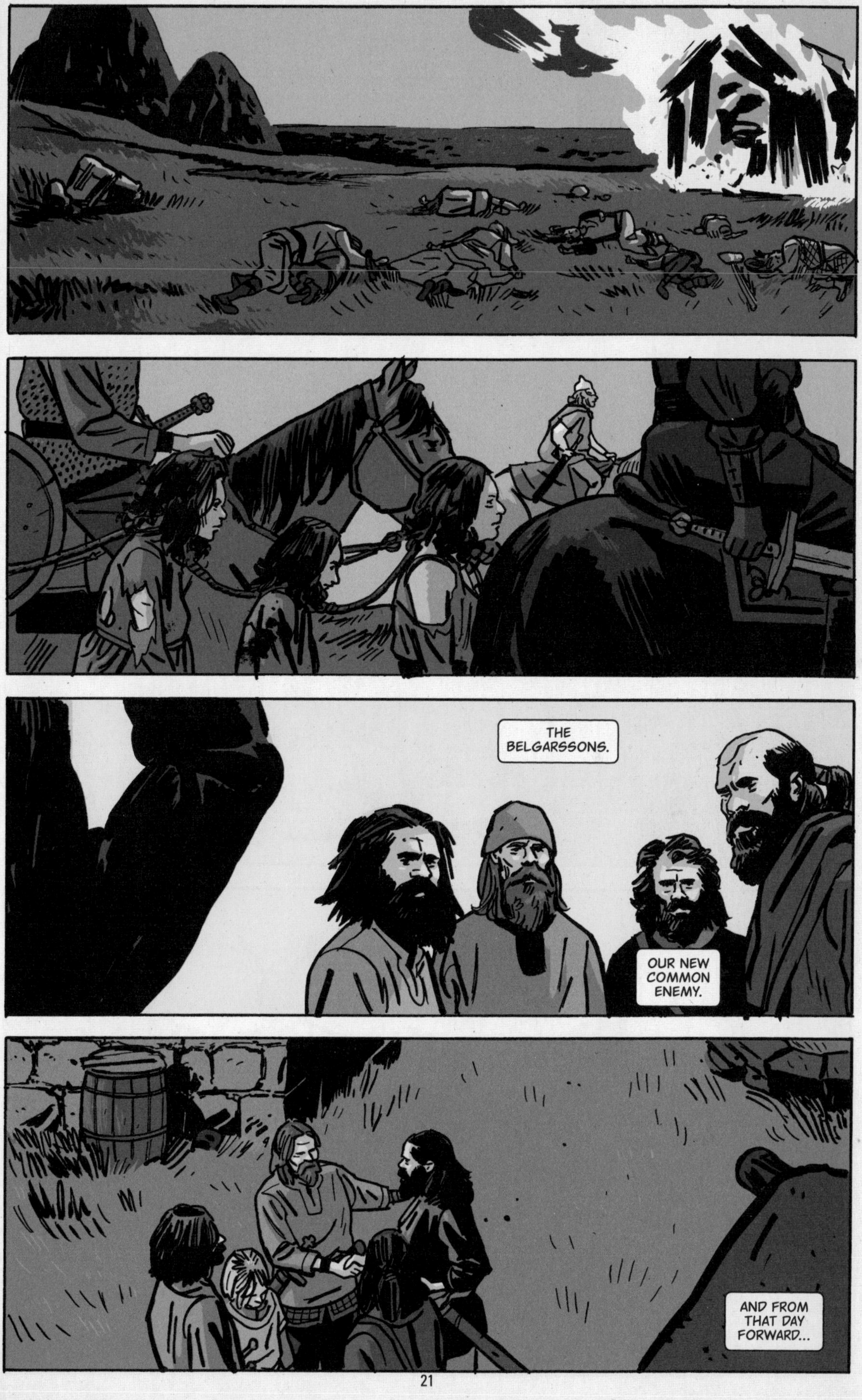
THE BELGARSSONS.
OUR NEW COMMON ENEMY.
AND FROM THAT DAY FORWARD...

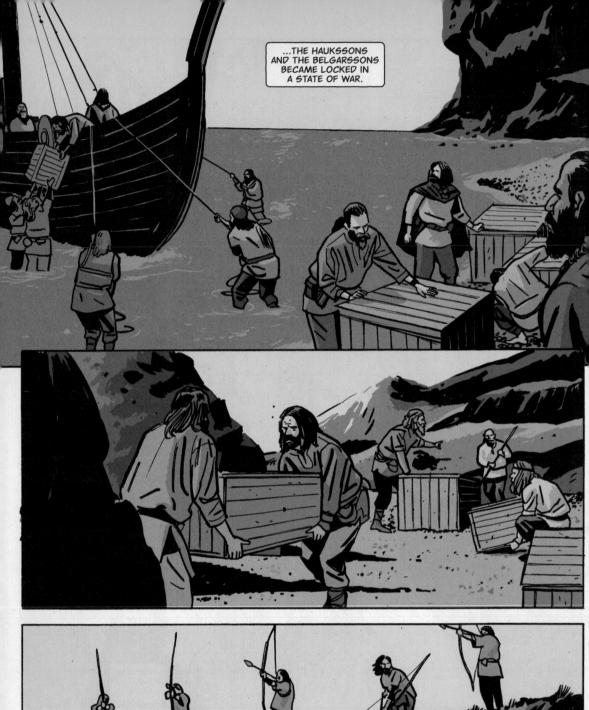

...THE HAUKSSONS AND THE BELGARSSONS BECAME LOCKED IN A STATE OF WAR.

MY MOTHER DISAPPROVED, TO PUT IT MILDLY.

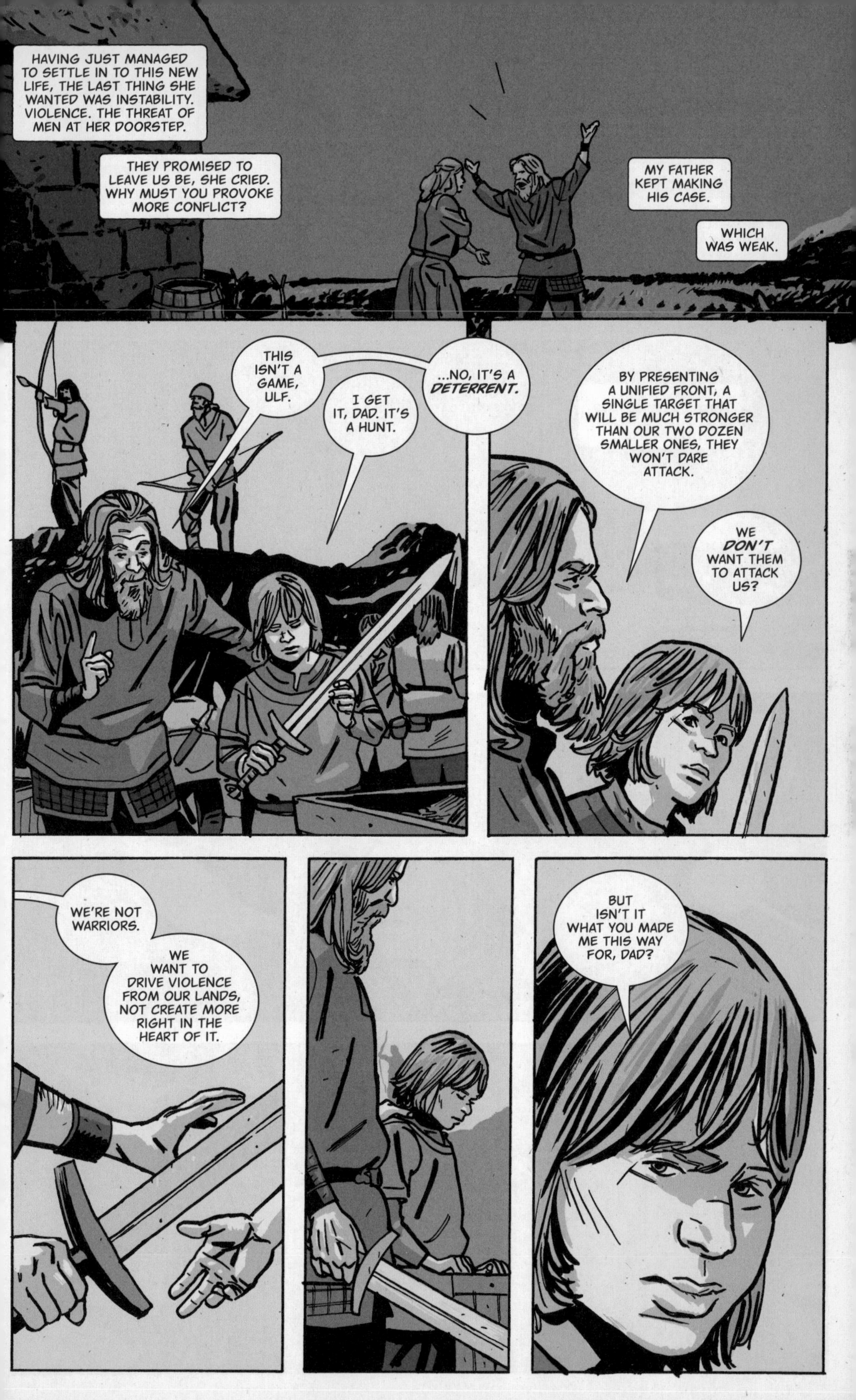
HAVING JUST MANAGED TO SETTLE IN TO THIS NEW LIFE, THE LAST THING SHE WANTED WAS INSTABILITY. VIOLENCE. THE THREAT OF MEN AT HER DOORSTEP.
THEY PROMISED TO LEAVE US BE, SHE CRIED. WHY MUST YOU PROVOKE MORE CONFLICT?
MY FATHER KEPT MAKING HIS CASE.
WHICH WAS WEAK.
THIS ISN'T A GAME, ULF.
I GET IT, DAD. IT'S A HUNT.
...NO, IT'S A *DETERRENT.*
BY PRESENTING A UNIFIED FRONT, A SINGLE TARGET THAT WILL BE MUCH STRONGER THAN OUR TWO DOZEN SMALLER ONES, THEY WON'T DARE ATTACK.
WE *DON'T* WANT THEM TO ATTACK US?
WE'RE NOT WARRIORS.
WE WANT TO DRIVE VIOLENCE FROM OUR LANDS, NOT CREATE MORE RIGHT IN THE HEART OF IT.
BUT ISN'T IT WHAT YOU MADE ME THIS WAY FOR, DAD?

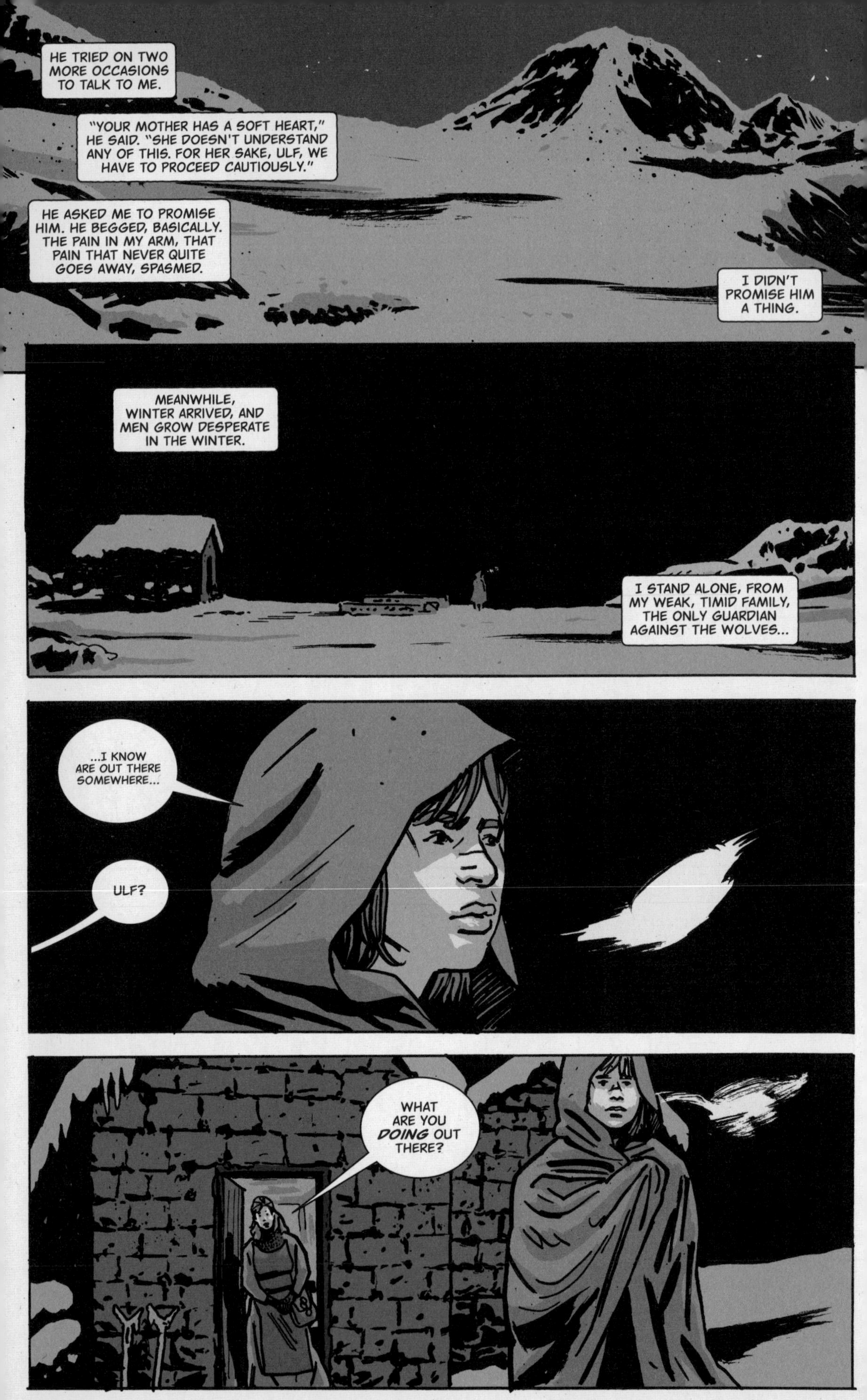
HE TRIED ON TWO MORE OCCASIONS TO TALK TO ME.
"YOUR MOTHER HAS A SOFT HEART," HE SAID. "SHE DOESN'T UNDERSTAND ANY OF THIS. FOR HER SAKE, ULF, WE HAVE TO PROCEED CAUTIOUSLY."
HE ASKED ME TO PROMISE HIM. HE BEGGED, BASICALLY. THE PAIN IN MY ARM, THAT PAIN THAT NEVER QUITE GOES AWAY, SPASMED.
I DIDN'T PROMISE HIM A THING.
MEANWHILE, WINTER ARRIVED, AND MEN GROW DESPERATE IN THE WINTER.
I STAND ALONE, FROM MY WEAK, TIMID FAMILY, THE ONLY GUARDIAN AGAINST THE WOLVES...
...I KNOW ARE OUT THERE SOMEWHERE...
ULF?
WHAT ARE YOU DOING OUT THERE?

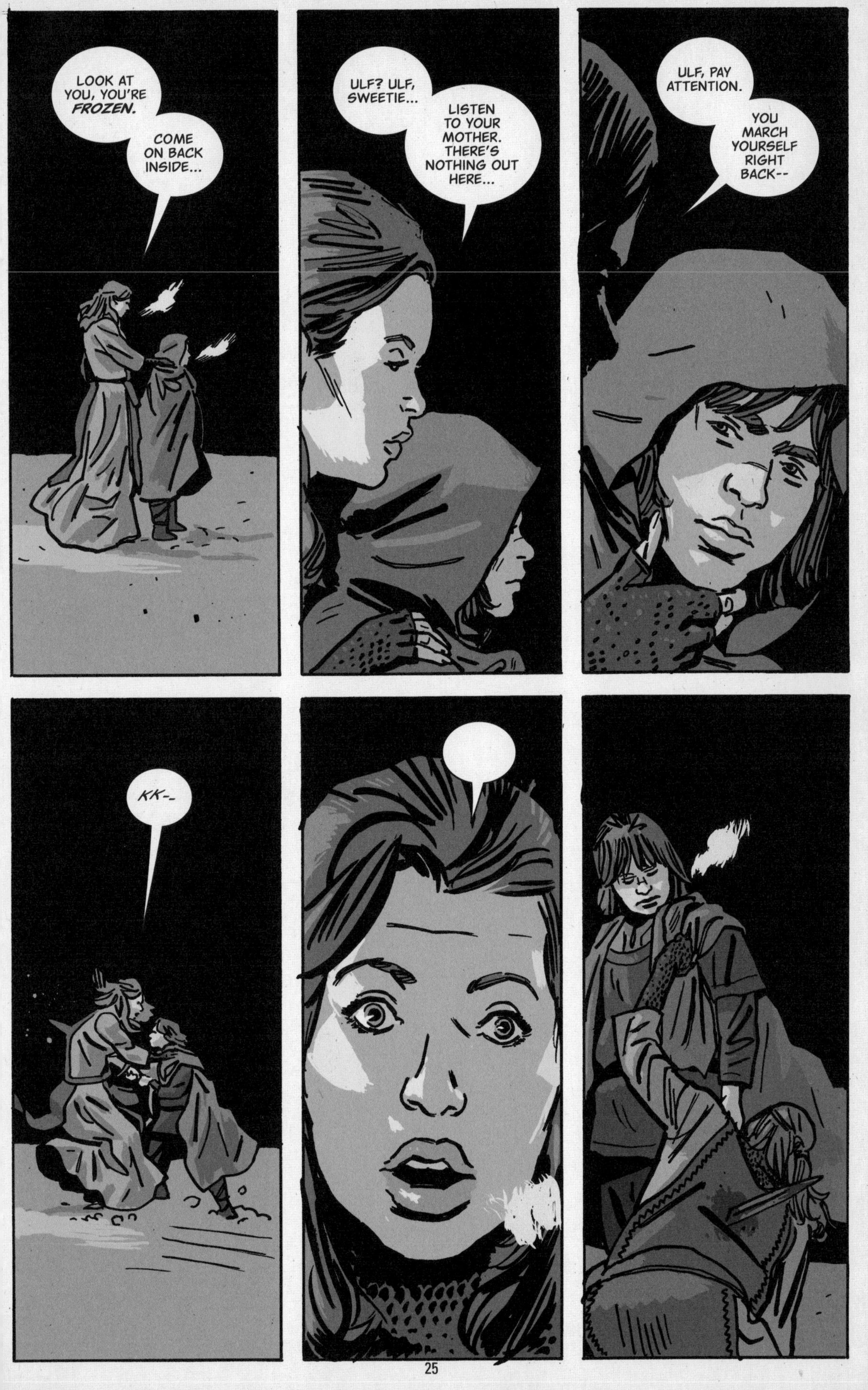
LOOK AT YOU, YOU'RE *FROZEN.*
COME ON BACK INSIDE...
ULF? ULF, SWEETIE...
LISTEN TO YOUR MOTHER. THERE'S NOTHING OUT HERE...
ULF, PAY ATTENTION.
YOU MARCH YOURSELF RIGHT BACK--
KK--

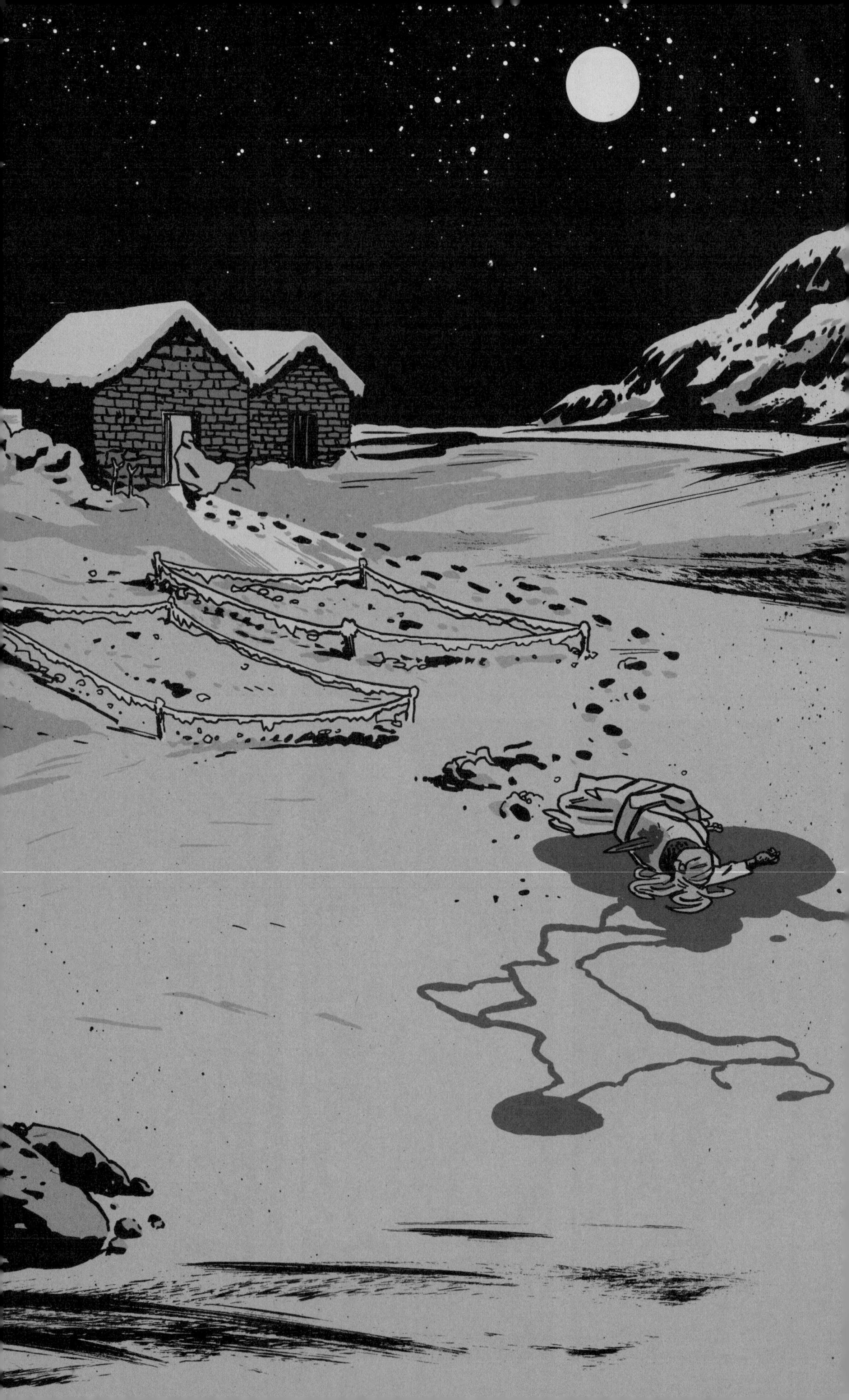

Part Two: Security 880

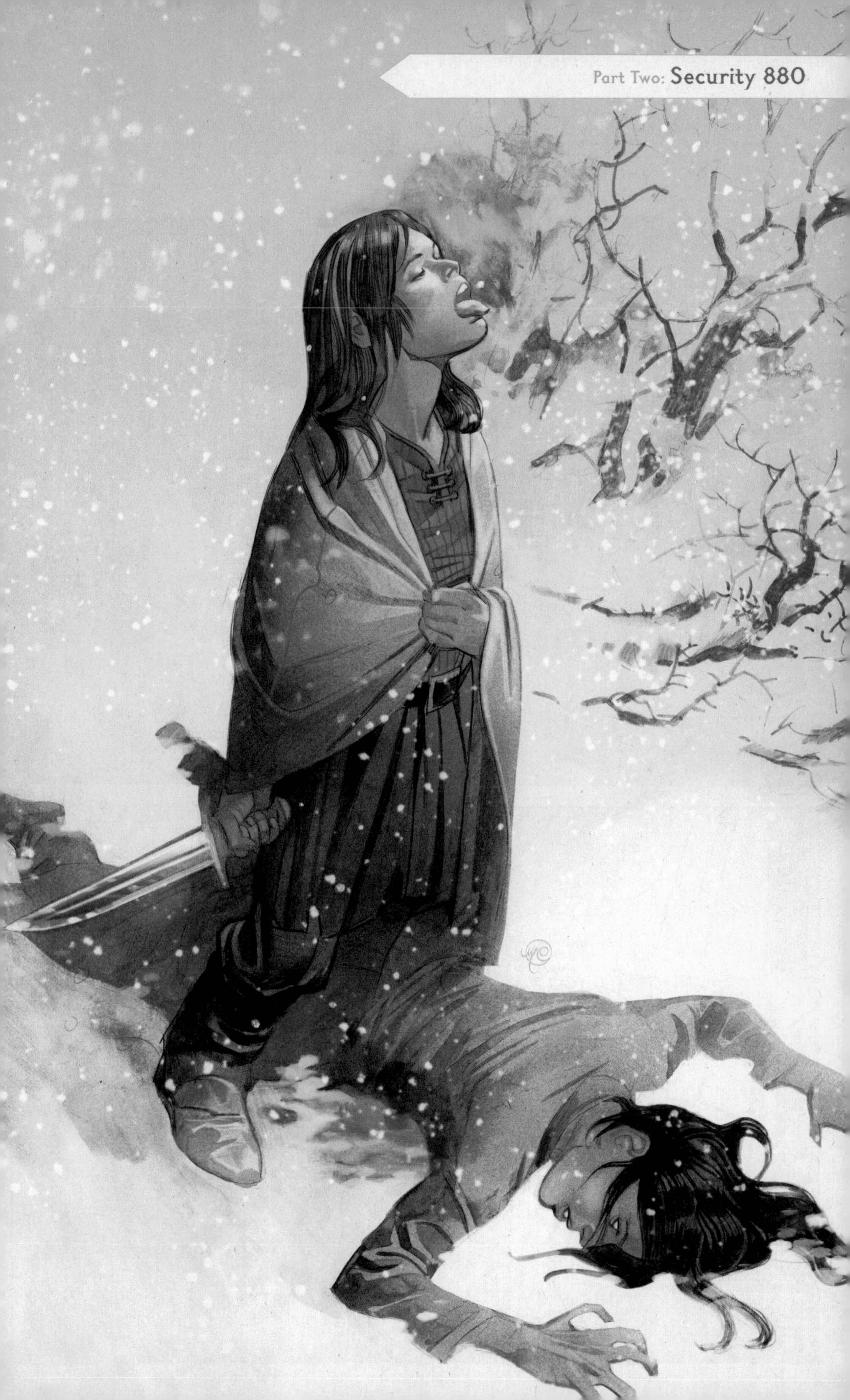

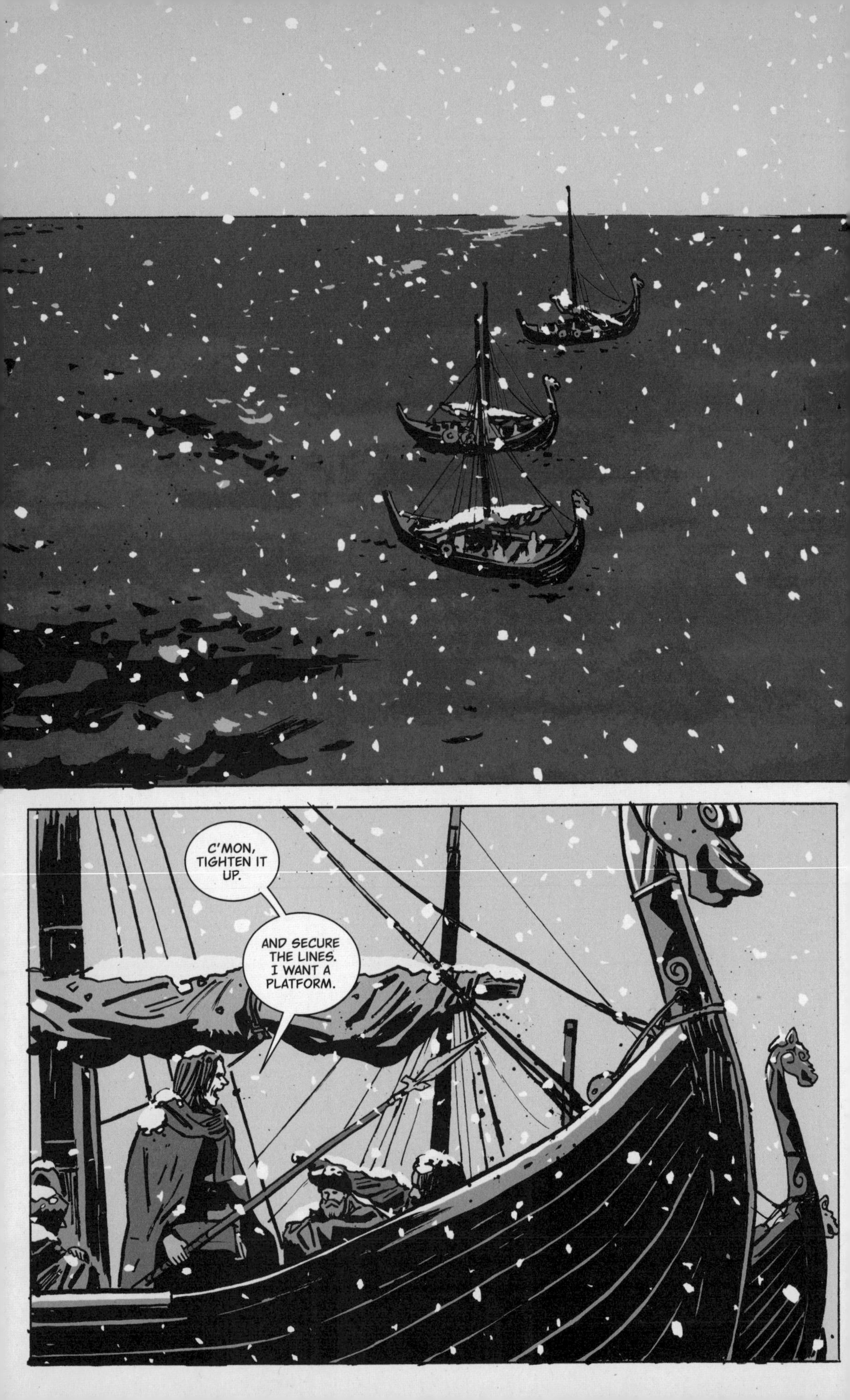
C'MON, TIGHTEN IT UP.
AND SECURE THE LINES. I WANT A PLATFORM.

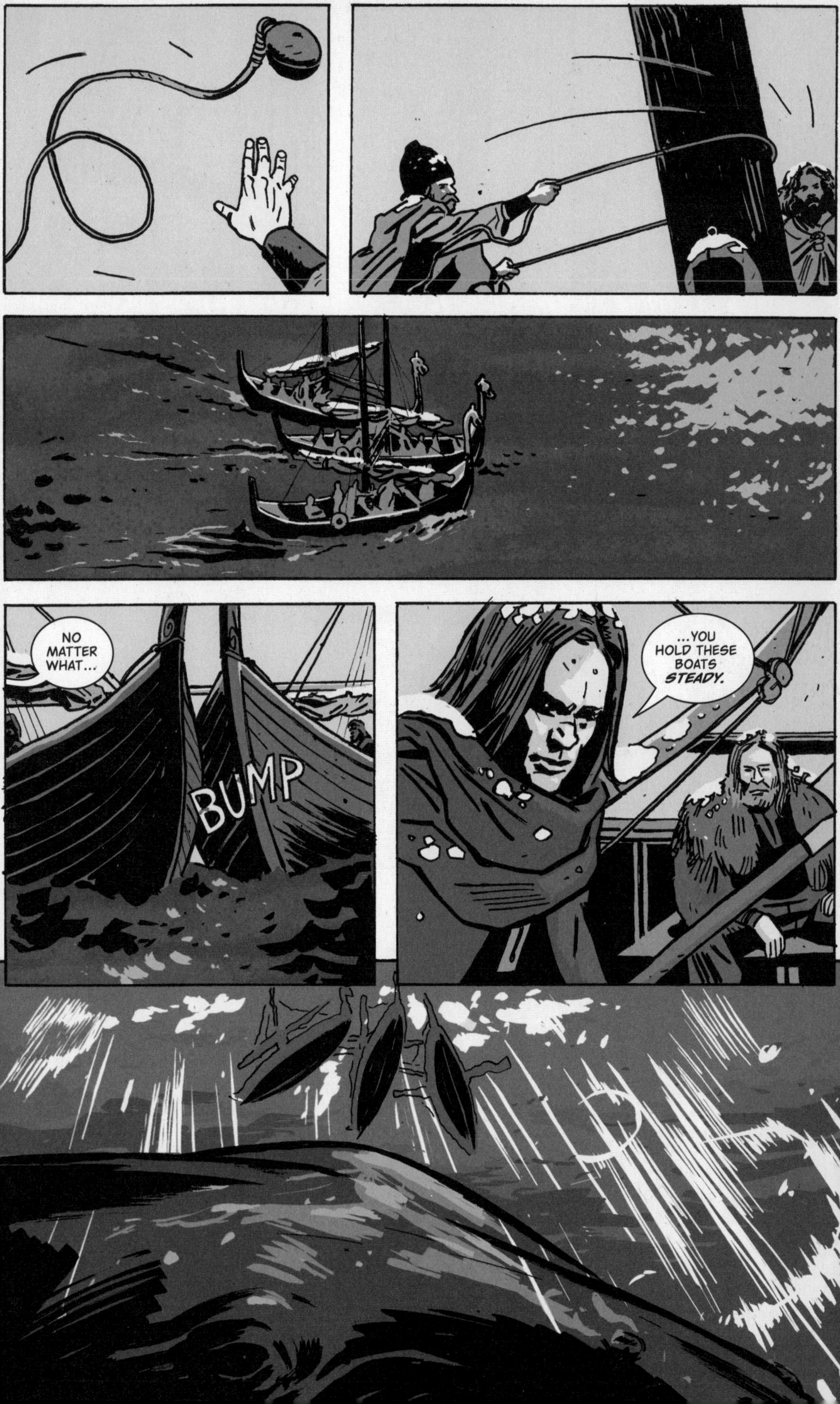
NO MATTER WHAT...
BUMP
...YOU HOLD THESE BOATS STEADY.

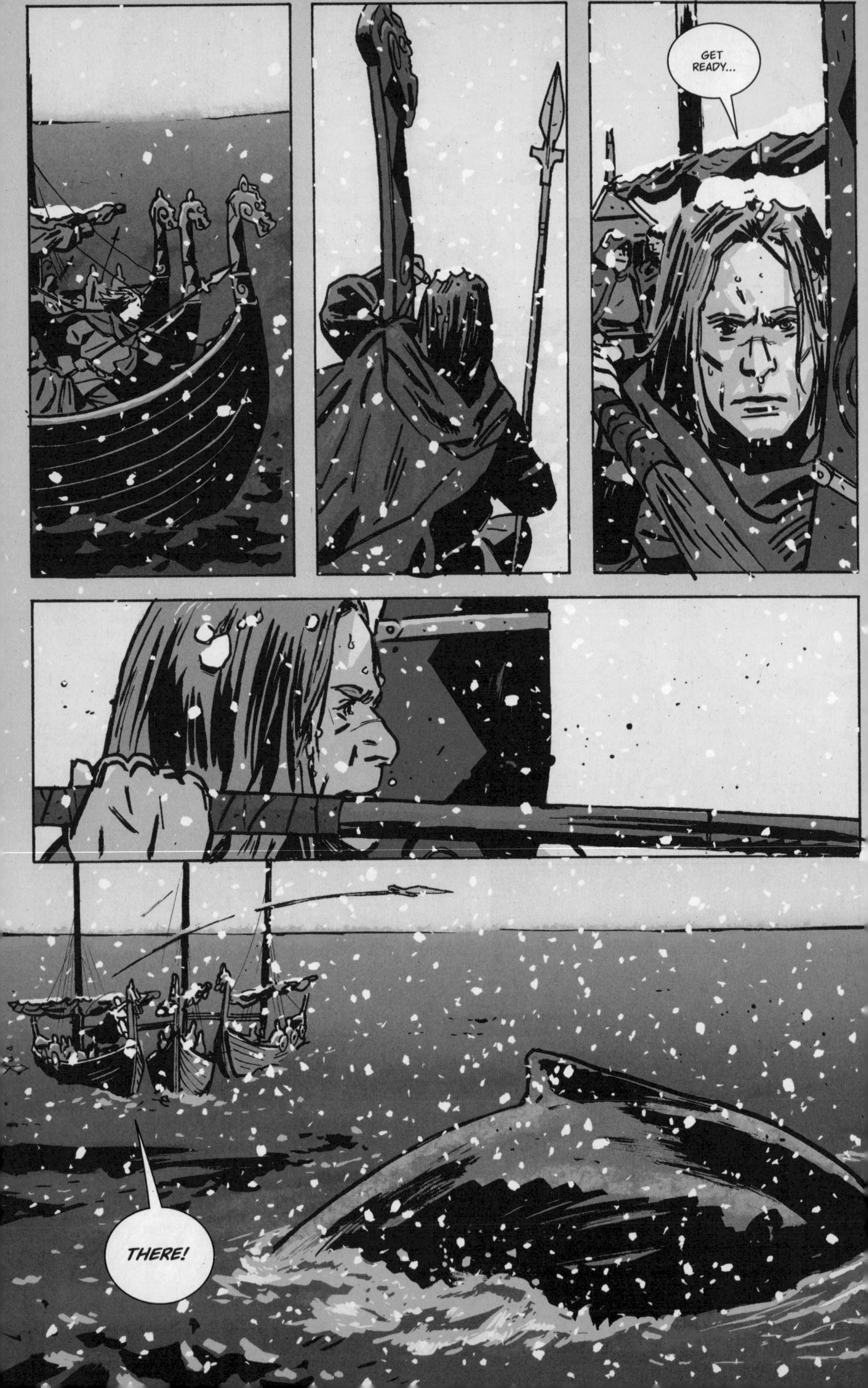
GET READY...
THERE!

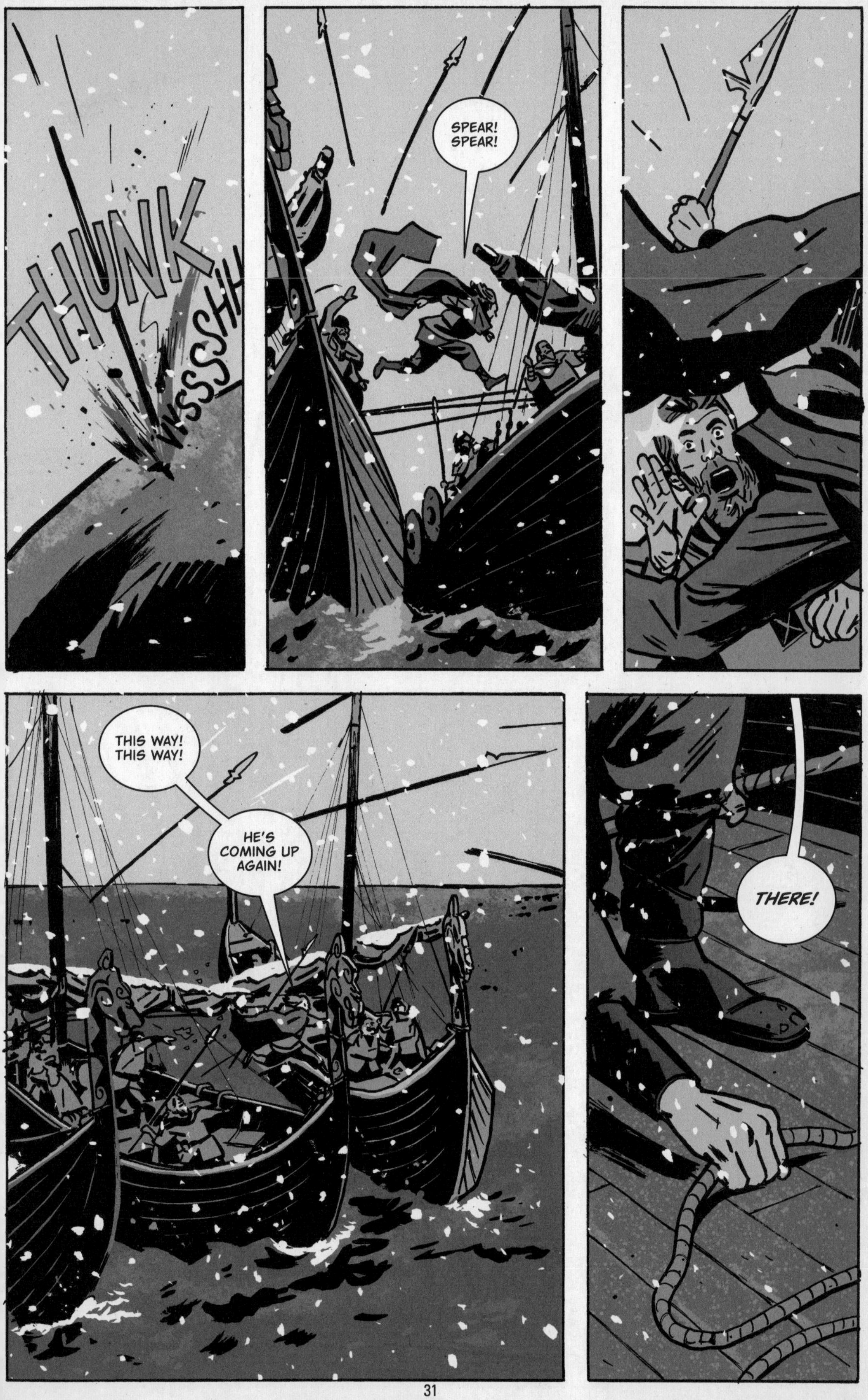
THUNK
WHSSSSHH
SPEAR! SPEAR!
THIS WAY! THIS WAY!
HE'S COMING UP AGAIN!
THERE!

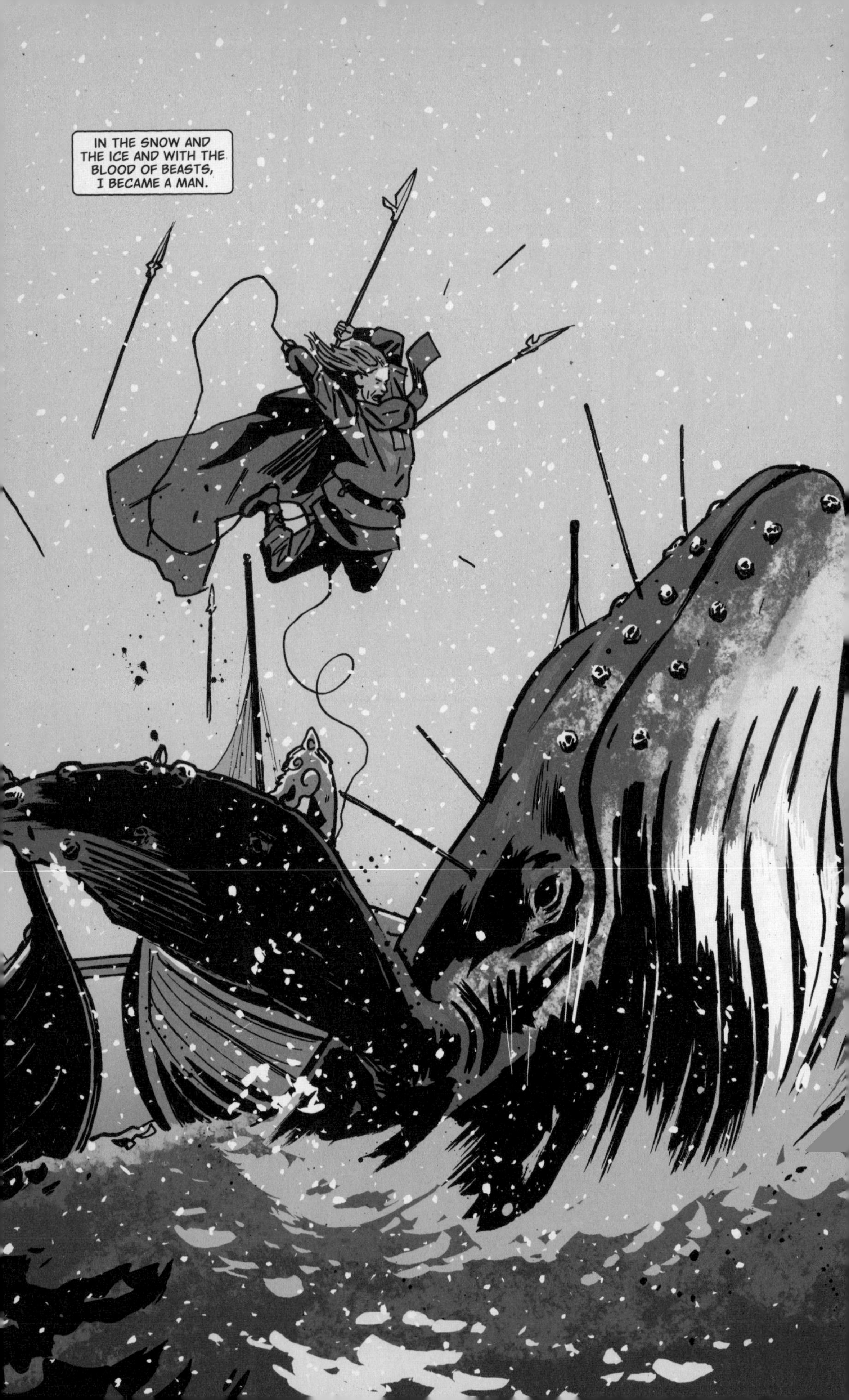
IN THE SNOW AND THE ICE AND WITH THE BLOOD OF BEASTS, I BECAME A MAN.

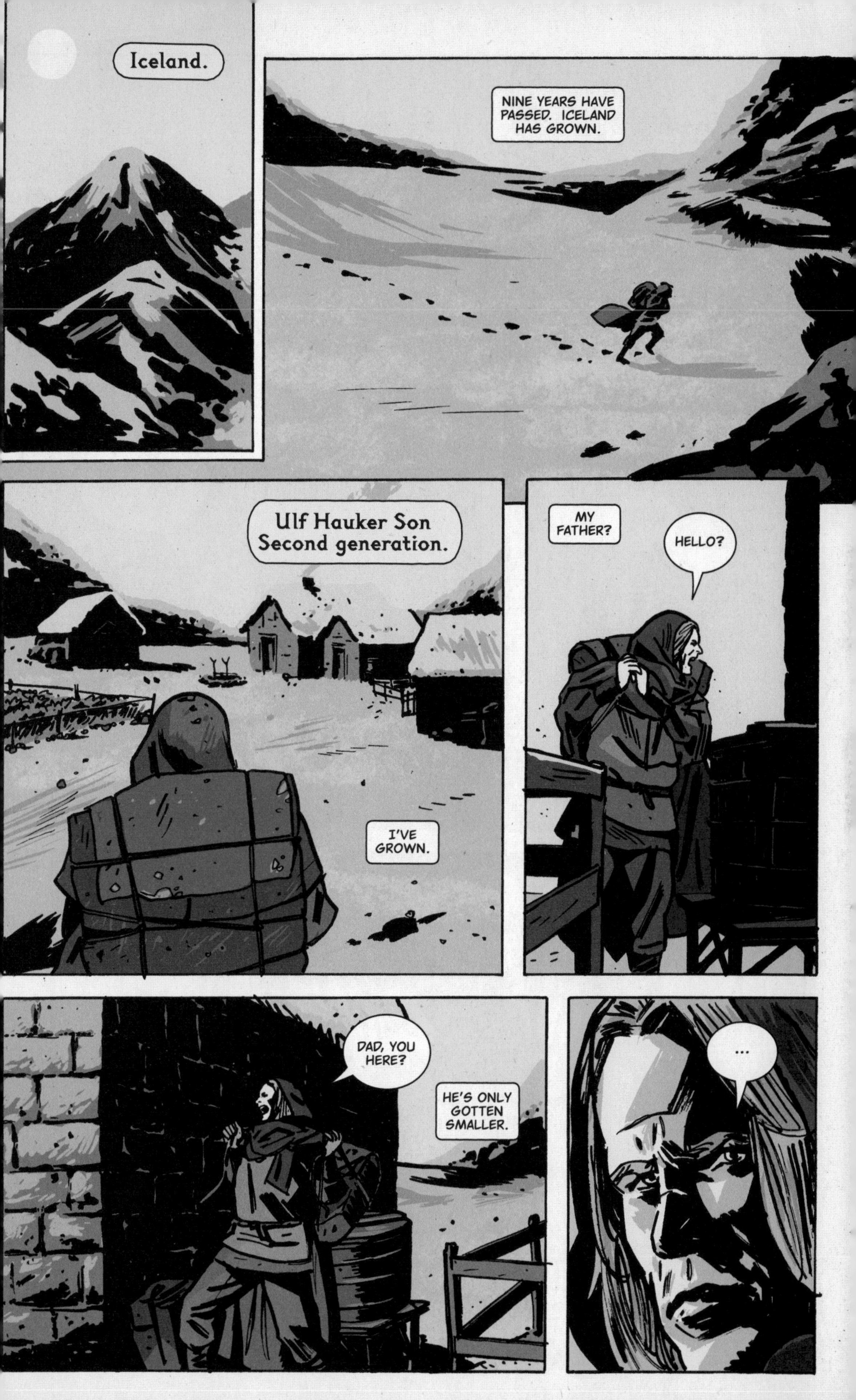
Iceland.
NINE YEARS HAVE PASSED. ICELAND HAS GROWN.
Ulf Hauker Son
Second generation.
I'VE GROWN.
MY FATHER?
HELLO?
DAD, YOU HERE?
HE'S ONLY GOTTEN SMALLER.
...

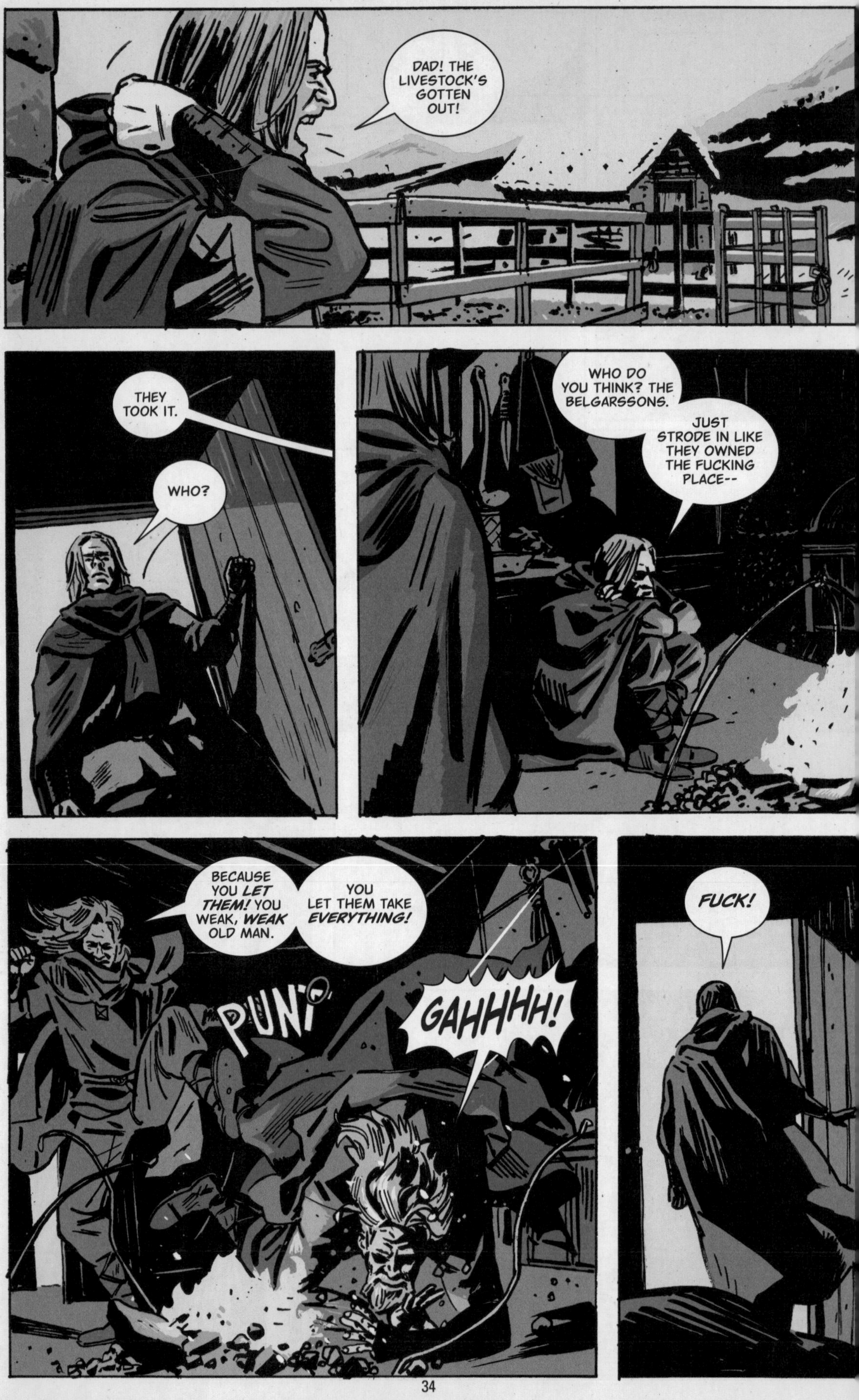
DAD! THE LIVESTOCK'S GOTTEN OUT!
THEY TOOK IT.
WHO?
WHO DO YOU THINK? THE BELGARSSONS.
JUST STRODE IN LIKE THEY OWNED THE FUCKING PLACE--
BECAUSE YOU *LET THEM!* YOU WEAK, *WEAK* OLD MAN.
YOU LET THEM TAKE *EVERYTHING!*
PUNT
GAHHHH!
FUCK!

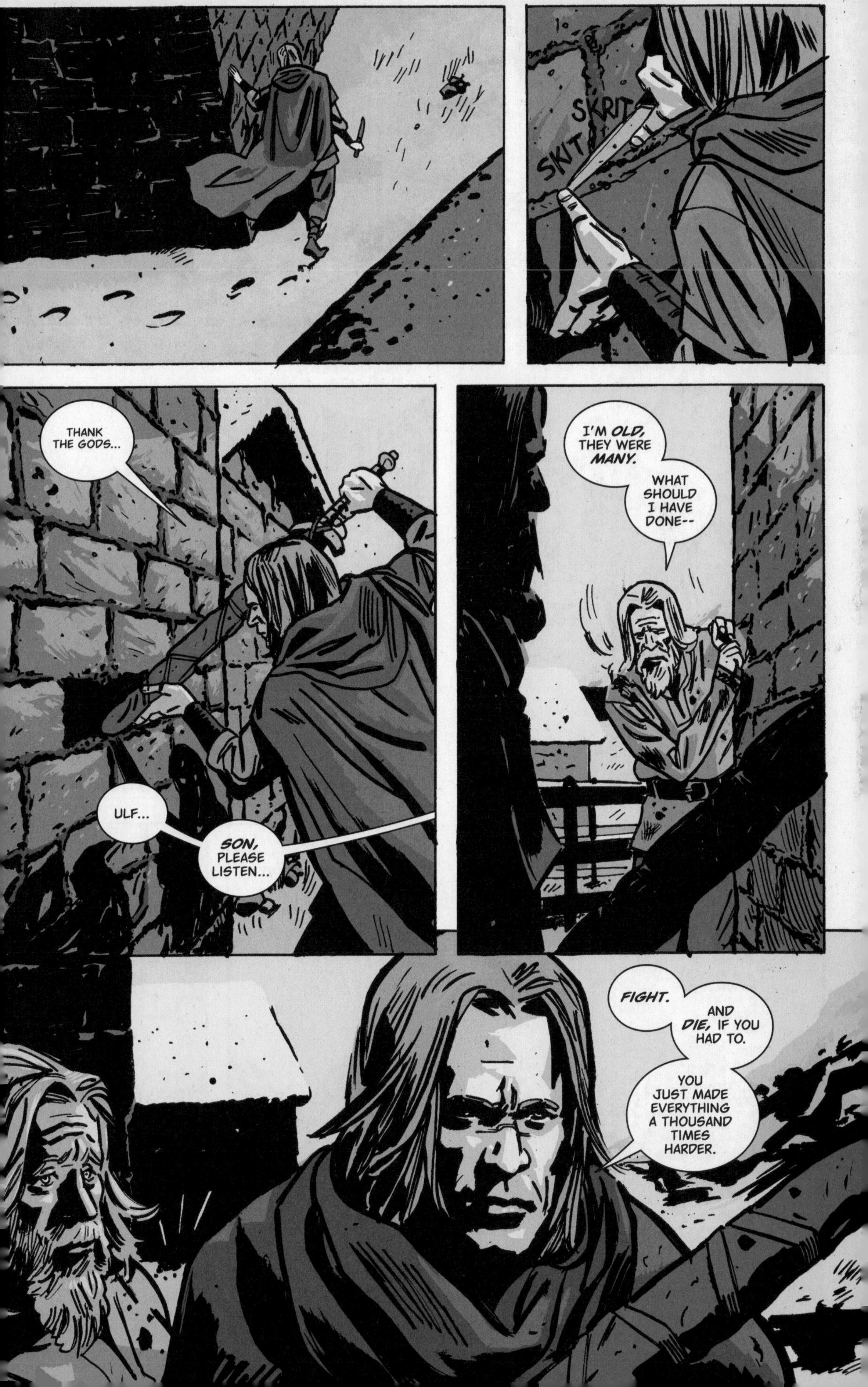
SKRIT
SKIT
THANK THE GODS...
ULF...
SON, PLEASE LISTEN...
I'M OLD, THEY WERE MANY.
WHAT SHOULD I HAVE DONE--
FIGHT.
AND DIE, IF YOU HAD TO.
YOU JUST MADE EVERYTHING A THOUSAND TIMES HARDER.

Belgarssons' Territory.

EIGHT HOMESTEADS, LOOKS LIKE. MAYBE TWENTY BUILDINGS IN ALL.

SO FIGURE... FORTY MEN.

BAD ODDS.

WE SURPRISE THEM, WE'LL HAVE WON BEFORE IT EVEN GETS UNDER WAY.

YOU RUN LIKE HEL HERSELF IS POKING YOUR ARSE. ONCE THERE, KILL ANYTHING ON TWO LEGS.

AYE, THAT'S FINE.

IF YOU'RE SURE, ULF. THIS IS NO LITTLE THING, WHAT WE'RE DOING. THIS IS MOST CERTAINLY AN ESCALATION. THIS IS A DECLARATION OF WAR.

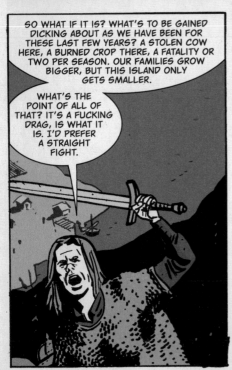

SO WHAT IF IT IS? WHAT'S TO BE GAINED DICKING ABOUT AS WE HAVE BEEN FOR THESE LAST FEW YEARS? A STOLEN COW HERE, A BURNED CROP THERE, A FATALITY OR TWO PER SEASON. OUR FAMILIES GROW BIGGER, BUT THIS ISLAND ONLY GETS SMALLER.

WHAT'S THE POINT OF ALL OF THAT? IT'S A FUCKING DRAG, IS WHAT IT IS. I'D PREFER A STRAIGHT FIGHT.

WE'LL BACK YOU UP, ULF HAUKER, LIKE WE ALWAYS DID YOUR FATHER.

FUCK MY FATHER.

FROM NOW ON, YOU DO FOR ME.

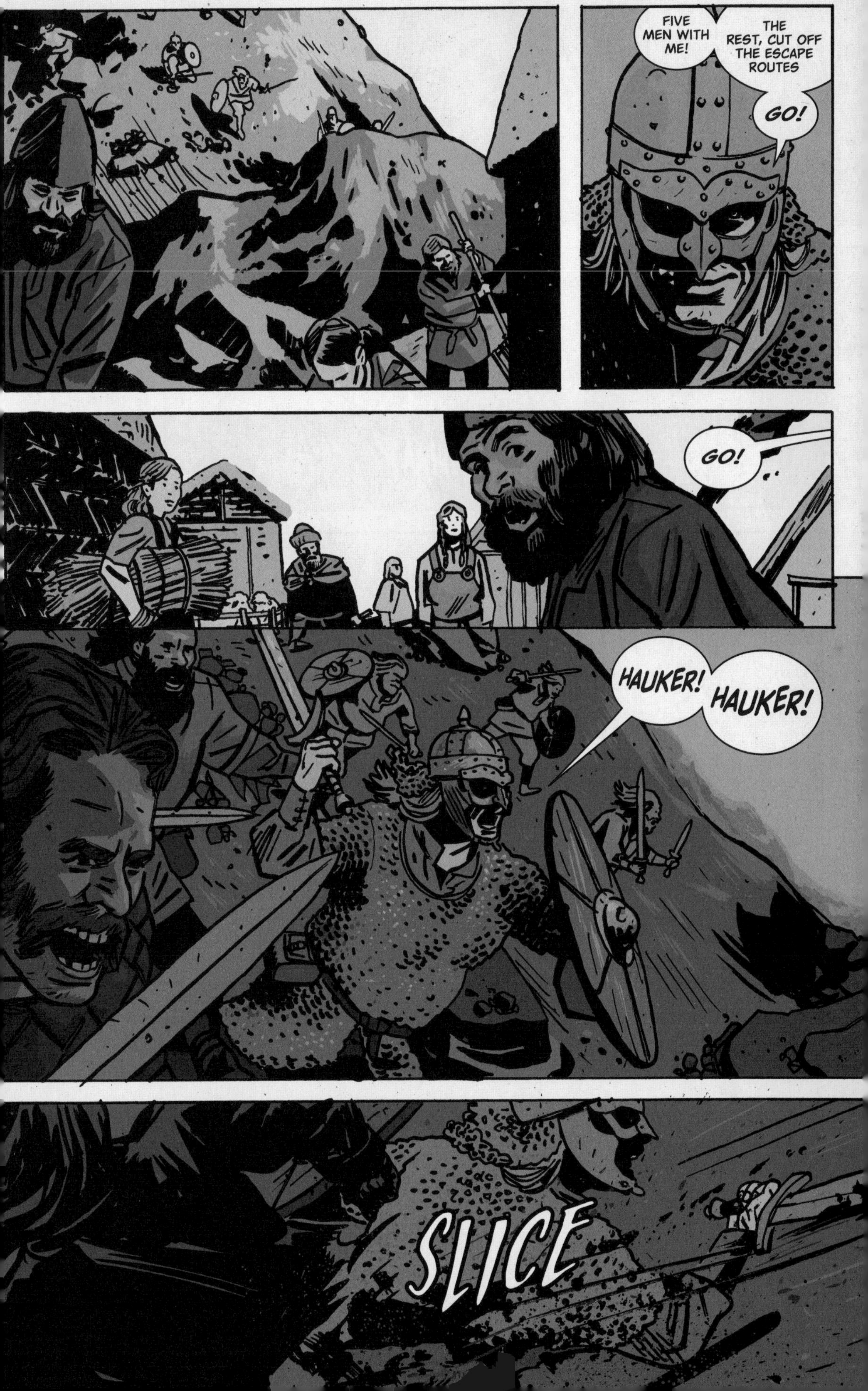

FIVE MEN WITH ME!
THE REST, CUT OFF THE ESCAPE ROUTES
GO!
GO!
HAUKER!
HAUKER!
SLICE

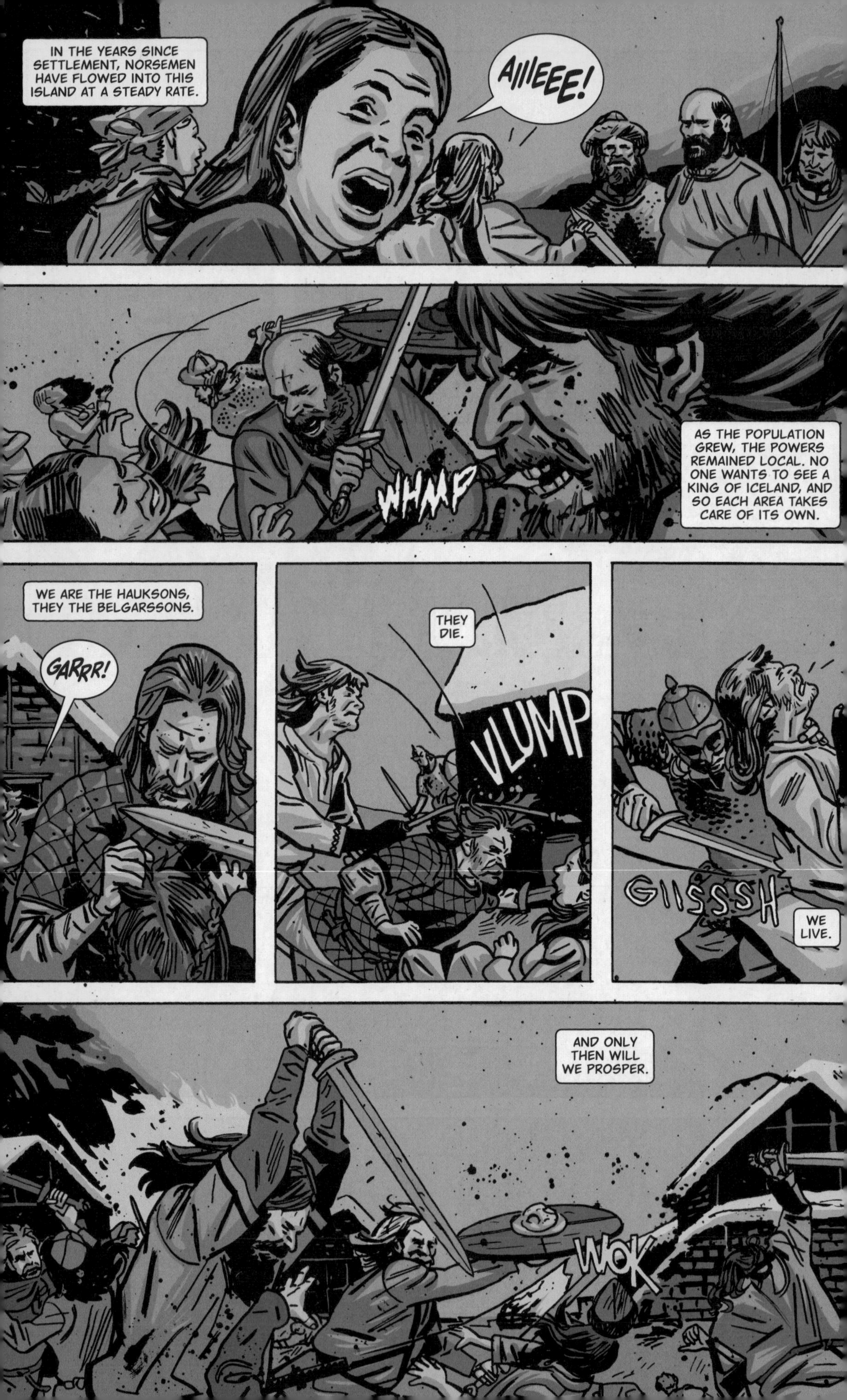
IN THE YEARS SINCE SETTLEMENT, NORSEMEN HAVE FLOWED INTO THIS ISLAND AT A STEADY RATE.
AIIIEEE!
WHMP
AS THE POPULATION GREW, THE POWERS REMAINED LOCAL. NO ONE WANTS TO SEE A KING OF ICELAND, AND SO EACH AREA TAKES CARE OF ITS OWN.
WE ARE THE HAUKSONS, THEY THE BELGARSSONS.
GARRR!
THEY DIE.
VLUMP
GIISSSH
WE LIVE.
AND ONLY THEN WILL WE PROSPER.
WOK

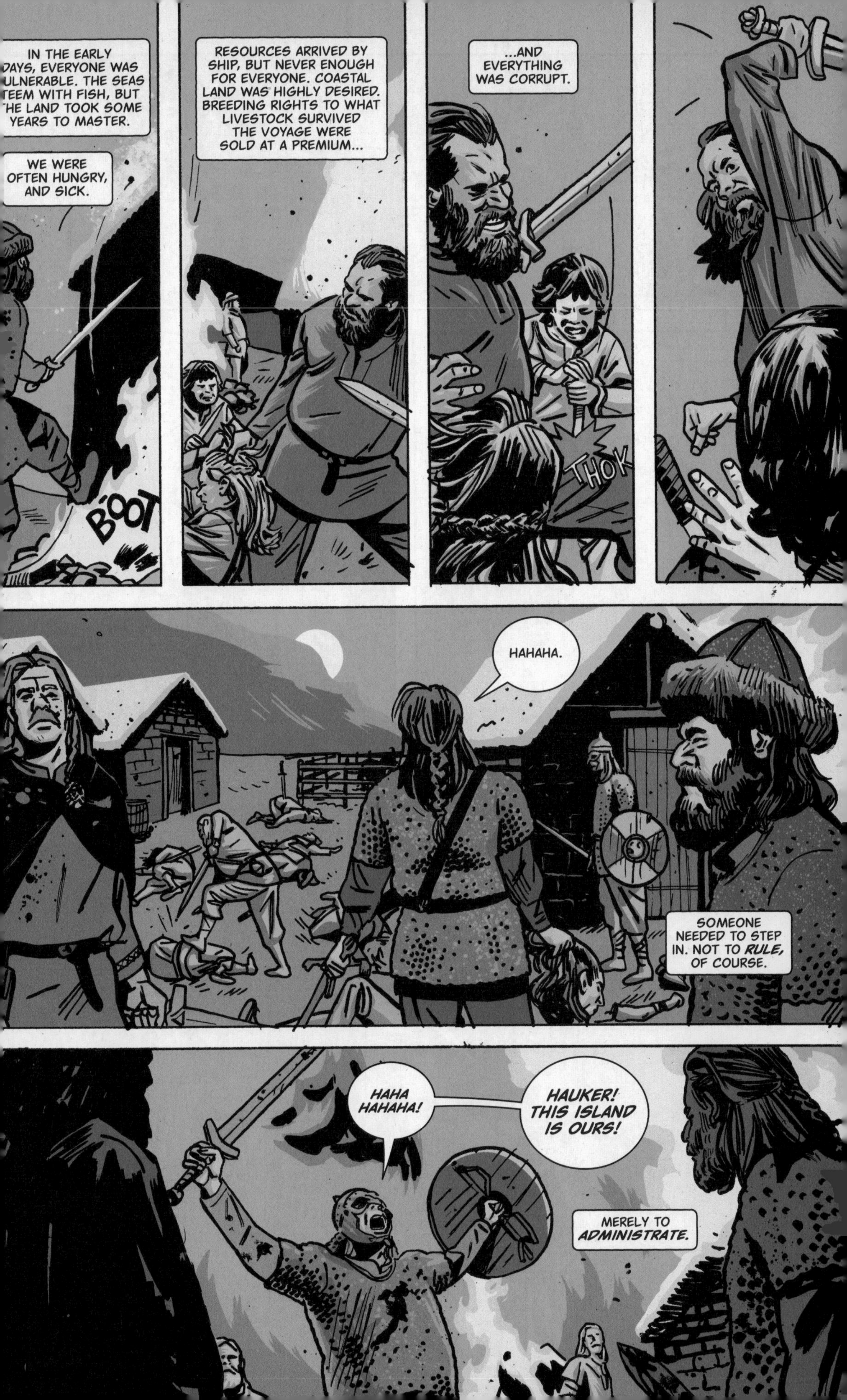

IN THE EARLY DAYS, EVERYONE WAS ULNERABLE. THE SEAS TEEM WITH FISH, BUT THE LAND TOOK SOME YEARS TO MASTER.
WE WERE OFTEN HUNGRY, AND SICK.
BOOT
RESOURCES ARRIVED BY SHIP, BUT NEVER ENOUGH FOR EVERYONE. COASTAL LAND WAS HIGHLY DESIRED. BREEDING RIGHTS TO WHAT LIVESTOCK SURVIVED THE VOYAGE WERE SOLD AT A PREMIUM...
...AND EVERYTHING WAS CORRUPT.
THOK
HAHAHA.
SOMEONE NEEDED TO STEP IN. NOT TO *RULE*, OF COURSE.
HAHA HAHAHA!
HAUKER! THIS ISLAND IS OURS!
MERELY TO *ADMINISTRATE.*

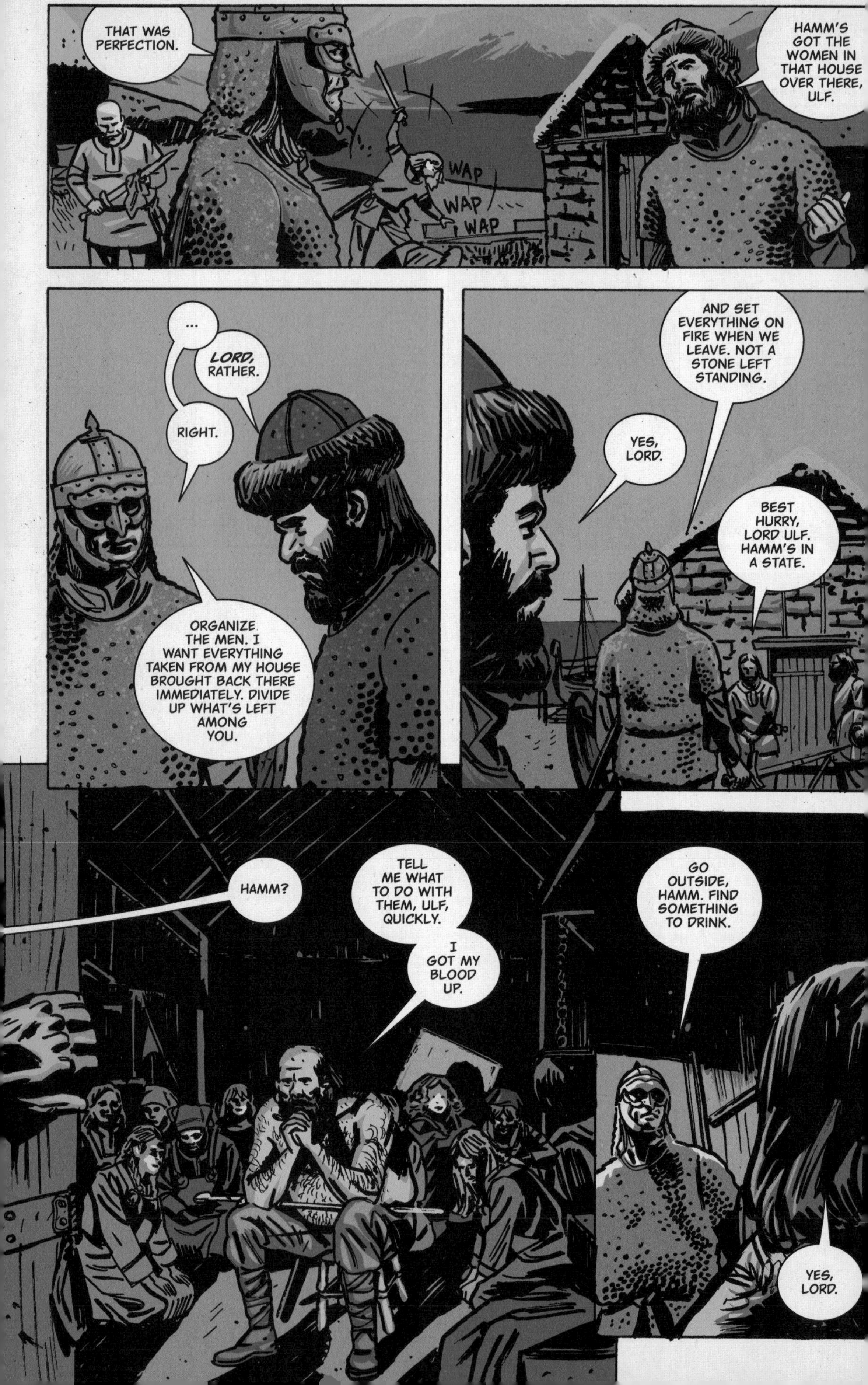
THAT WAS PERFECTION.
WAP
WAP
WAP
HAMM'S GOT THE WOMEN IN THAT HOUSE OVER THERE, ULF.
...
LORD, RATHER.
RIGHT.
ORGANIZE THE MEN. I WANT EVERYTHING TAKEN FROM MY HOUSE BROUGHT BACK THERE IMMEDIATELY. DIVIDE UP WHAT'S LEFT AMONG YOU.
AND SET EVERYTHING ON FIRE WHEN WE LEAVE. NOT A STONE LEFT STANDING.
YES, LORD.
BEST HURRY, LORD ULF. HAMM'S IN A STATE.
HAMM?
TELL ME WHAT TO DO WITH THEM, ULF, QUICKLY.
I GOT MY BLOOD UP.
GO OUTSIDE, HAMM. FIND SOMETHING TO DRINK.
YES, LORD.

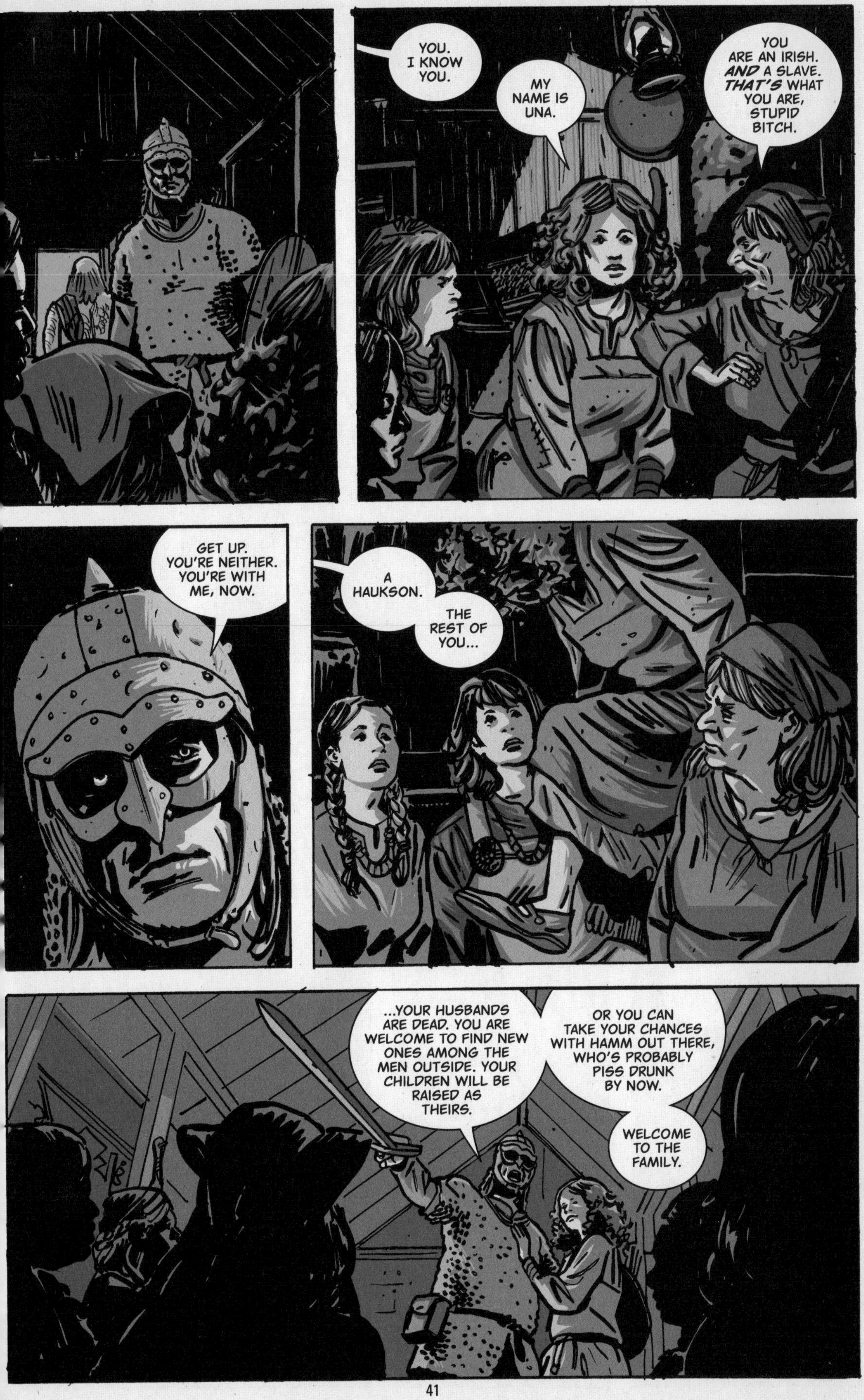

YOU. I KNOW YOU.
MY NAME IS UNA.
YOU ARE AN IRISH. AND A SLAVE. THAT'S WHAT YOU ARE, STUPID BITCH.
GET UP. YOU'RE NEITHER. YOU'RE WITH ME, NOW.
A HAUKSON.
THE REST OF YOU...
...YOUR HUSBANDS ARE DEAD. YOU ARE WELCOME TO FIND NEW ONES AMONG THE MEN OUTSIDE. YOUR CHILDREN WILL BE RAISED AS THEIRS.
OR YOU CAN TAKE YOUR CHANCES WITH HAMM OUT THERE, WHO'S PROBABLY PISS DRUNK BY NOW.
WELCOME TO THE FAMILY.

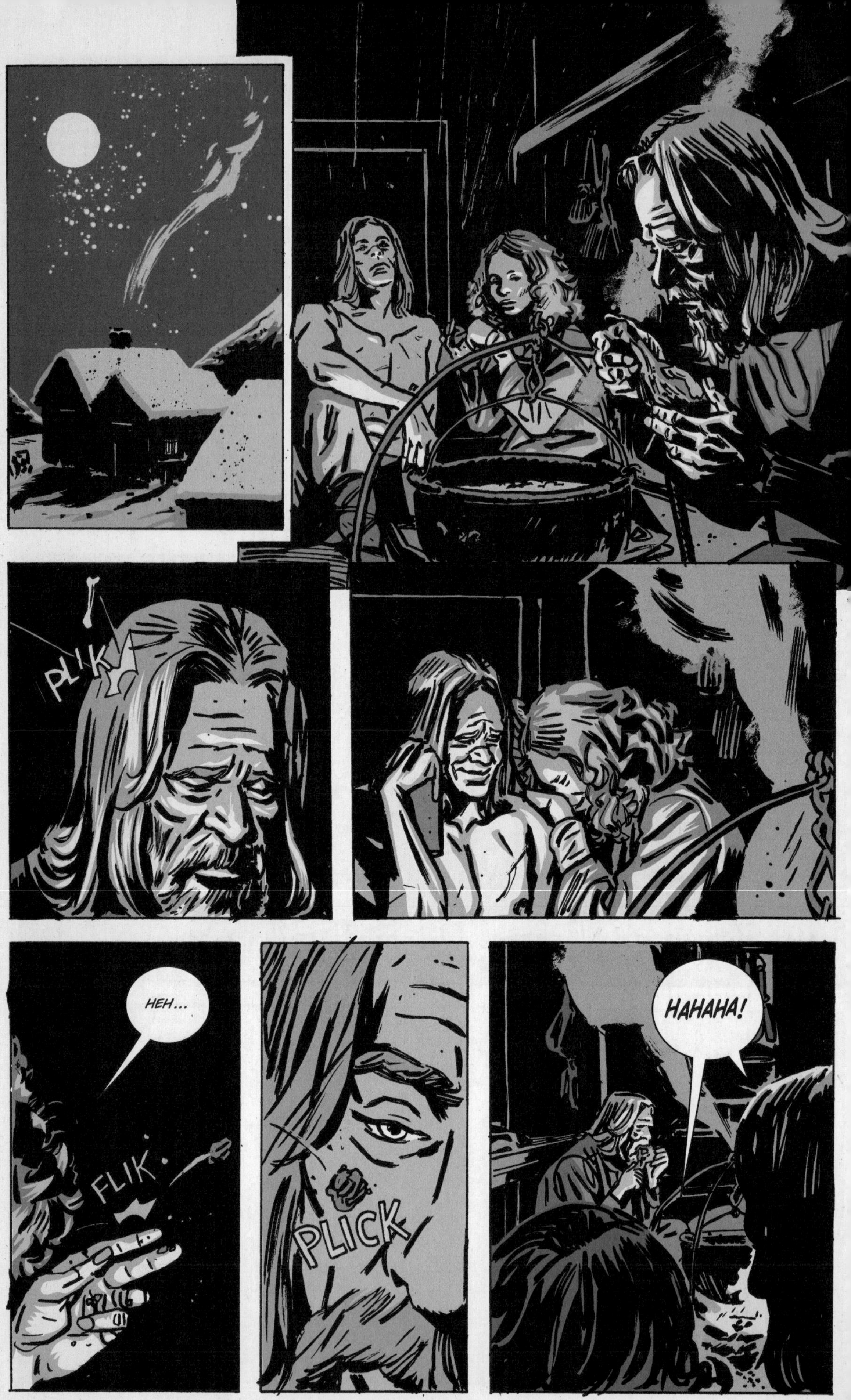
PLIK
HEH...
FLIK
PLICK
HAHAHA!

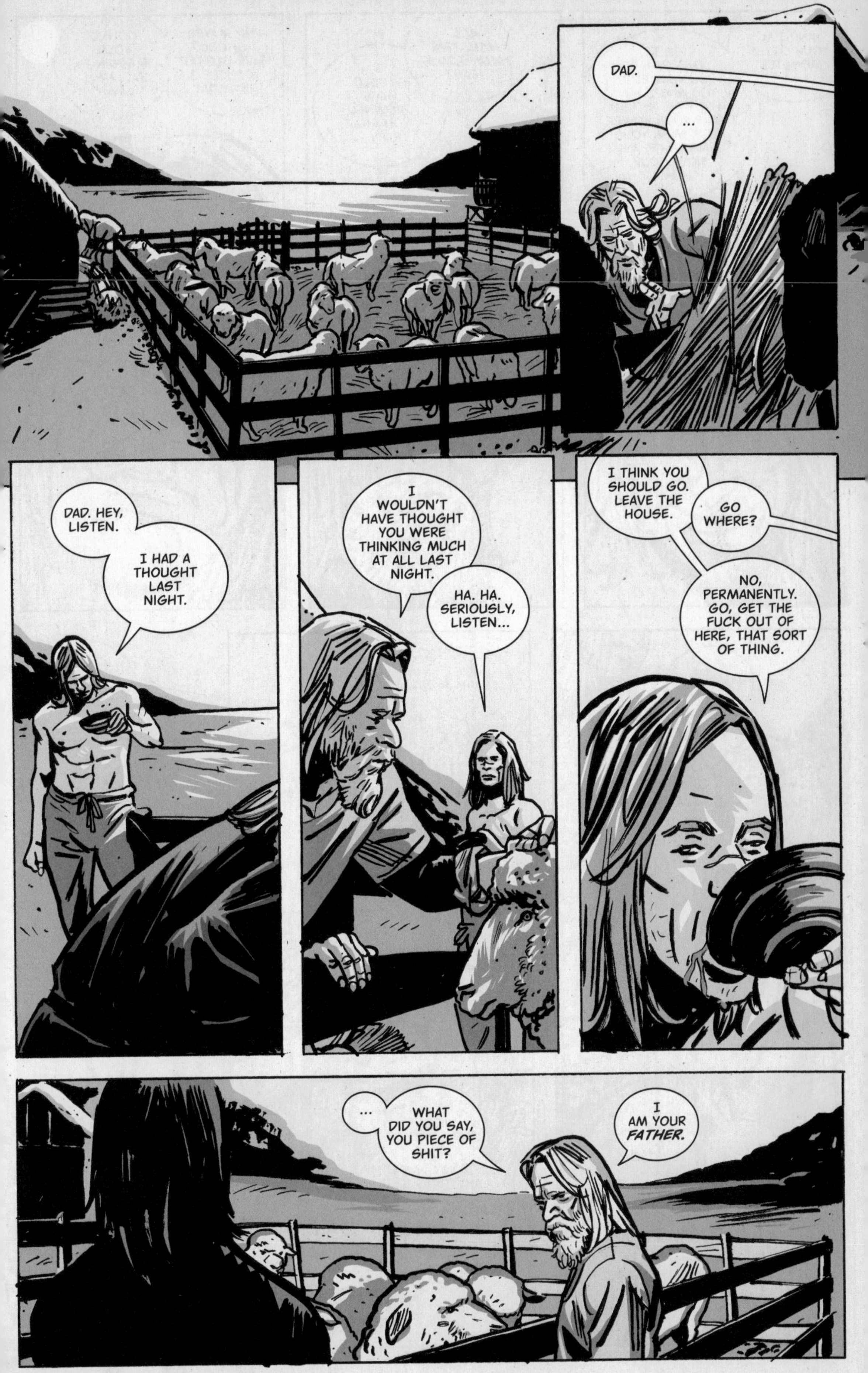
DAD.
...
DAD. HEY, LISTEN.
I HAD A THOUGHT LAST NIGHT.
I WOULDN'T HAVE THOUGHT YOU WERE THINKING MUCH AT ALL LAST NIGHT.
HA. HA. SERIOUSLY, LISTEN...
I THINK YOU SHOULD GO. LEAVE THE HOUSE.
GO WHERE?
NO, PERMANENTLY. GO, GET THE FUCK OUT OF HERE, THAT SORT OF THING.
...
WHAT DID YOU SAY, YOU PIECE OF SHIT?
I AM YOUR FATHER.

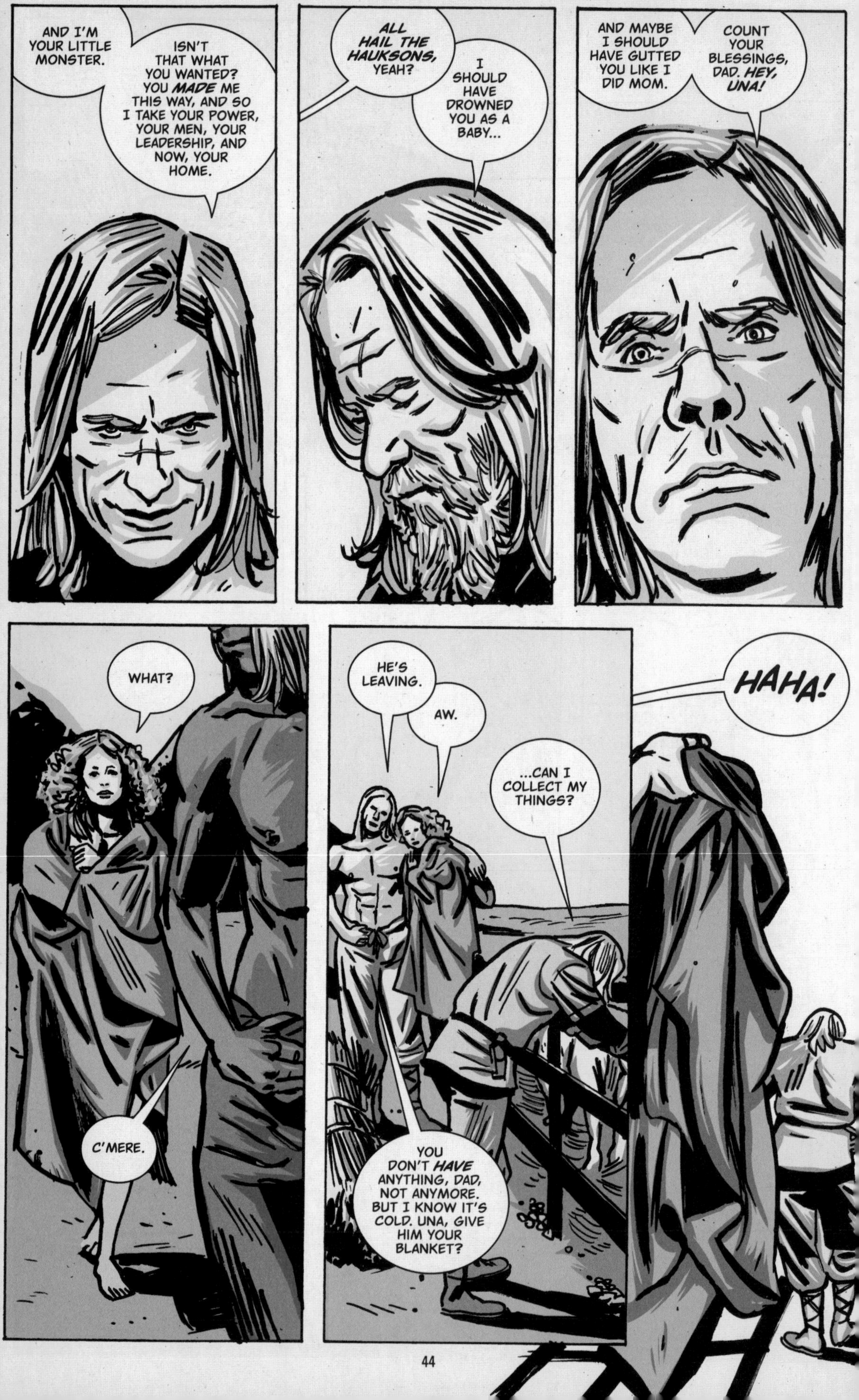
AND I'M YOUR LITTLE MONSTER.
ISN'T THAT WHAT YOU WANTED? YOU MADE ME THIS WAY, AND SO I TAKE YOUR POWER, YOUR MEN, YOUR LEADERSHIP, AND NOW, YOUR HOME.
ALL HAIL THE HAUKSONS, YEAH?
I SHOULD HAVE DROWNED YOU AS A BABY...
AND MAYBE I SHOULD HAVE GUTTED YOU LIKE I DID MOM.
COUNT YOUR BLESSINGS, DAD. HEY, UNA!
WHAT?
C'MERE.
HE'S LEAVING.
AW.
...CAN I COLLECT MY THINGS?
YOU DON'T HAVE ANYTHING, DAD, NOT ANYMORE. BUT I KNOW IT'S COLD. UNA, GIVE HIM YOUR BLANKET?
HAHA!

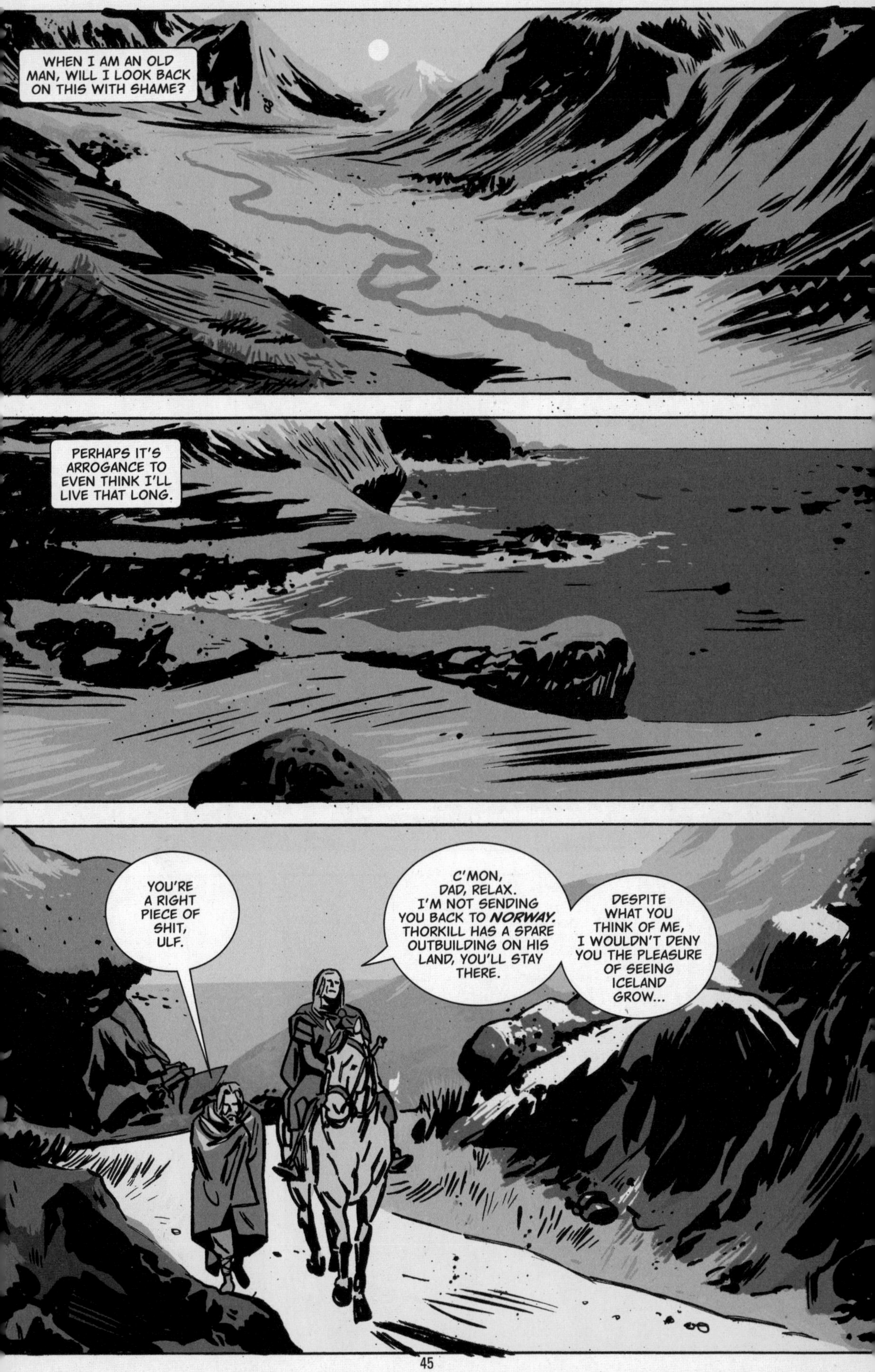
WHEN I AM AN OLD MAN, WILL I LOOK BACK ON THIS WITH SHAME?
PERHAPS IT'S ARROGANCE TO EVEN THINK I'LL LIVE THAT LONG.
YOU'RE A RIGHT PIECE OF SHIT, ULF.
C'MON, DAD, RELAX. I'M NOT SENDING YOU BACK TO *NORWAY.* THORKILL HAS A SPARE OUTBUILDING ON HIS LAND, YOU'LL STAY THERE.
DESPITE WHAT YOU THINK OF ME, I WOULDN'T DENY YOU THE PLEASURE OF SEEING ICELAND GROW...

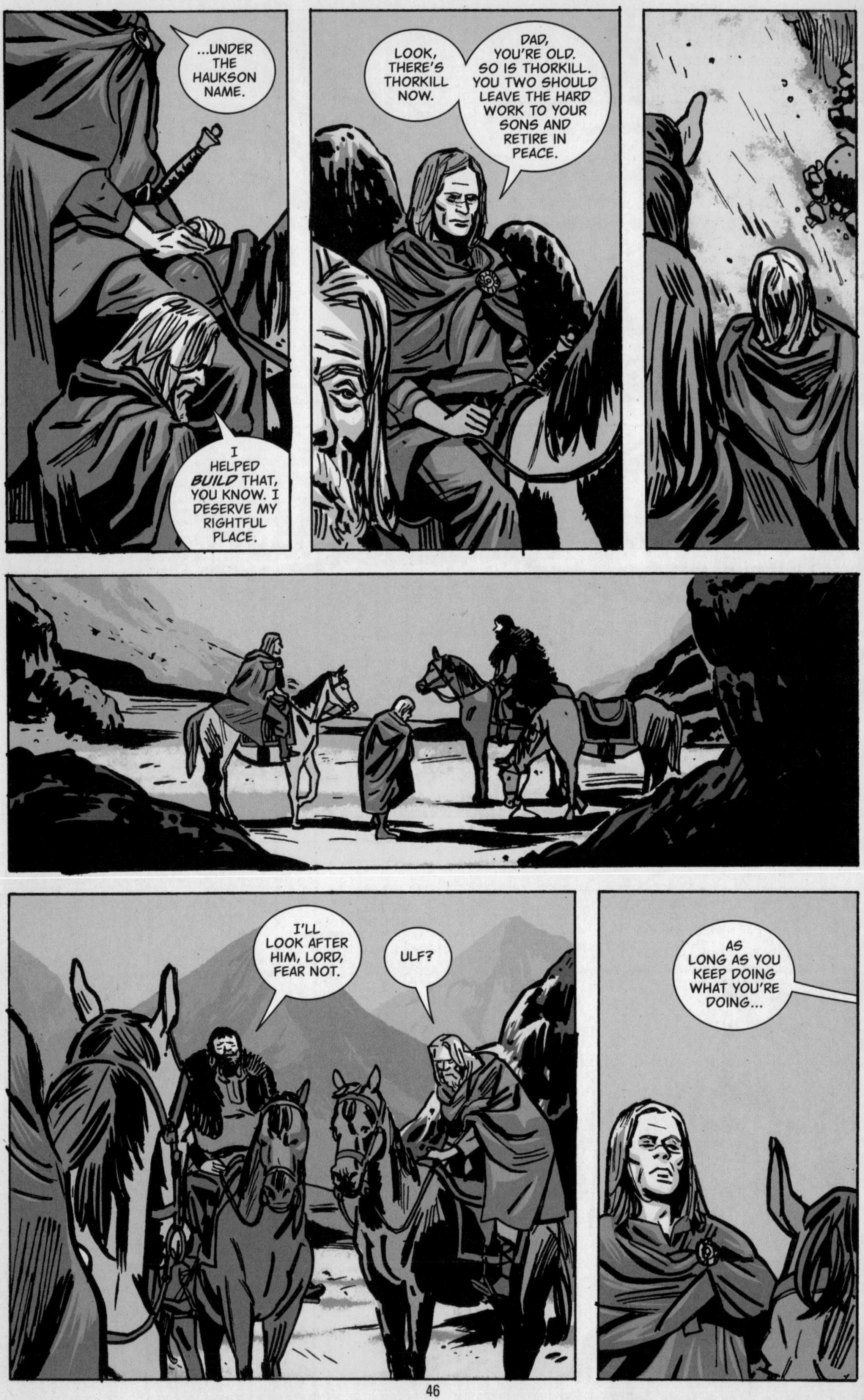
...UNDER THE HAUKSON NAME.
I HELPED BUILD THAT, YOU KNOW. I DESERVE MY RIGHTFUL PLACE.
LOOK, THERE'S THORKILL NOW.
DAD, YOU'RE OLD. SO IS THORKILL. YOU TWO SHOULD LEAVE THE HARD WORK TO YOUR SONS AND RETIRE IN PEACE.
I'LL LOOK AFTER HIM, LORD, FEAR NOT.
ULF?
AS LONG AS YOU KEEP DOING WHAT YOU'RE DOING...

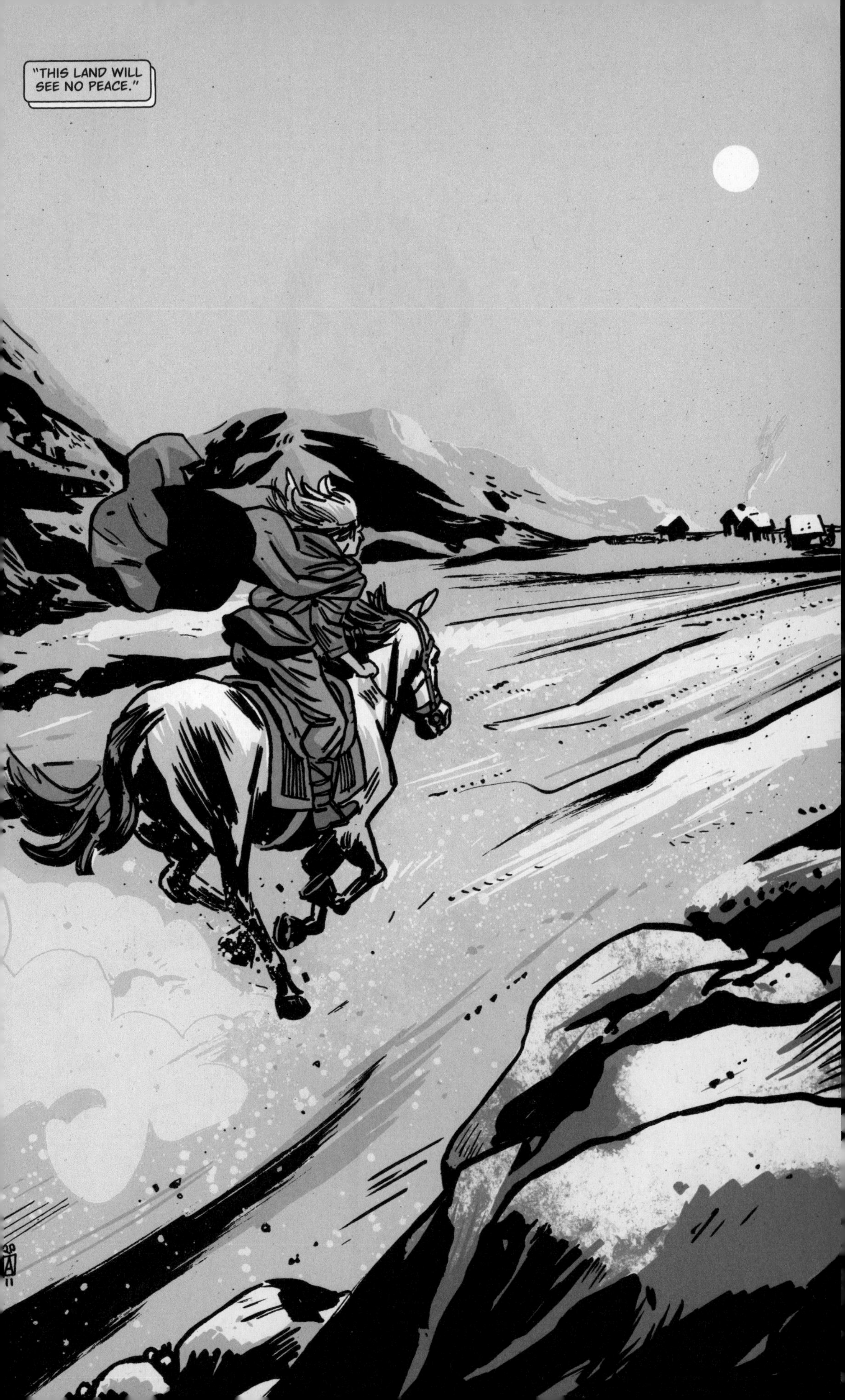
"THIS LAND WILL SEE NO PEACE."

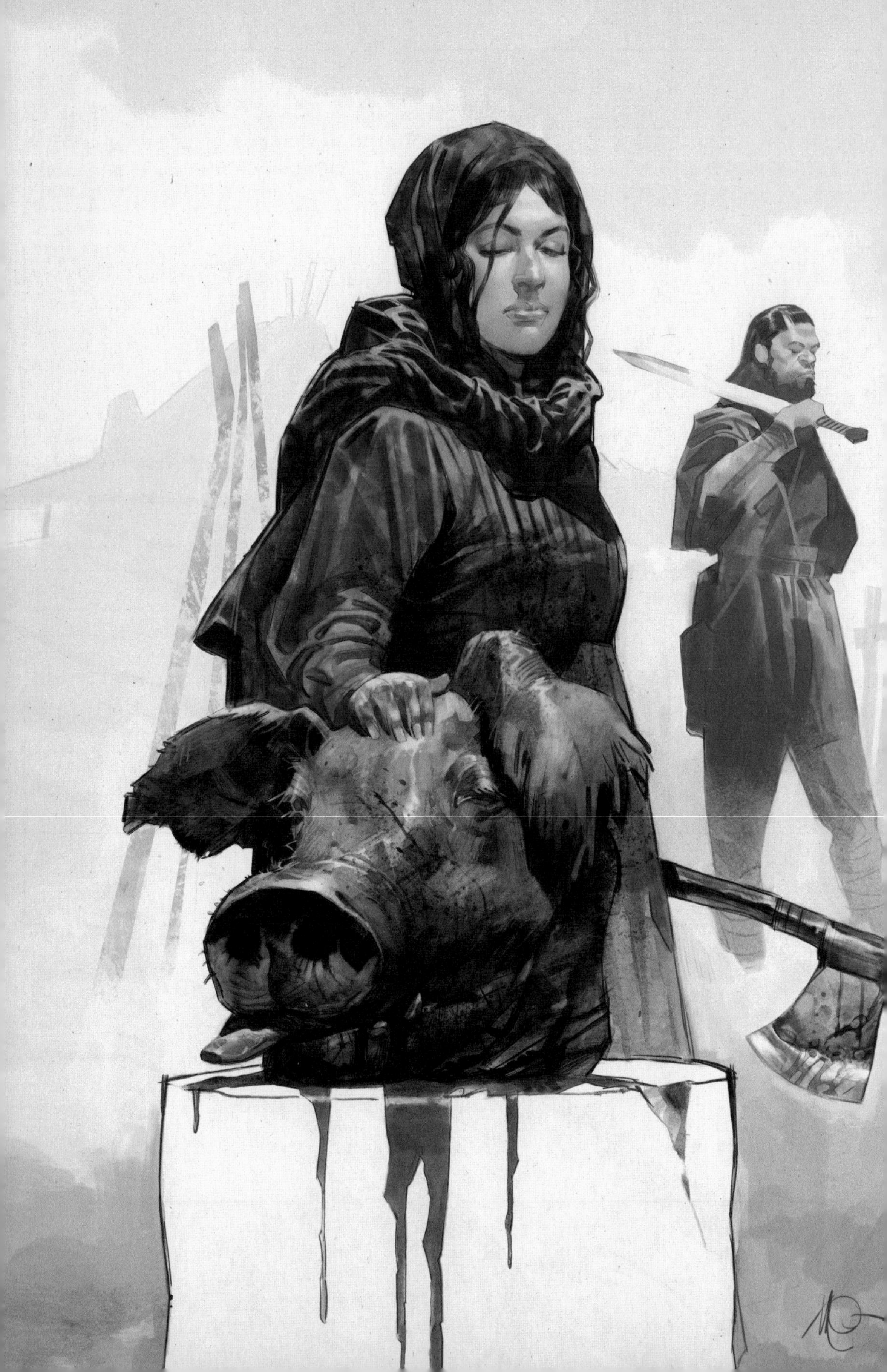

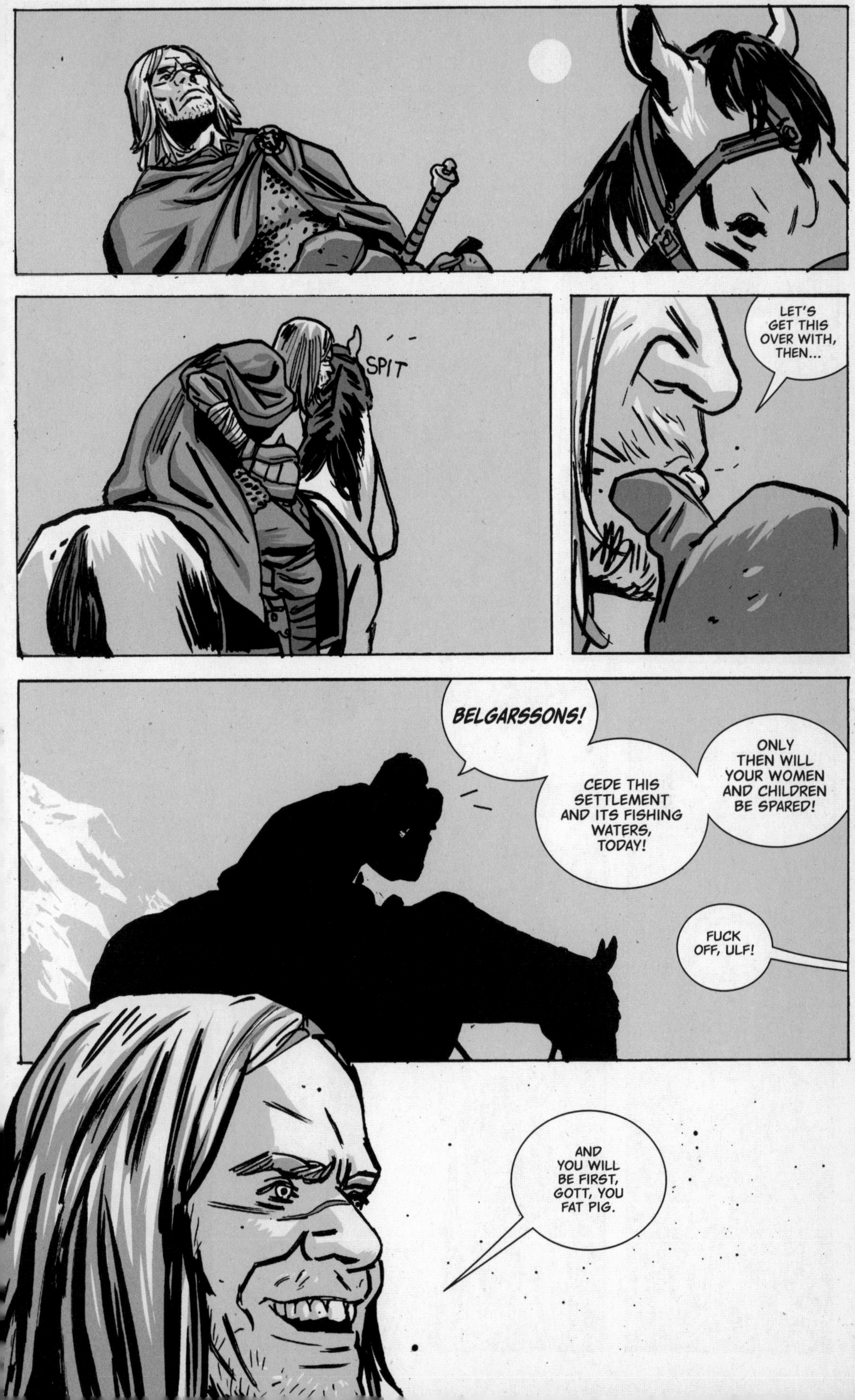
SPIT
LET'S GET THIS OVER WITH, THEN...
BELGARSSONS!
CEDE THIS SETTLEMENT AND ITS FISHING WATERS, TODAY!
ONLY THEN WILL YOUR WOMEN AND CHILDREN BE SPARED!
FUCK OFF, ULF!
AND YOU WILL BE FIRST, GOTT, YOU FAT PIG.

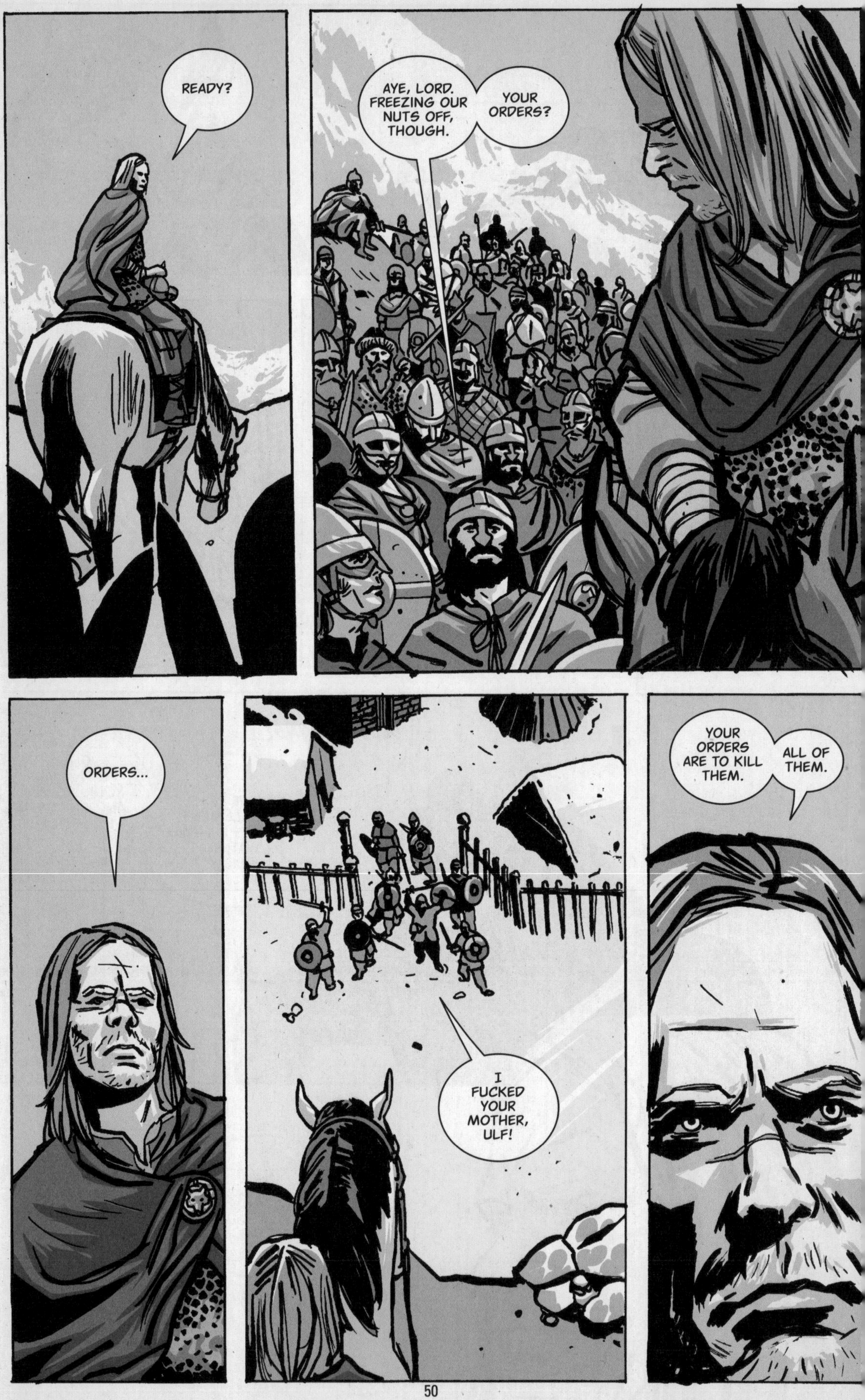
READY?
AYE, LORD. FREEZING OUR NUTS OFF, THOUGH.
YOUR ORDERS?
ORDERS...
I FUCKED YOUR MOTHER, ULF!
YOUR ORDERS ARE TO KILL THEM.
ALL OF THEM.

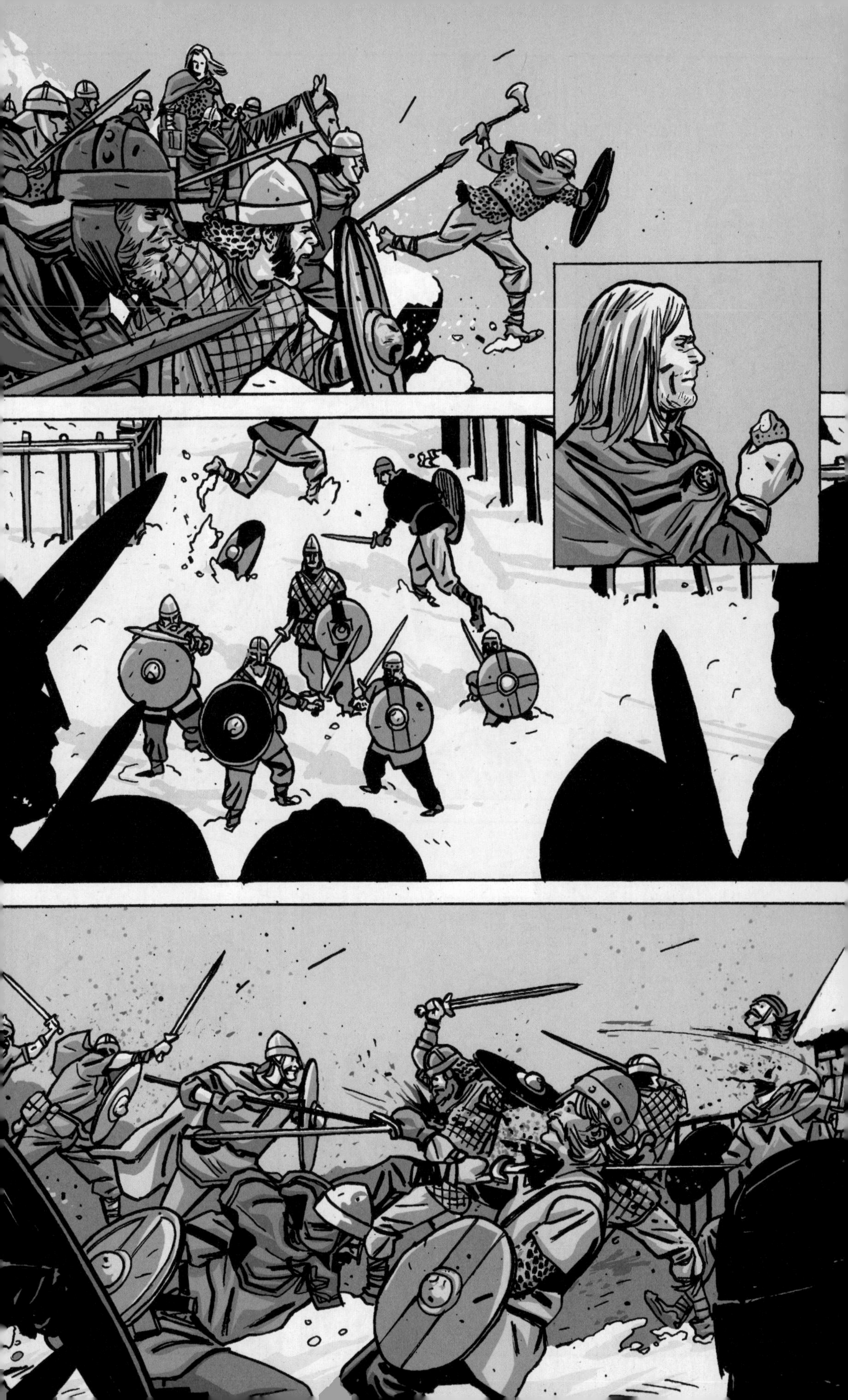

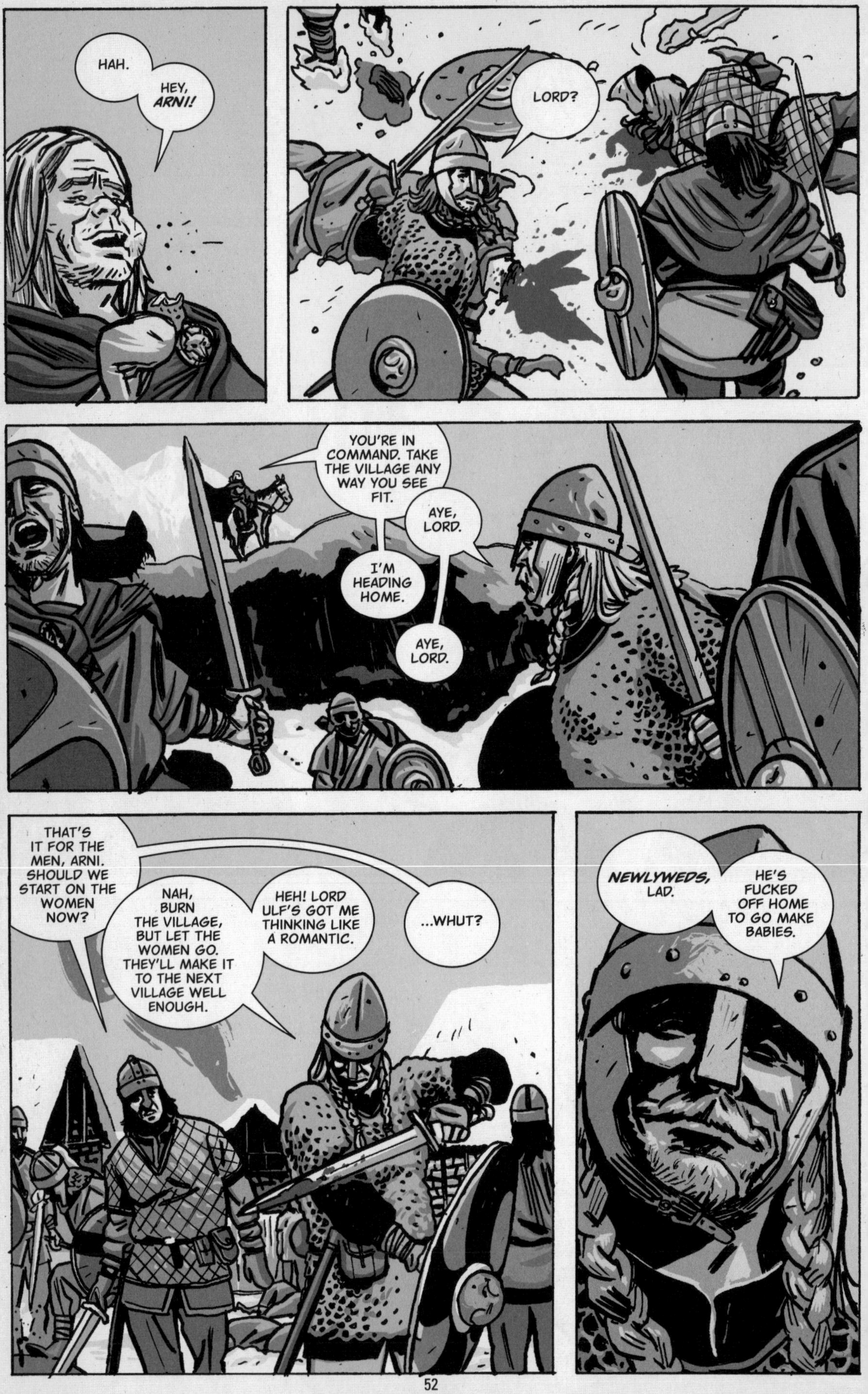
HAH.
HEY, ARNI!
LORD?
YOU'RE IN COMMAND. TAKE THE VILLAGE ANY WAY YOU SEE FIT.
AYE, LORD.
I'M HEADING HOME.
AYE, LORD.
THAT'S IT FOR THE MEN, ARNI. SHOULD WE START ON THE WOMEN NOW?
NAH, BURN THE VILLAGE, BUT LET THE WOMEN GO. THEY'LL MAKE IT TO THE NEXT VILLAGE WELL ENOUGH.
HEH! LORD ULF'S GOT ME THINKING LIKE A ROMANTIC.
...WHUT?
NEWLYWEDS, LAD.
HE'S FUCKED OFF HOME TO GO MAKE BABIES.

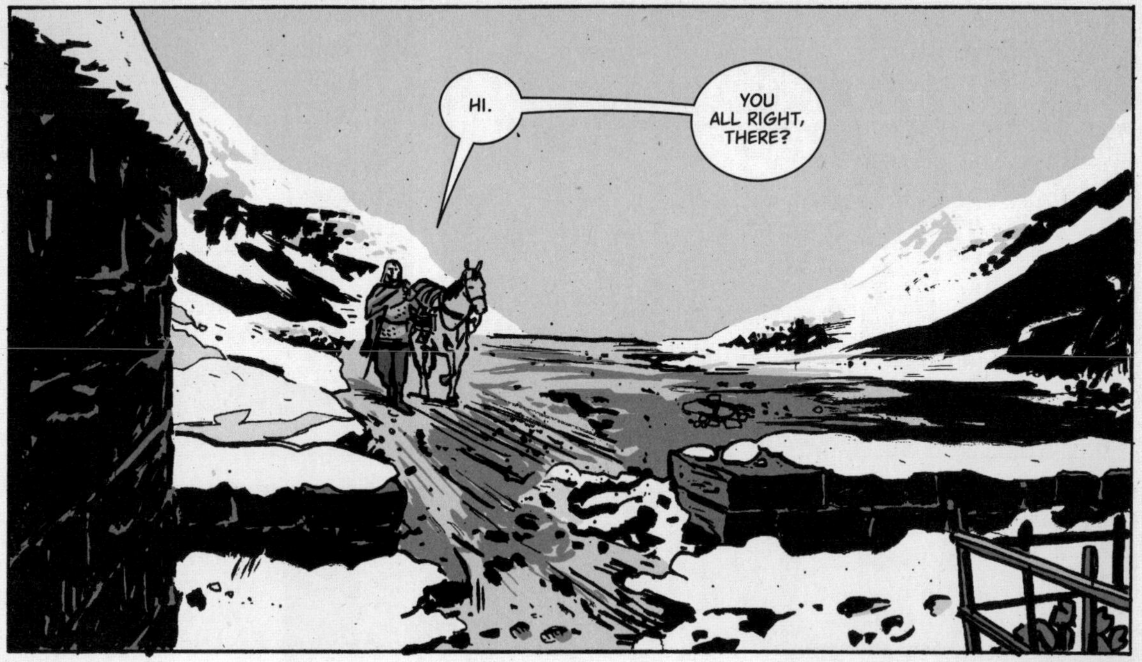
HI.
YOU ALL RIGHT, THERE?

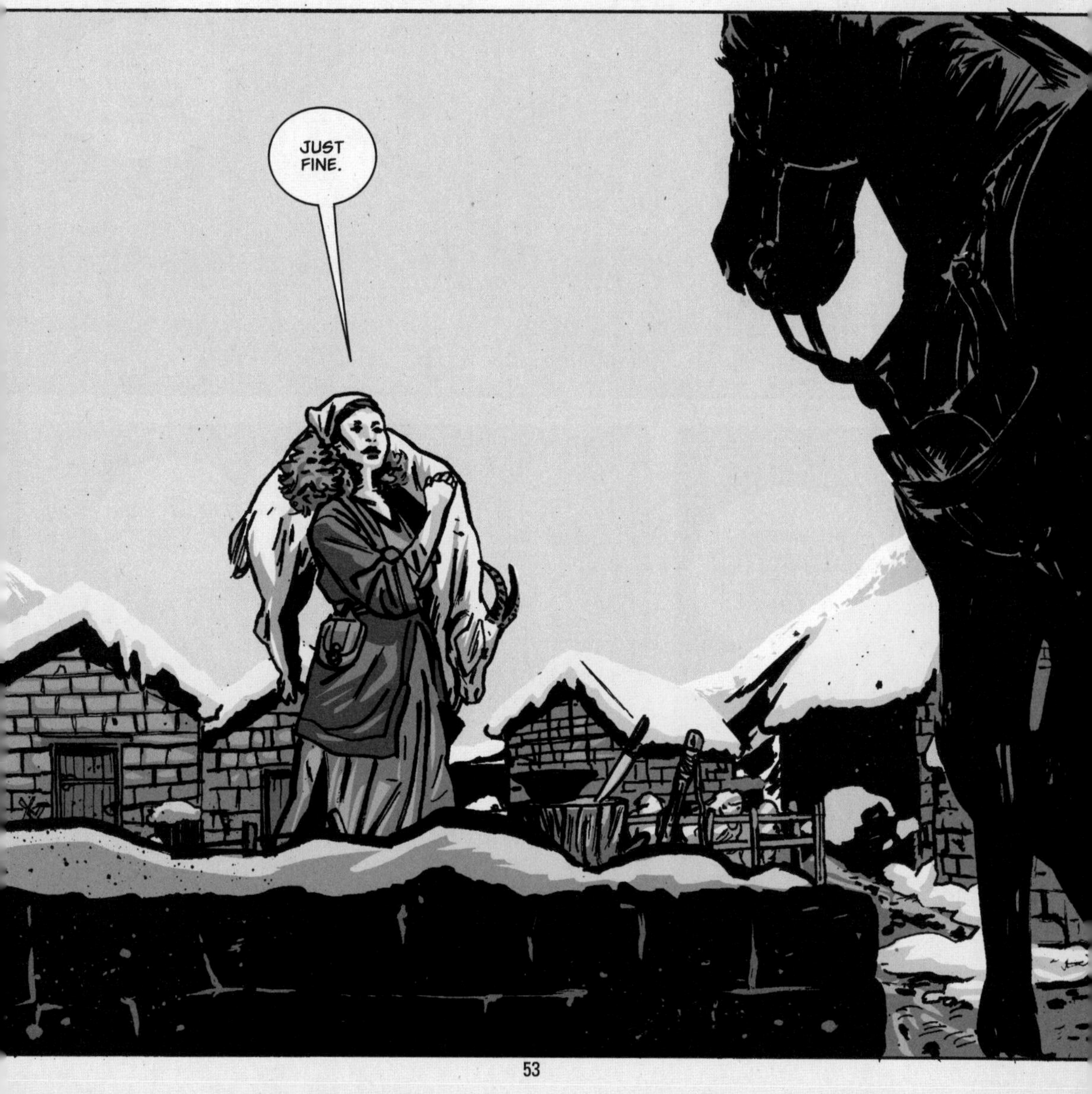
JUST FINE.

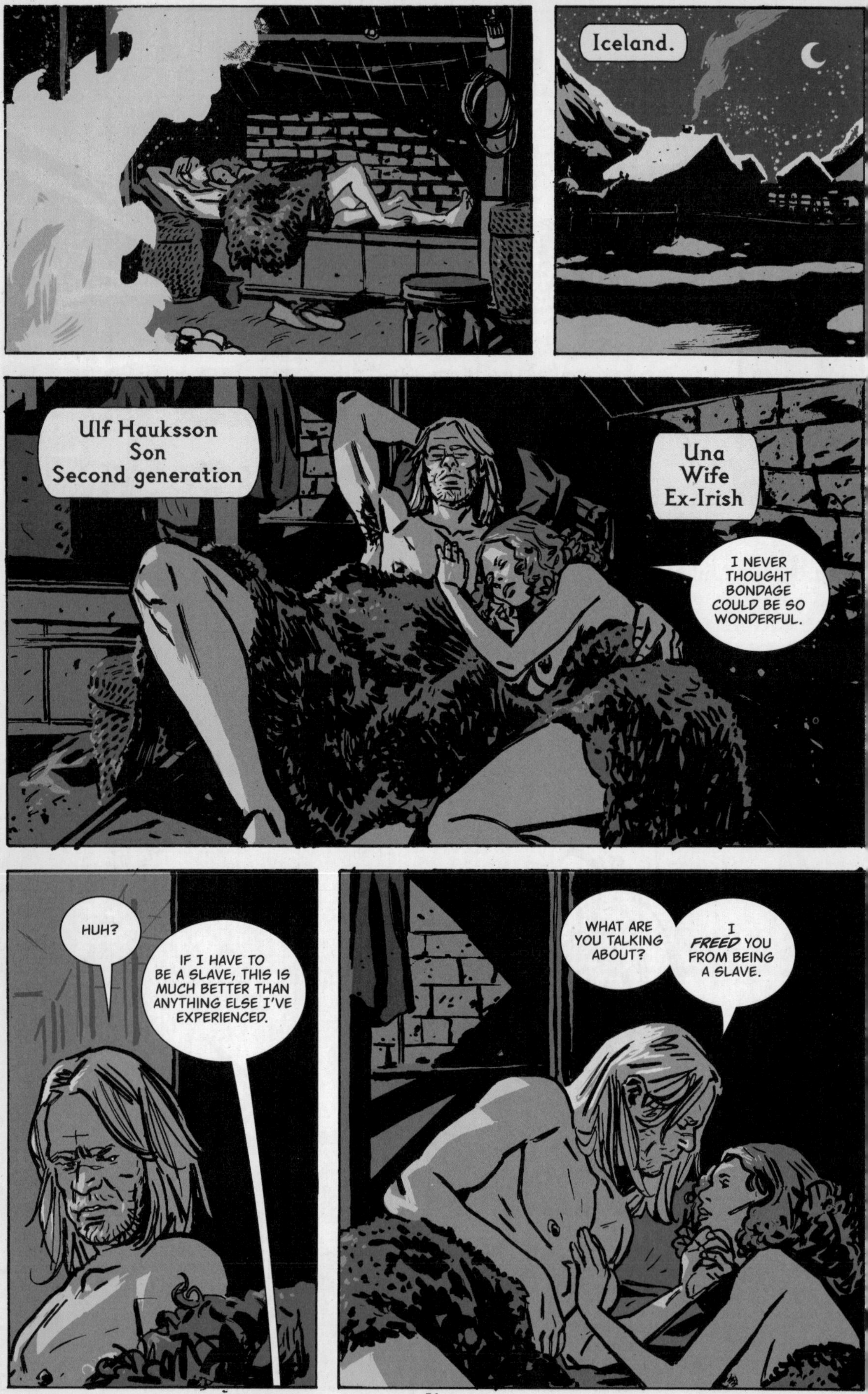
Iceland.
Ulf Hauksson Son Second generation
Una Wife Ex-Irish
I NEVER THOUGHT BONDAGE COULD BE SO WONDERFUL.
HUH?
IF I HAVE TO BE A SLAVE, THIS IS MUCH BETTER THAN ANYTHING ELSE I'VE EXPERIENCED.
WHAT ARE YOU TALKING ABOUT?
I *FREED* YOU FROM BEING A SLAVE.

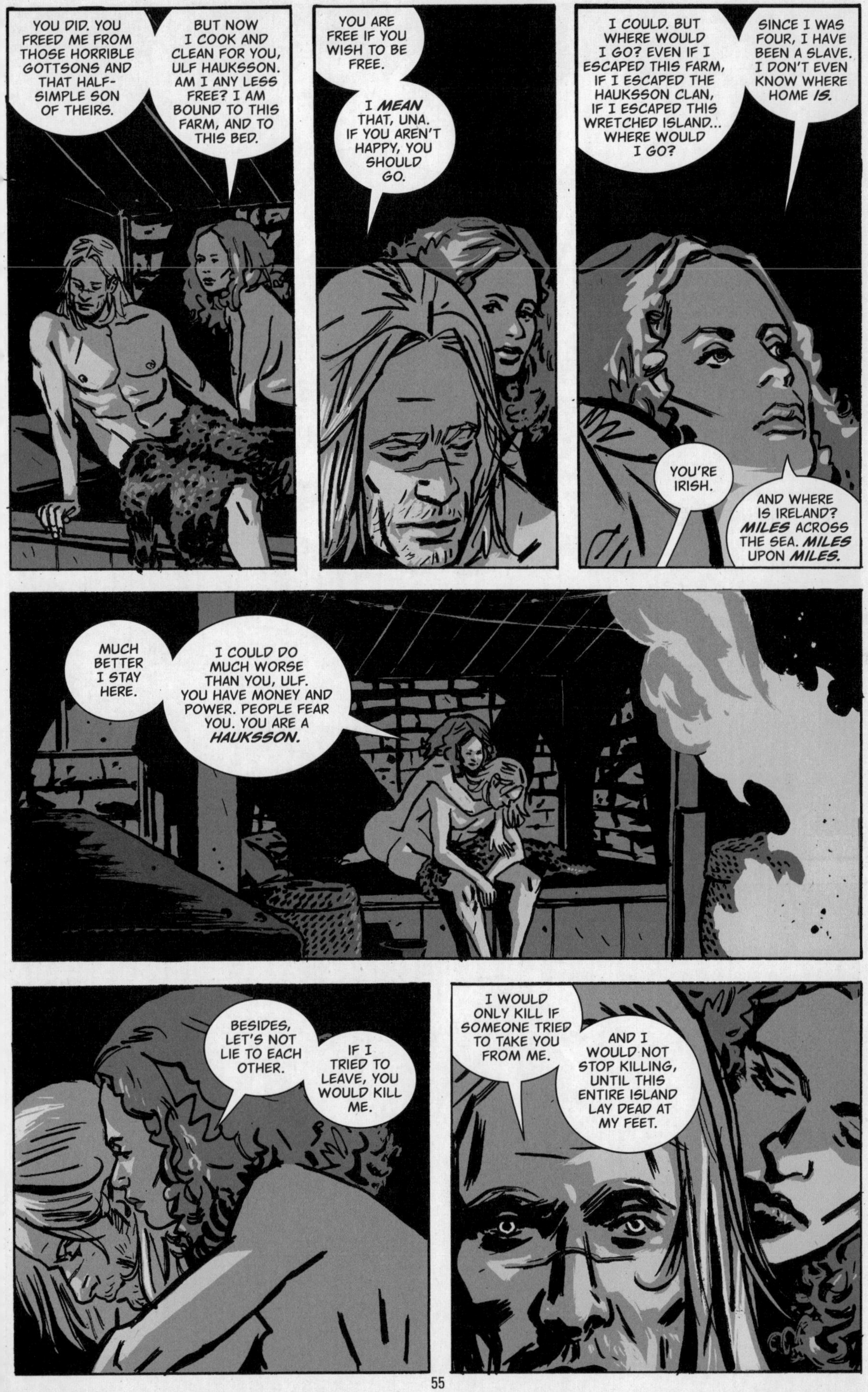
YOU DID. YOU FREED ME FROM THOSE HORRIBLE GOTTSONS AND THAT HALF-SIMPLE SON OF THEIRS.
BUT NOW I COOK AND CLEAN FOR YOU, ULF HAUKSSON. AM I ANY LESS FREE? I AM BOUND TO THIS FARM, AND TO THIS BED.
YOU ARE FREE IF YOU WISH TO BE FREE.
I MEAN THAT, UNA. IF YOU AREN'T HAPPY, YOU SHOULD GO.
I COULD. BUT WHERE WOULD I GO? EVEN IF I ESCAPED THIS FARM, IF I ESCAPED THE HAUKSSON CLAN, IF I ESCAPED THIS WRETCHED ISLAND... WHERE WOULD I GO?
SINCE I WAS FOUR, I HAVE BEEN A SLAVE. I DON'T EVEN KNOW WHERE HOME IS.
YOU'RE IRISH.
AND WHERE IS IRELAND? MILES ACROSS THE SEA. MILES UPON MILES.
MUCH BETTER I STAY HERE.
I COULD DO MUCH WORSE THAN YOU, ULF. YOU HAVE MONEY AND POWER. PEOPLE FEAR YOU. YOU ARE A HAUKSSON.
BESIDES, LET'S NOT LIE TO EACH OTHER.
IF I TRIED TO LEAVE, YOU WOULD KILL ME.
I WOULD ONLY KILL IF SOMEONE TRIED TO TAKE YOU FROM ME.
AND I WOULD NOT STOP KILLING, UNTIL THIS ENTIRE ISLAND LAY DEAD AT MY FEET.

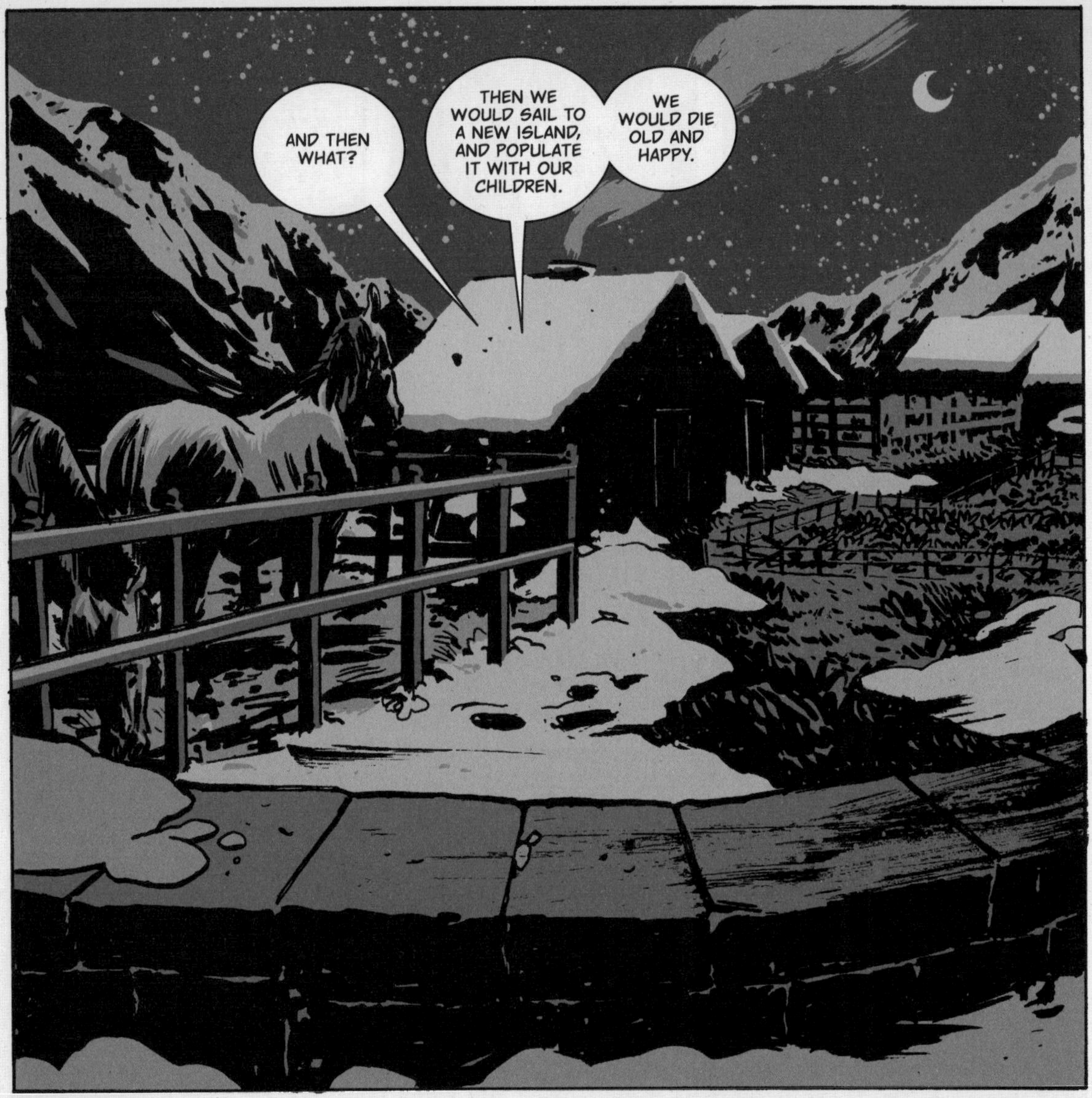
AND THEN WHAT?
THEN WE WOULD SAIL TO A NEW ISLAND, AND POPULATE IT WITH OUR CHILDREN.
WE WOULD DIE OLD AND HAPPY.

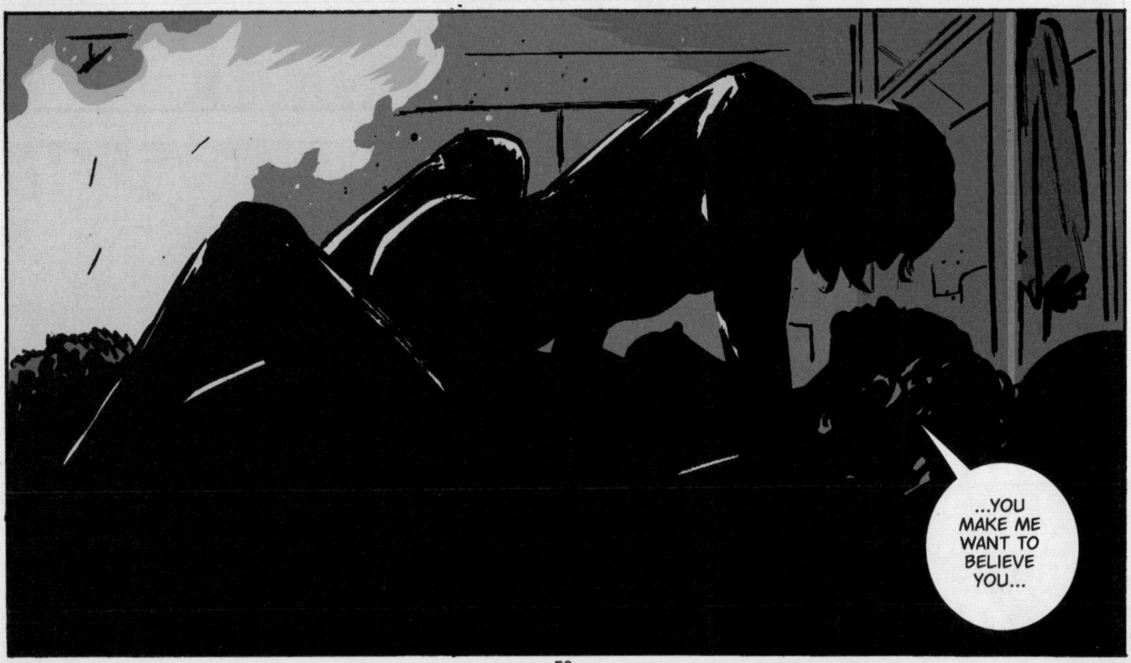
...YOU MAKE ME WANT TO BELIEVE YOU...

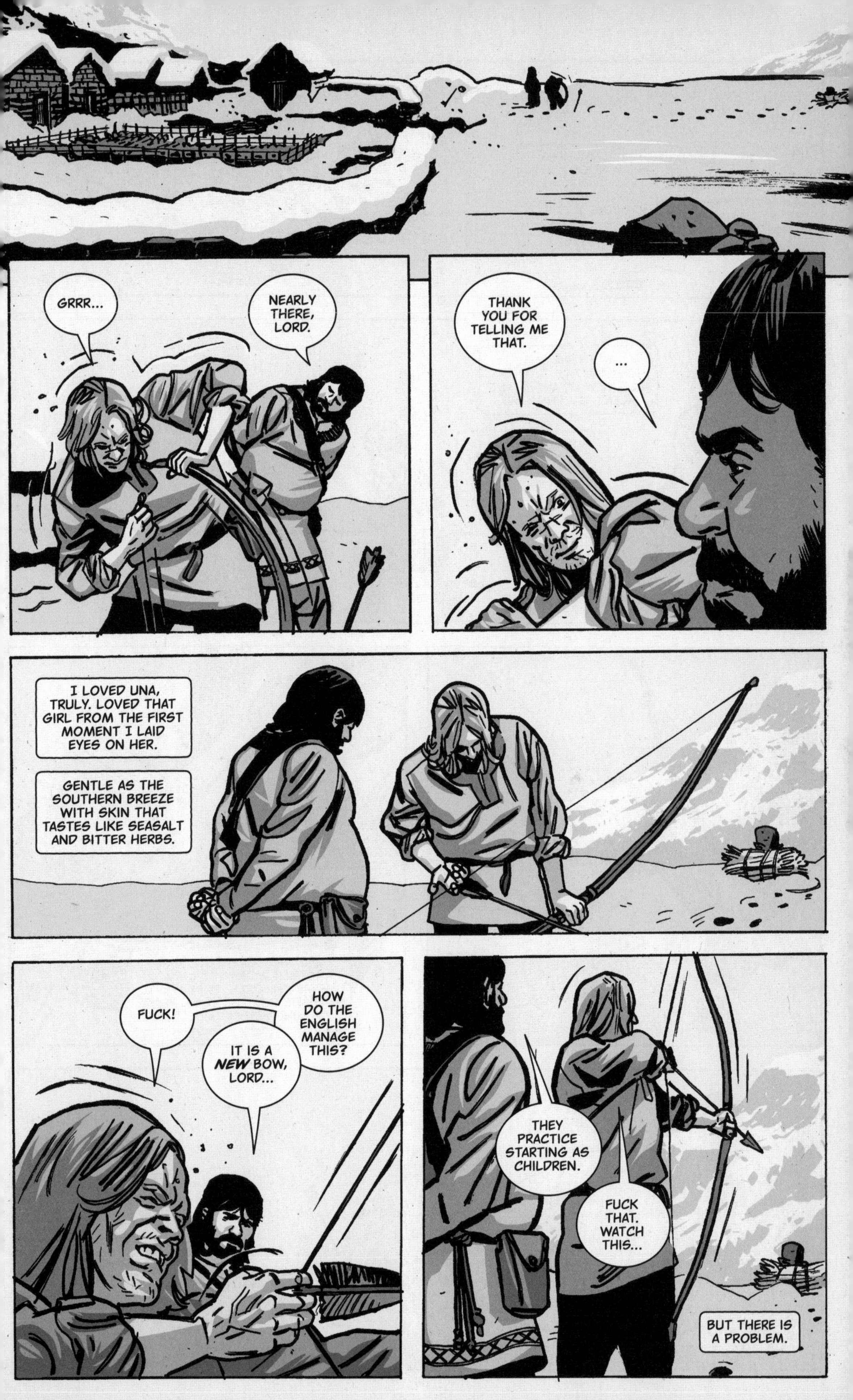
GRRR...
NEARLY THERE, LORD.
THANK YOU FOR TELLING ME THAT.
...
I LOVED UNA, TRULY. LOVED THAT GIRL FROM THE FIRST MOMENT I LAID EYES ON HER.
GENTLE AS THE SOUTHERN BREEZE WITH SKIN THAT TASTES LIKE SEASALT AND BITTER HERBS.
FUCK!
HOW DO THE ENGLISH MANAGE THIS?
IT IS A *NEW* BOW, LORD...
THEY PRACTICE STARTING AS CHILDREN.
FUCK THAT. WATCH THIS...
BUT THERE IS A PROBLEM.

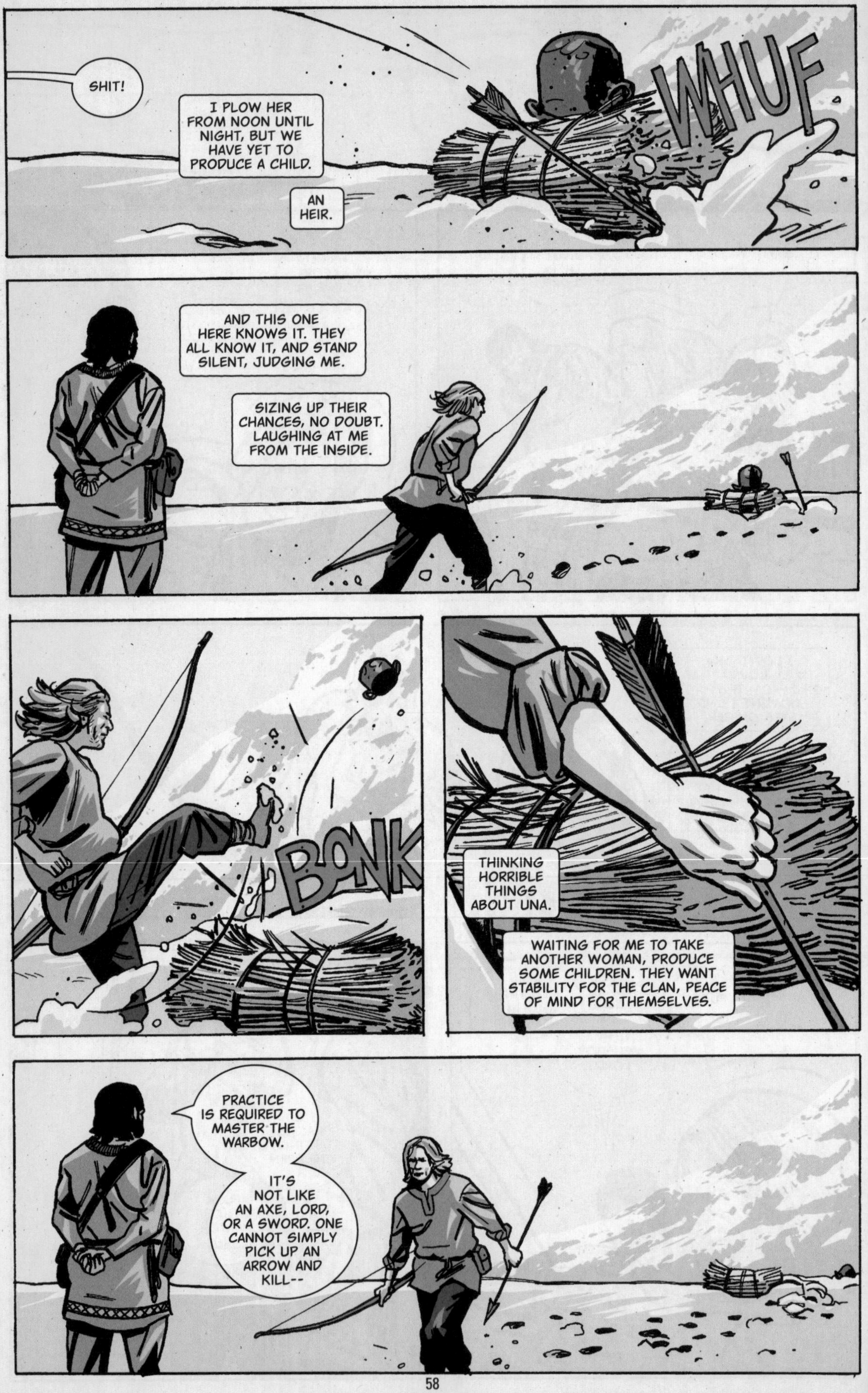
SHIT!
I PLOW HER FROM NOON UNTIL NIGHT, BUT WE HAVE YET TO PRODUCE A CHILD.
AN HEIR.
WHUF
AND THIS ONE HERE KNOWS IT. THEY ALL KNOW IT, AND STAND SILENT, JUDGING ME.
SIZING UP THEIR CHANCES, NO DOUBT. LAUGHING AT ME FROM THE INSIDE.
BONK
THINKING HORRIBLE THINGS ABOUT UNA.
WAITING FOR ME TO TAKE ANOTHER WOMAN, PRODUCE SOME CHILDREN. THEY WANT STABILITY FOR THE CLAN, PEACE OF MIND FOR THEMSELVES.
PRACTICE IS REQUIRED TO MASTER THE WARBOW.
IT'S NOT LIKE AN AXE, LORD, OR A SWORD. ONE CANNOT SIMPLY PICK UP AN ARROW AND KILL--

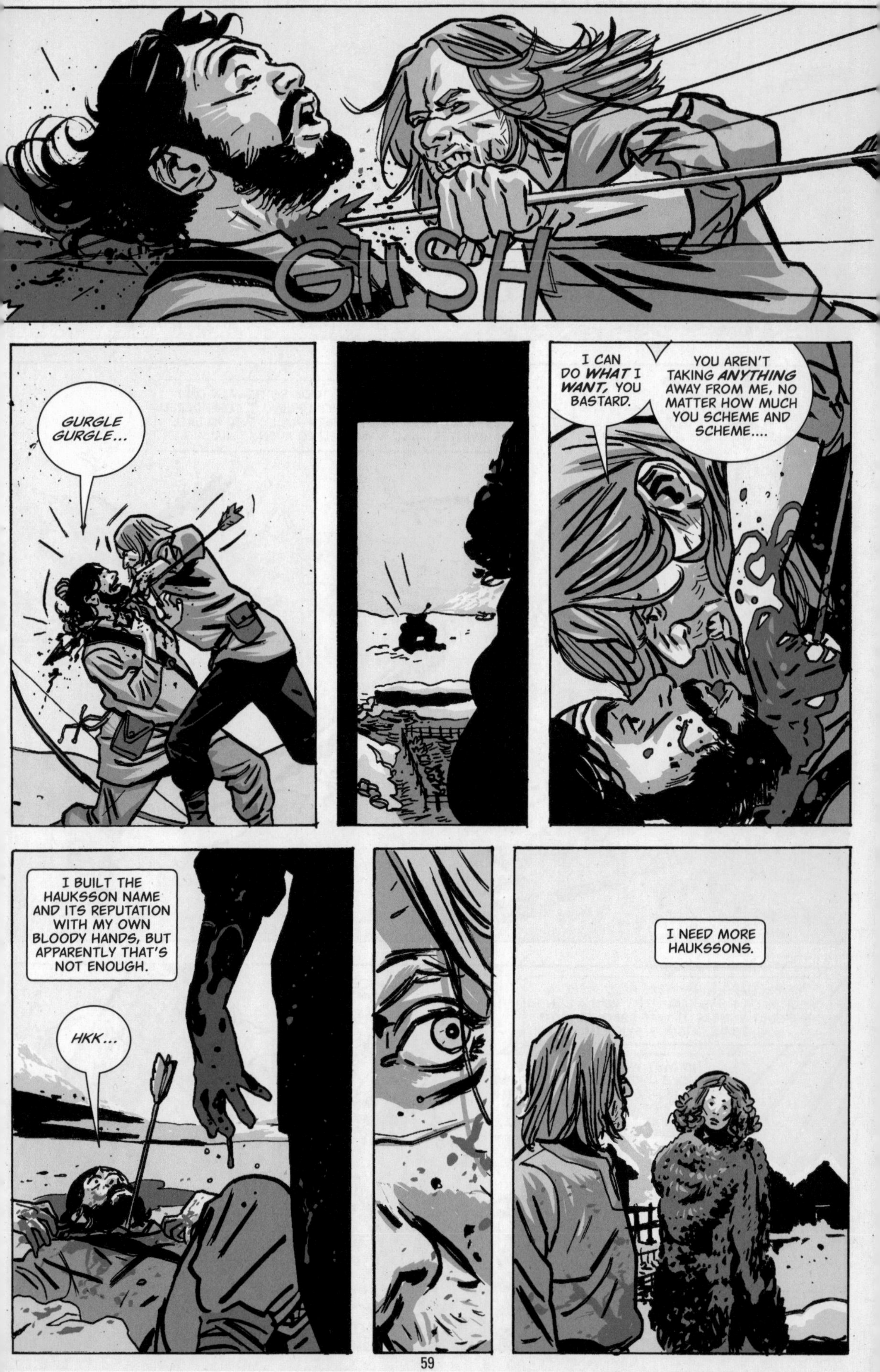
GUSH
GURGLE GURGLE...
I CAN DO WHAT I WANT, YOU BASTARD.
YOU AREN'T TAKING ANYTHING AWAY FROM ME, NO MATTER HOW MUCH YOU SCHEME AND SCHEME....
I BUILT THE HAUKSSON NAME AND ITS REPUTATION WITH MY OWN BLOODY HANDS, BUT APPARENTLY THAT'S NOT ENOUGH.
HKK...
I NEED MORE HAUKSSONS.

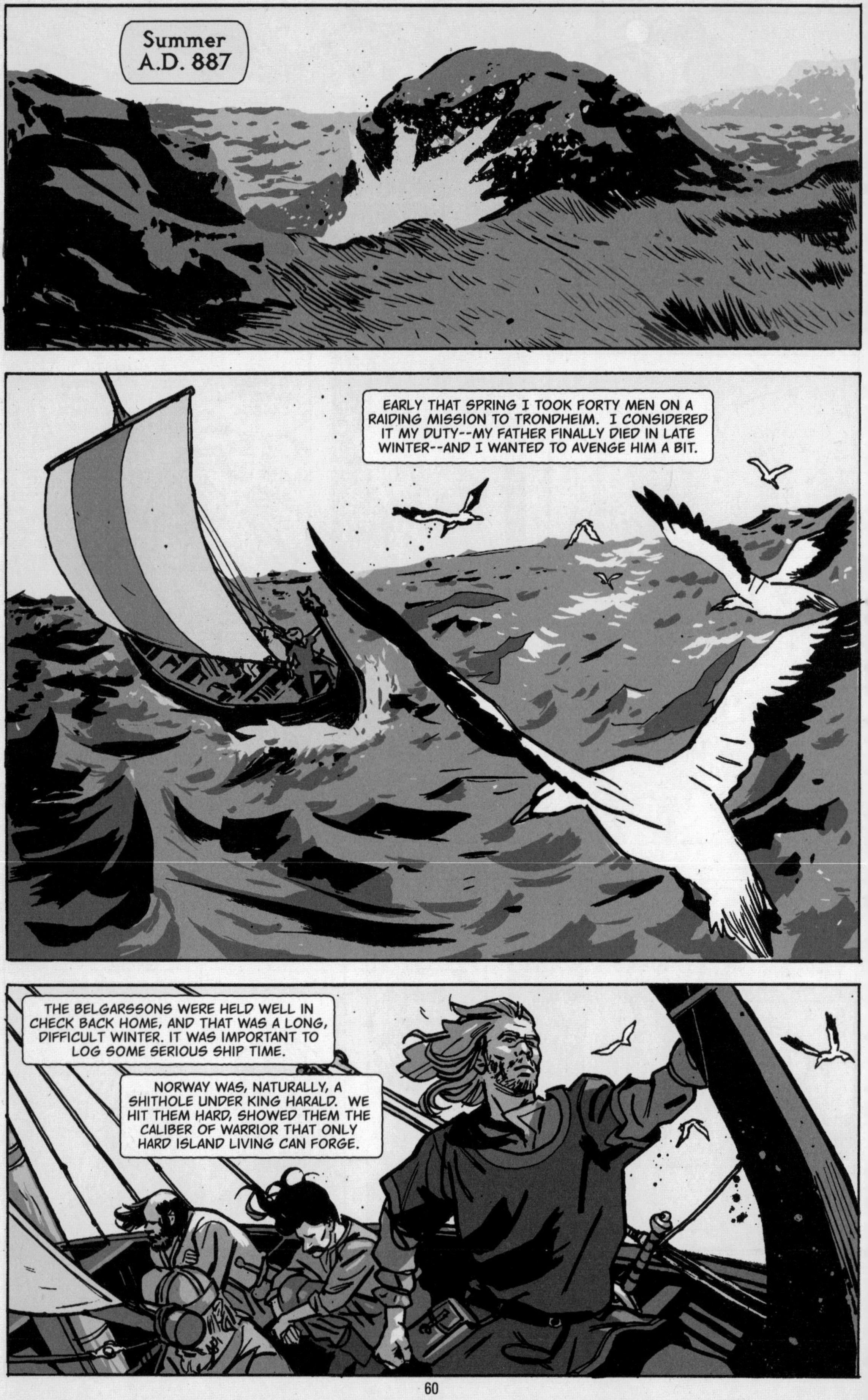
Summer
A.D. 887
EARLY THAT SPRING I TOOK FORTY MEN ON A RAIDING MISSION TO TRONDHEIM. I CONSIDERED IT MY DUTY--MY FATHER FINALLY DIED IN LATE WINTER--AND I WANTED TO AVENGE HIM A BIT.
THE BELGARSSONS WERE HELD WELL IN CHECK BACK HOME, AND THAT WAS A LONG, DIFFICULT WINTER. IT WAS IMPORTANT TO LOG SOME SERIOUS SHIP TIME.
NORWAY WAS, NATURALLY, A SHITHOLE UNDER KING HARALD. WE HIT THEM HARD, SHOWED THEM THE CALIBER OF WARRIOR THAT ONLY HARD ISLAND LIVING CAN FORGE.

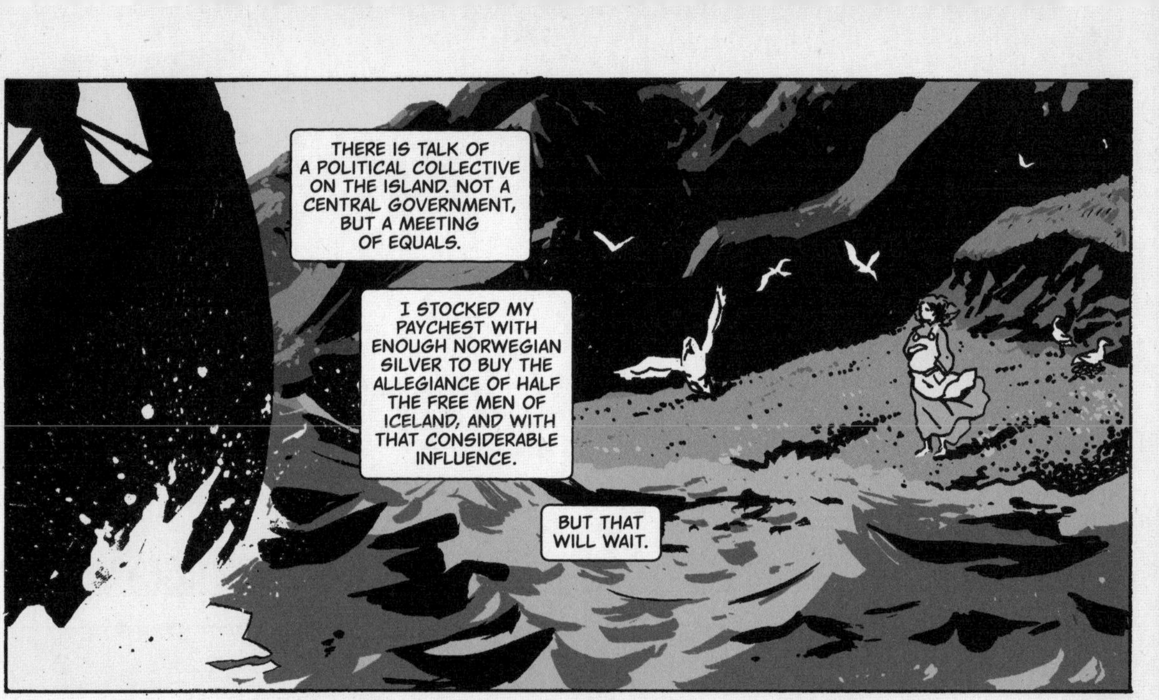
THERE IS TALK OF A POLITICAL COLLECTIVE ON THE ISLAND. NOT A CENTRAL GOVERNMENT, BUT A MEETING OF EQUALS.
I STOCKED MY PAYCHEST WITH ENOUGH NORWEGIAN SILVER TO BUY THE ALLEGIANCE OF HALF THE FREE MEN OF ICELAND, AND WITH THAT CONSIDERABLE INFLUENCE.
BUT THAT WILL WAIT.

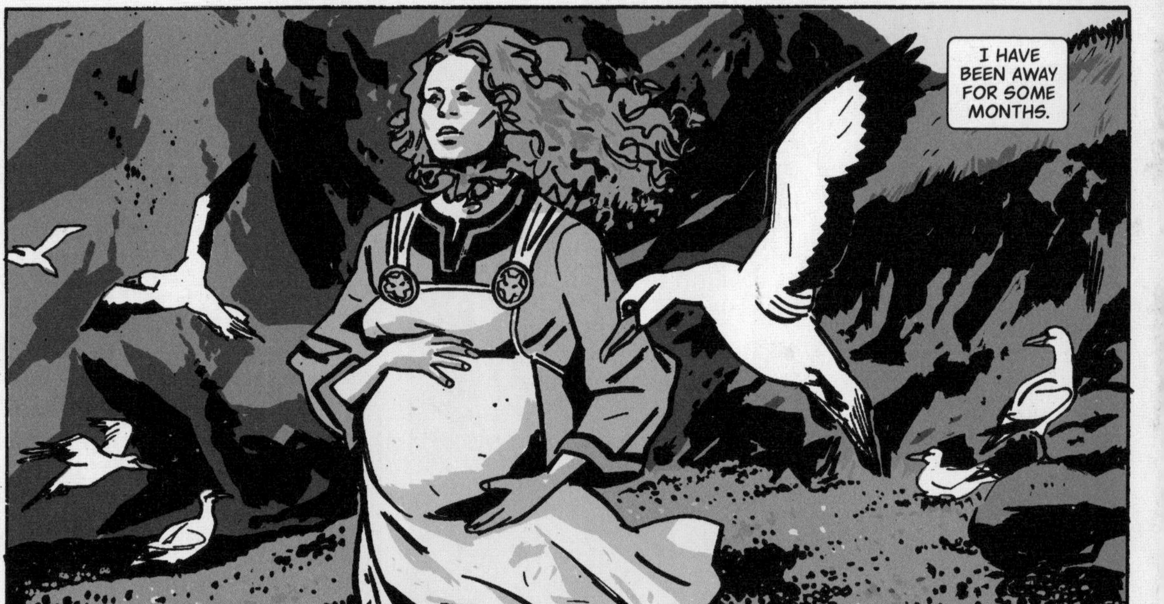
I HAVE BEEN AWAY FOR SOME MONTHS.

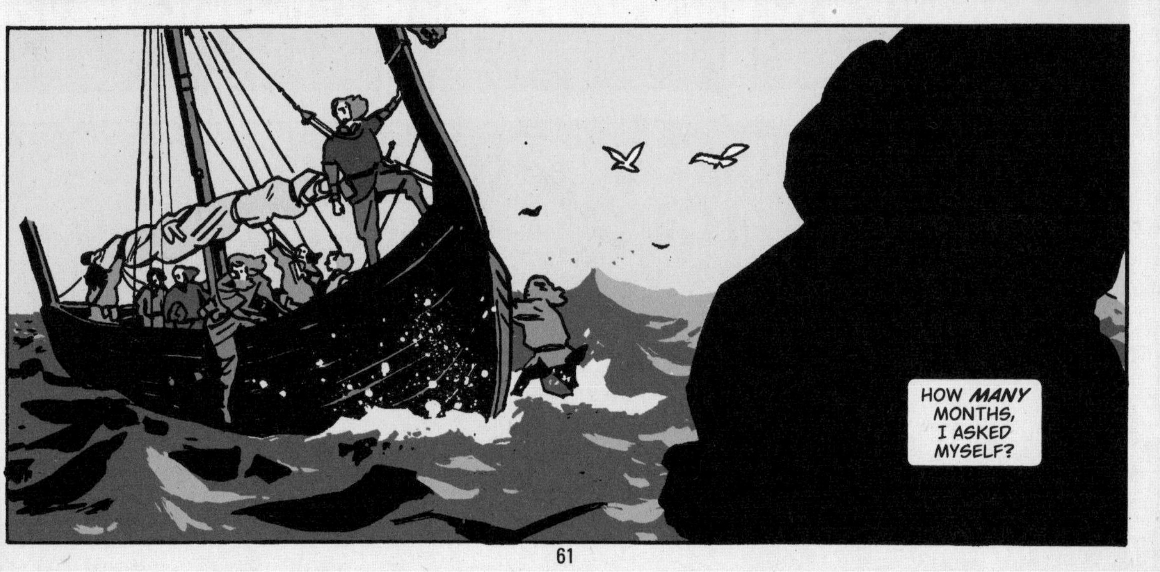
HOW *MANY* MONTHS, I ASKED MYSELF?

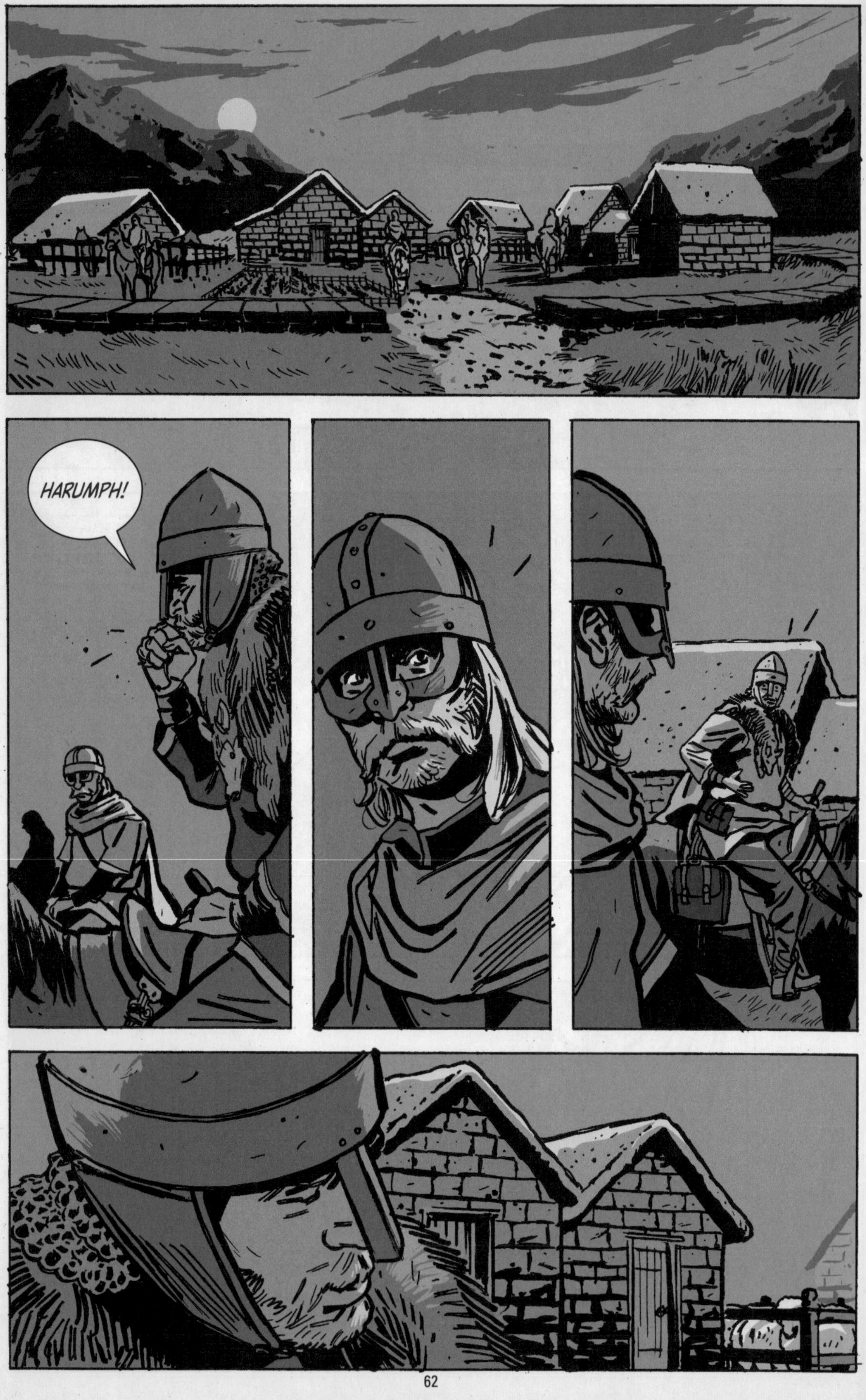
HARUMPH!

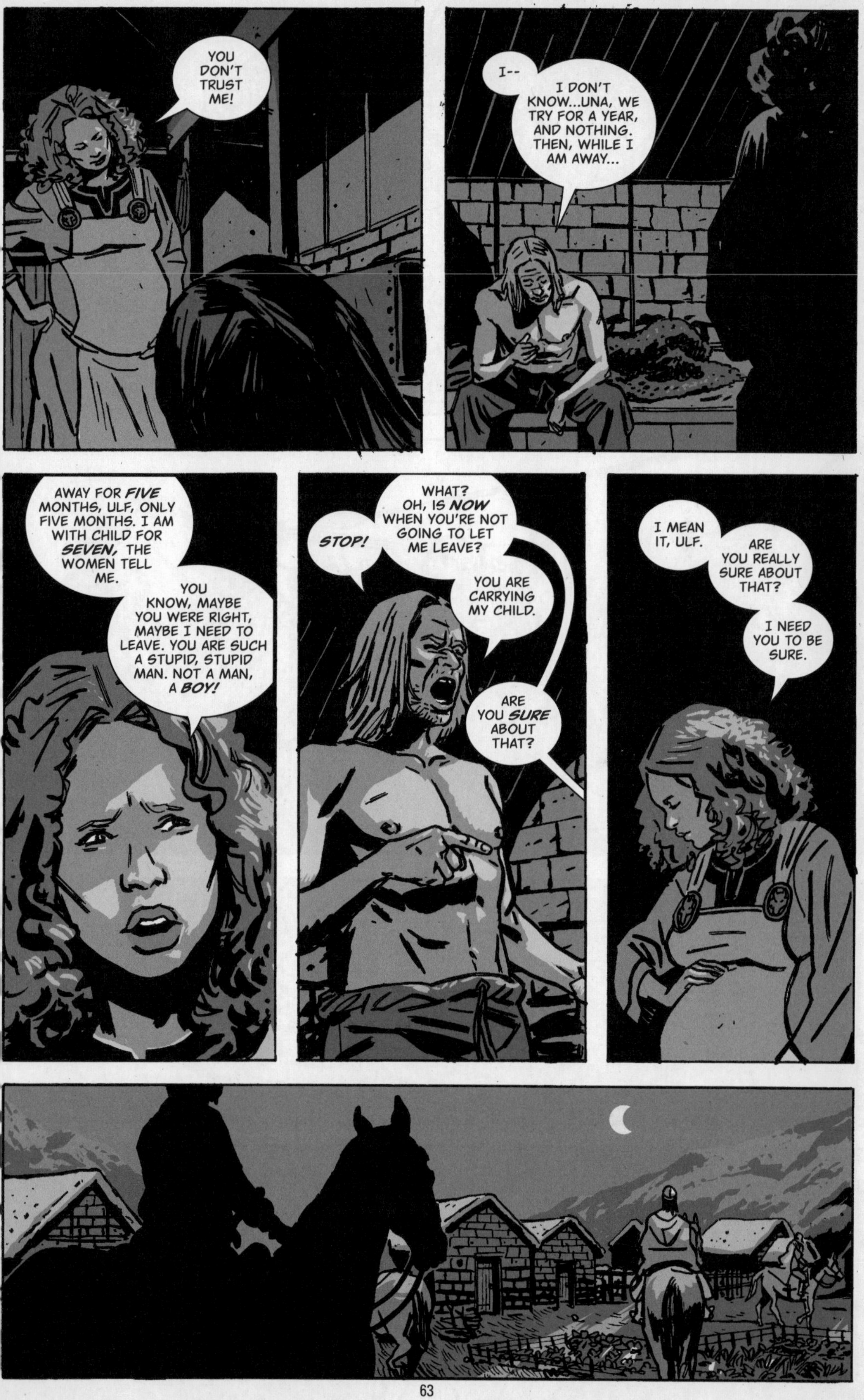
YOU DON'T TRUST ME!
I--
I DON'T KNOW...UNA, WE TRY FOR A YEAR, AND NOTHING. THEN, WHILE I AM AWAY...
AWAY FOR FIVE MONTHS, ULF, ONLY FIVE MONTHS. I AM WITH CHILD FOR SEVEN, THE WOMEN TELL ME.
YOU KNOW, MAYBE YOU WERE RIGHT, MAYBE I NEED TO LEAVE. YOU ARE SUCH A STUPID, STUPID MAN. NOT A MAN, A BOY!
STOP!
WHAT? OH, IS NOW WHEN YOU'RE NOT GOING TO LET ME LEAVE?
YOU ARE CARRYING MY CHILD.
ARE YOU SURE ABOUT THAT?
I MEAN IT, ULF.
ARE YOU REALLY SURE ABOUT THAT?
I NEED YOU TO BE SURE.

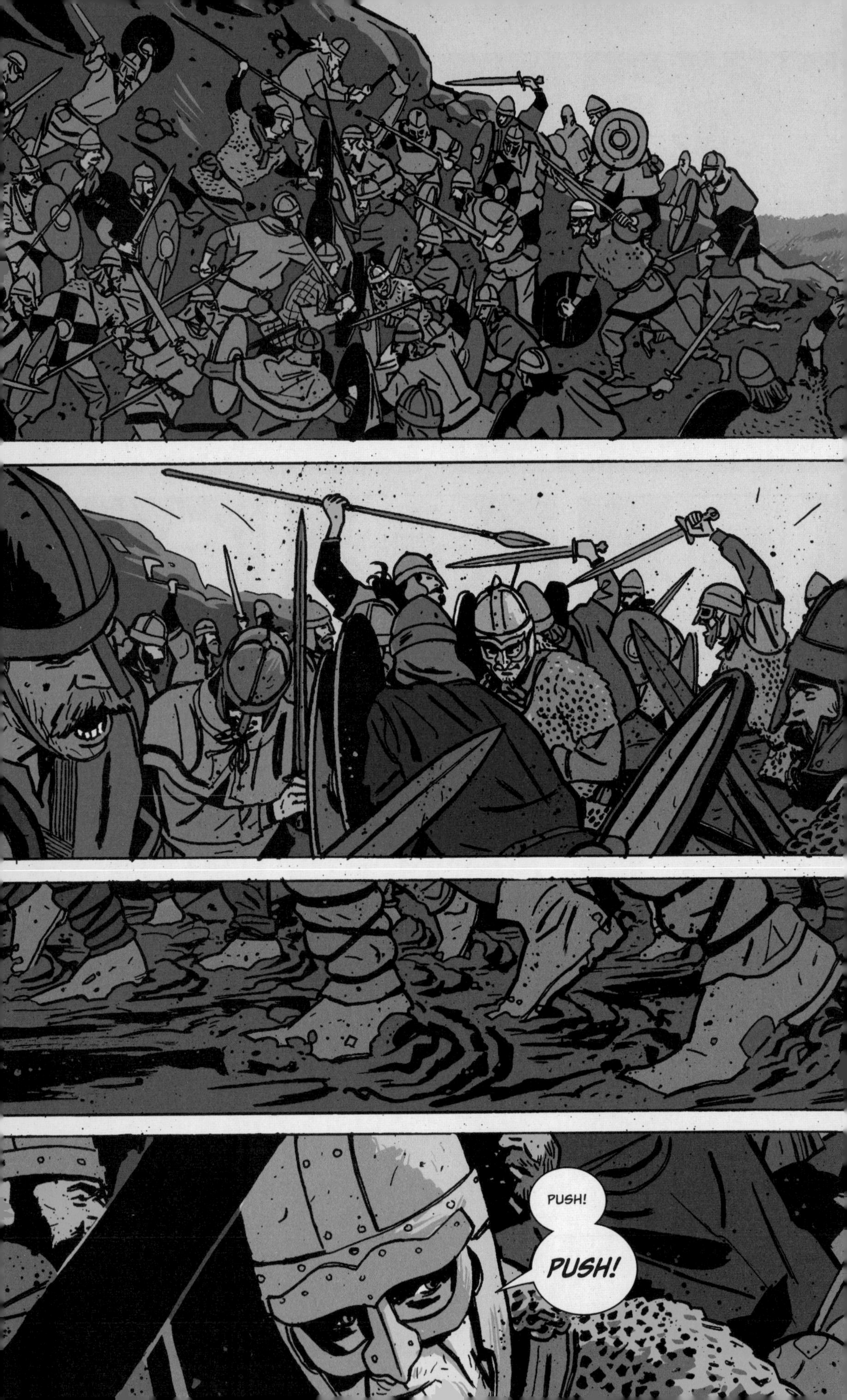
PUSH!
PUSH!

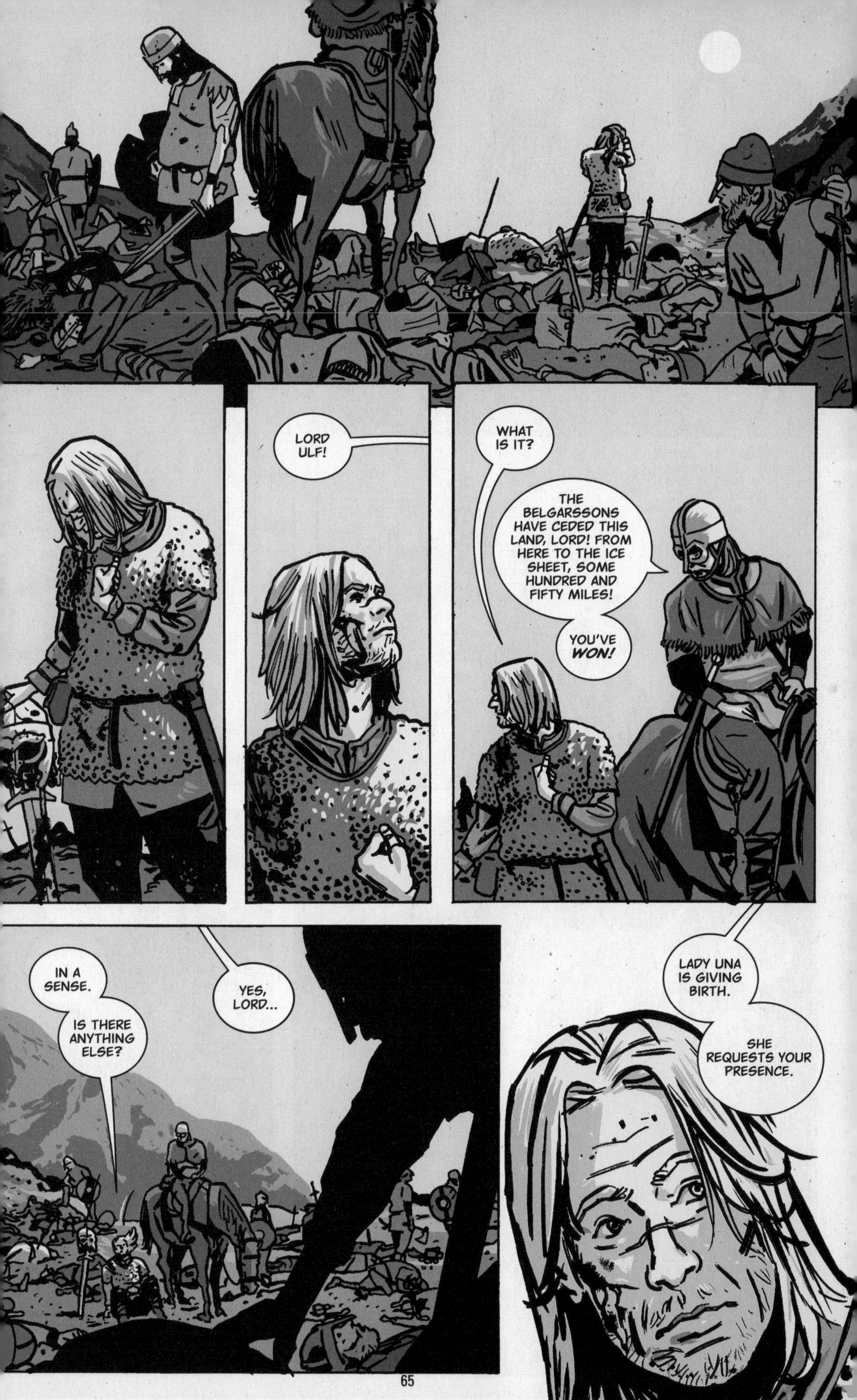
LORD ULF!
WHAT IS IT?
THE BELGARSSONS HAVE CEDED THIS LAND, LORD! FROM HERE TO THE ICE SHEET, SOME HUNDRED AND FIFTY MILES!
YOU'VE WON!
IN A SENSE.
YES, LORD...
IS THERE ANYTHING ELSE?
LADY UNA IS GIVING BIRTH.
SHE REQUESTS YOUR PRESENCE.

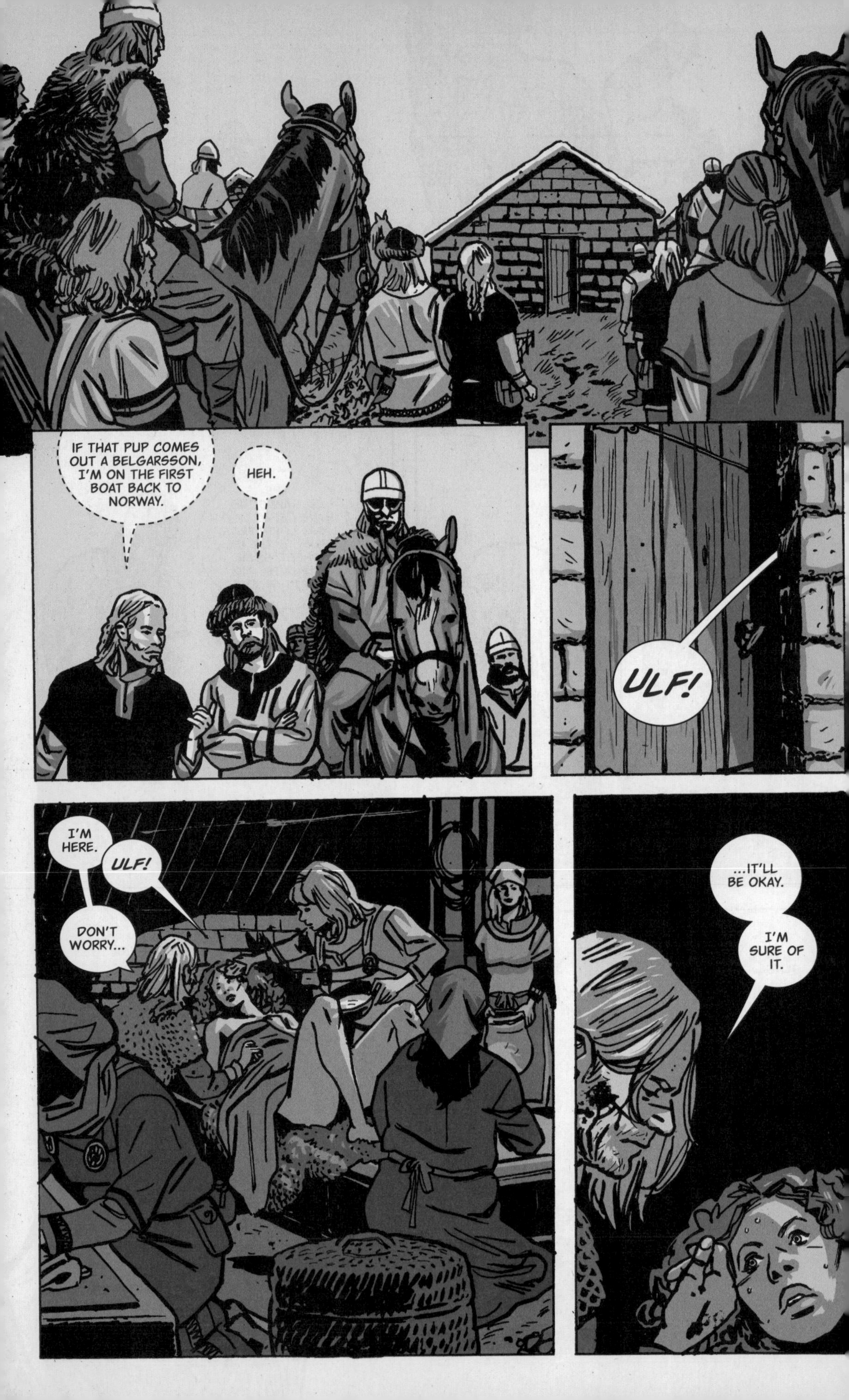
IF THAT PUP COMES OUT A BELGARSSON, I'M ON THE FIRST BOAT BACK TO NORWAY.
HEH.
ULF!
I'M HERE.
ULF!
DON'T WORRY...
...IT'LL BE OKAY.
I'M SURE OF IT.

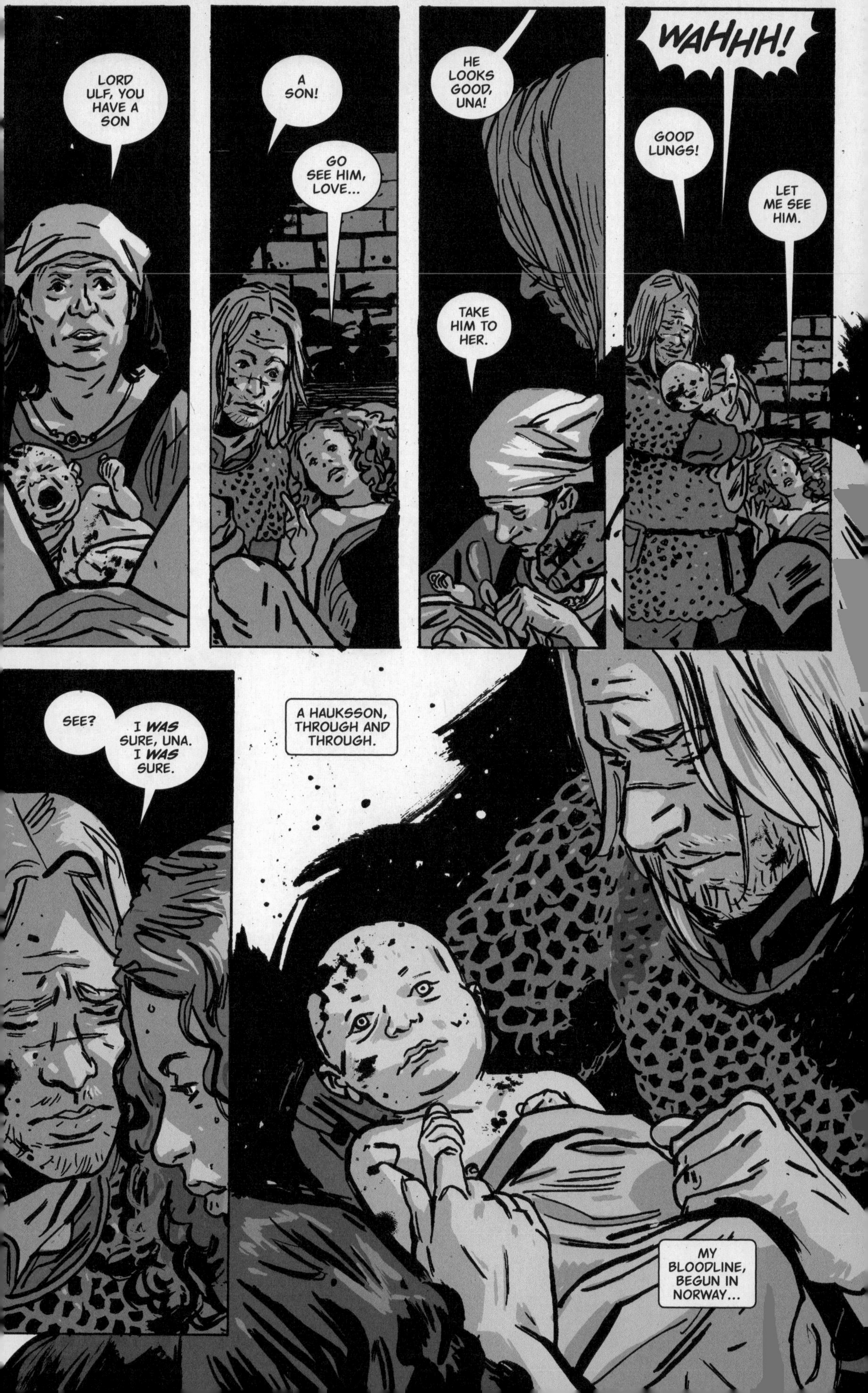
LORD ULF, YOU HAVE A SON
A SON!
GO SEE HIM, LOVE...
HE LOOKS GOOD, UNA!
TAKE HIM TO HER.
WAHHH!
GOOD LUNGS!
LET ME SEE HIM.
SEE?
I WAS SURE, UNA. I WAS SURE.
A HAUKSSON, THROUGH AND THROUGH.
MY BLOODLINE, BEGUN IN NORWAY...

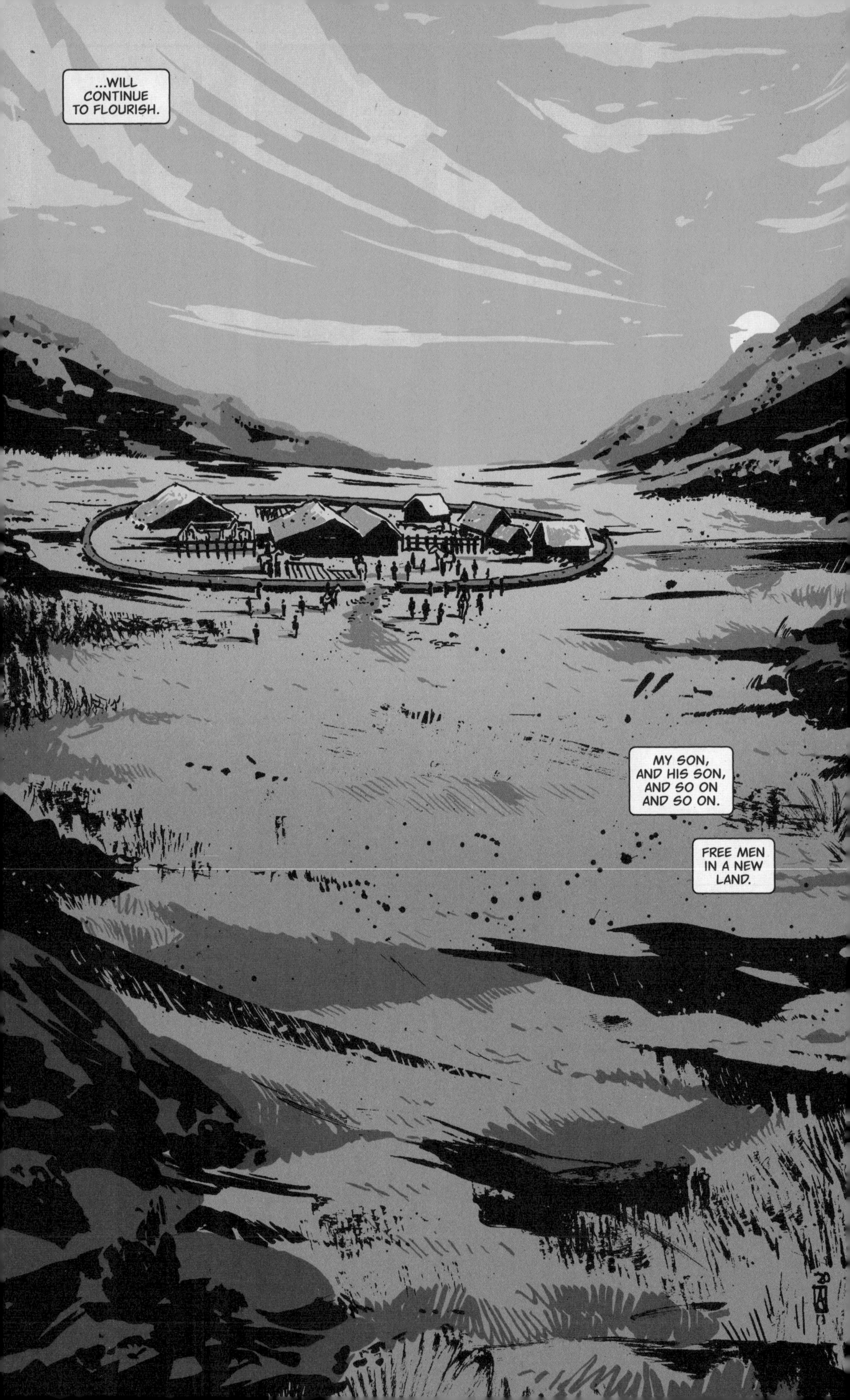
...WILL CONTINUE TO FLOURISH.
MY SON, AND HIS SON, AND SO ON AND SO ON.
FREE MEN IN A NEW LAND.

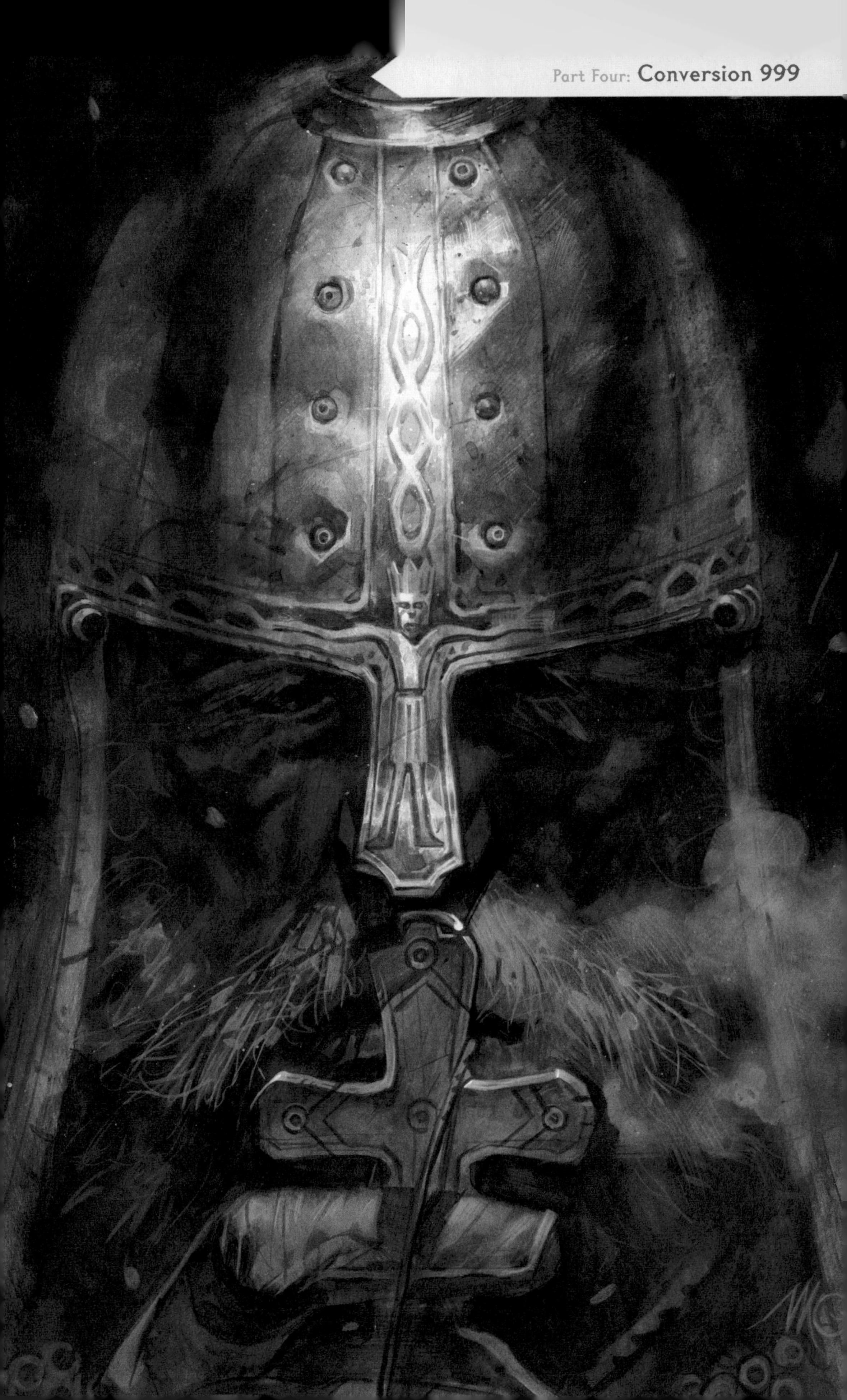

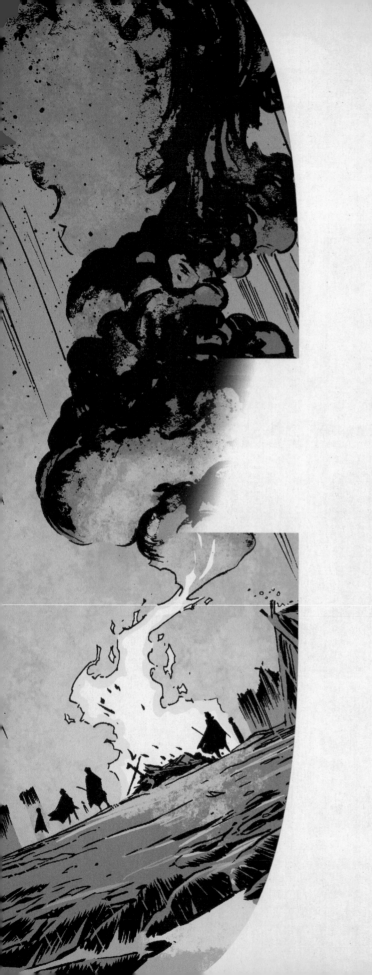

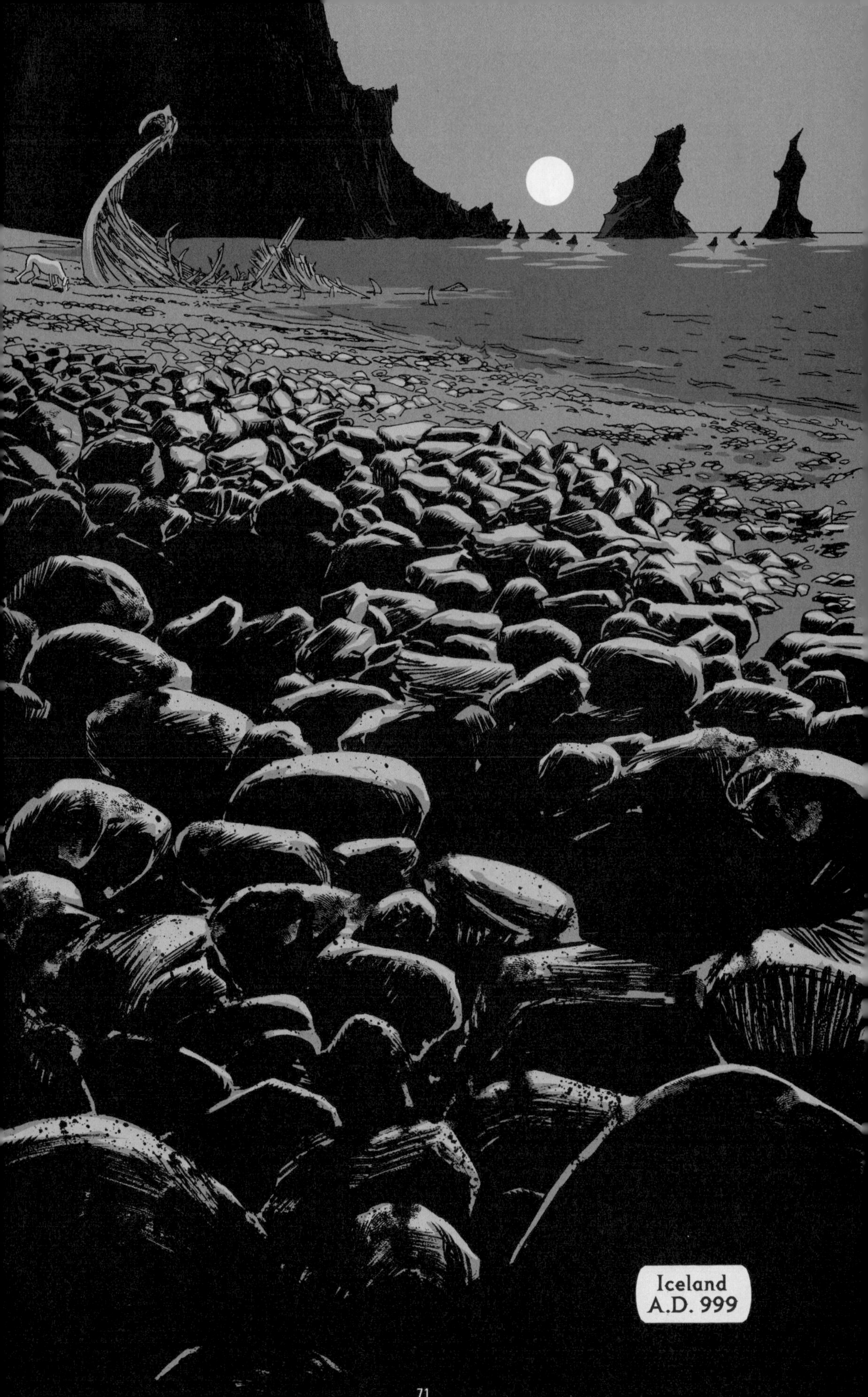
Iceland
A.D. 999

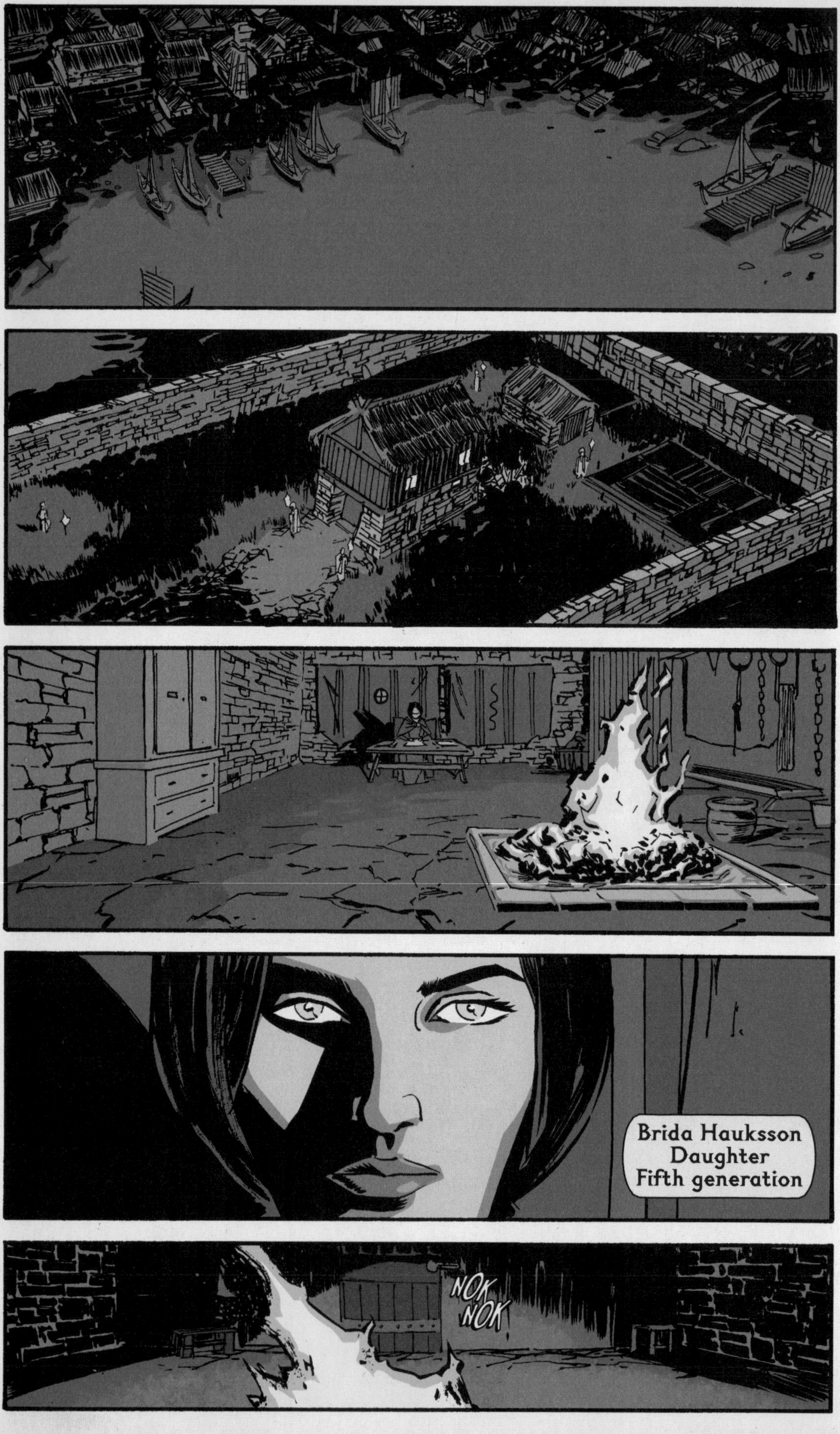
Brida Hauksson
Daughter
Fifth generation
NOK
NOK

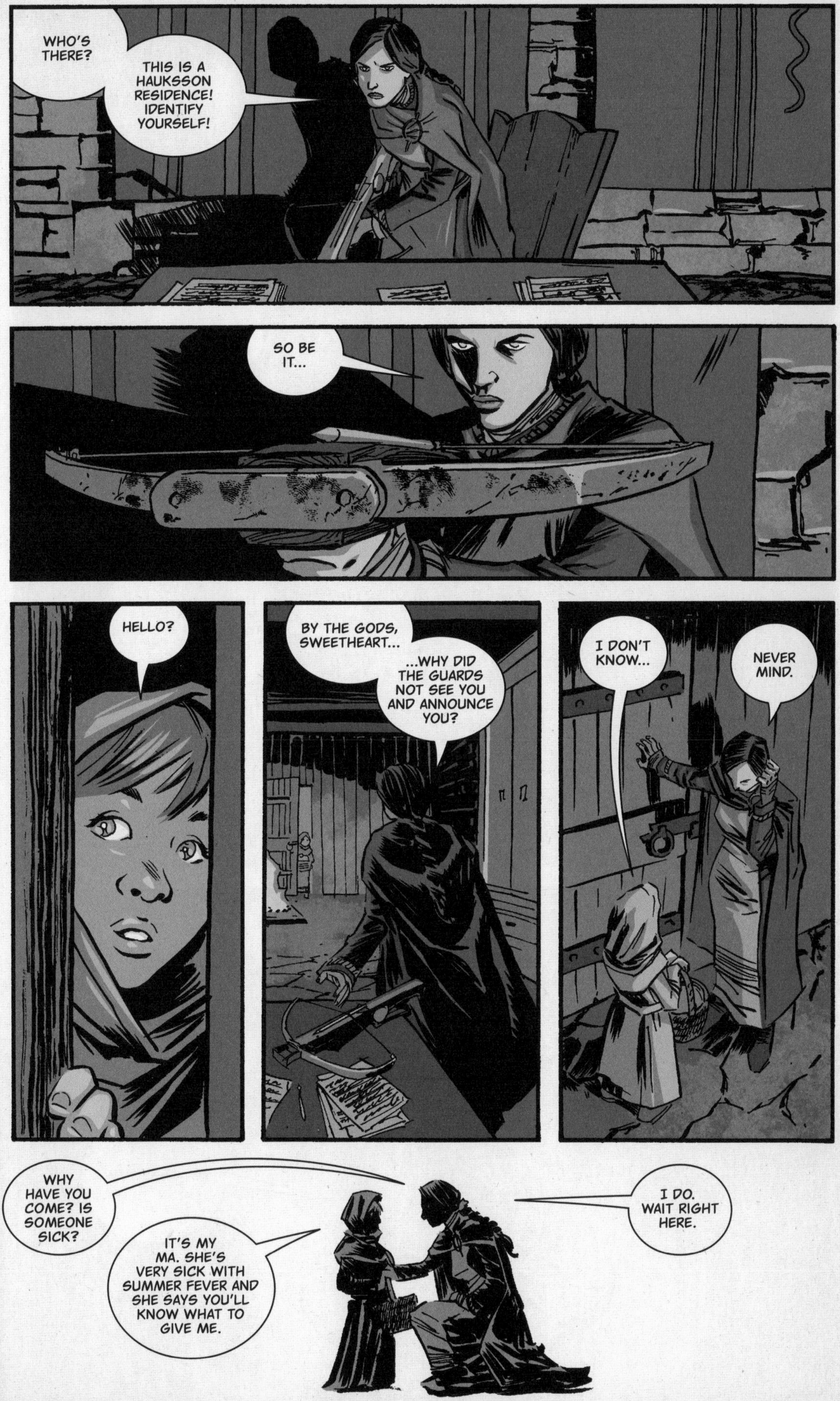
WHO'S THERE?
THIS IS A HAUKSSON RESIDENCE! IDENTIFY YOURSELF!
SO BE IT...
HELLO?
BY THE GODS, SWEETHEART...
...WHY DID THE GUARDS NOT SEE YOU AND ANNOUNCE YOU?
I DON'T KNOW...
NEVER MIND.
WHY HAVE YOU COME? IS SOMEONE SICK?
IT'S MY MA. SHE'S VERY SICK WITH SUMMER FEVER AND SHE SAYS YOU'LL KNOW WHAT TO GIVE ME.
I DO. WAIT RIGHT HERE.

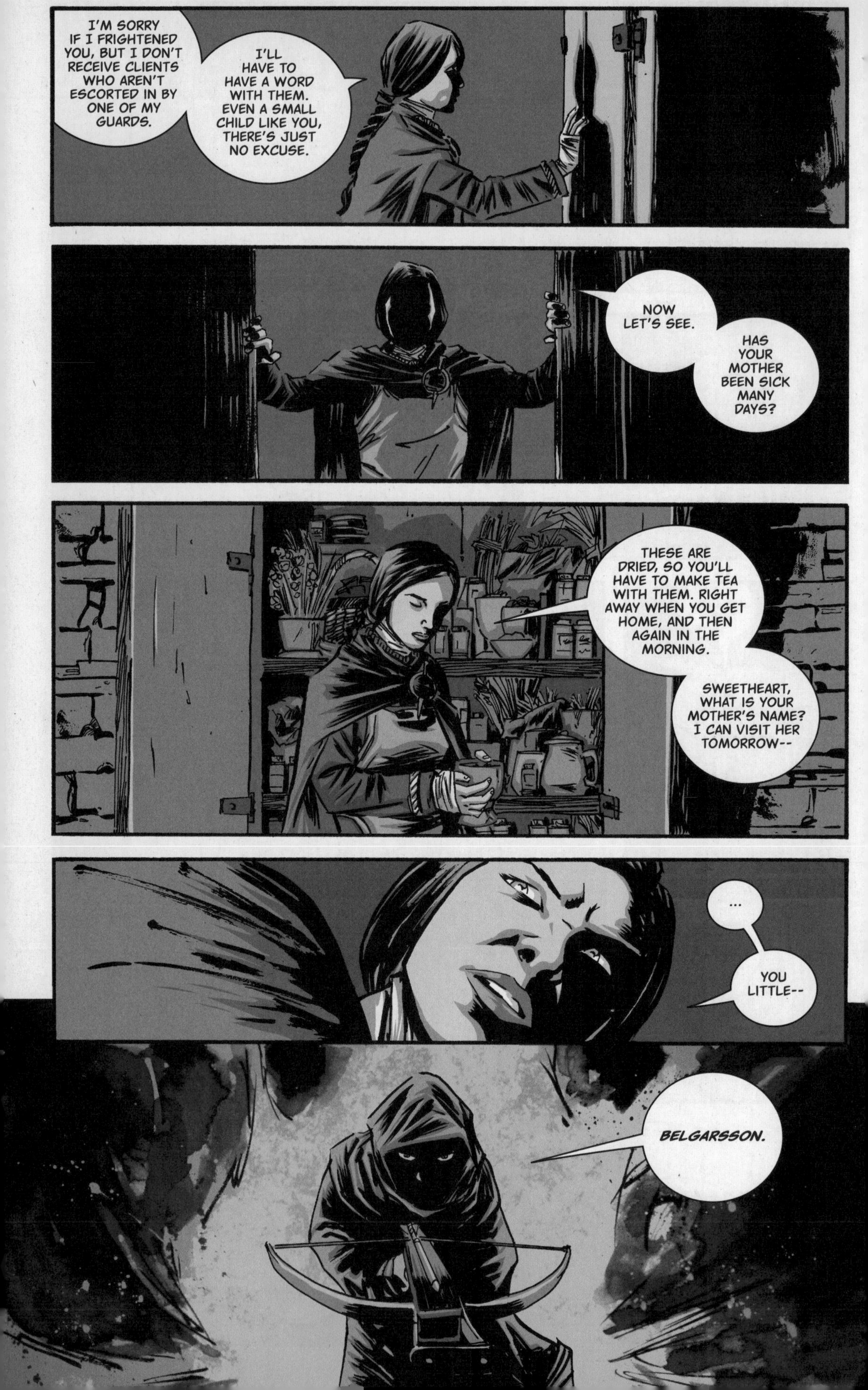
I'M SORRY IF I FRIGHTENED YOU, BUT I DON'T RECEIVE CLIENTS WHO AREN'T ESCORTED IN BY ONE OF MY GUARDS.
I'LL HAVE TO HAVE A WORD WITH THEM. EVEN A SMALL CHILD LIKE YOU, THERE'S JUST NO EXCUSE.
NOW LET'S SEE.
HAS YOUR MOTHER BEEN SICK MANY DAYS?
THESE ARE DRIED, SO YOU'LL HAVE TO MAKE TEA WITH THEM. RIGHT AWAY WHEN YOU GET HOME, AND THEN AGAIN IN THE MORNING.
SWEETHEART, WHAT IS YOUR MOTHER'S NAME? I CAN VISIT HER TOMORROW--
...
YOU LITTLE--
BELGARSSON.

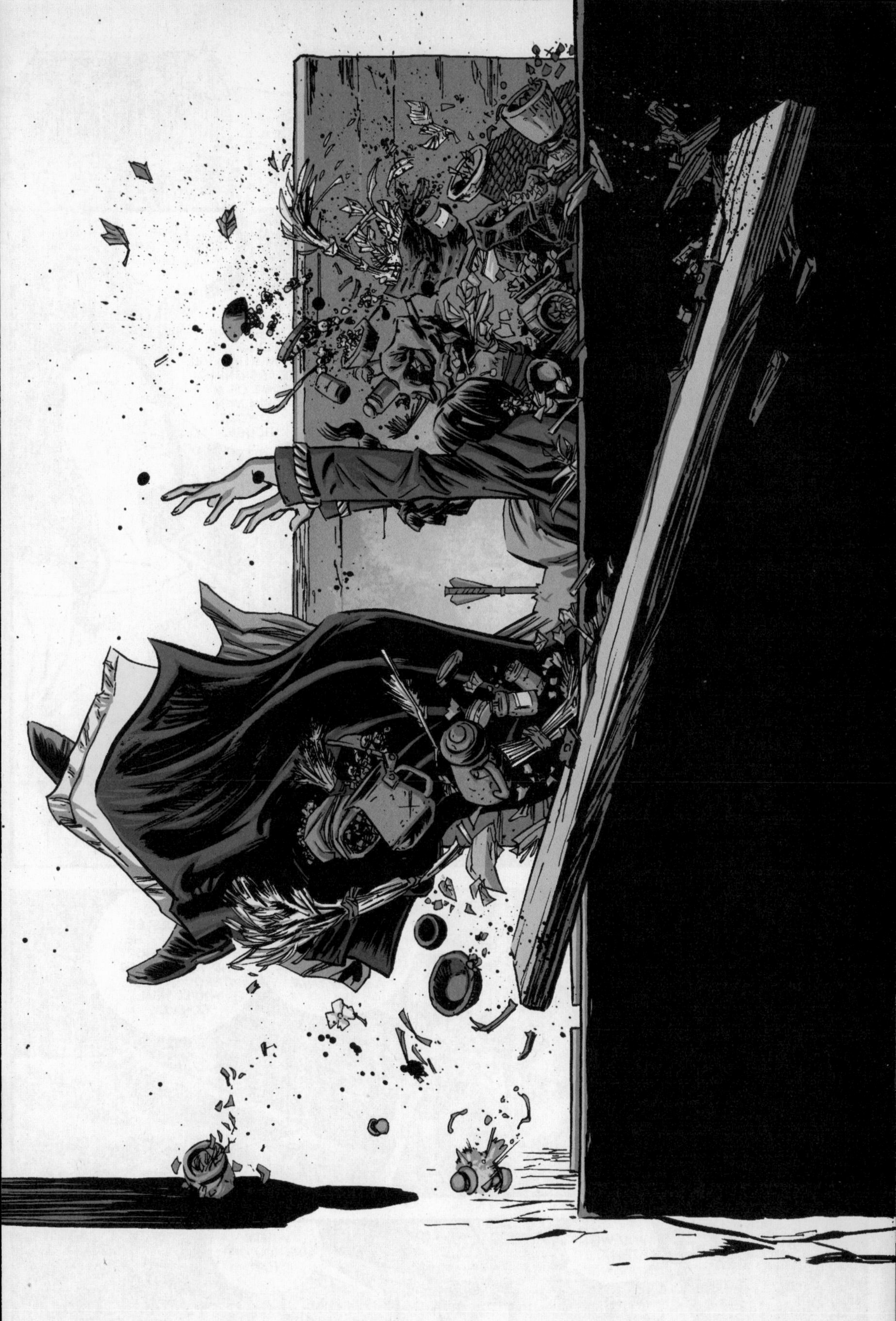

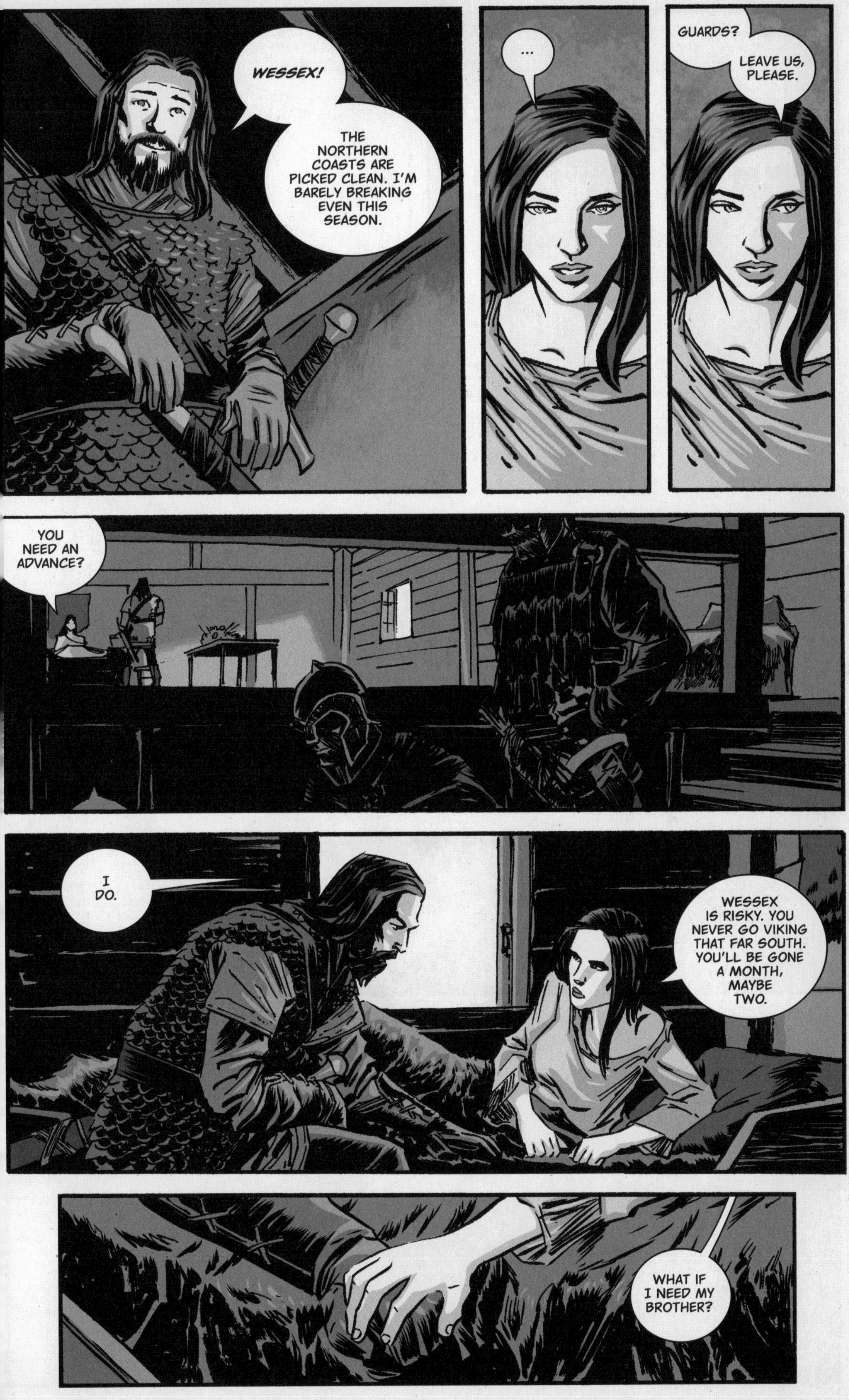
WESSEX!
THE NORTHERN COASTS ARE PICKED CLEAN. I'M BARELY BREAKING EVEN THIS SEASON.
...
GUARDS?
LEAVE US, PLEASE.
YOU NEED AN ADVANCE?
I DO.
WESSEX IS RISKY. YOU NEVER GO VIKING THAT FAR SOUTH. YOU'LL BE GONE A MONTH, MAYBE TWO.
WHAT IF I NEED MY BROTHER?

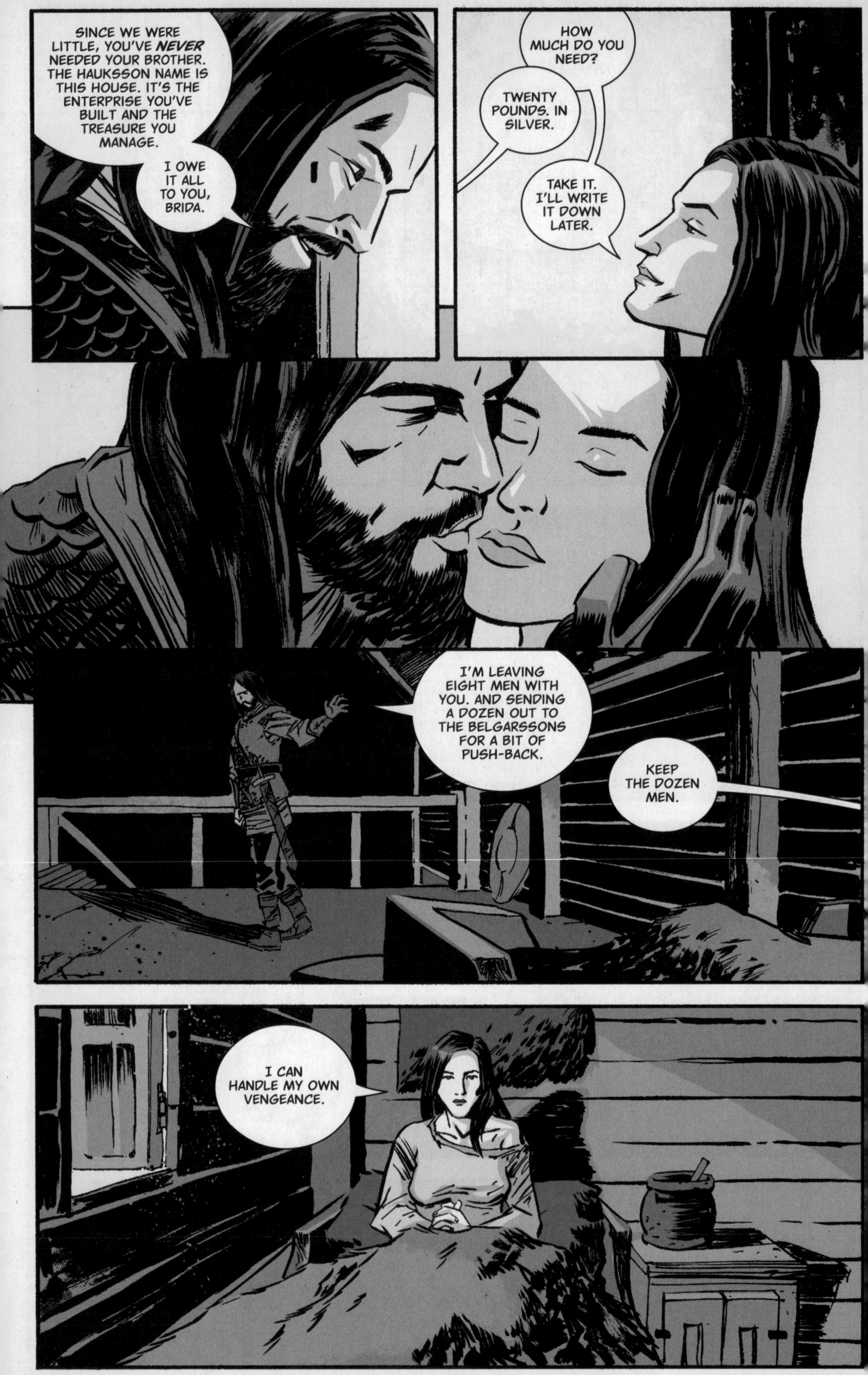
SINCE WE WERE LITTLE, YOU'VE ***NEVER*** NEEDED YOUR BROTHER. THE HAUKSSON NAME IS THIS HOUSE. IT'S THE ENTERPRISE YOU'VE BUILT AND THE TREASURE YOU MANAGE.
I OWE IT ALL TO YOU, BRIDA.
HOW MUCH DO YOU NEED?
TWENTY POUNDS. IN SILVER.
TAKE IT. I'LL WRITE IT DOWN LATER.
I'M LEAVING EIGHT MEN WITH YOU. AND SENDING A DOZEN OUT TO THE BELGARSSONS FOR A BIT OF PUSH-BACK.
KEEP THE DOZEN MEN.
I CAN HANDLE MY OWN VENGEANCE.

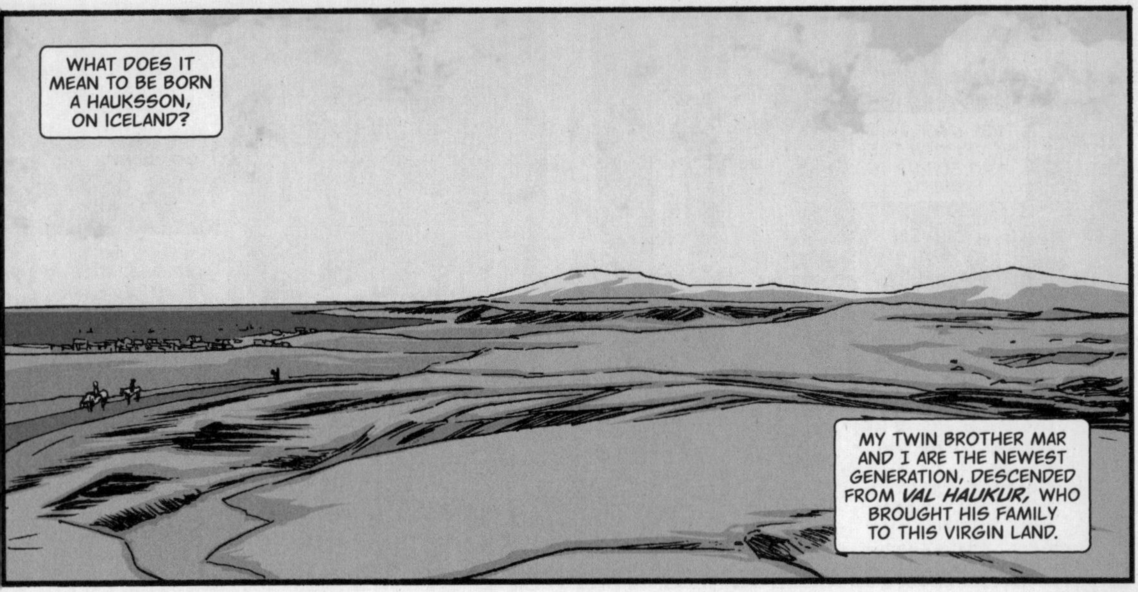
WHAT DOES IT MEAN TO BE BORN A HAUKSSON, ON ICELAND?
MY TWIN BROTHER MAR AND I ARE THE NEWEST GENERATION, DESCENDED FROM VAL HAUKUR, WHO BROUGHT HIS FAMILY TO THIS VIRGIN LAND.

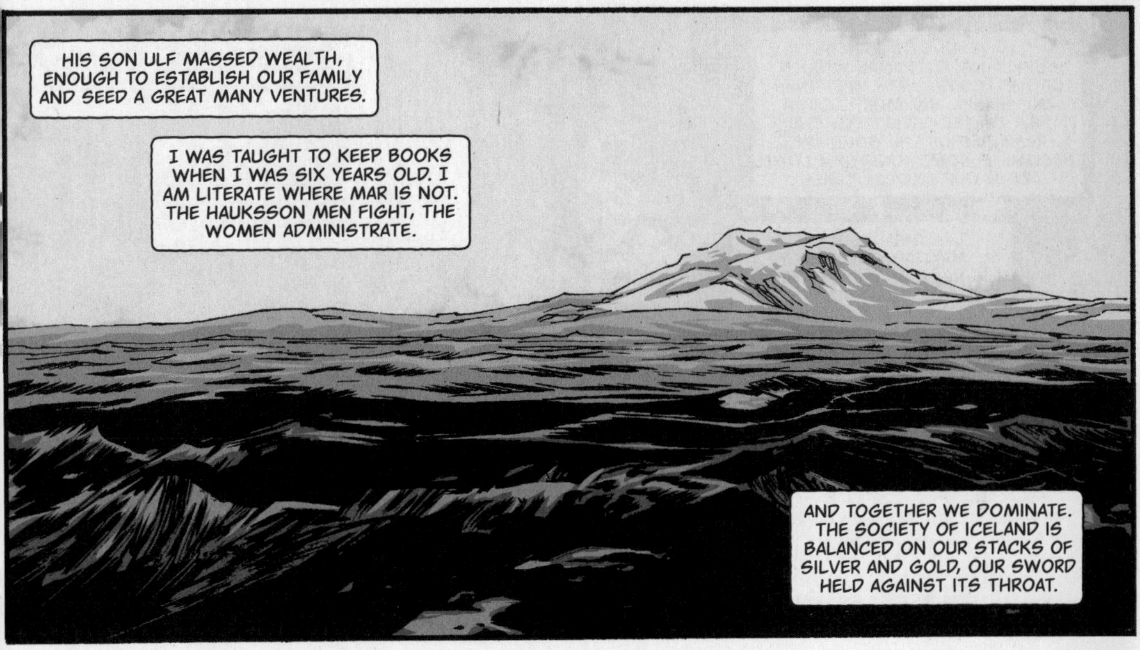
HIS SON ULF MASSED WEALTH, ENOUGH TO ESTABLISH OUR FAMILY AND SEED A GREAT MANY VENTURES.
I WAS TAUGHT TO KEEP BOOKS WHEN I WAS SIX YEARS OLD. I AM LITERATE WHERE MAR IS NOT. THE HAUKSSON MEN FIGHT, THE WOMEN ADMINISTRATE.
AND TOGETHER WE DOMINATE. THE SOCIETY OF ICELAND IS BALANCED ON OUR STACKS OF SILVER AND GOLD, OUR SWORD HELD AGAINST ITS THROAT.

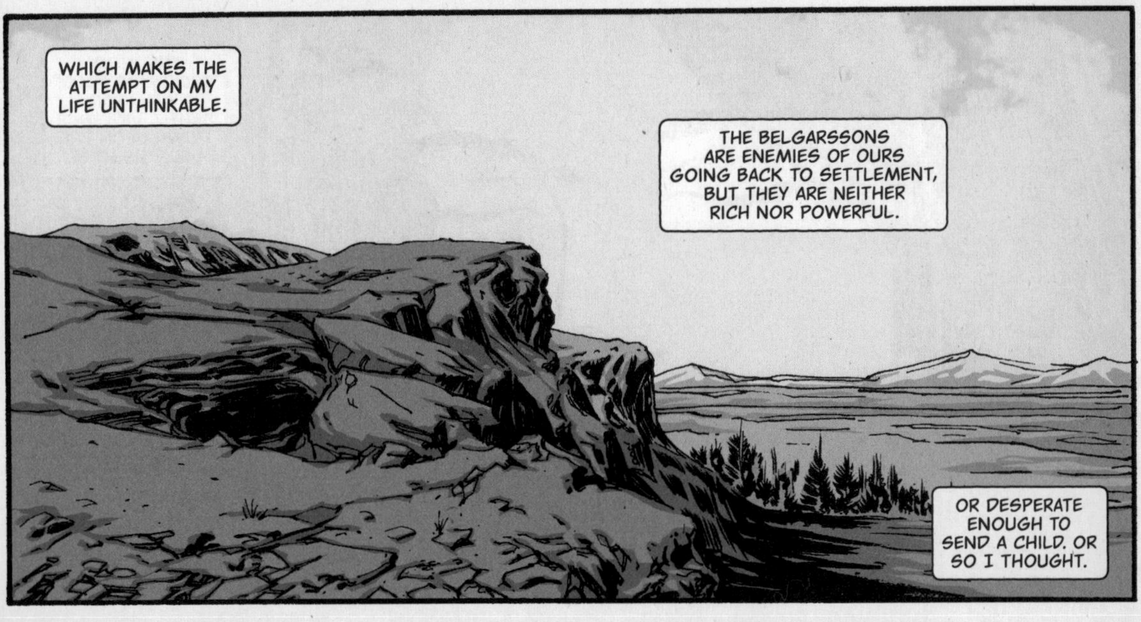
WHICH MAKES THE ATTEMPT ON MY LIFE UNTHINKABLE.
THE BELGARSSONS ARE ENEMIES OF OURS GOING BACK TO SETTLEMENT, BUT THEY ARE NEITHER RICH NOR POWERFUL.
OR DESPERATE ENOUGH TO SEND A CHILD. OR SO I THOUGHT.

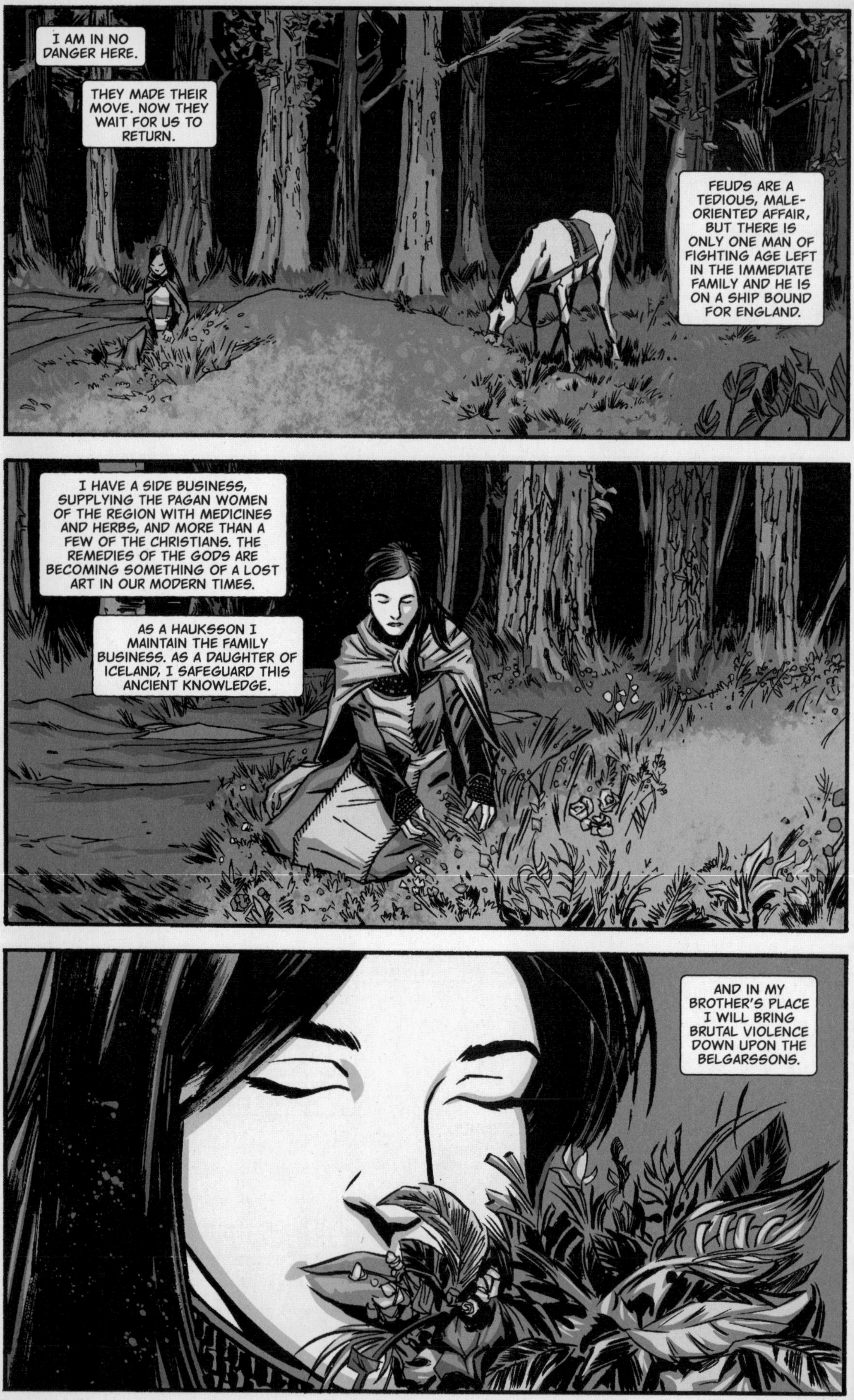

I AM IN NO DANGER HERE.
THEY MADE THEIR MOVE. NOW THEY WAIT FOR US TO RETURN.
FEUDS ARE A TEDIOUS, MALE-ORIENTED AFFAIR, BUT THERE IS ONLY ONE MAN OF FIGHTING AGE LEFT IN THE IMMEDIATE FAMILY AND HE IS ON A SHIP BOUND FOR ENGLAND.
I HAVE A SIDE BUSINESS, SUPPLYING THE PAGAN WOMEN OF THE REGION WITH MEDICINES AND HERBS, AND MORE THAN A FEW OF THE CHRISTIANS. THE REMEDIES OF THE GODS ARE BECOMING SOMETHING OF A LOST ART IN OUR MODERN TIMES.
AS A HAUKSSON I MAINTAIN THE FAMILY BUSINESS. AS A DAUGHTER OF ICELAND, I SAFEGUARD THIS ANCIENT KNOWLEDGE.
AND IN MY BROTHER'S PLACE I WILL BRING BRUTAL VIOLENCE DOWN UPON THE BELGARSSONS.

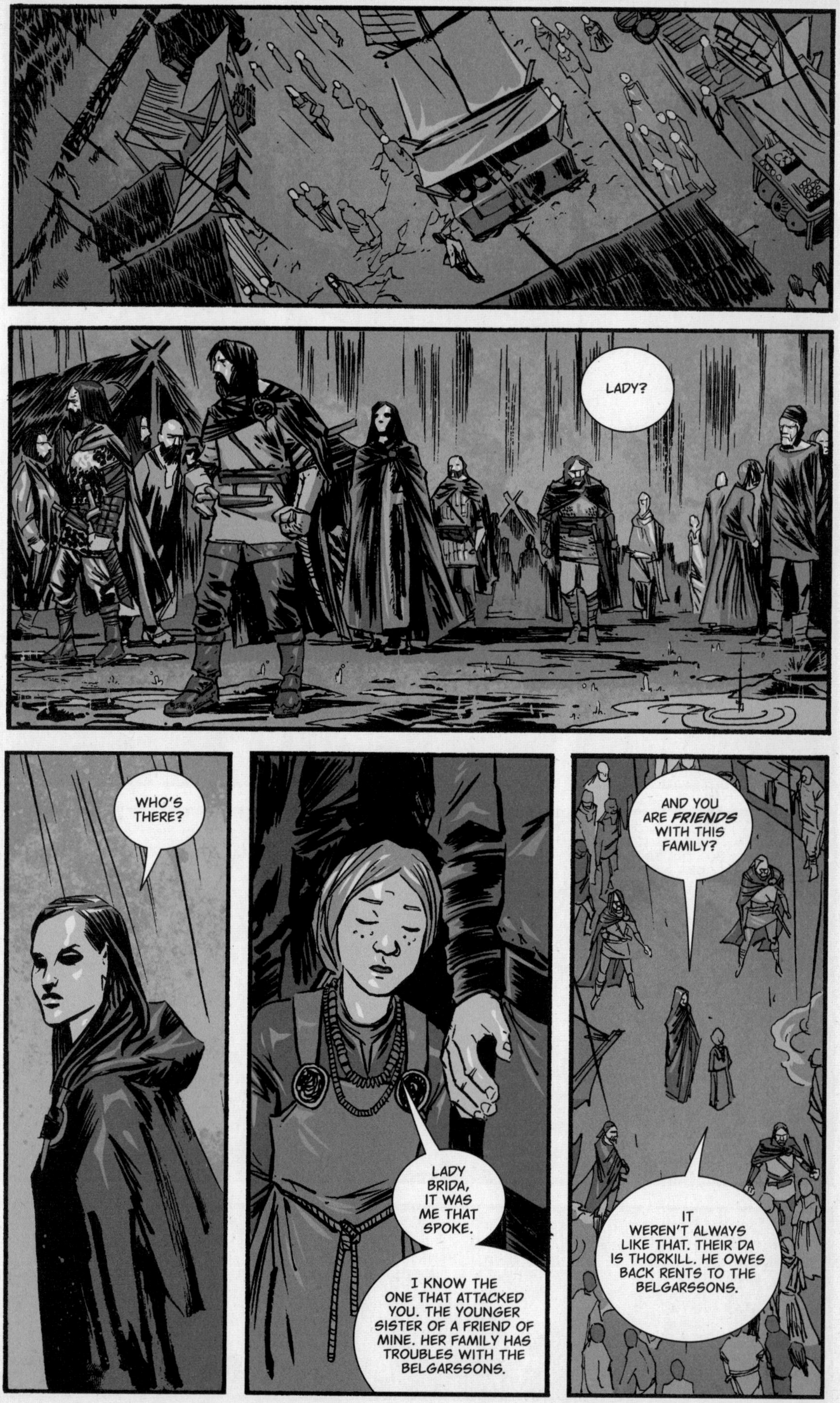
LADY?
WHO'S THERE?
LADY BRIDA, IT WAS ME THAT SPOKE.
I KNOW THE ONE THAT ATTACKED YOU. THE YOUNGER SISTER OF A FRIEND OF MINE. HER FAMILY HAS TROUBLES WITH THE BELGARSSONS.
AND YOU ARE FRIENDS WITH THIS FAMILY?
IT WEREN'T ALWAYS LIKE THAT. THEIR DA IS THORKILL. HE OWES BACK RENTS TO THE BELGARSSONS.

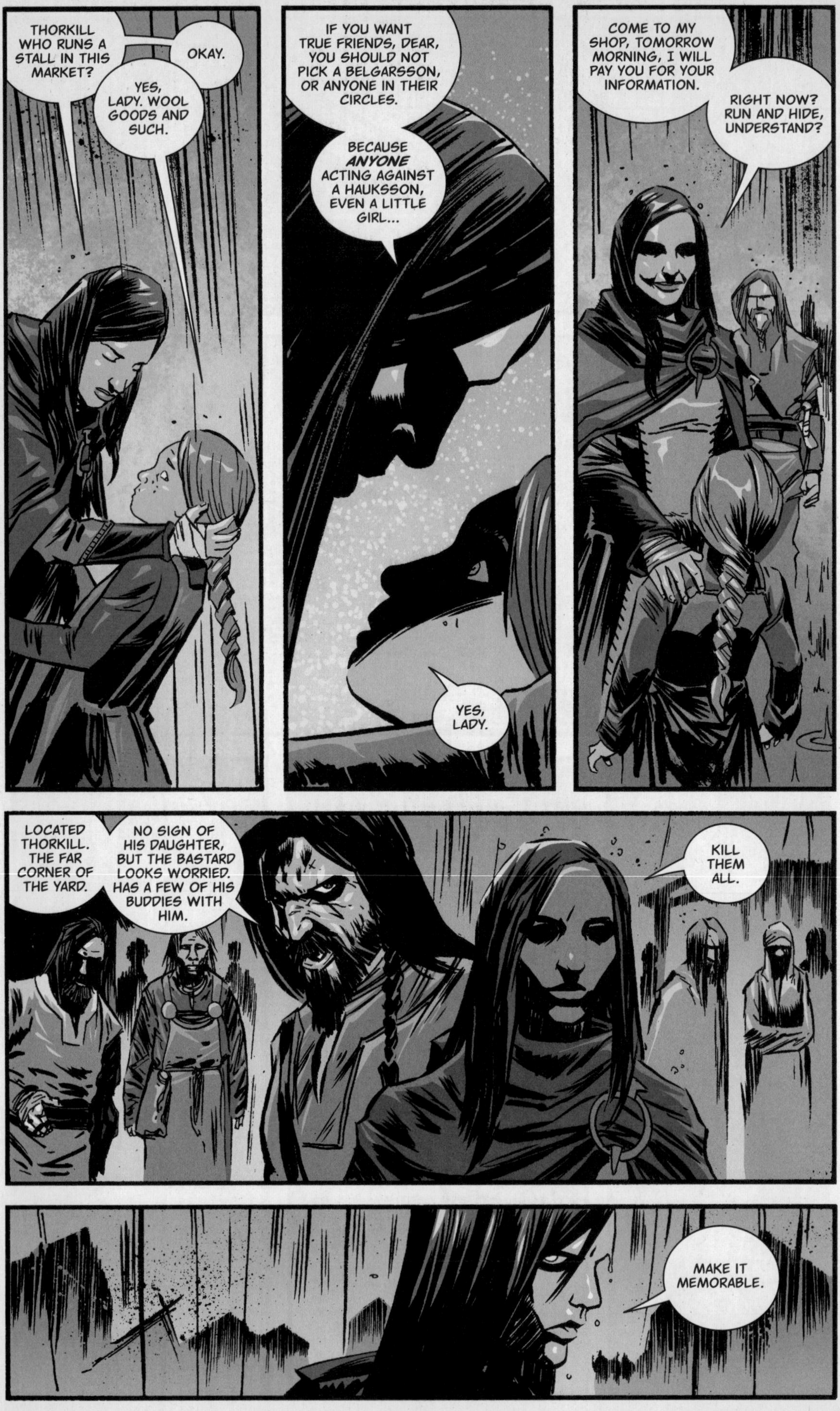
THORKILL WHO RUNS A STALL IN THIS MARKET?
OKAY.
YES, LADY. WOOL GOODS AND SUCH.
IF YOU WANT TRUE FRIENDS, DEAR, YOU SHOULD NOT PICK A BELGARSSON, OR ANYONE IN THEIR CIRCLES.
BECAUSE *ANYONE* ACTING AGAINST A HAUKSSON, EVEN A LITTLE GIRL...
YES, LADY.
COME TO MY SHOP, TOMORROW MORNING, I WILL PAY YOU FOR YOUR INFORMATION.
RIGHT NOW? RUN AND HIDE, UNDERSTAND?
LOCATED THORKILL. THE FAR CORNER OF THE YARD.
NO SIGN OF HIS DAUGHTER, BUT THE BASTARD LOOKS WORRIED. HAS A FEW OF HIS BUDDIES WITH HIM.
KILL THEM ALL.
MAKE IT MEMORABLE.

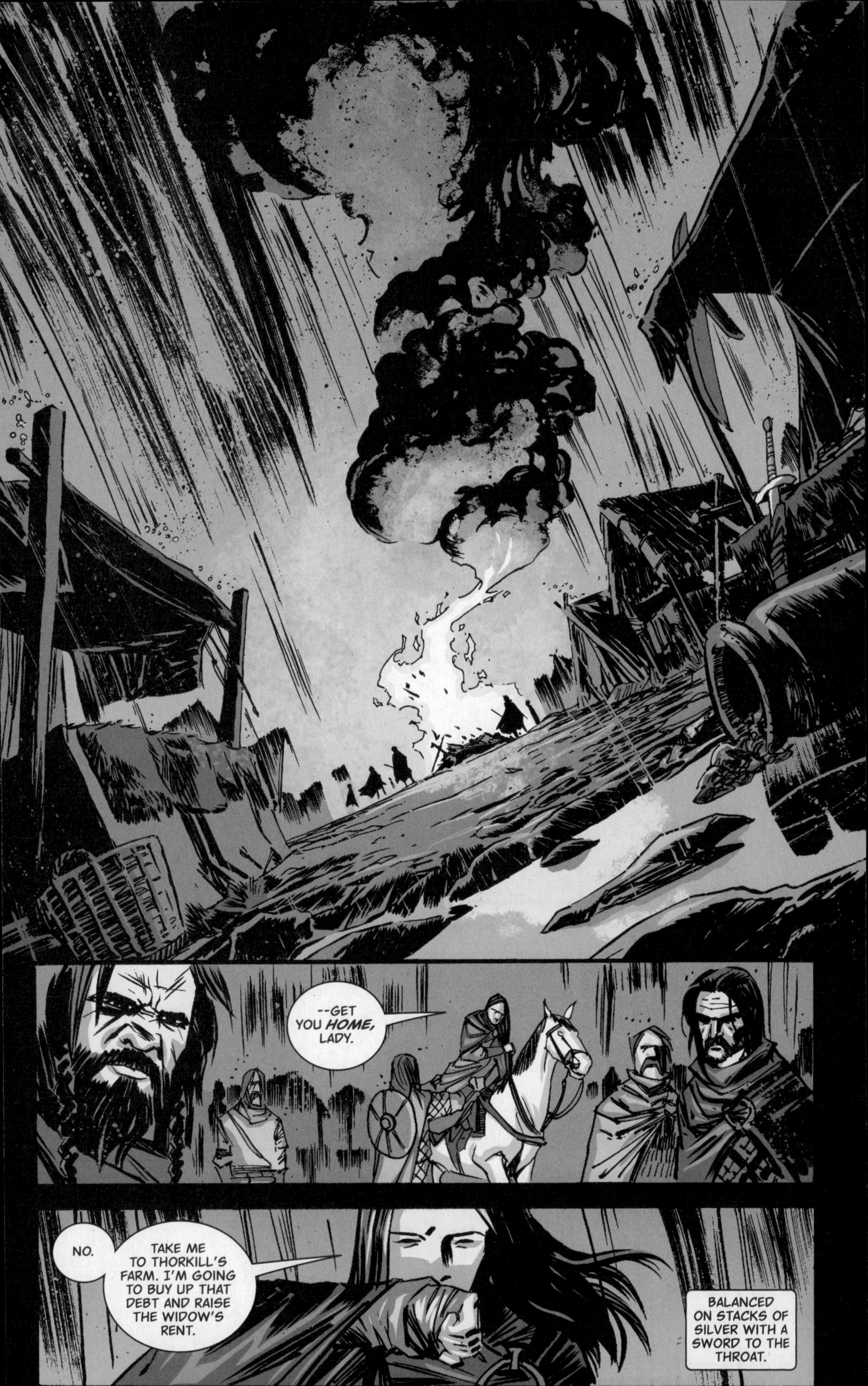
--GET YOU *HOME*, LADY.
NO.
TAKE ME TO THORKILL'S FARM. I'M GOING TO BUY UP THAT DEBT AND RAISE THE WIDOW'S RENT.
BALANCED ON STACKS OF SILVER WITH A SWORD TO THE THROAT.

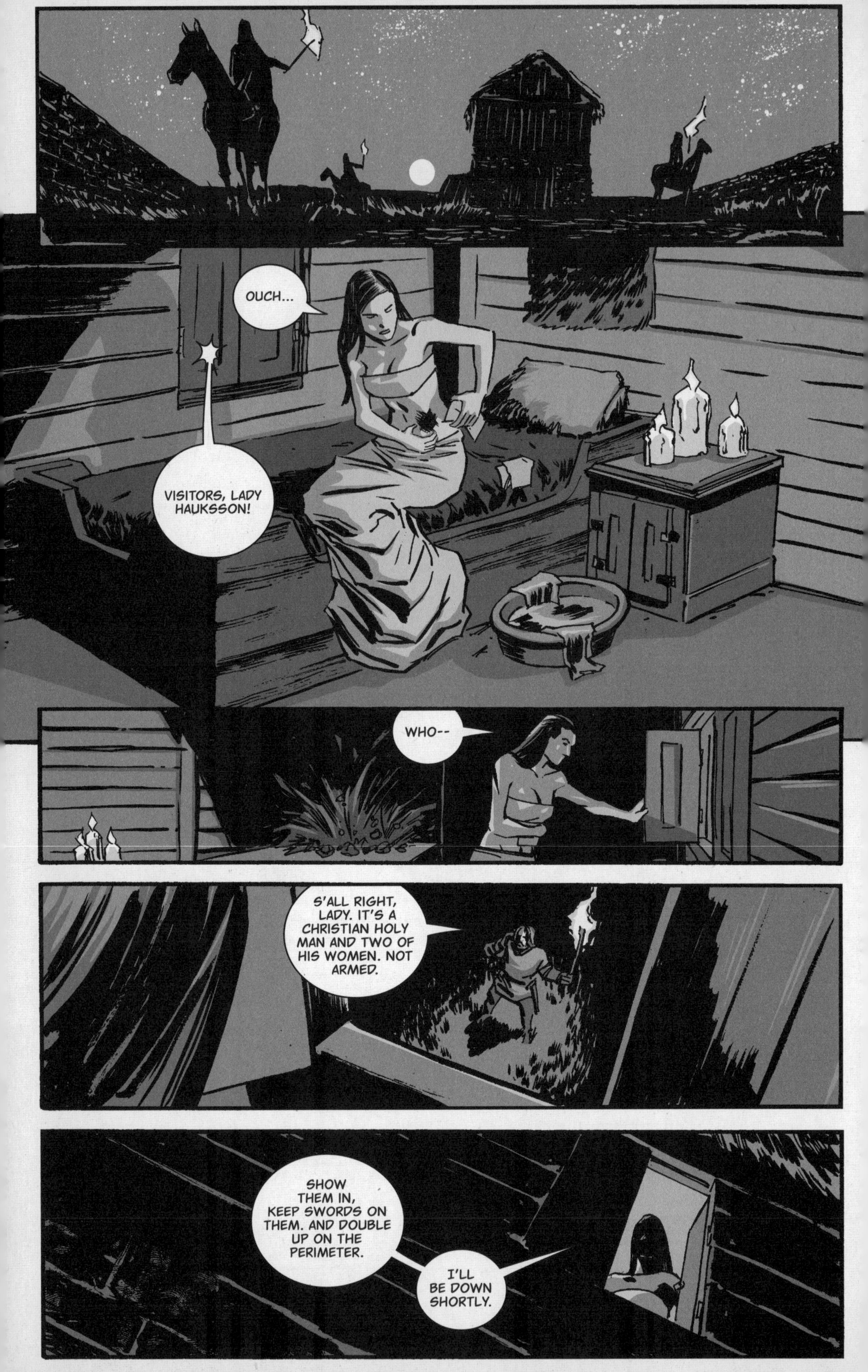
OUCH...
VISITORS, LADY HAUKSSON!
WHO--
S'ALL RIGHT, LADY. IT'S A CHRISTIAN HOLY MAN AND TWO OF HIS WOMEN. NOT ARMED.
SHOW THEM IN, KEEP SWORDS ON THEM. AND DOUBLE UP ON THE PERIMETER.
I'LL BE DOWN SHORTLY.

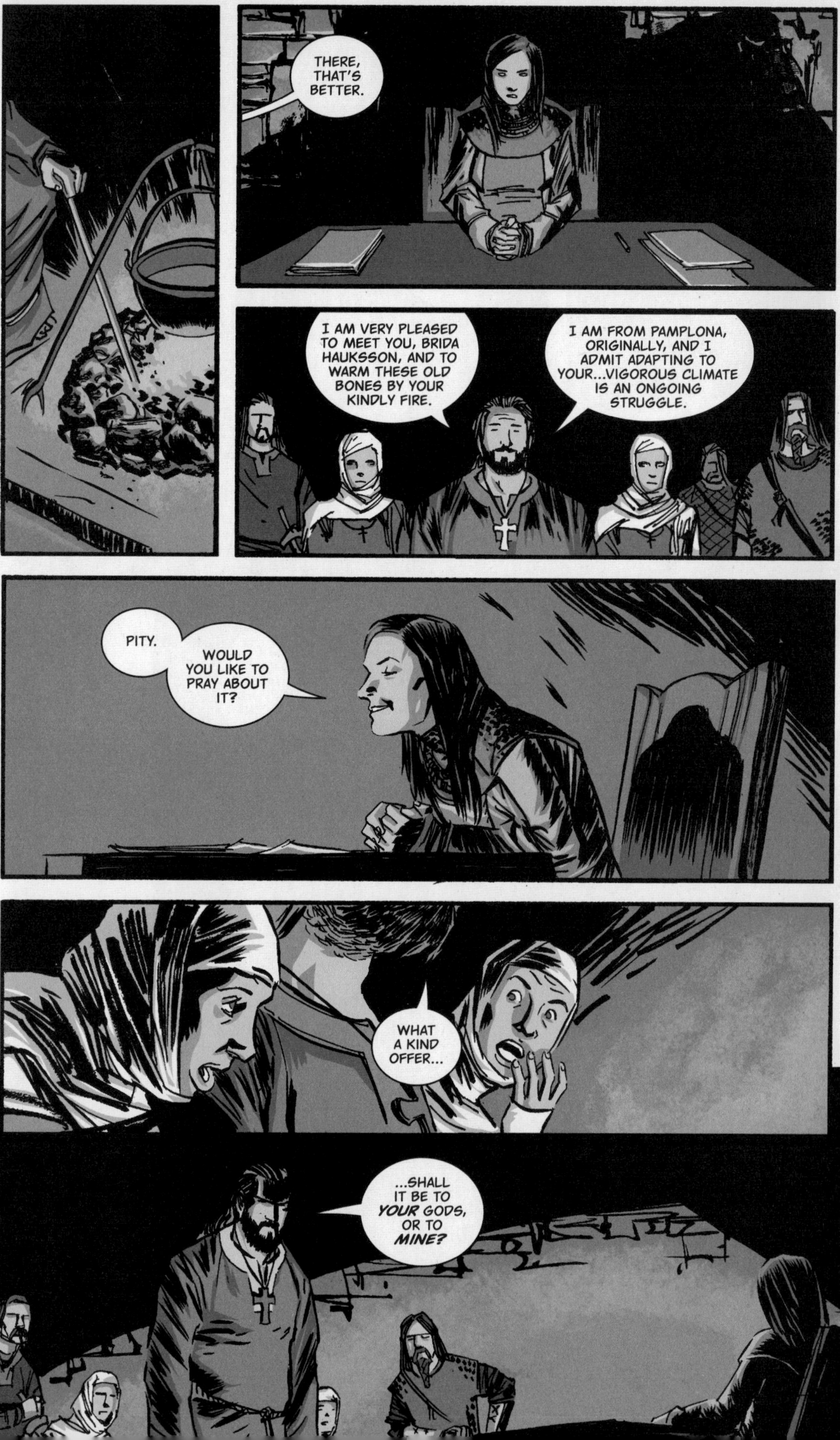
THERE, THAT'S BETTER.
I AM VERY PLEASED TO MEET YOU, BRIDA HAUKSSON, AND TO WARM THESE OLD BONES BY YOUR KINDLY FIRE.
I AM FROM PAMPLONA, ORIGINALLY, AND I ADMIT ADAPTING TO YOUR...VIGOROUS CLIMATE IS AN ONGOING STRUGGLE.
PITY.
WOULD YOU LIKE TO PRAY ABOUT IT?
WHAT A KIND OFFER...
...SHALL IT BE TO *YOUR* GODS, OR TO *MINE?*

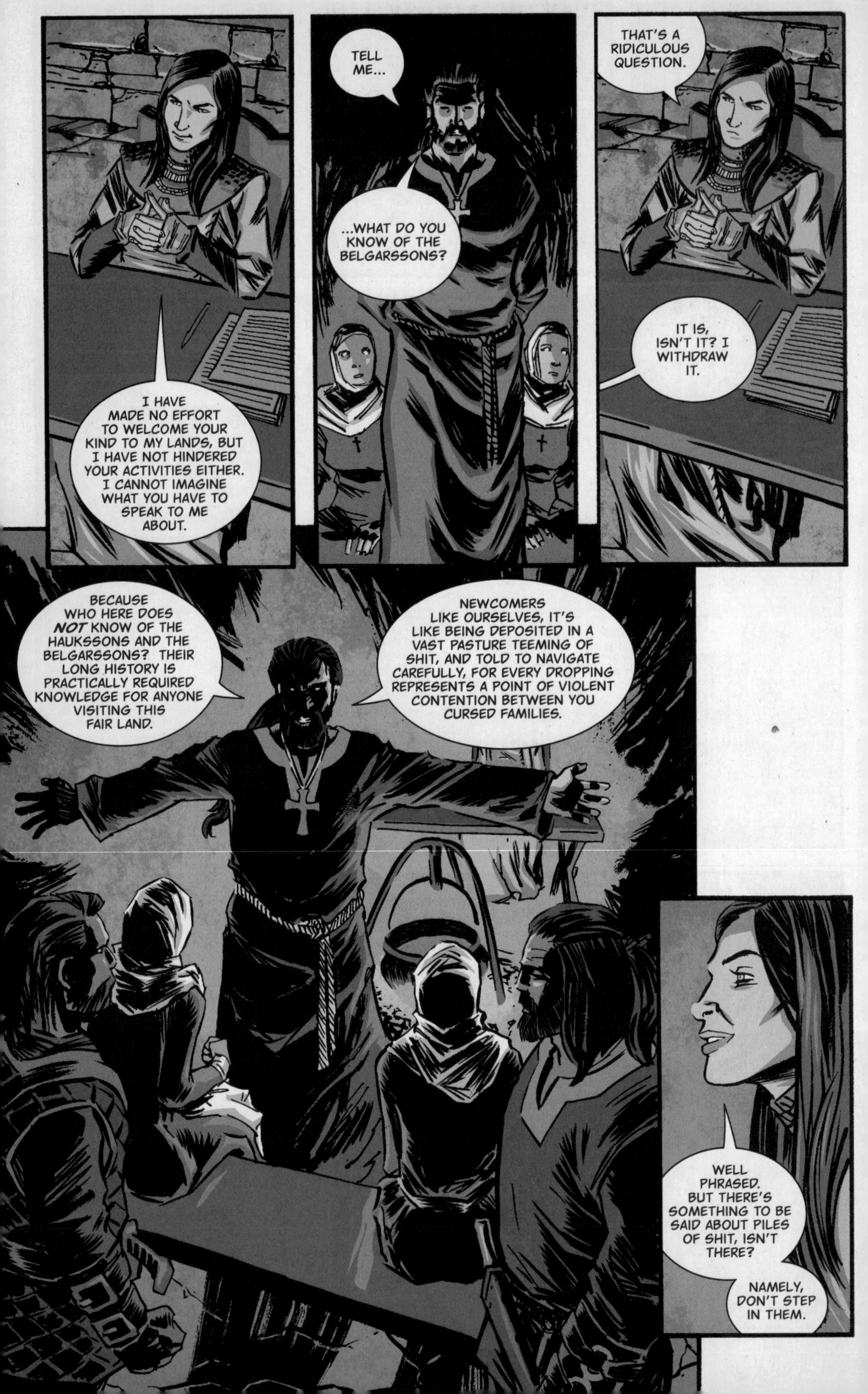
I HAVE MADE NO EFFORT TO WELCOME YOUR KIND TO MY LANDS, BUT I HAVE NOT HINDERED YOUR ACTIVITIES EITHER. I CANNOT IMAGINE WHAT YOU HAVE TO SPEAK TO ME ABOUT.
TELL ME...
...WHAT DO YOU KNOW OF THE BELGARSSONS?
THAT'S A RIDICULOUS QUESTION.
IT IS, ISN'T IT? I WITHDRAW IT.
BECAUSE WHO HERE DOES *NOT* KNOW OF THE HAUKSSONS AND THE BELGARSSONS? THEIR LONG HISTORY IS PRACTICALLY REQUIRED KNOWLEDGE FOR ANYONE VISITING THIS FAIR LAND.
NEWCOMERS LIKE OURSELVES, IT'S LIKE BEING DEPOSITED IN A VAST PASTURE TEEMING OF SHIT, AND TOLD TO NAVIGATE CAREFULLY, FOR EVERY DROPPING REPRESENTS A POINT OF VIOLENT CONTENTION BETWEEN YOU CURSED FAMILIES.
WELL PHRASED. BUT THERE'S SOMETHING TO BE SAID ABOUT PILES OF SHIT, ISN'T THERE?
NAMELY, DON'T STEP IN THEM.

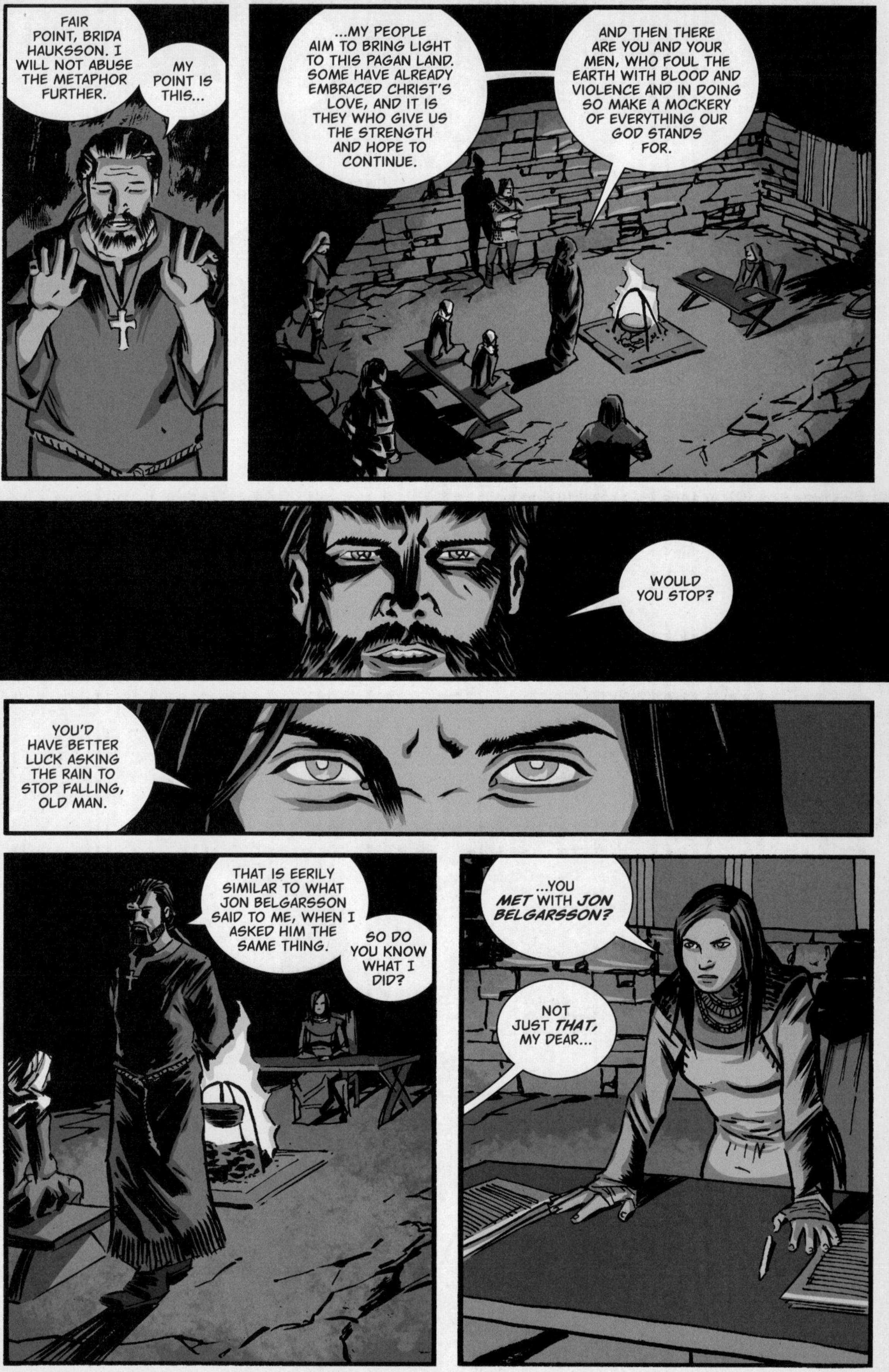
FAIR POINT, BRIDA HAUKSSON. I WILL NOT ABUSE THE METAPHOR FURTHER.
MY POINT IS THIS...
...MY PEOPLE AIM TO BRING LIGHT TO THIS PAGAN LAND. SOME HAVE ALREADY EMBRACED CHRIST'S LOVE, AND IT IS THEY WHO GIVE US THE STRENGTH AND HOPE TO CONTINUE.
AND THEN THERE ARE YOU AND YOUR MEN, WHO FOUL THE EARTH WITH BLOOD AND VIOLENCE AND IN DOING SO MAKE A MOCKERY OF EVERYTHING OUR GOD STANDS FOR.
WOULD YOU STOP?
YOU'D HAVE BETTER LUCK ASKING THE RAIN TO STOP FALLING, OLD MAN.
THAT IS EERILY SIMILAR TO WHAT JON BELGARSSON SAID TO ME, WHEN I ASKED HIM THE SAME THING.
SO DO YOU KNOW WHAT I DID?
...YOU *MET* WITH *JON BELGARSSON?*
NOT JUST *THAT,* MY DEAR...

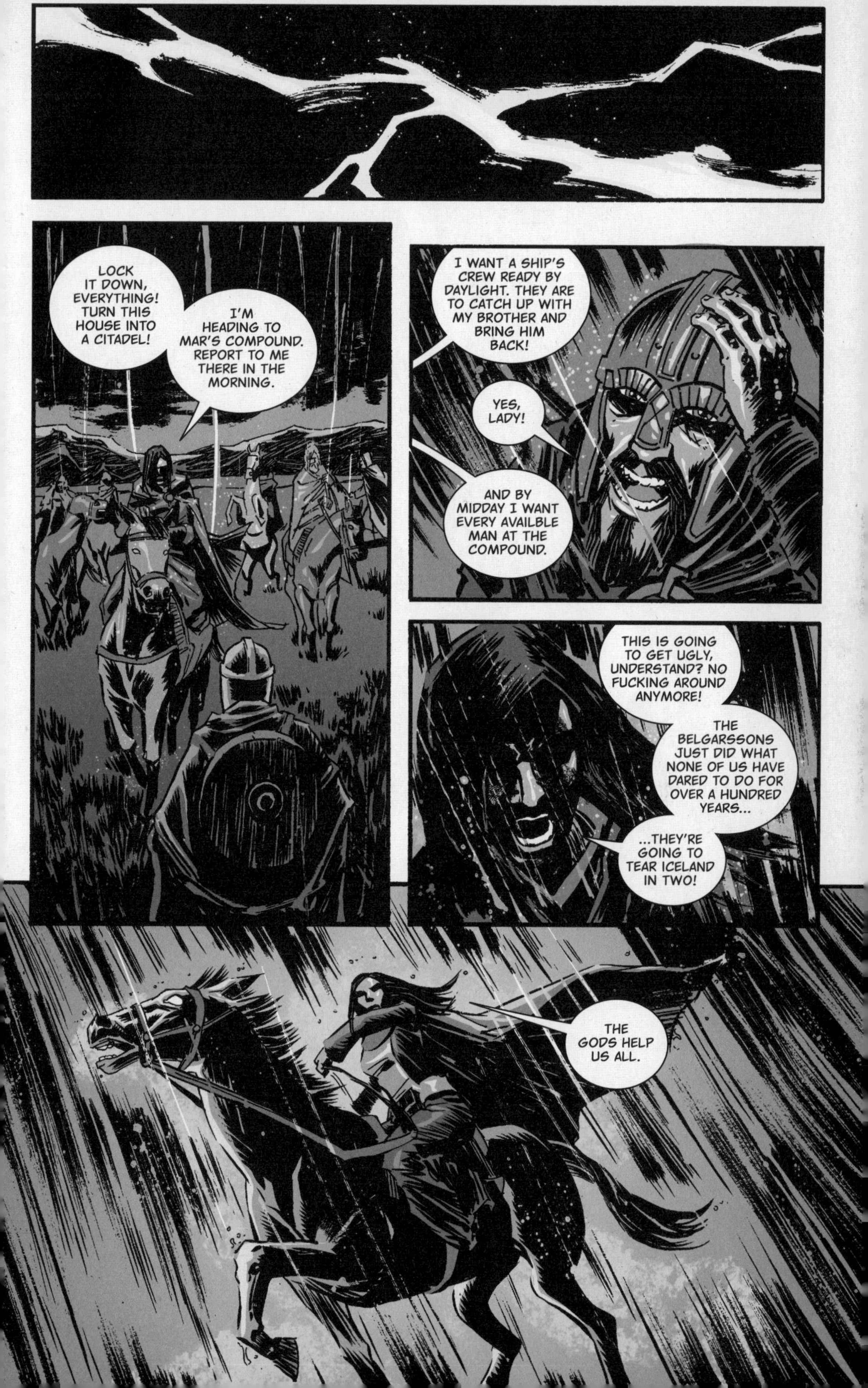
LOCK IT DOWN, EVERYTHING! TURN THIS HOUSE INTO A CITADEL!
I'M HEADING TO MAR'S COMPOUND. REPORT TO ME THERE IN THE MORNING.
I WANT A SHIP'S CREW READY BY DAYLIGHT. THEY ARE TO CATCH UP WITH MY BROTHER AND BRING HIM BACK!
YES, LADY!
AND BY MIDDAY I WANT EVERY AVAILBLE MAN AT THE COMPOUND.
THIS IS GOING TO GET UGLY, UNDERSTAND? NO FUCKING AROUND ANYMORE!
THE BELGARSSONS JUST DID WHAT NONE OF US HAVE DARED TO DO FOR OVER A HUNDRED YEARS...
...THEY'RE GOING TO TEAR ICELAND IN TWO!
THE GODS HELP US ALL.

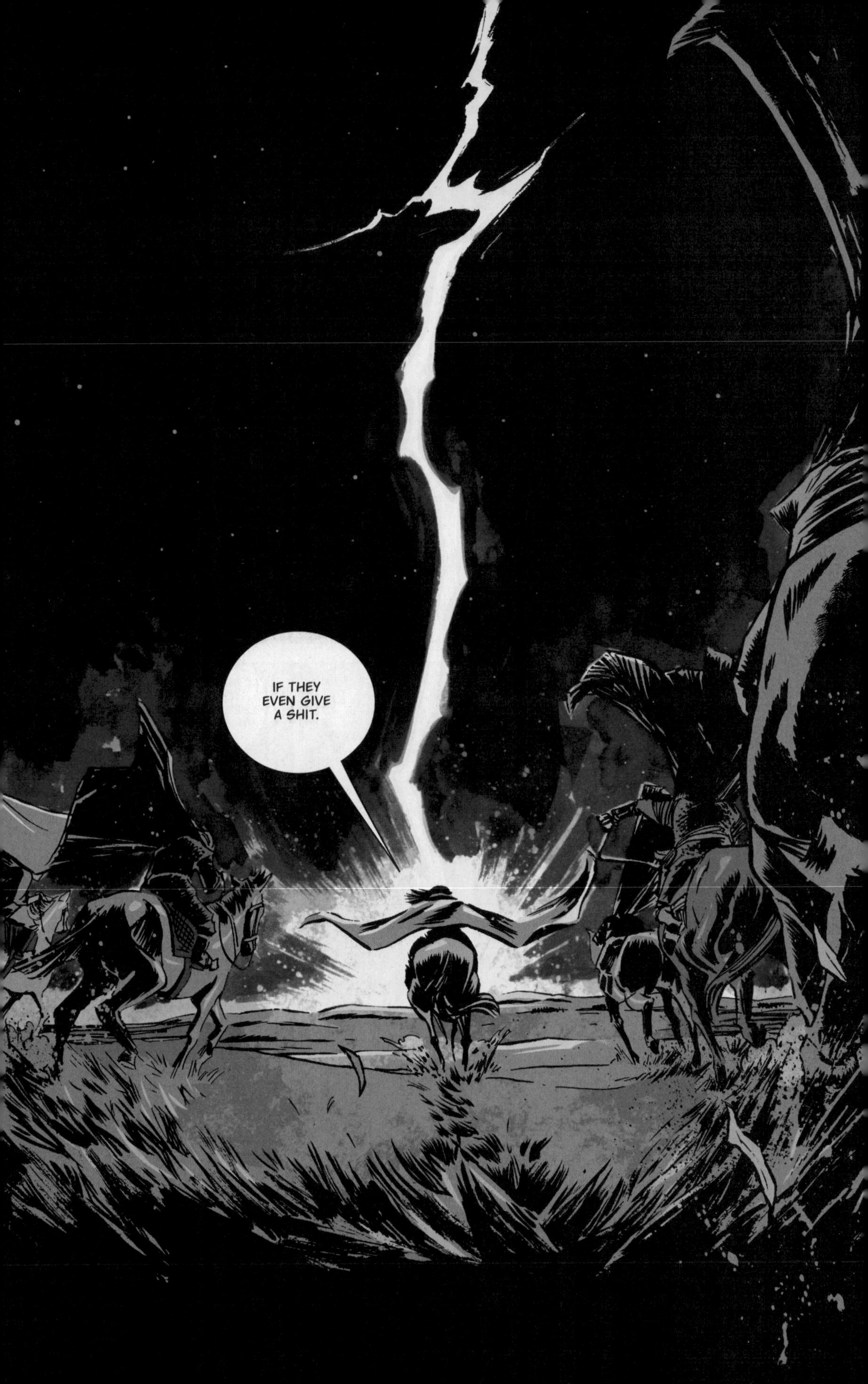
IF THEY EVEN GIVE A SHIT.

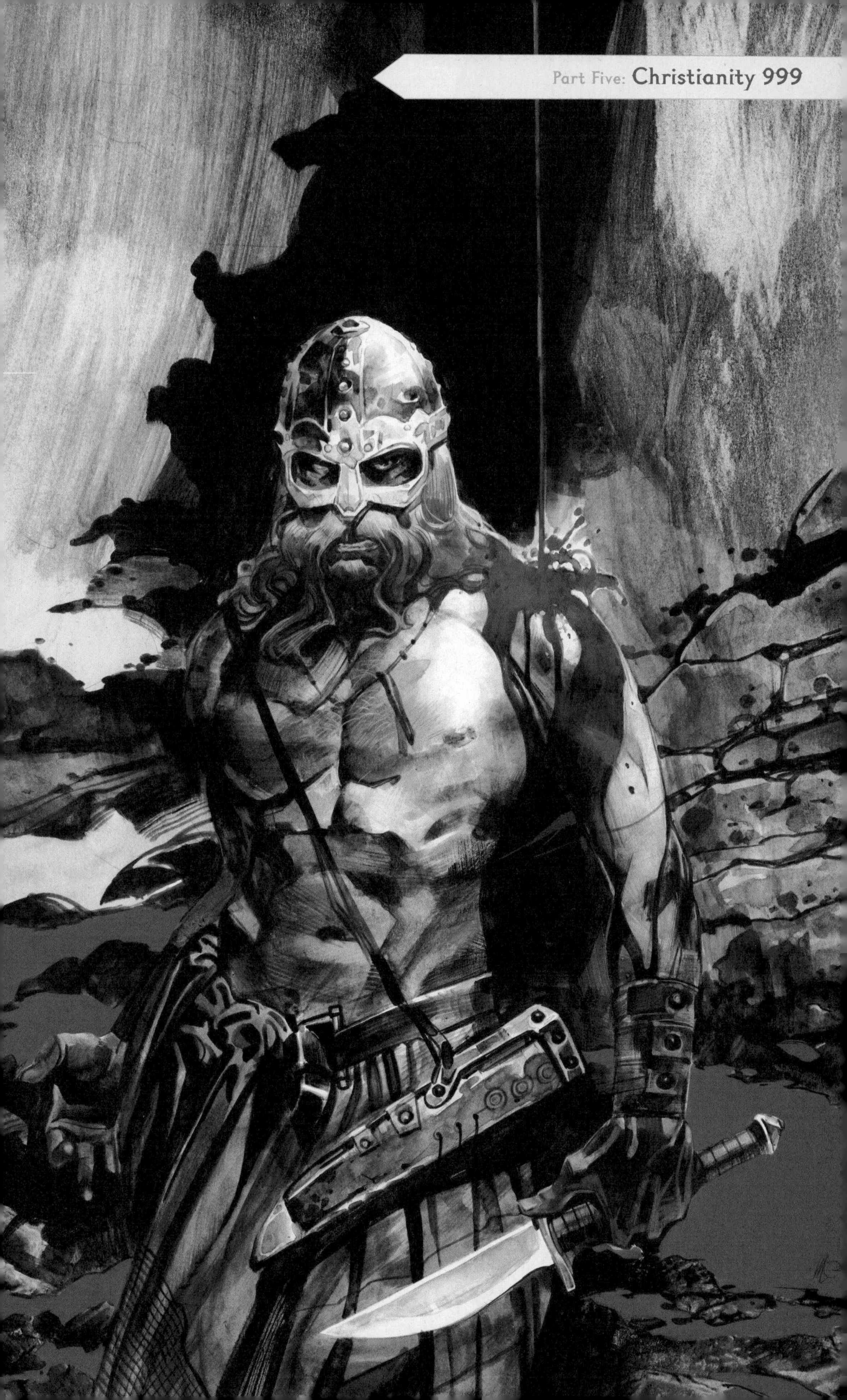

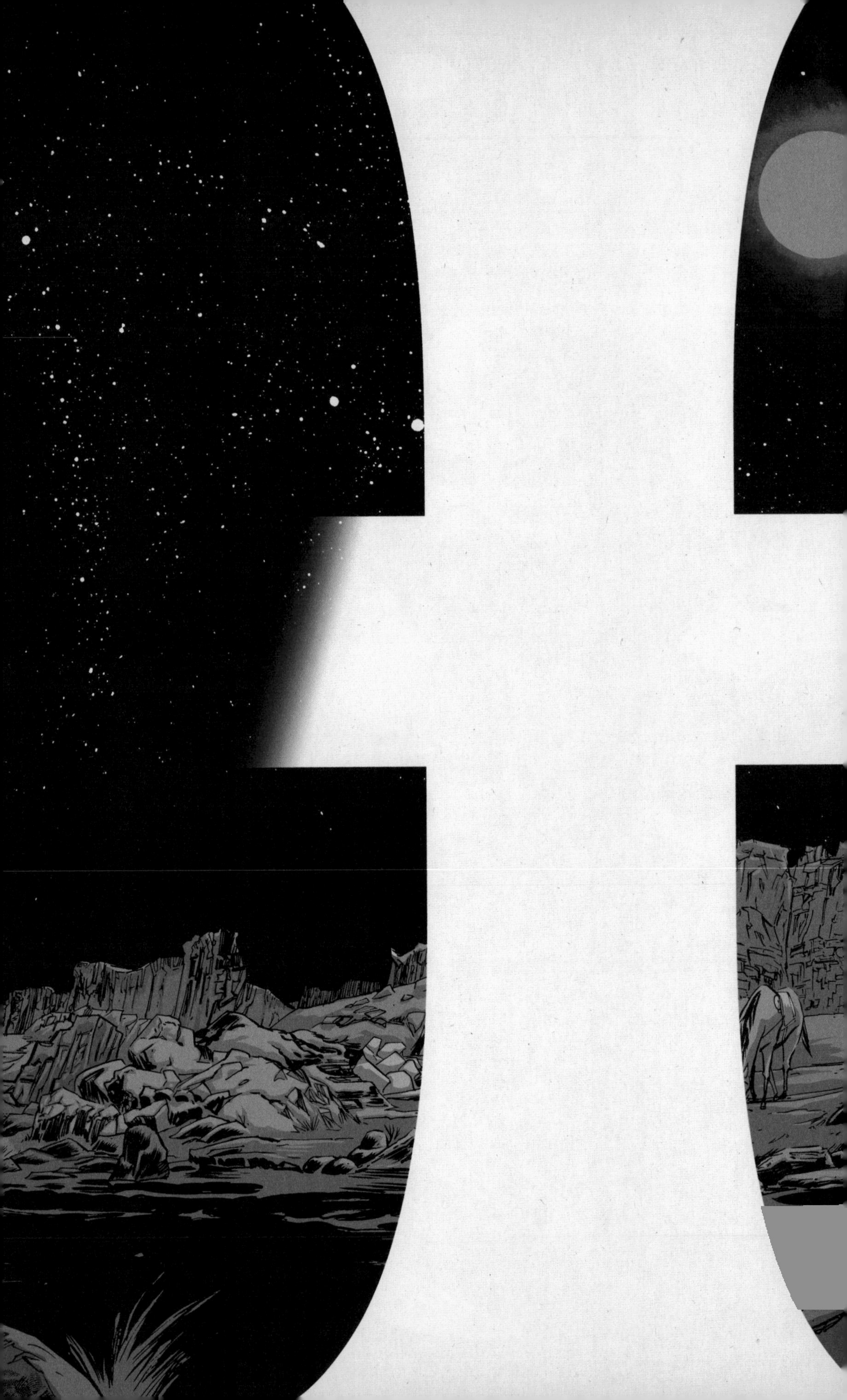

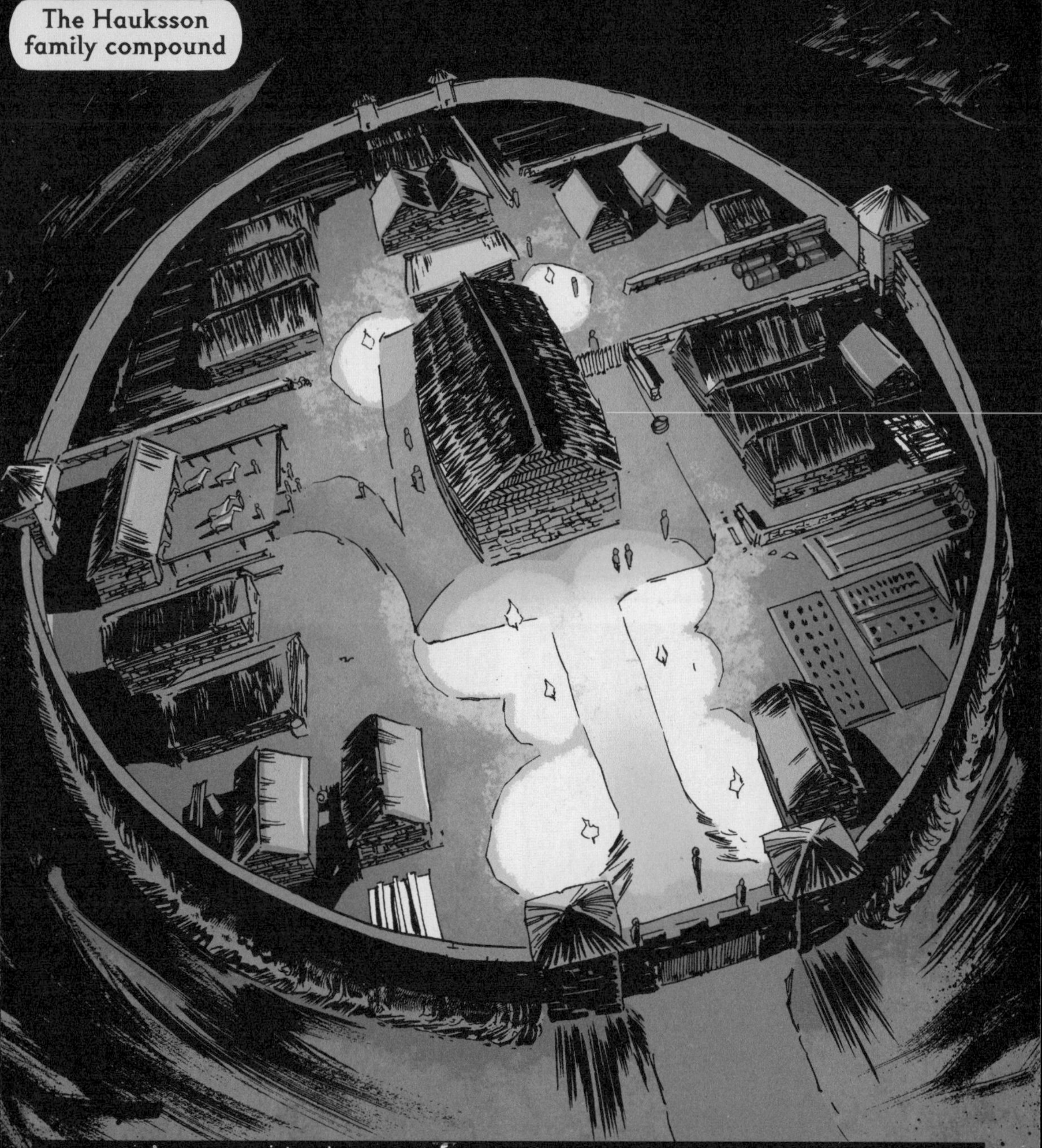
The Hauksson family compound

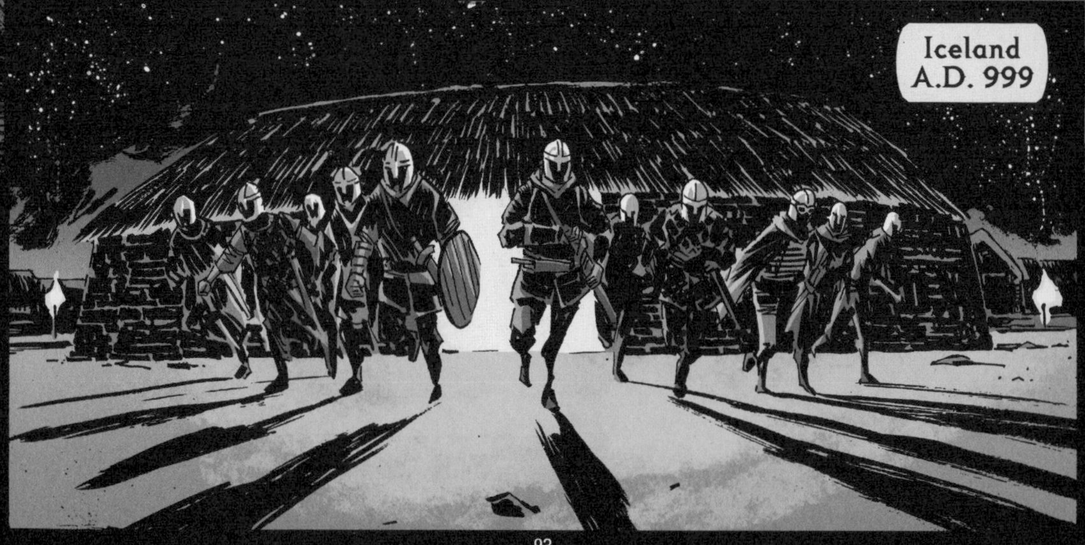
Iceland A.D. 999

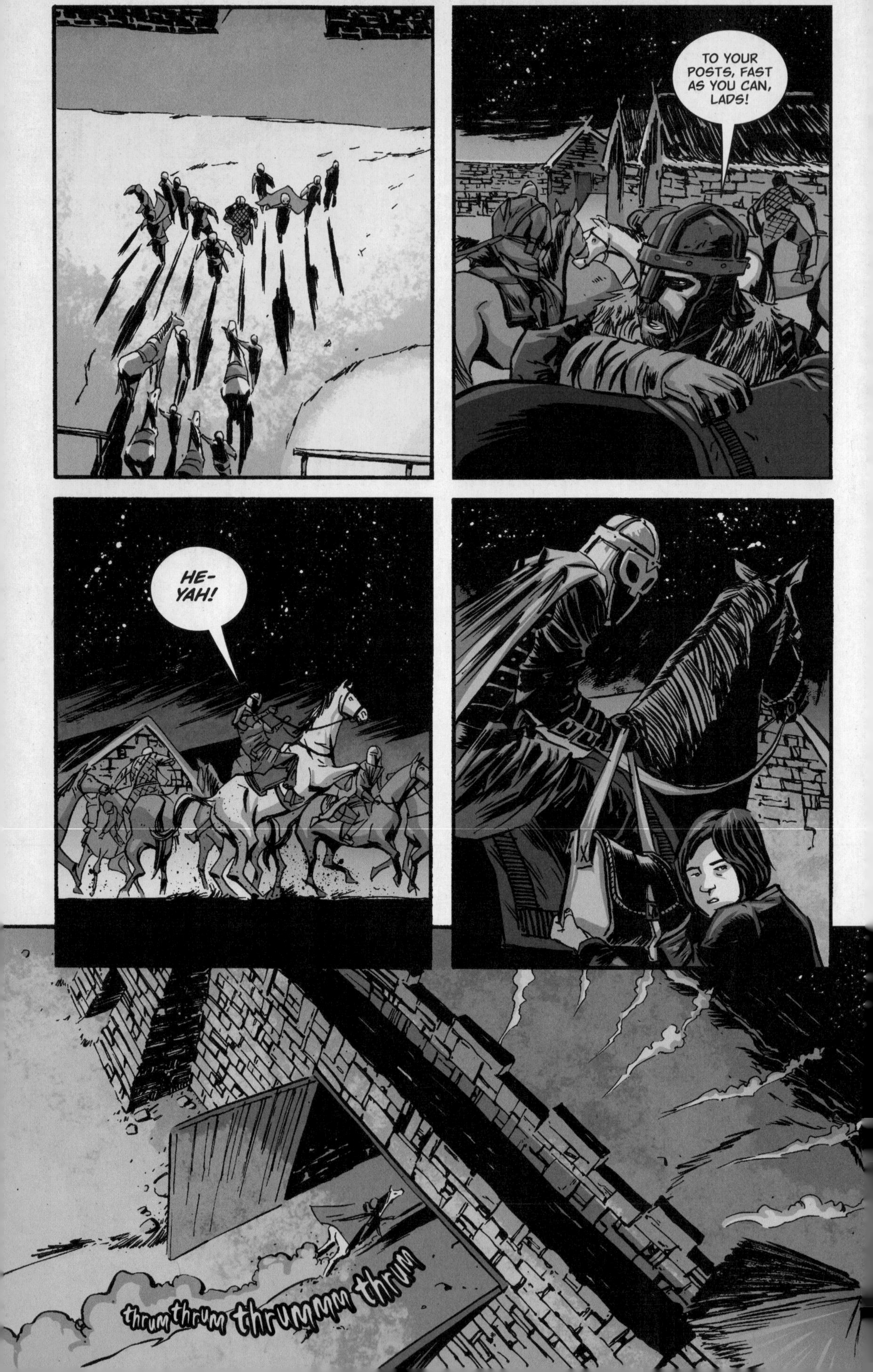

TO YOUR POSTS, FAST AS YOU CAN, LADS!
HE-YAH!
thrum thrum thrummm thrum

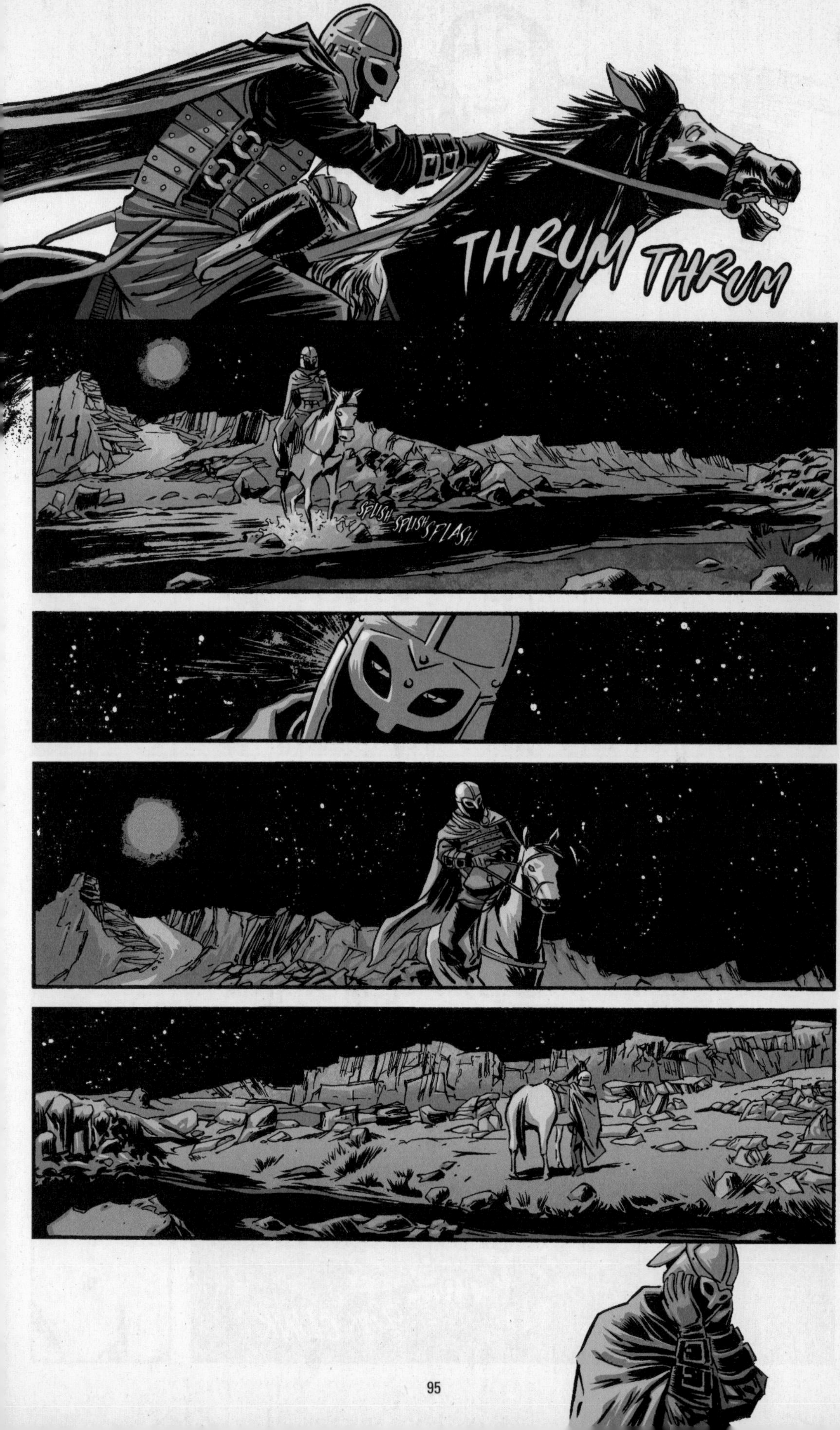
THRUM THRUM
SPLISH SPLISH SPLASH

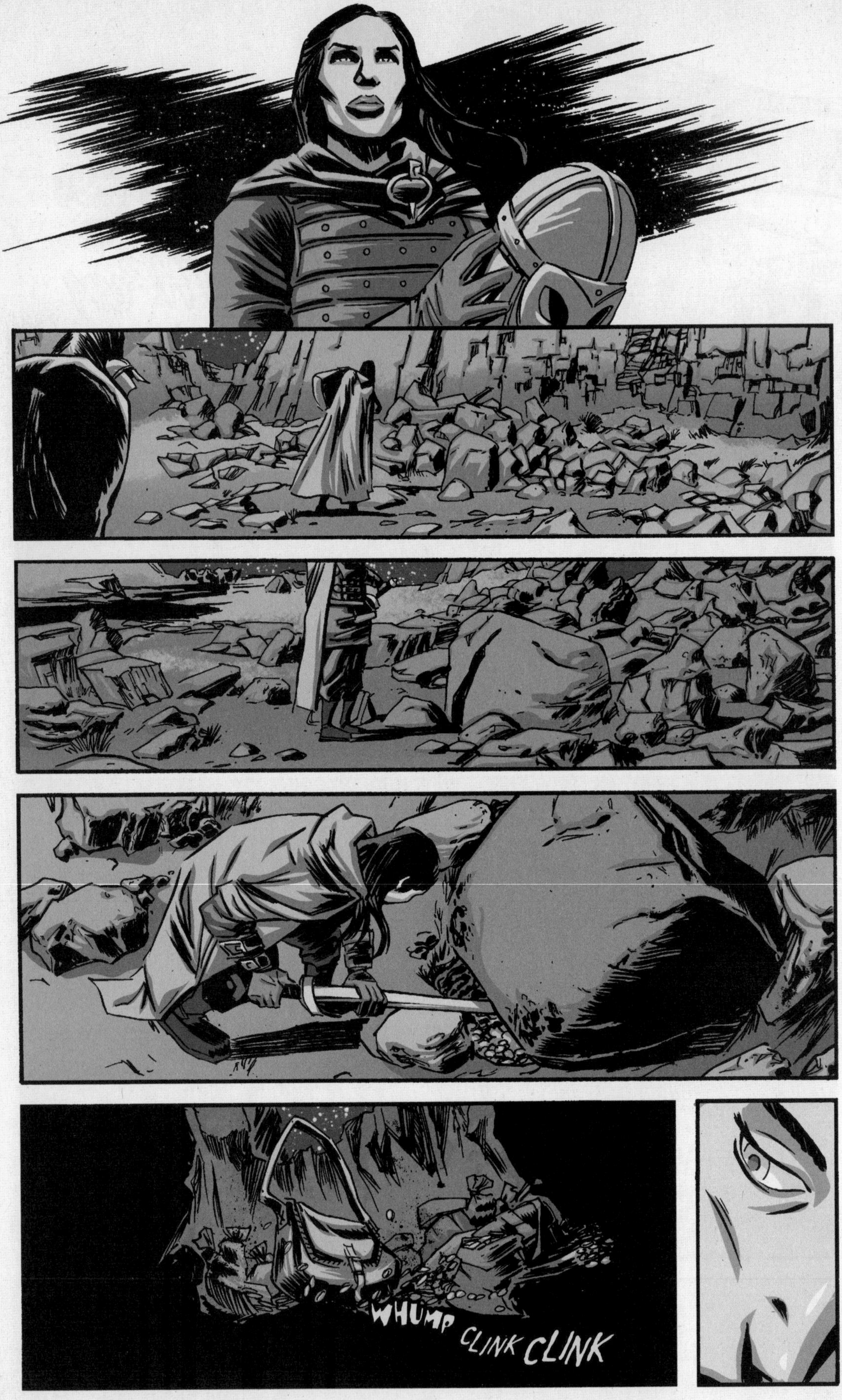
WHUMP
CLINK CLINK

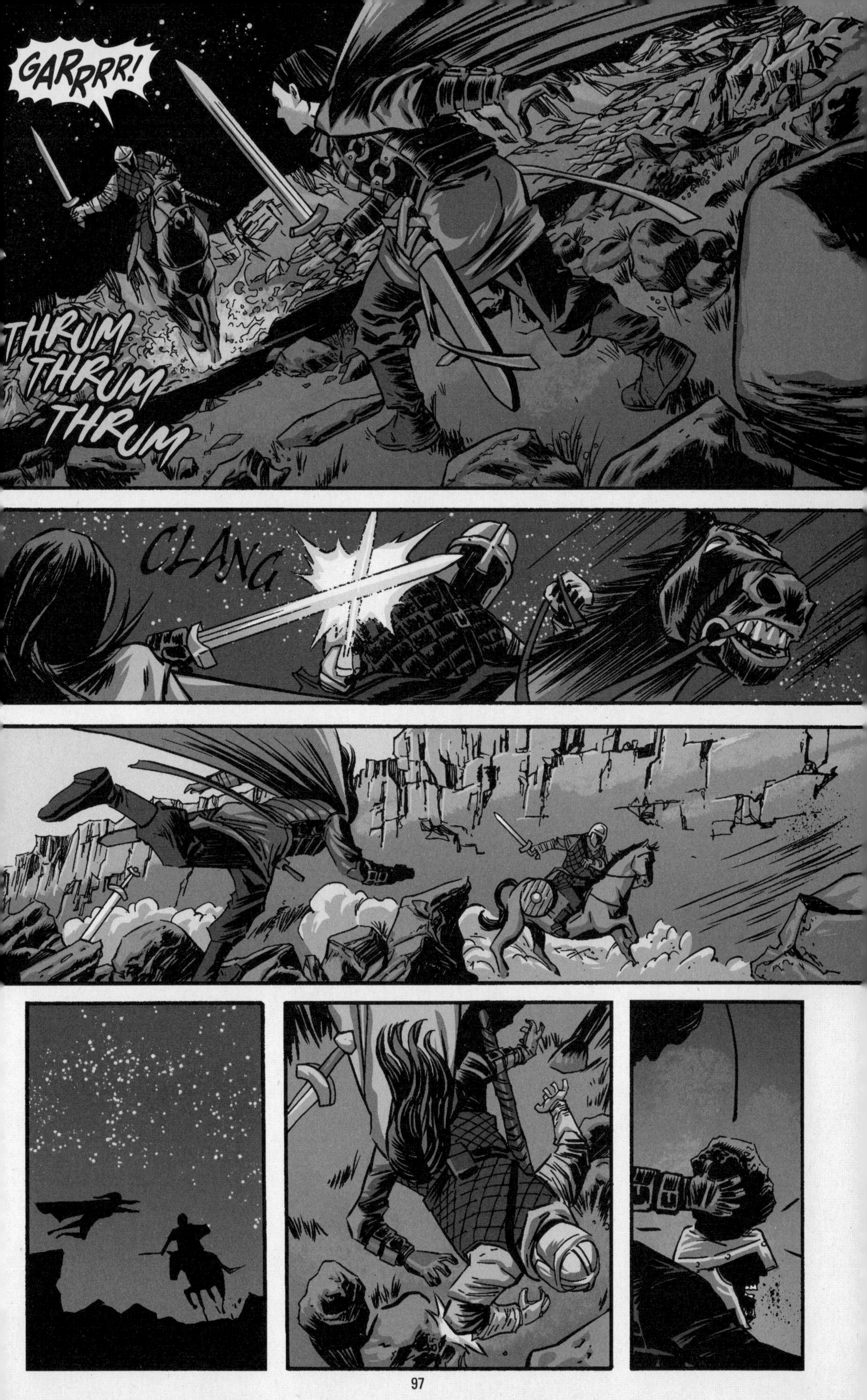
GARRRR!
THRUM THRUM THRUM
CLANG

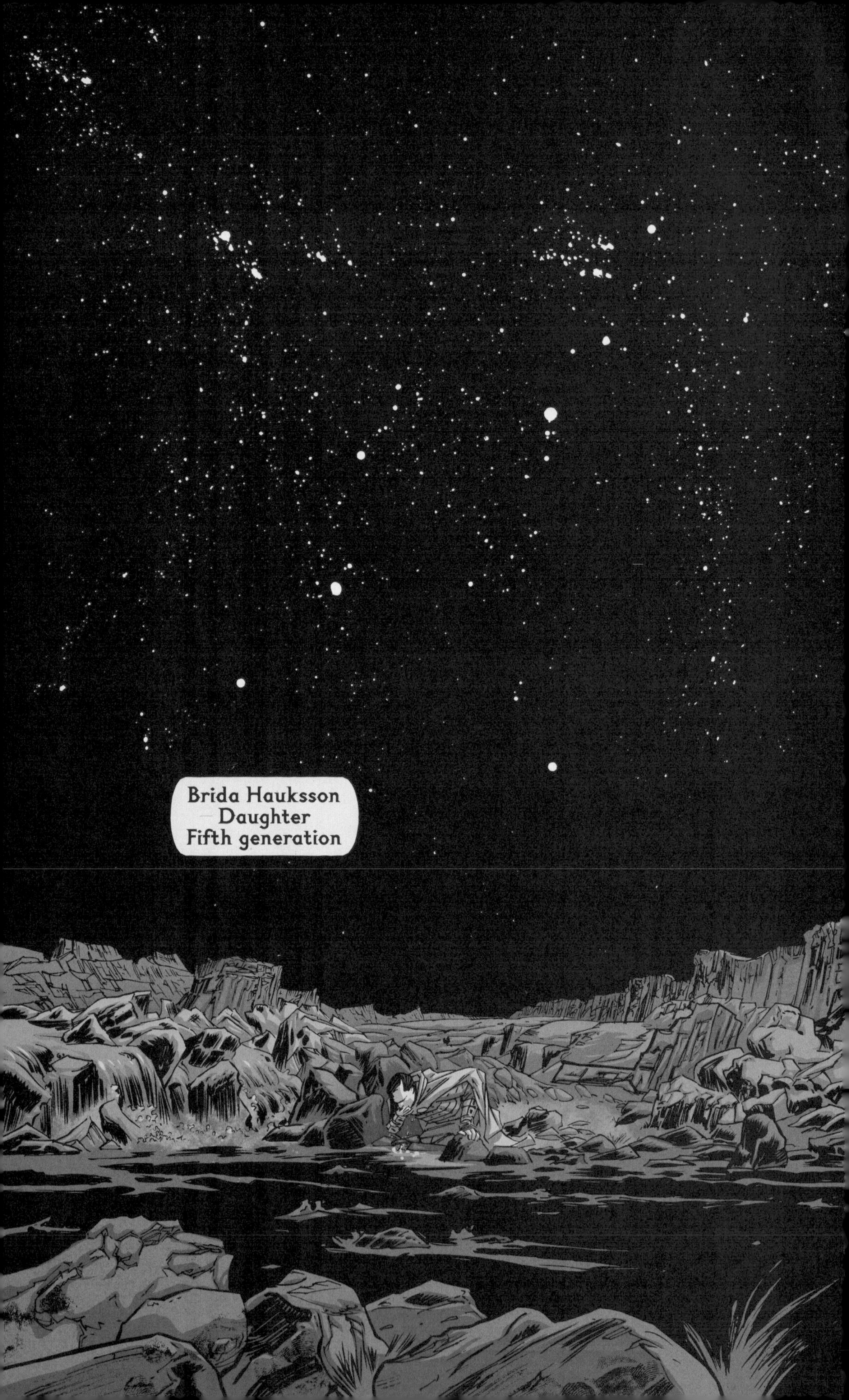
Brida Hauksson — Daughter Fifth generation

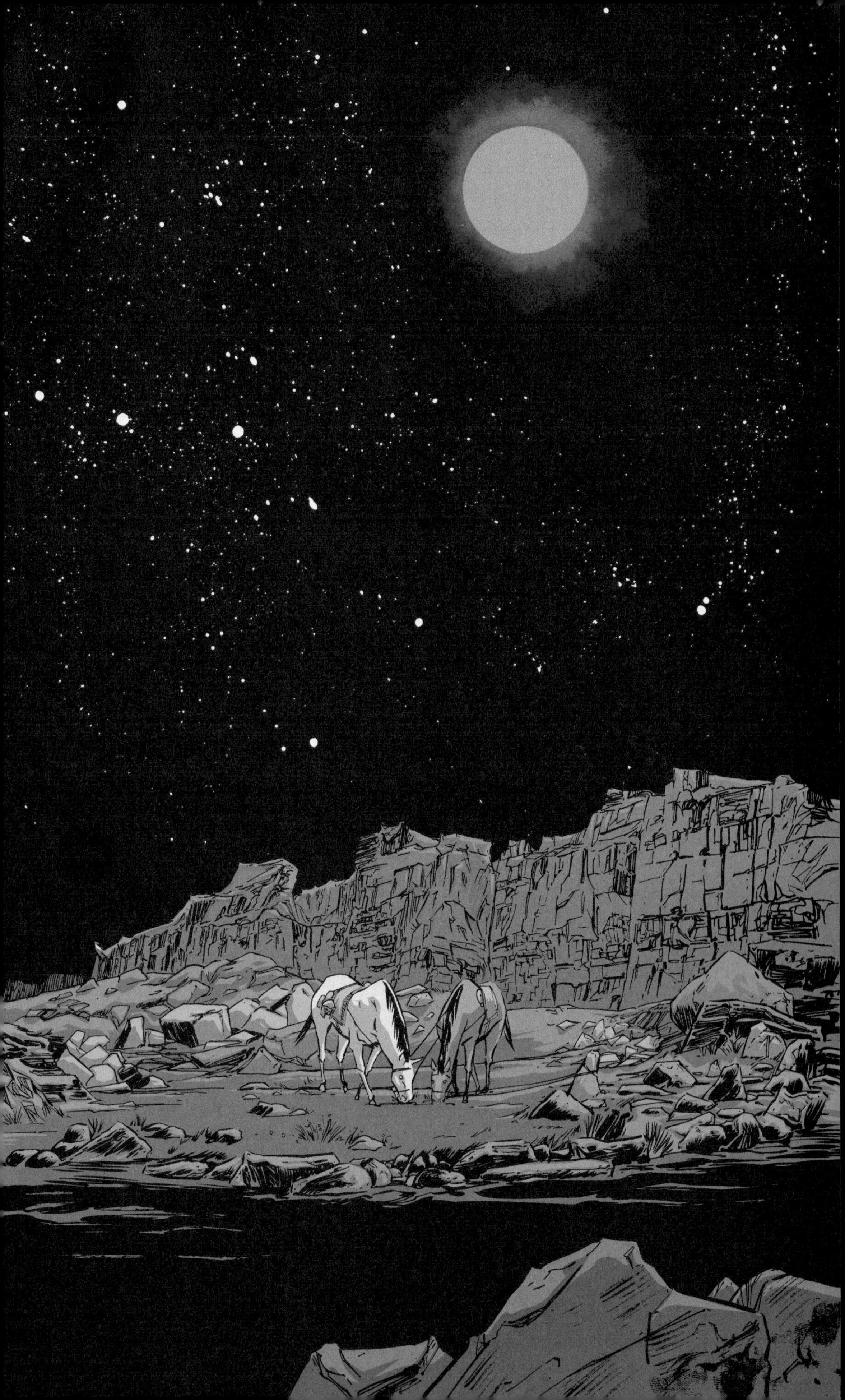

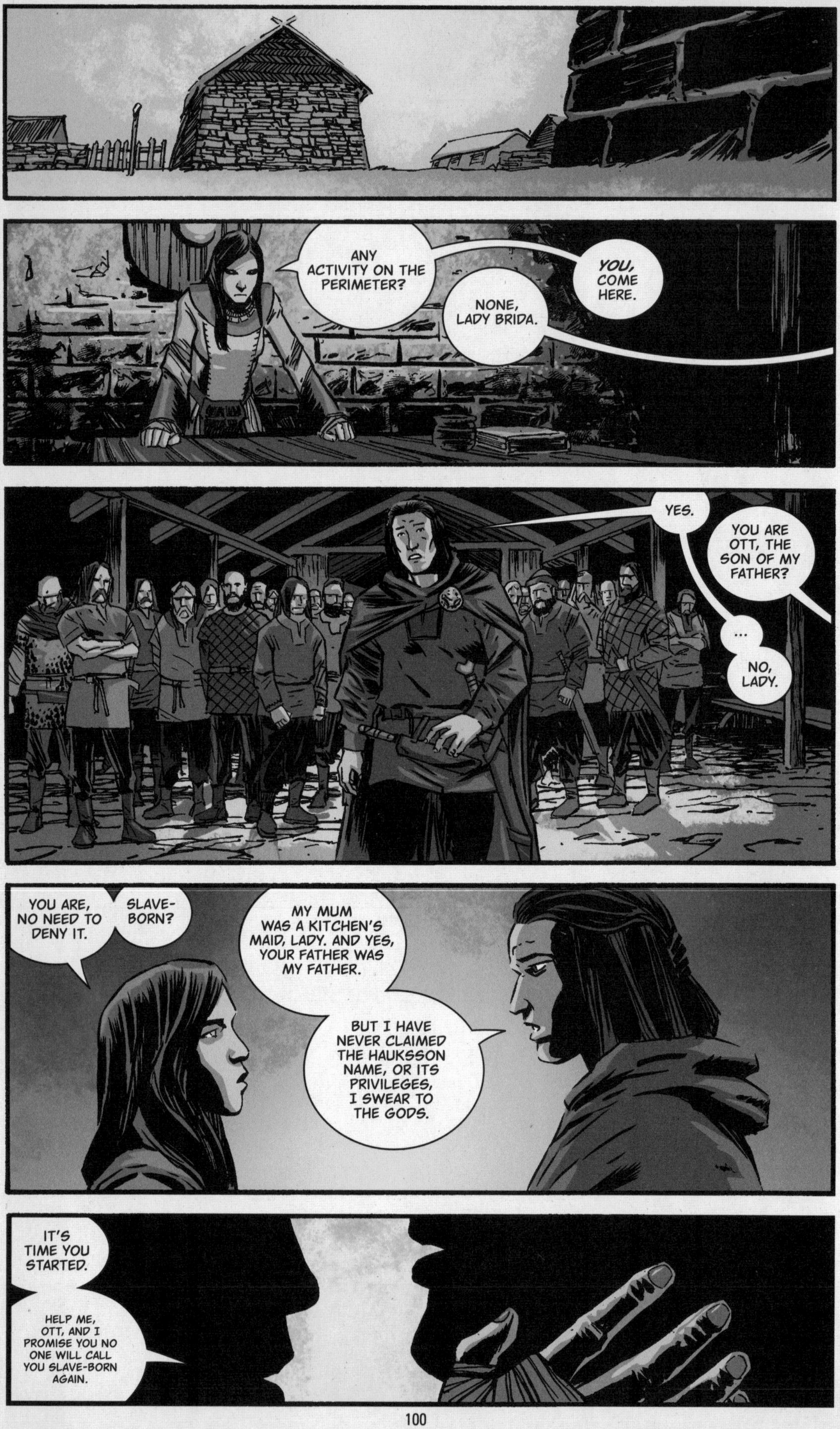
ANY ACTIVITY ON THE PERIMETER?
NONE, LADY BRIDA.
YOU, COME HERE.
YES.
YOU ARE OTT, THE SON OF MY FATHER?
...
NO, LADY.
YOU ARE, NO NEED TO DENY IT.
SLAVE-BORN?
MY MUM WAS A KITCHEN'S MAID, LADY. AND YES, YOUR FATHER WAS MY FATHER.
BUT I HAVE NEVER CLAIMED THE HAUKSSON NAME, OR ITS PRIVILEGES, I SWEAR TO THE GODS.
IT'S TIME YOU STARTED.
HELP ME, OTT, AND I PROMISE YOU NO ONE WILL CALL YOU SLAVE-BORN AGAIN.

OTT IS A MEMBER OF THE HOUSEHOLD NOW. HE IS A HAUKSSON BY BIRTHRIGHT.

TELL ME, HOW ARE THINGS OUT THERE?

AHEM--

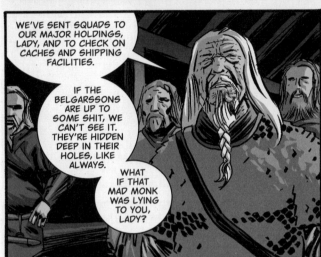

WE'VE SENT SQUADS TO OUR MAJOR HOLDINGS, LADY, AND TO CHECK ON CACHES AND SHIPPING FACILITIES.

IF THE BELGARSSONS ARE UP TO SOME SHIT, WE CAN'T SEE IT. THEY'RE HIDDEN DEEP IN THEIR HOLES, LIKE ALWAYS.

WHAT IF THAT MAD MONK WAS LYING TO YOU, LADY?

ANY NEWS OF MY BROTHER?

NO NEWS, LADY.

CHECK CHURCHES, AND BUILDING SITES. IF THE PRIEST WAS TELLING ME THE TRUTH, THE BELGARSSONS WILL BE SUPPLYING SECURITY.

I ALSO WANT THIS COMPOUND LIT, FROM SUNDOWN TO SUNRISE, LIKE IT'S MIDDAY IN SUMMER. I DON'T WANT TO SEE A SINGLE CAST SHADOW LARGE ENOUGH FOR A MAN TO HIDE IN.

AND YOU...

YES.

YOU ARE LOYAL AND WELL PAID, YOUR FUTURE AND THAT OF YOUR CHILDREN'S TIED UP IN MY OWN.

YES, LADY.

IF THERE'S ANOTHER ATTEMPT ON MY LIFE, *YOU* ARE TO BE HELD RESPONSIBLE.

SO SEE TO IT THERE IS NOT.

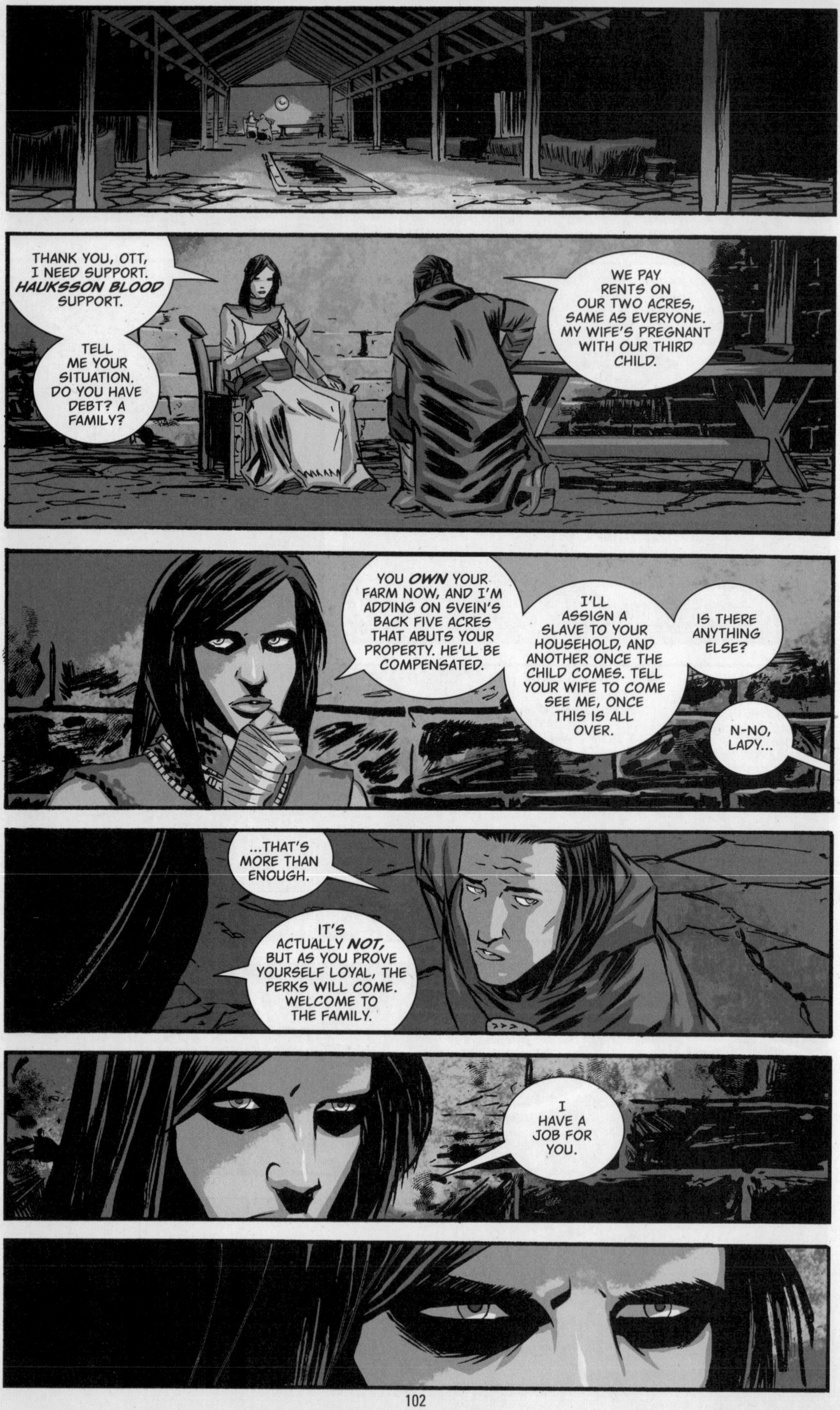

THANK YOU, OTT, I NEED SUPPORT. HAUKSSON BLOOD SUPPORT.
TELL ME YOUR SITUATION. DO YOU HAVE DEBT? A FAMILY?
WE PAY RENTS ON OUR TWO ACRES, SAME AS EVERYONE. MY WIFE'S PREGNANT WITH OUR THIRD CHILD.
YOU OWN YOUR FARM NOW, AND I'M ADDING ON SVEIN'S BACK FIVE ACRES THAT ABUTS YOUR PROPERTY. HE'LL BE COMPENSATED.
I'LL ASSIGN A SLAVE TO YOUR HOUSEHOLD, AND ANOTHER ONCE THE CHILD COMES. TELL YOUR WIFE TO COME SEE ME, ONCE THIS IS ALL OVER.
IS THERE ANYTHING ELSE?
N-NO, LADY...
...THAT'S MORE THAN ENOUGH.
IT'S ACTUALLY NOT, BUT AS YOU PROVE YOURSELF LOYAL, THE PERKS WILL COME. WELCOME TO THE FAMILY.
I HAVE A JOB FOR YOU.

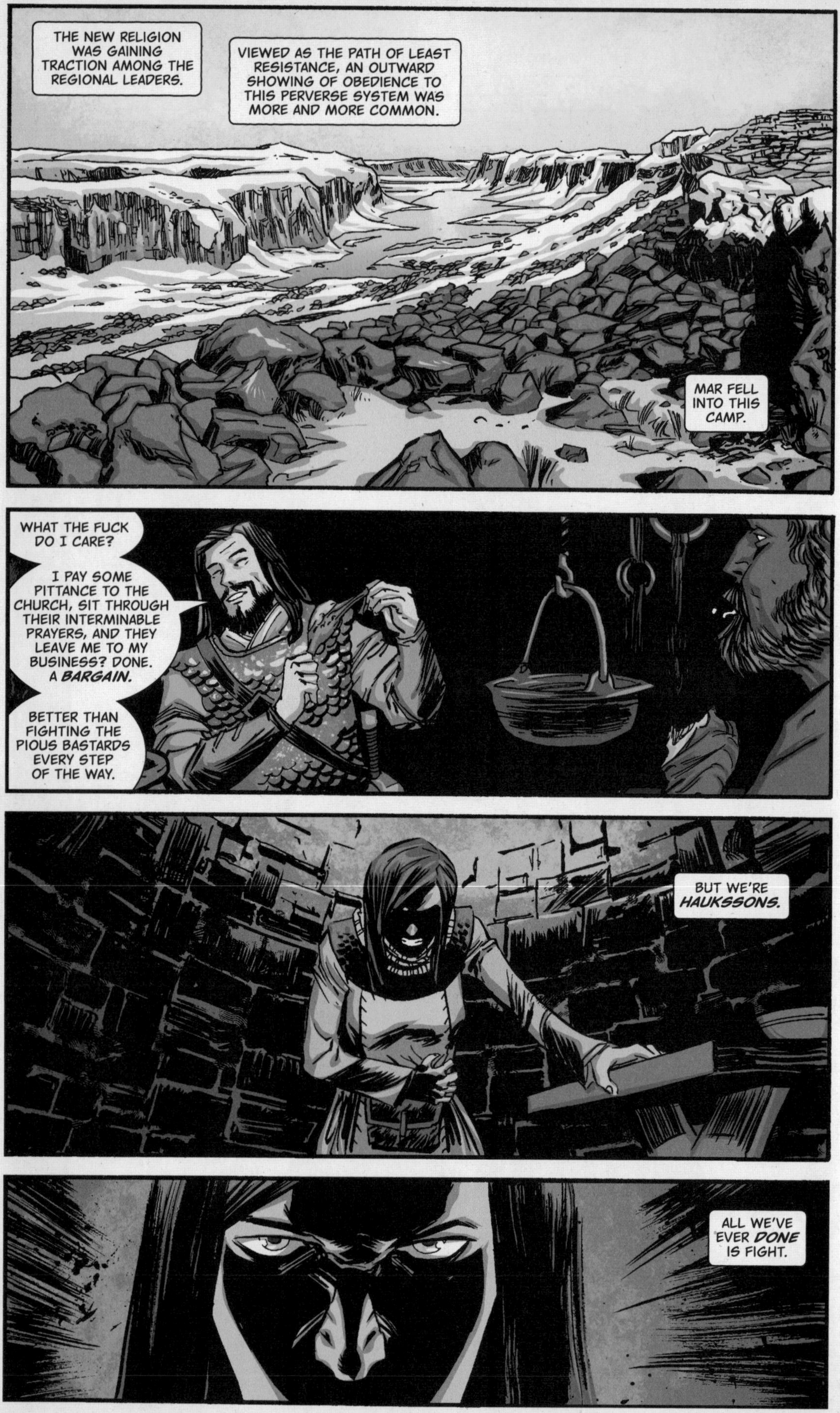
THE NEW RELIGION WAS GAINING TRACTION AMONG THE REGIONAL LEADERS.
VIEWED AS THE PATH OF LEAST RESISTANCE, AN OUTWARD SHOWING OF OBEDIENCE TO THIS PERVERSE SYSTEM WAS MORE AND MORE COMMON.
MAR FELL INTO THIS CAMP.
WHAT THE FUCK DO I CARE?
I PAY SOME PITTANCE TO THE CHURCH, SIT THROUGH THEIR INTERMINABLE PRAYERS, AND THEY LEAVE ME TO MY BUSINESS? DONE. A *BARGAIN.*
BETTER THAN FIGHTING THE PIOUS BASTARDS EVERY STEP OF THE WAY.
BUT WE'RE *HAUKSSONS.*
ALL WE'VE EVER *DONE* IS FIGHT.

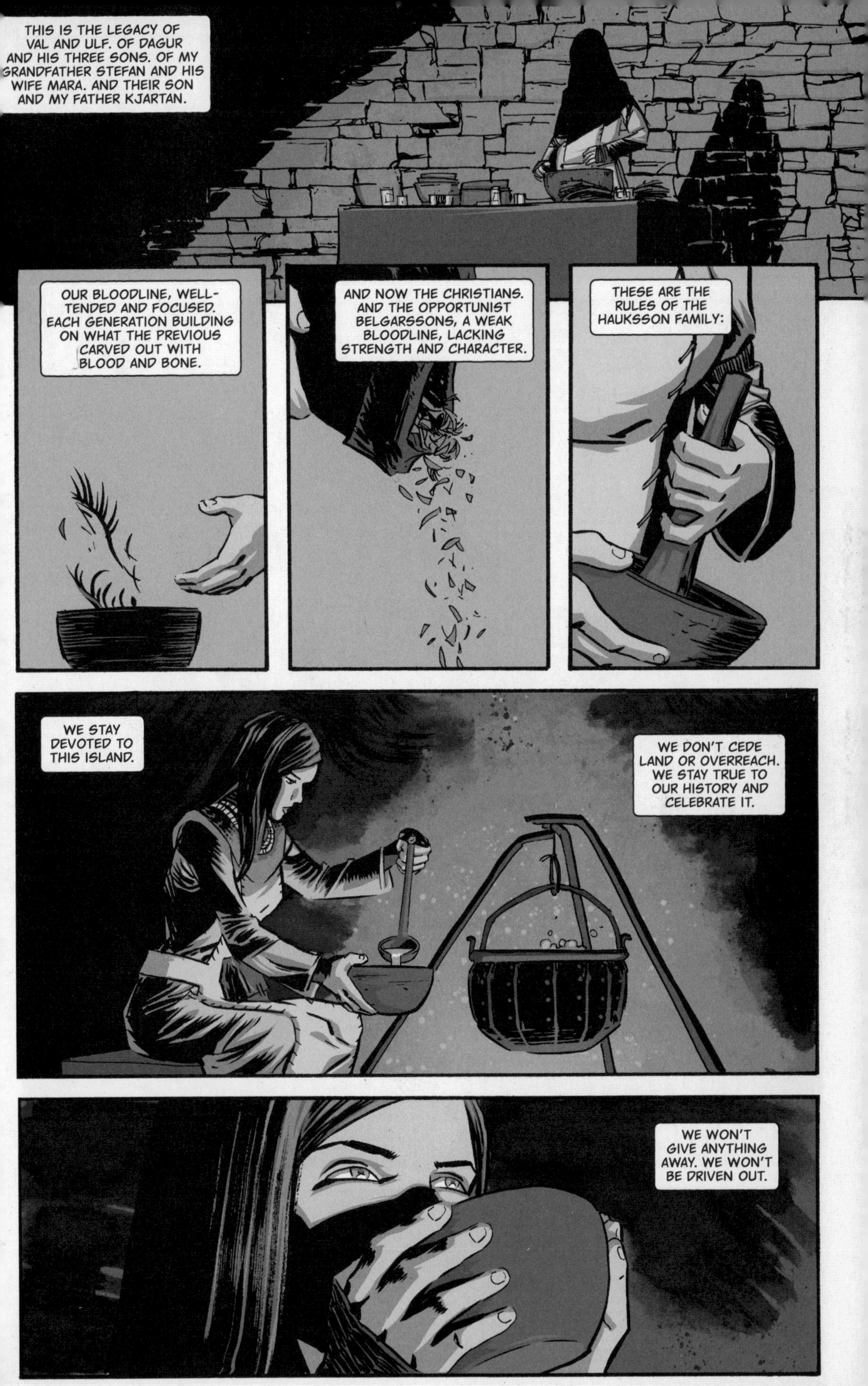
THIS IS THE LEGACY OF VAL AND ULF. OF DAGUR AND HIS THREE SONS. OF MY GRANDFATHER STEFAN AND HIS WIFE MARA. AND THEIR SON AND MY FATHER KJARTAN.
OUR BLOODLINE, WELL-TENDED AND FOCUSED. EACH GENERATION BUILDING ON WHAT THE PREVIOUS CARVED OUT WITH BLOOD AND BONE.
AND NOW THE CHRISTIANS. AND THE OPPORTUNIST BELGARSSONS, A WEAK BLOODLINE, LACKING STRENGTH AND CHARACTER.
THESE ARE THE RULES OF THE HAUKSSON FAMILY:
WE STAY DEVOTED TO THIS ISLAND.
WE DON'T CEDE LAND OR OVERREACH. WE STAY TRUE TO OUR HISTORY AND CELEBRATE IT.
WE WON'T GIVE ANYTHING AWAY. WE WON'T BE DRIVEN OUT.

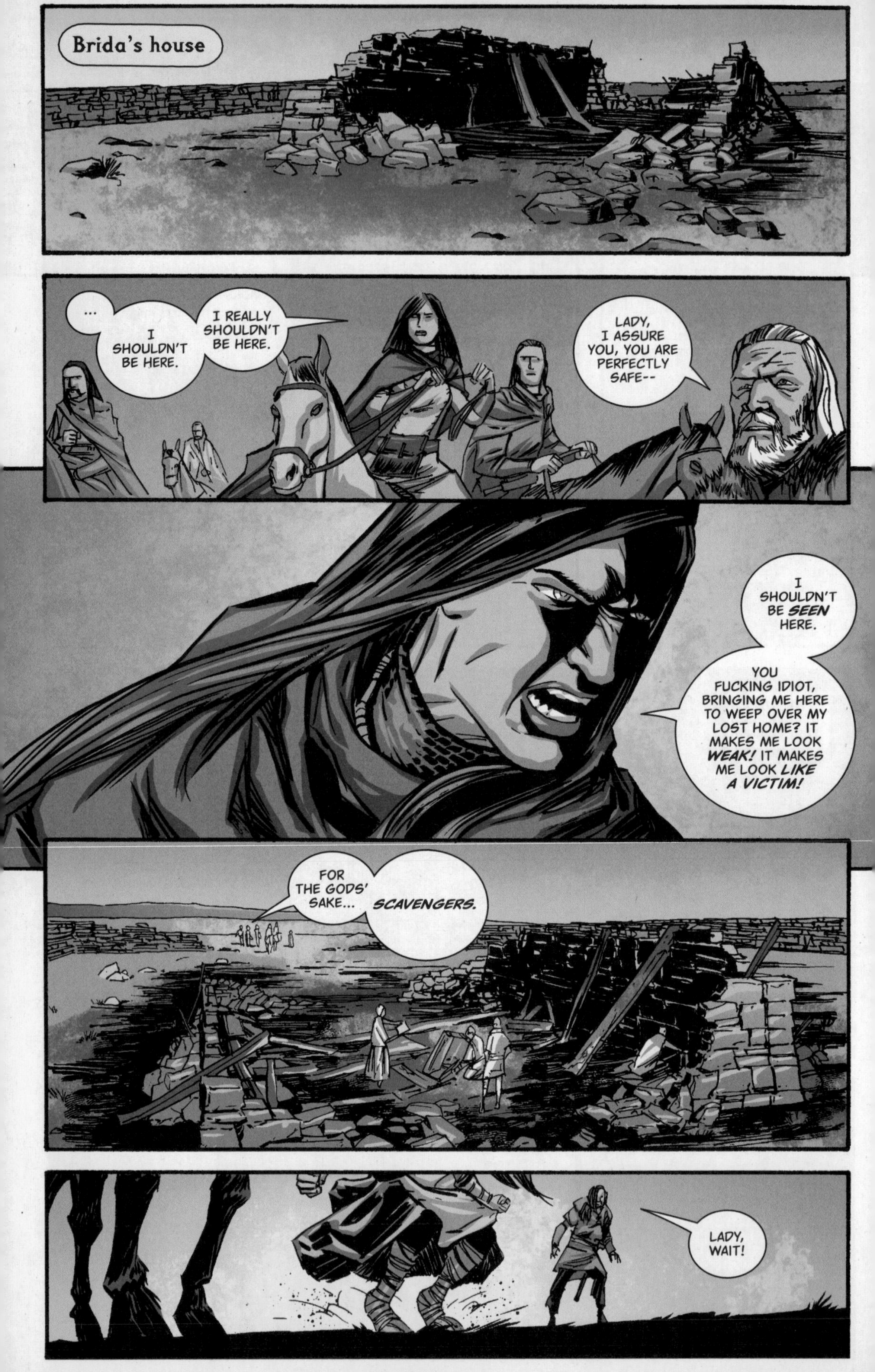
Brida's house
...
I SHOULDN'T BE HERE.
I REALLY SHOULDN'T BE HERE.
LADY, I ASSURE YOU, YOU ARE PERFECTLY SAFE--
I SHOULDN'T BE *SEEN* HERE.
YOU FUCKING IDIOT, BRINGING ME HERE TO WEEP OVER MY LOST HOME? IT MAKES ME LOOK *WEAK!* IT MAKES ME LOOK *LIKE A VICTIM!*
FOR THE GODS' SAKE...
SCAVENGERS.
LADY, WAIT!

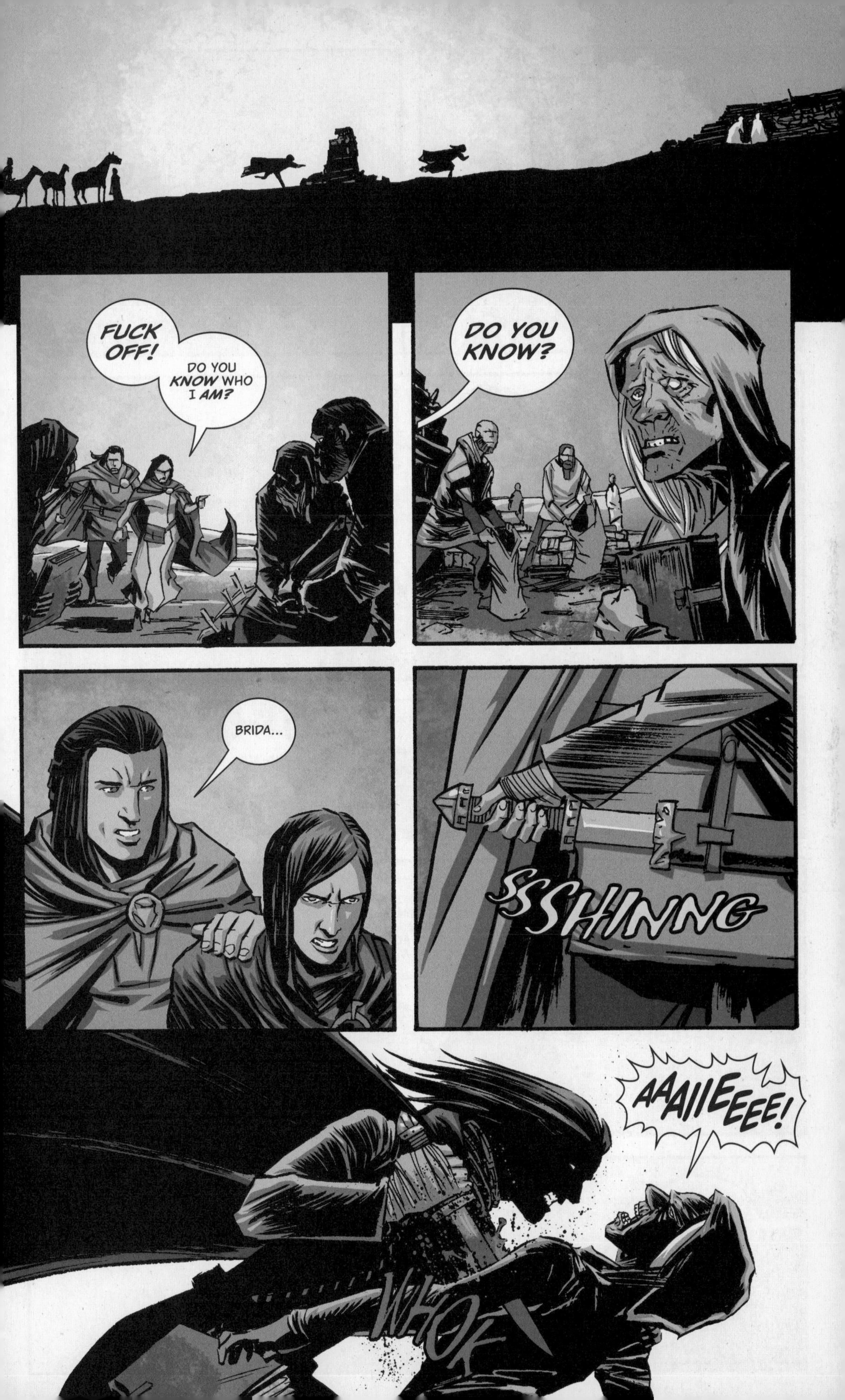
FUCK OFF!
DO YOU KNOW WHO I AM?
DO YOU KNOW?
BRIDA...
SSHINNG
AAAIIEEEE!
WHOK

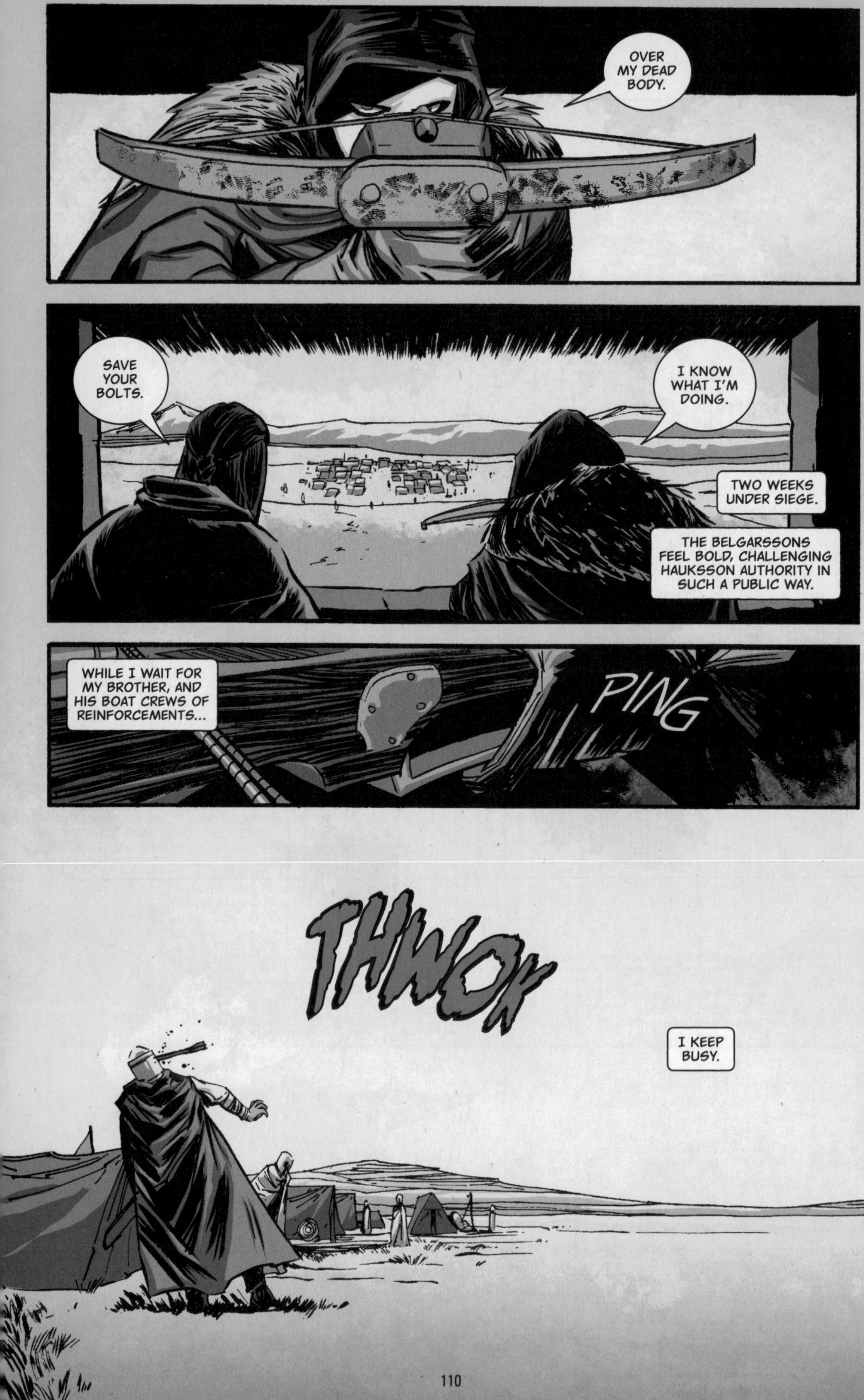
OVER MY DEAD BODY.
SAVE YOUR BOLTS.
I KNOW WHAT I'M DOING.
TWO WEEKS UNDER SIEGE.
THE BELGARSSONS FEEL BOLD, CHALLENGING HAUKSSON AUTHORITY IN SUCH A PUBLIC WAY.
WHILE I WAIT FOR MY BROTHER, AND HIS BOAT CREWS OF REINFORCEMENTS...
PING
THWOK
I KEEP BUSY.

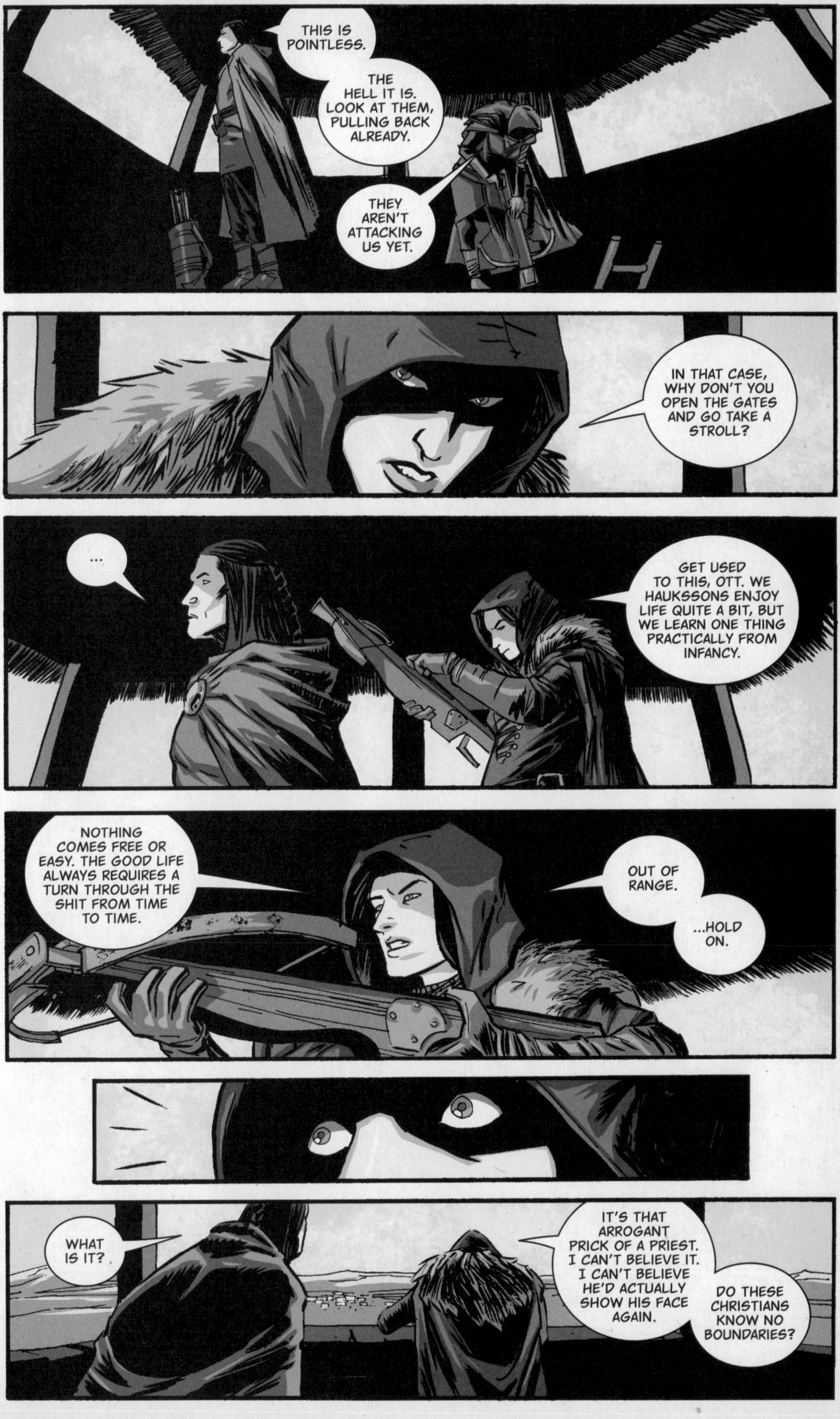

THIS IS POINTLESS.
THE HELL IT IS. LOOK AT THEM, PULLING BACK ALREADY.
THEY AREN'T ATTACKING US YET.
IN THAT CASE, WHY DON'T YOU OPEN THE GATES AND GO TAKE A STROLL?
...
GET USED TO THIS, OTT. WE HAUKSSONS ENJOY LIFE QUITE A BIT, BUT WE LEARN ONE THING PRACTICALLY FROM INFANCY.
NOTHING COMES FREE OR EASY. THE GOOD LIFE ALWAYS REQUIRES A TURN THROUGH THE SHIT FROM TIME TO TIME.
OUT OF RANGE.
...HOLD ON.
WHAT IS IT?
IT'S THAT ARROGANT PRICK OF A PRIEST. I CAN'T BELIEVE IT. I CAN'T BELIEVE HE'D ACTUALLY SHOW HIS FACE AGAIN.
DO THESE CHRISTIANS KNOW NO BOUNDARIES?

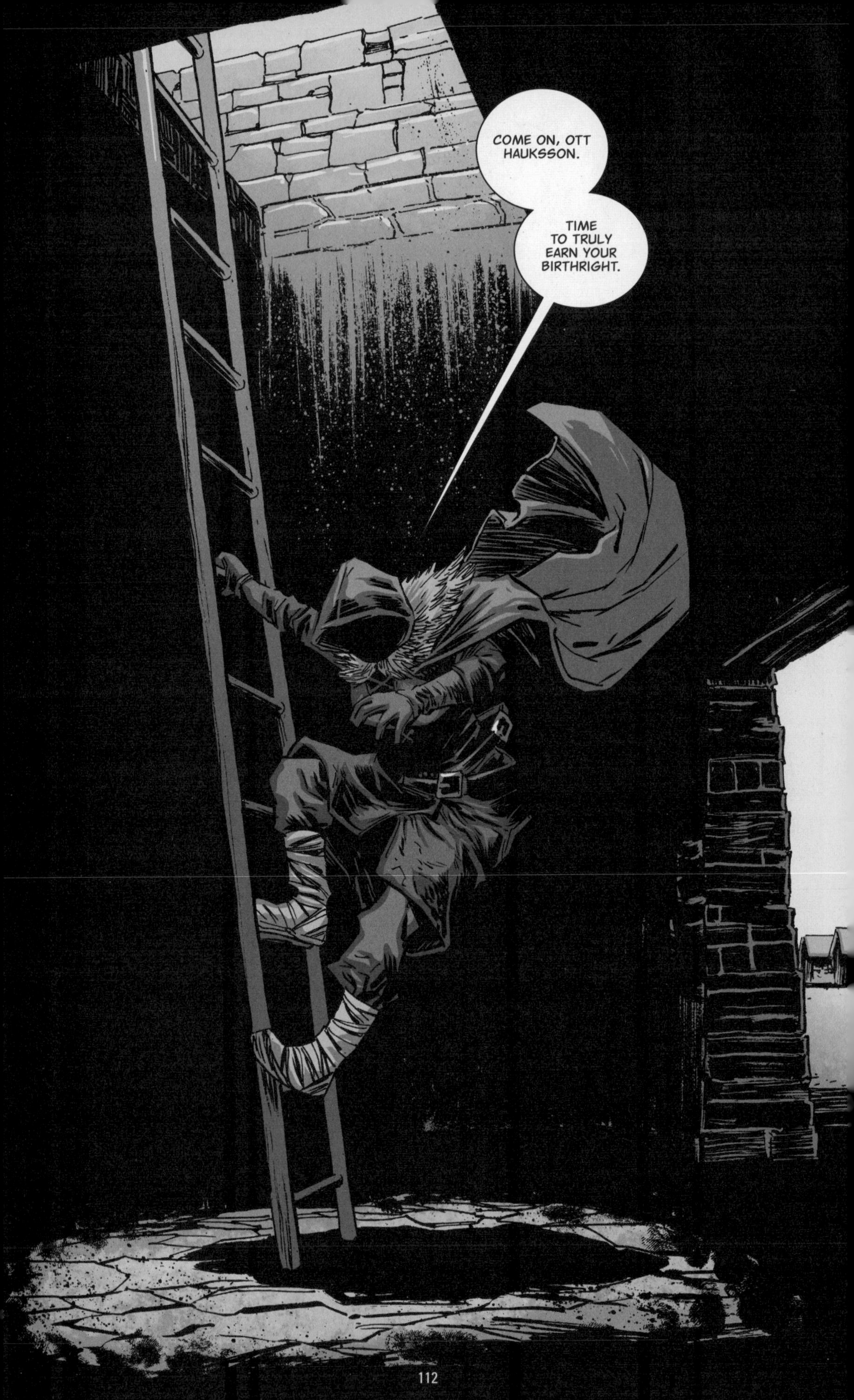
COME ON, OTT HAUKSSON.
TIME TO TRULY EARN YOUR BIRTHRIGHT.

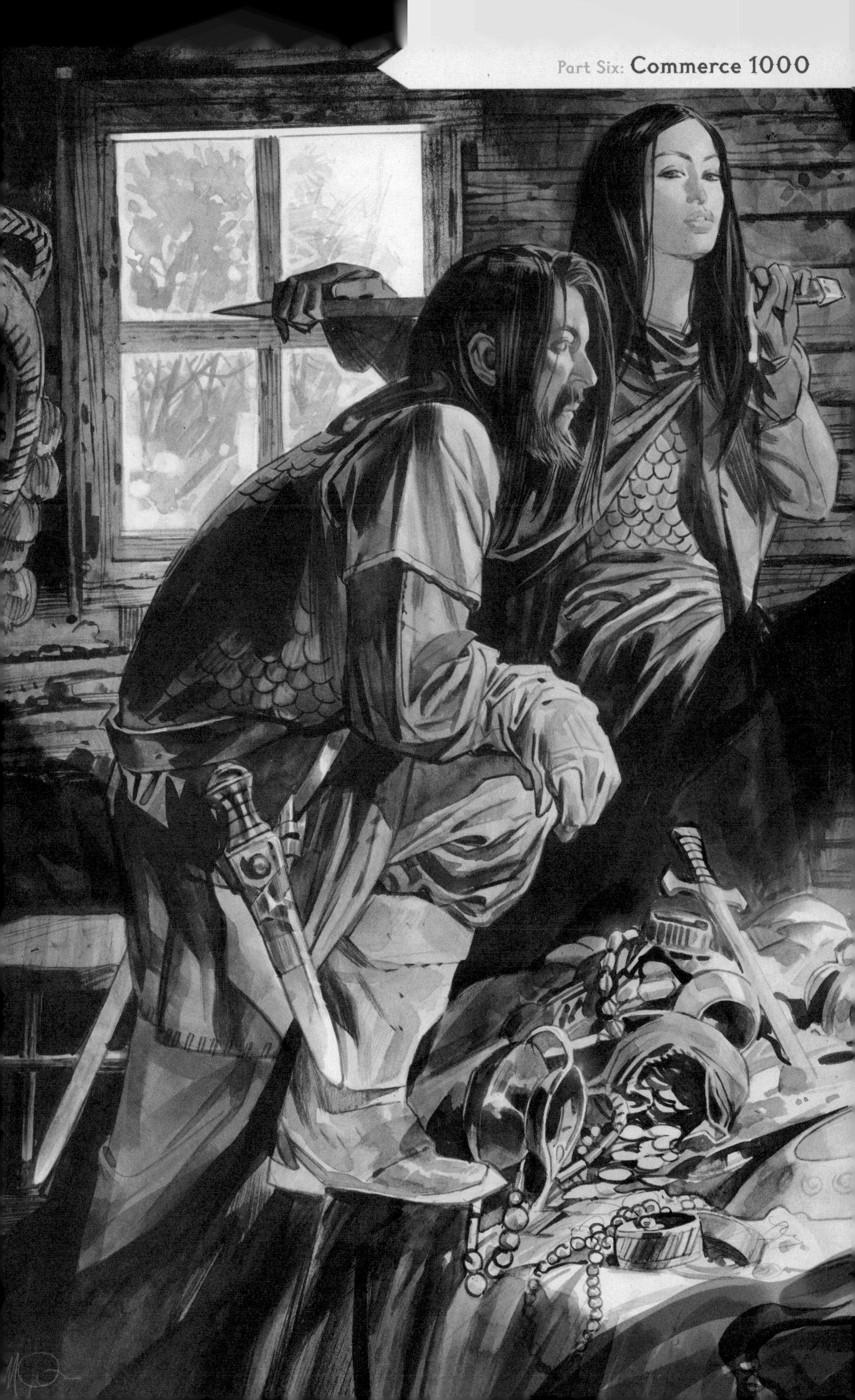

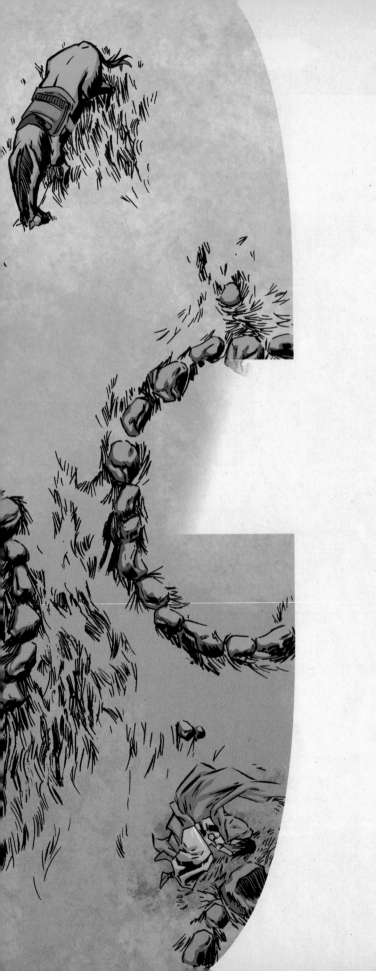

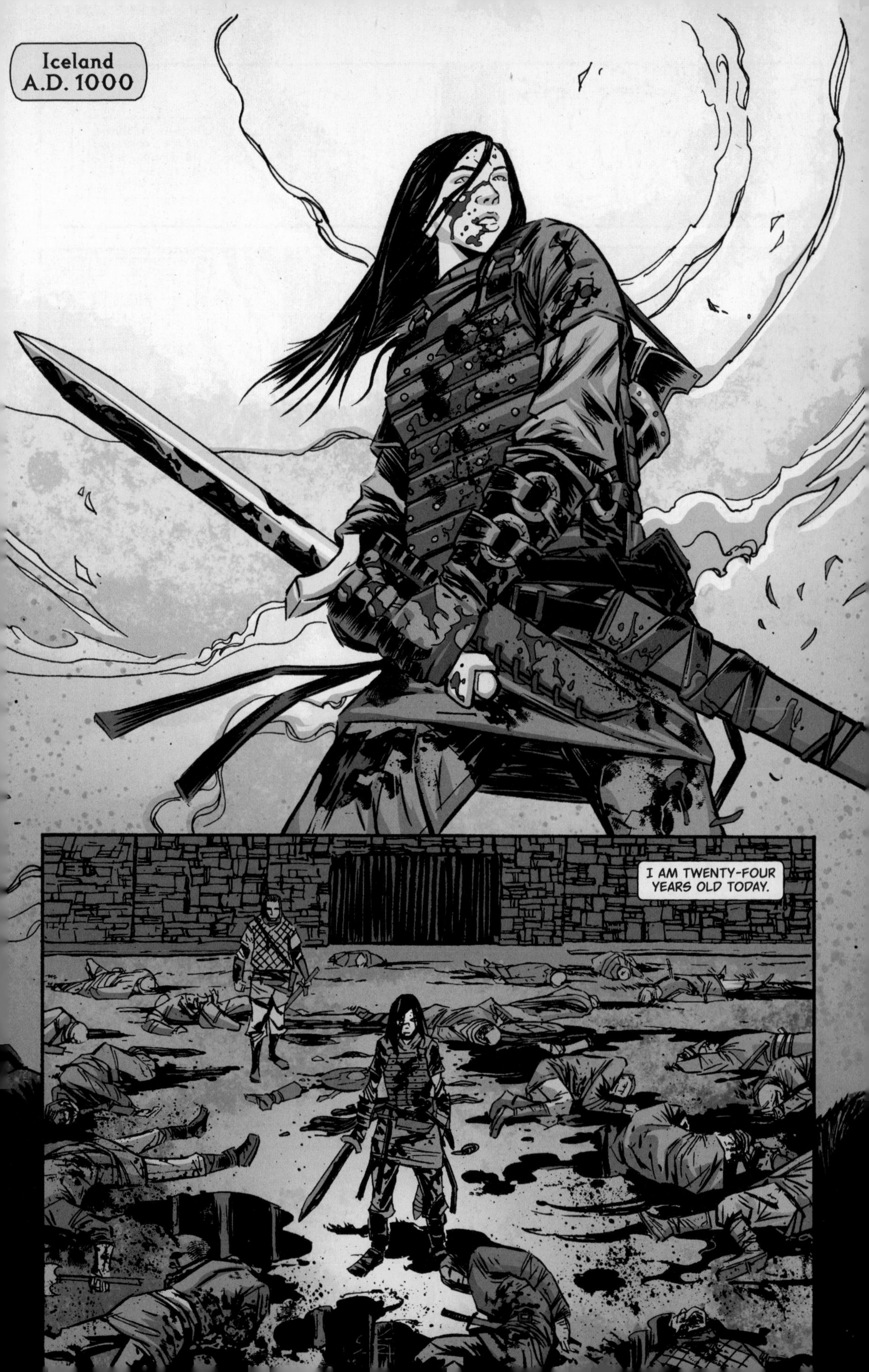
Iceland
A.D. 1000
I AM TWENTY-FOUR YEARS OLD TODAY.

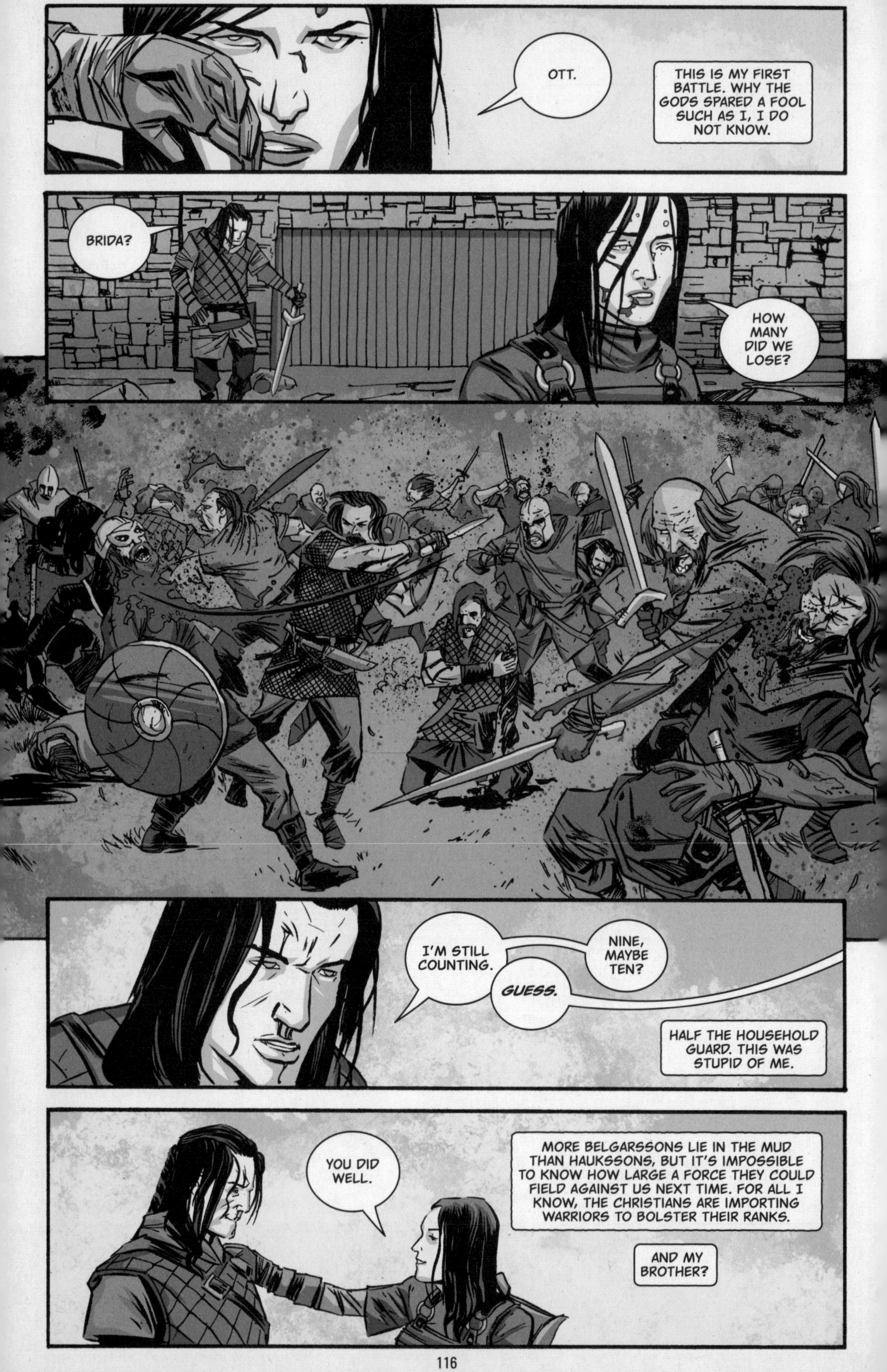
OTT.
THIS IS MY FIRST BATTLE. WHY THE GODS SPARED A FOOL SUCH AS I, I DO NOT KNOW.
BRIDA?
HOW MANY DID WE LOSE?
I'M STILL COUNTING.
NINE, MAYBE TEN?
GUESS.
HALF THE HOUSEHOLD GUARD. THIS WAS STUPID OF ME.
YOU DID WELL.
MORE BELGARSSONS LIE IN THE MUD THAN HAUKSSONS, BUT IT'S IMPOSSIBLE TO KNOW HOW LARGE A FORCE THEY COULD FIELD AGAINST US NEXT TIME. FOR ALL I KNOW, THE CHRISTIANS ARE IMPORTING WARRIORS TO BOLSTER THEIR RANKS.
AND MY BROTHER?

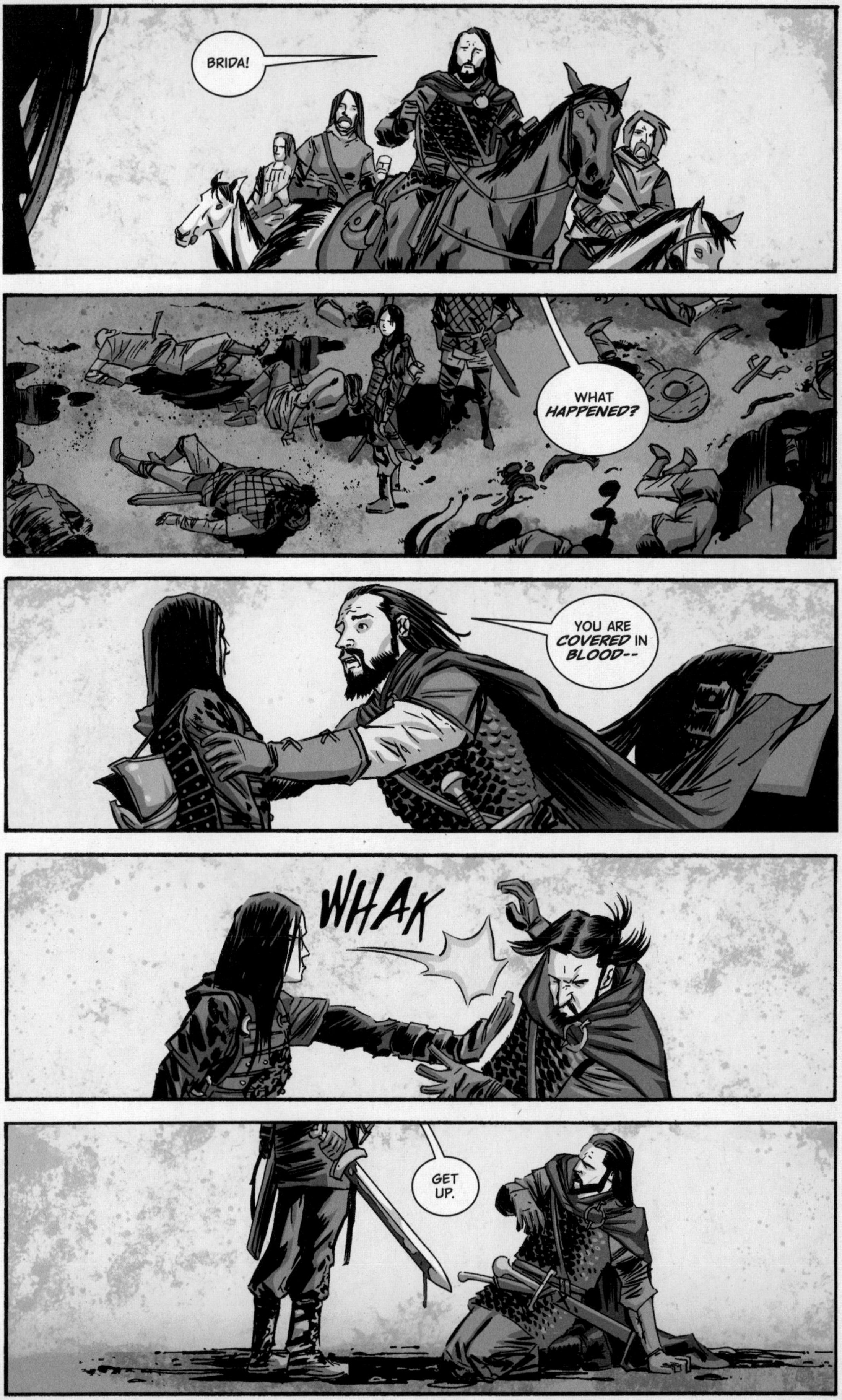
BRIDA!
WHAT HAPPENED?
YOU ARE COVERED IN BLOOD--
WHAK
GET UP.

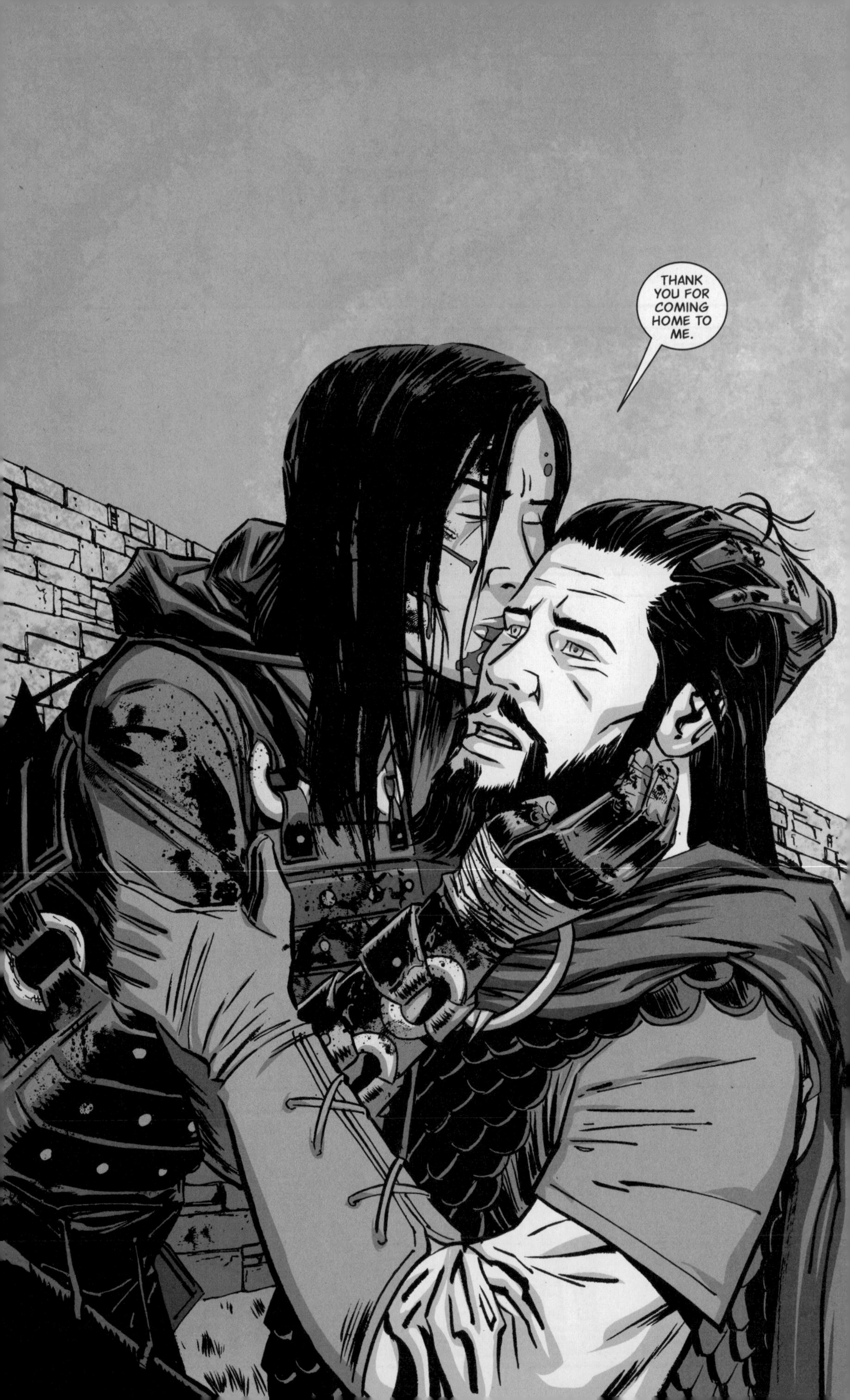
THANK YOU FOR COMING HOME TO ME.

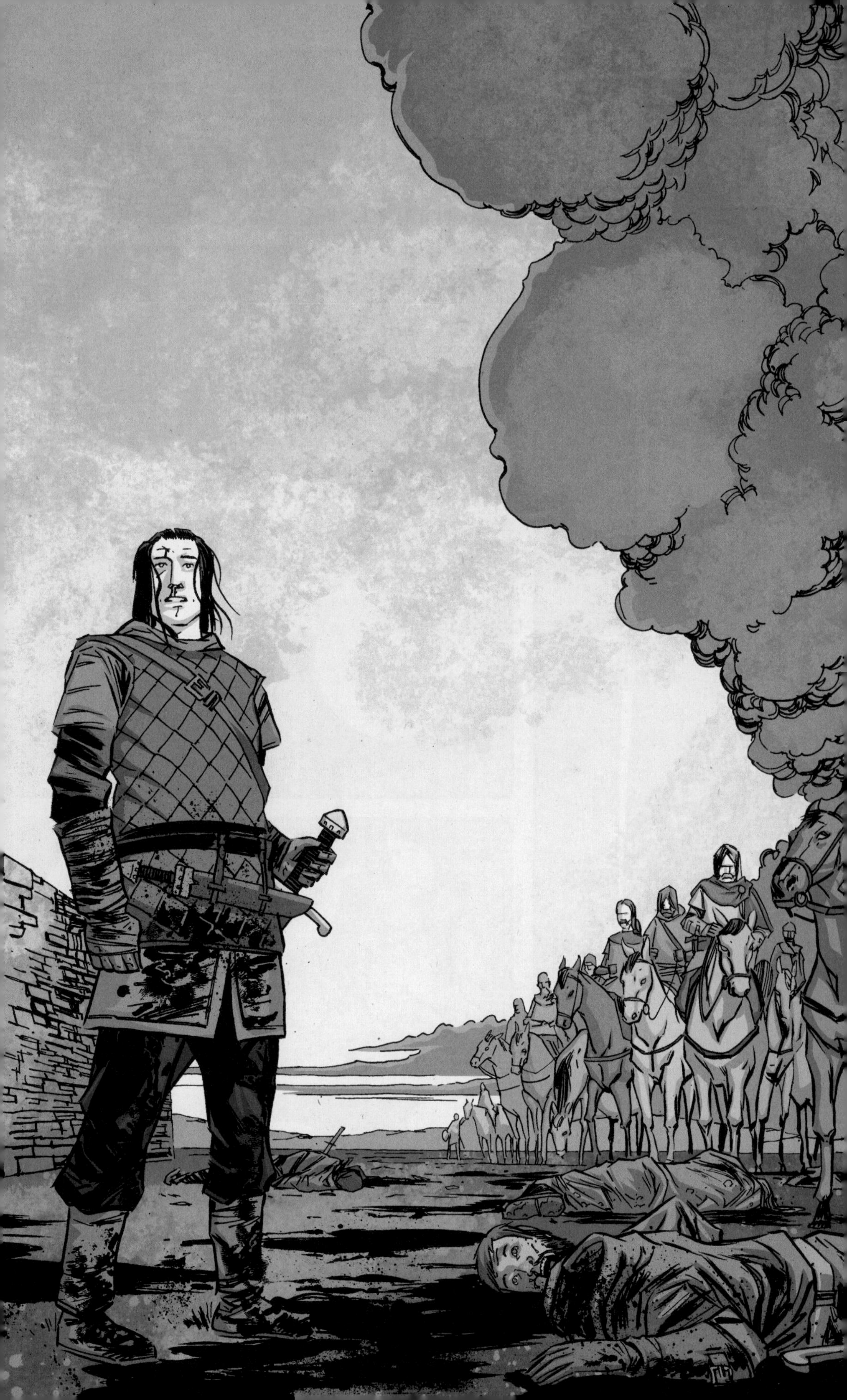

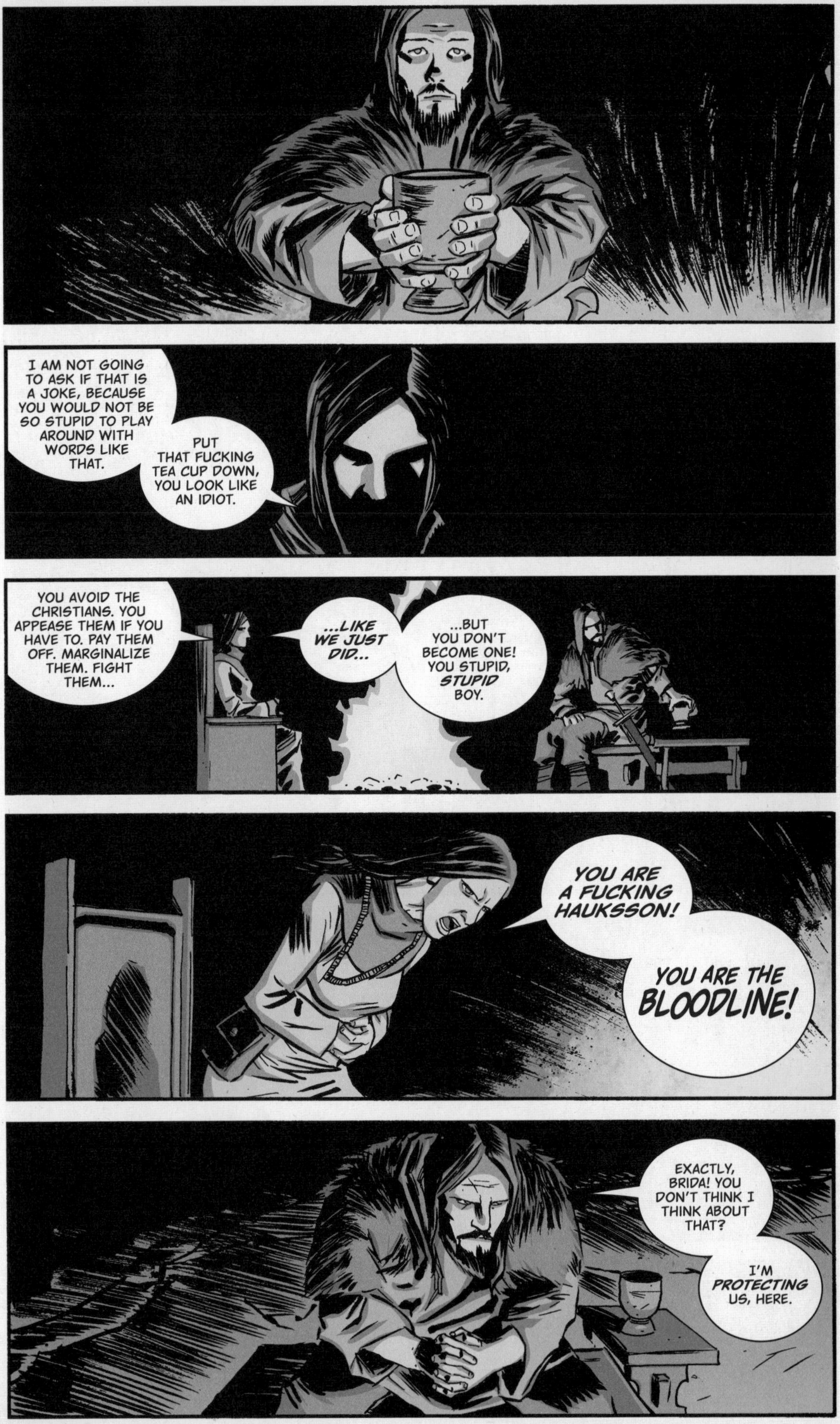

I AM NOT GOING TO ASK IF THAT IS A JOKE, BECAUSE YOU WOULD NOT BE SO STUPID TO PLAY AROUND WITH WORDS LIKE THAT.
PUT THAT FUCKING TEA CUP DOWN, YOU LOOK LIKE AN IDIOT.
YOU AVOID THE CHRISTIANS. YOU APPEASE THEM IF YOU HAVE TO. PAY THEM OFF. MARGINALIZE THEM. FIGHT THEM...
...LIKE WE JUST DID...
...BUT YOU DON'T BECOME ONE! YOU STUPID, STUPID BOY.
YOU ARE A FUCKING HAUKSSON!
YOU ARE THE BLOODLINE!
EXACTLY, BRIDA! YOU DON'T THINK I THINK ABOUT THAT?
I'M PROTECTING US, HERE.

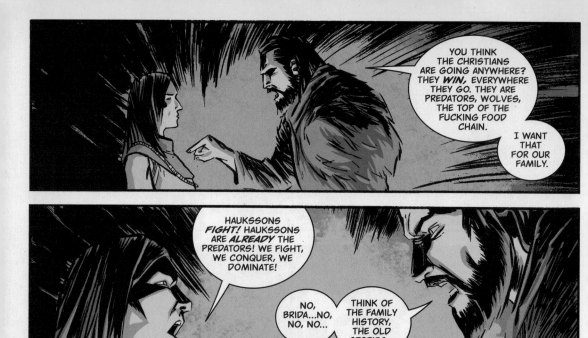

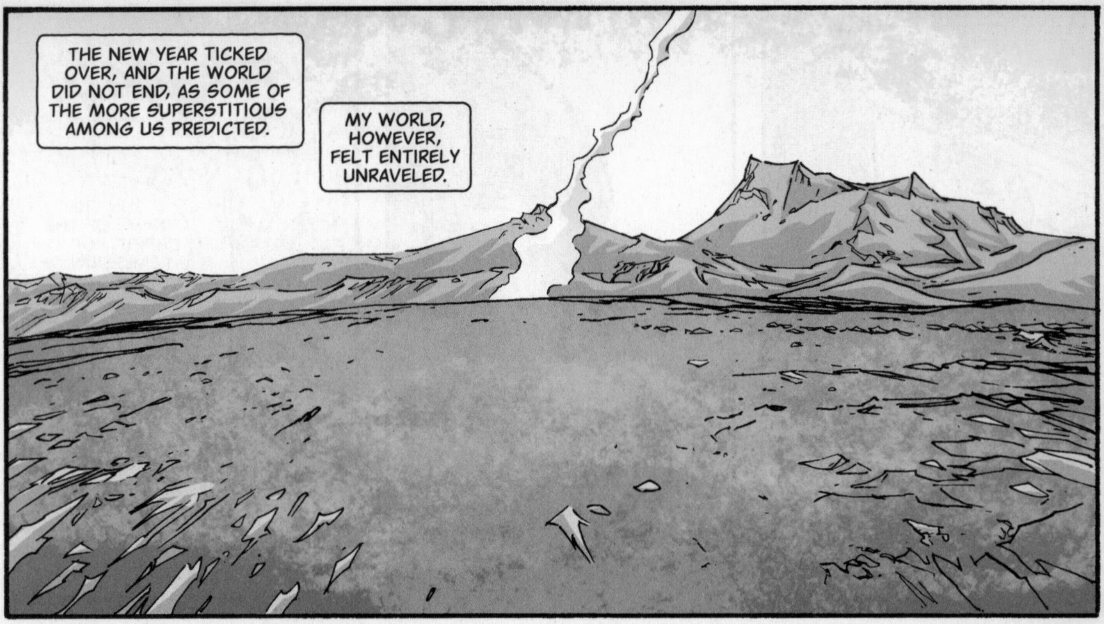
THE NEW YEAR TICKED OVER, AND THE WORLD DID NOT END, AS SOME OF THE MORE SUPERSTITIOUS AMONG US PREDICTED.
MY WORLD, HOWEVER, FELT ENTIRELY UNRAVELED.

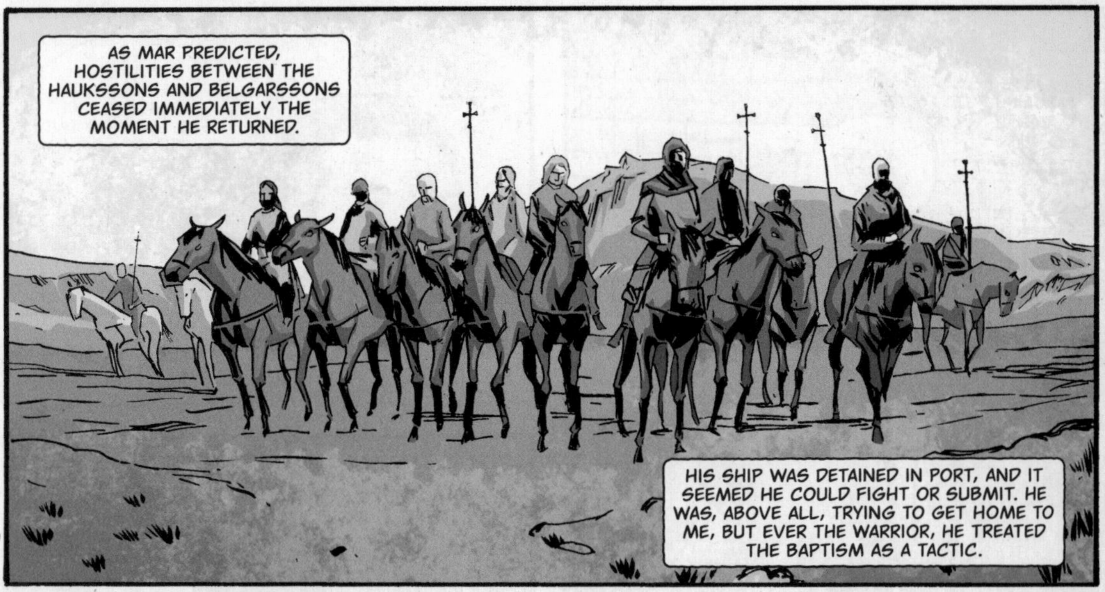
AS MAR PREDICTED, HOSTILITIES BETWEEN THE HAUKSSONS AND BELGARSSONS CEASED IMMEDIATELY THE MOMENT HE RETURNED.
HIS SHIP WAS DETAINED IN PORT, AND IT SEEMED HE COULD FIGHT OR SUBMIT. HE WAS, ABOVE ALL, TRYING TO GET HOME TO ME, BUT EVER THE WARRIOR, HE TREATED THE BAPTISM AS A TACTIC.

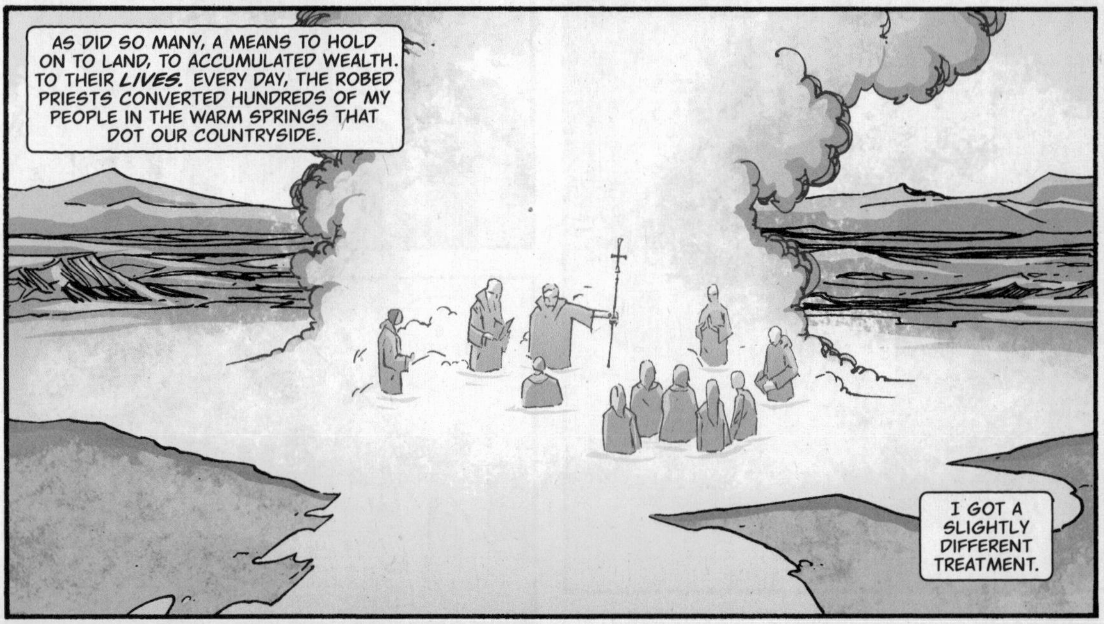
AS DID SO MANY, A MEANS TO HOLD ON TO LAND, TO ACCUMULATED WEALTH. TO THEIR *LIVES.* EVERY DAY, THE ROBED PRIESTS CONVERTED HUNDREDS OF MY PEOPLE IN THE WARM SPRINGS THAT DOT OUR COUNTRYSIDE.
I GOT A SLIGHTLY DIFFERENT TREATMENT.

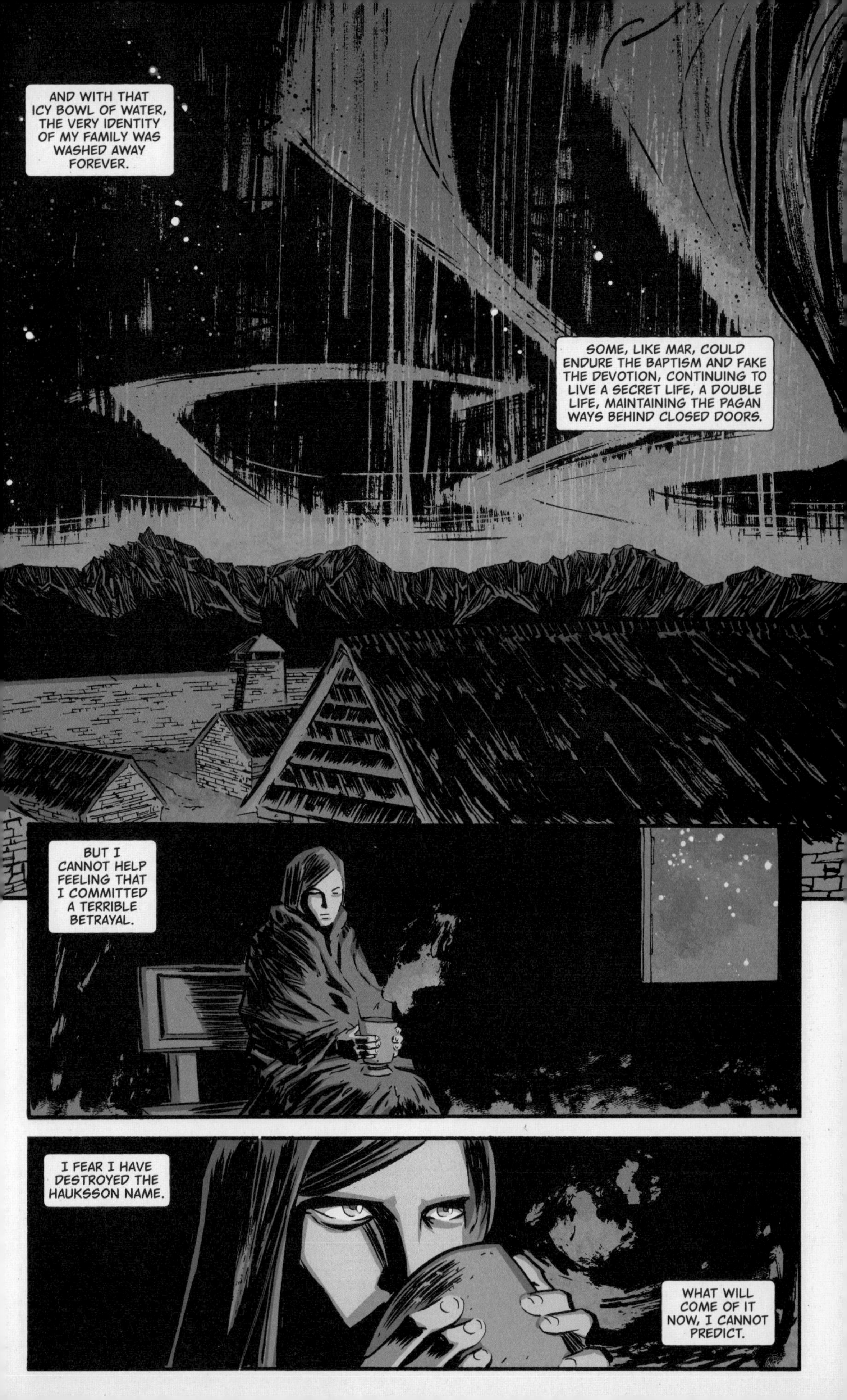
AND WITH THAT ICY BOWL OF WATER, THE VERY IDENTITY OF MY FAMILY WAS WASHED AWAY FOREVER.
SOME, LIKE MAR, COULD ENDURE THE BAPTISM AND FAKE THE DEVOTION, CONTINUING TO LIVE A SECRET LIFE, A DOUBLE LIFE, MAINTAINING THE PAGAN WAYS BEHIND CLOSED DOORS.
BUT I CANNOT HELP FEELING THAT I COMMITTED A TERRIBLE BETRAYAL.
I FEAR I HAVE DESTROYED THE HAUKSSON NAME.
WHAT WILL COME OF IT NOW, I CANNOT PREDICT.

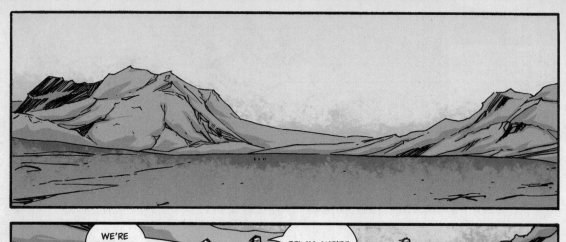

WE'RE EXPOSED.

RELAX, WE'RE PROTECTED.

YOU TRULY BELIEVE THAT? A CHRISTIAN HAS NEVER TURNED A SWORD ON ANOTHER CHRISTIAN? TRULY?

THAT'S NOT WHAT I MEAN...

...THAT'S WHAT *I* MEAN. WE HAVE SIGNIFICANT POWER OVER THE CHURCH. YOU SHOULD REALIZE THAT.

THEY COULD KILL US NOW AND SCORE BIG...

...OR THEY CAN BEFRIEND US, AND EARN OFF US FOR DECADES. I KNOW WHAT I WOULD DO.

SPOKEN LIKE A HAUKSSON.

LOOK.

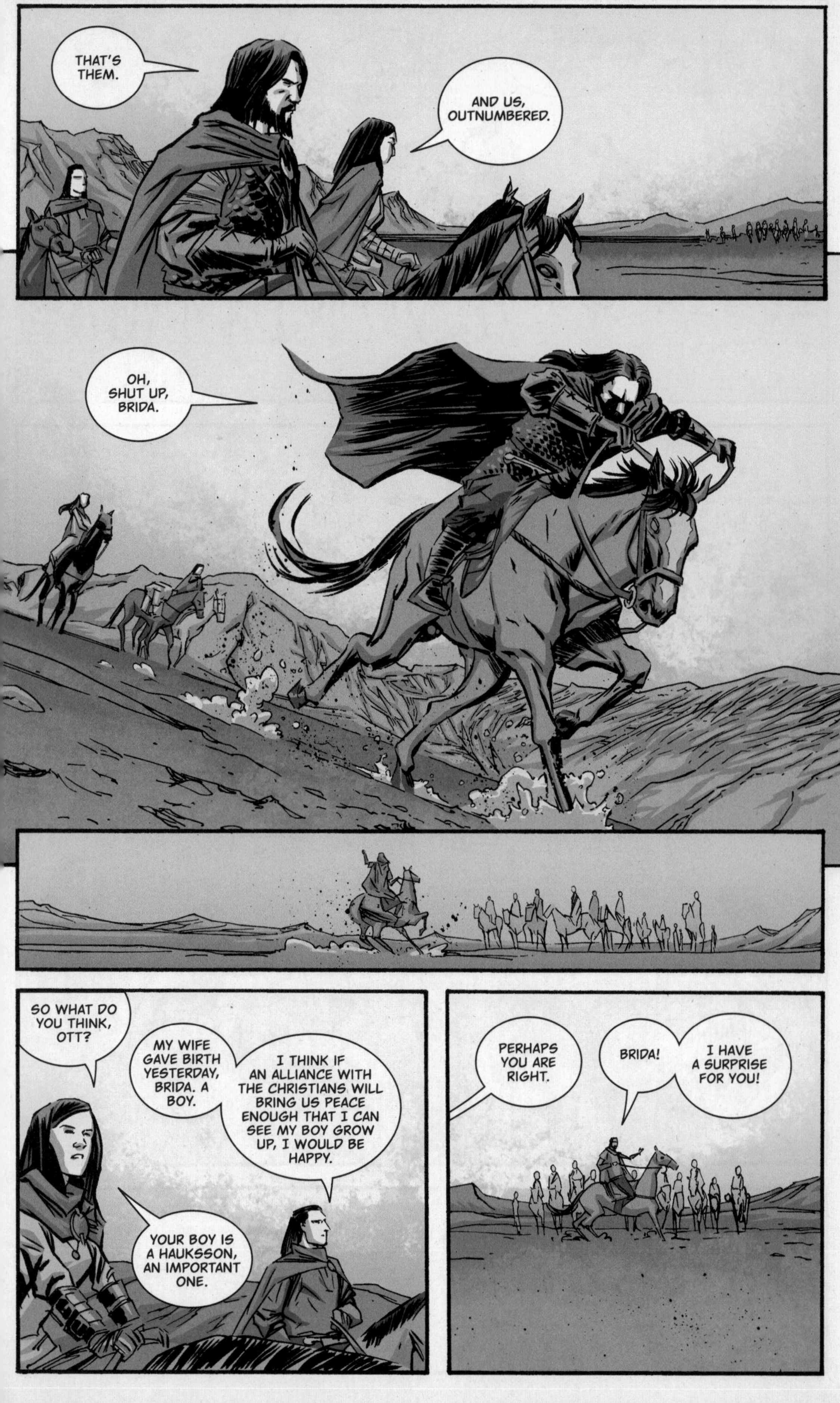
THAT'S THEM.
AND US, OUTNUMBERED.
OH, SHUT UP, BRIDA.
SO WHAT DO YOU THINK, OTT?
MY WIFE GAVE BIRTH YESTERDAY, BRIDA. A BOY.
I THINK IF AN ALLIANCE WITH THE CHRISTIANS WILL BRING US PEACE ENOUGH THAT I CAN SEE MY BOY GROW UP, I WOULD BE HAPPY.
YOUR BOY IS A HAUKSSON, AN IMPORTANT ONE.
PERHAPS YOU ARE RIGHT.
BRIDA!
I HAVE A SURPRISE FOR YOU!

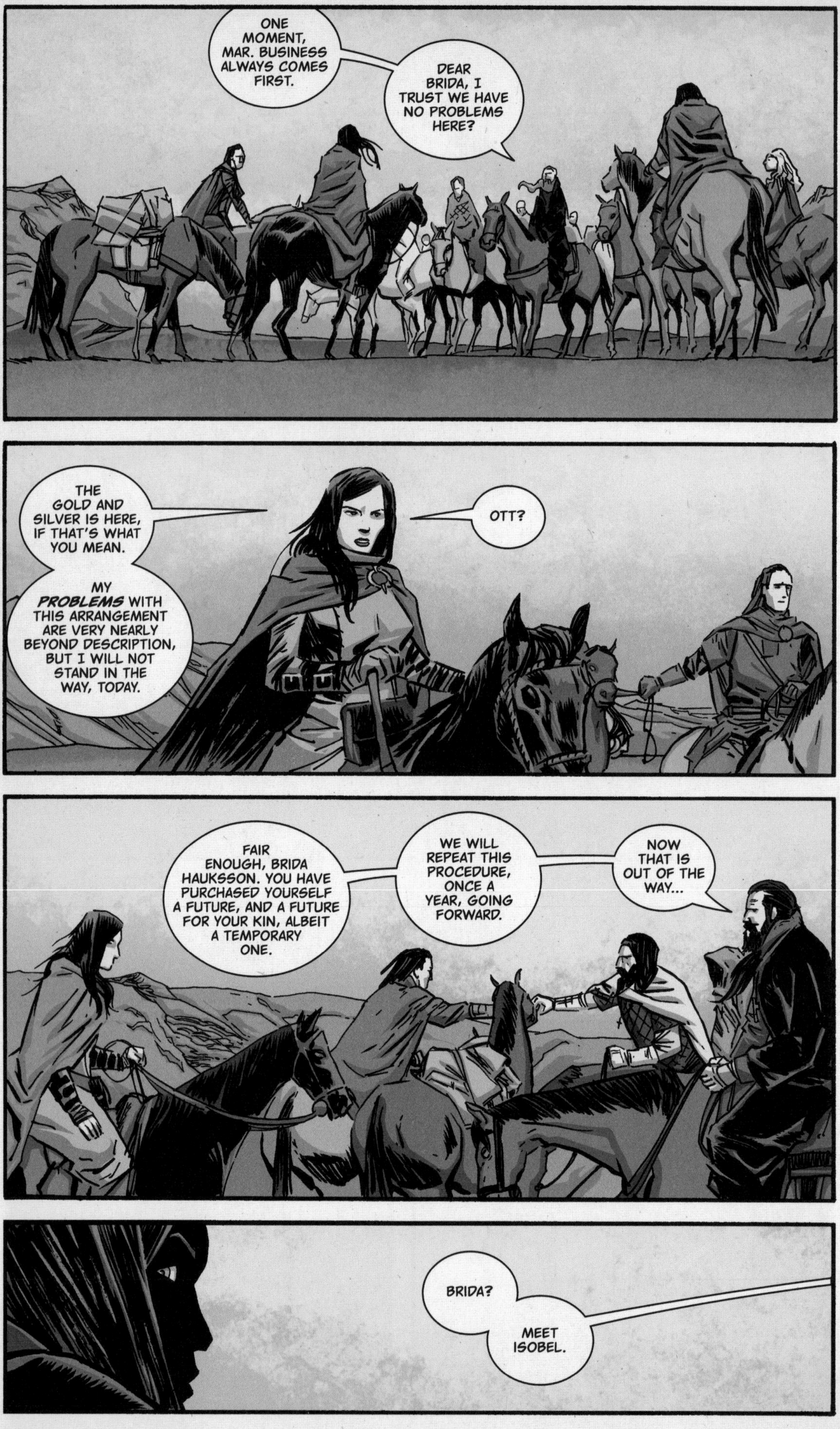
ONE MOMENT, MAR. BUSINESS ALWAYS COMES FIRST.
DEAR BRIDA, I TRUST WE HAVE NO PROBLEMS HERE?
THE GOLD AND SILVER IS HERE, IF THAT'S WHAT YOU MEAN.
MY *PROBLEMS* WITH THIS ARRANGEMENT ARE VERY NEARLY BEYOND DESCRIPTION, BUT I WILL NOT STAND IN THE WAY, TODAY.
OTT?
FAIR ENOUGH, BRIDA HAUKSSON. YOU HAVE PURCHASED YOURSELF A FUTURE, AND A FUTURE FOR YOUR KIN, ALBEIT A TEMPORARY ONE.
WE WILL REPEAT THIS PROCEDURE, ONCE A YEAR, GOING FORWARD.
NOW THAT IS OUT OF THE WAY...
BRIDA?
MEET ISOBEL.

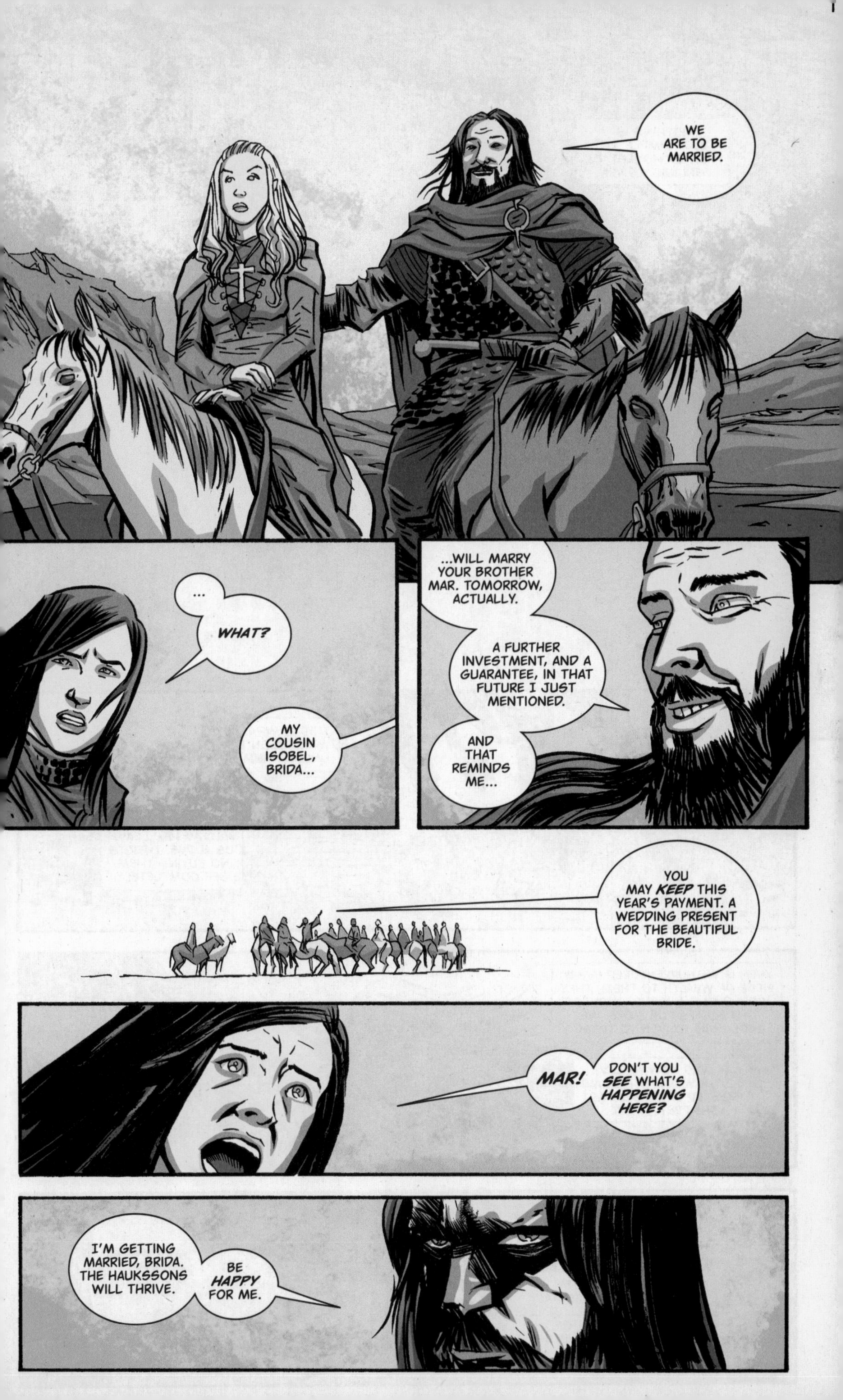
WE ARE TO BE MARRIED.
...
WHAT?
MY COUSIN ISOBEL, BRIDA...
...WILL MARRY YOUR BROTHER MAR. TOMORROW, ACTUALLY.
A FURTHER INVESTMENT, AND A GUARANTEE, IN THAT FUTURE I JUST MENTIONED.
AND THAT REMINDS ME...
YOU MAY KEEP THIS YEAR'S PAYMENT. A WEDDING PRESENT FOR THE BEAUTIFUL BRIDE.
MAR!
DON'T YOU SEE WHAT'S HAPPENING HERE?
I'M GETTING MARRIED, BRIDA. THE HAUKSSONS WILL THRIVE.
BE HAPPY FOR ME.

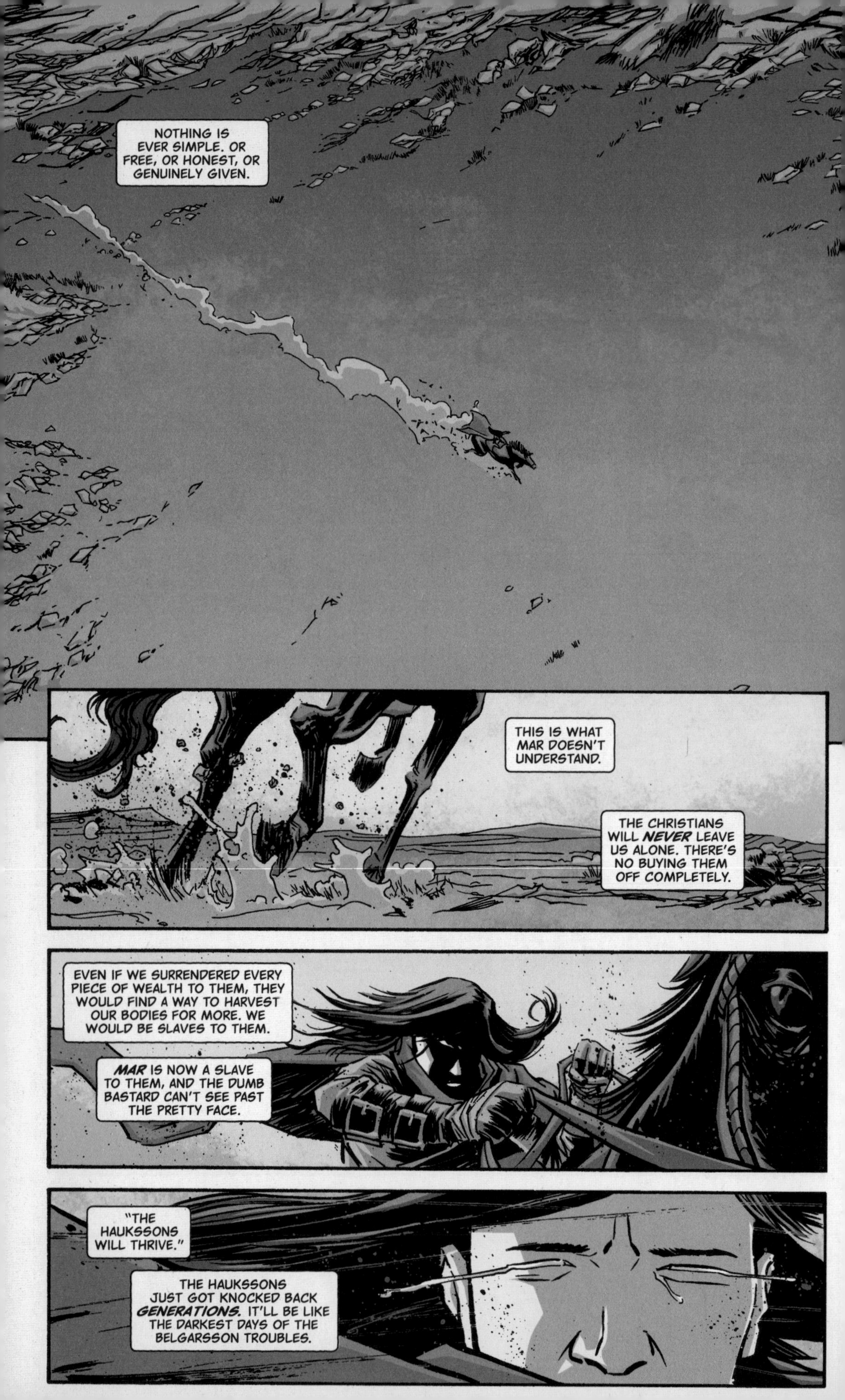
NOTHING IS EVER SIMPLE. OR FREE, OR HONEST, OR GENUINELY GIVEN.
THIS IS WHAT MAR DOESN'T UNDERSTAND.
THE CHRISTIANS WILL NEVER LEAVE US ALONE. THERE'S NO BUYING THEM OFF COMPLETELY.
EVEN IF WE SURRENDERED EVERY PIECE OF WEALTH TO THEM, THEY WOULD FIND A WAY TO HARVEST OUR BODIES FOR MORE. WE WOULD BE SLAVES TO THEM.
MAR IS NOW A SLAVE TO THEM, AND THE DUMB BASTARD CAN'T SEE PAST THE PRETTY FACE.
"THE HAUKSSONS WILL THRIVE."
THE HAUKSSONS JUST GOT KNOCKED BACK GENERATIONS. IT'LL BE LIKE THE DARKEST DAYS OF THE BELGARSSON TROUBLES.

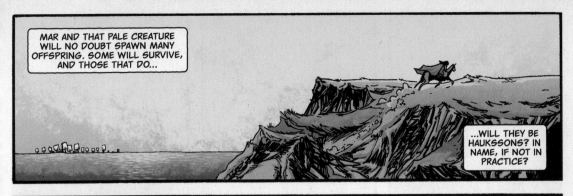

MAR AND THAT PALE CREATURE WILL NO DOUBT SPAWN MANY OFFSPRING. SOME WILL SURVIVE, AND THOSE THAT DO...

...WILL THEY BE HAUKSSONS? IN NAME, IF NOT IN PRACTICE?

THEY WILL BE CHRISTIANS, SURELY, BUT A GENERATION FROM NOW...TWO GENERATIONS...

THIS FAMILY I'VE HELPED SHEPHERD...

...WILL IT RESEMBLE US AT ALL, IN ANY WAY?

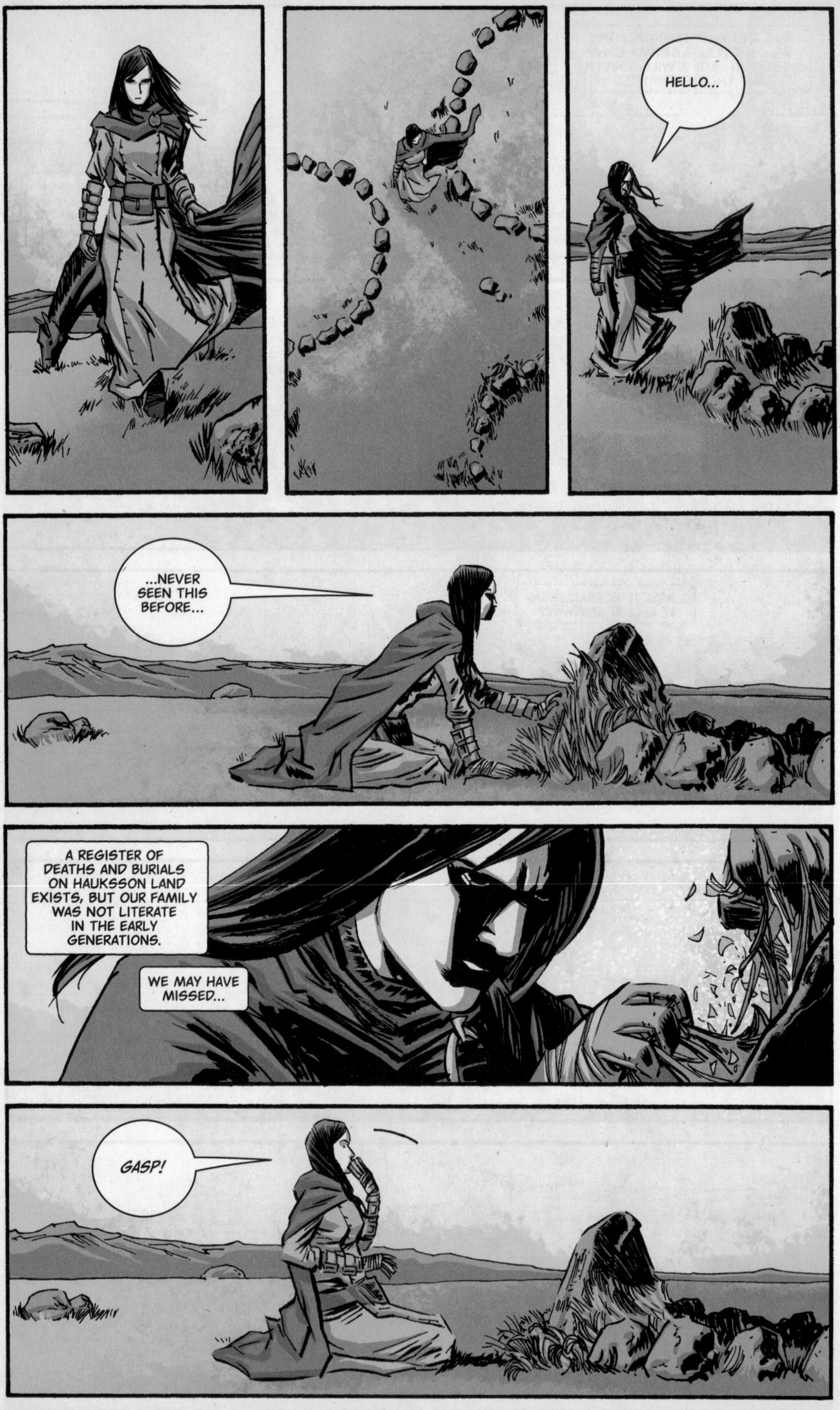
HELLO...
...NEVER SEEN THIS BEFORE...
A REGISTER OF DEATHS AND BURIALS ON HAUKSSON LAND EXISTS, BUT OUR FAMILY WAS NOT LITERATE IN THE EARLY GENERATIONS.
WE MAY HAVE MISSED...
GASP!

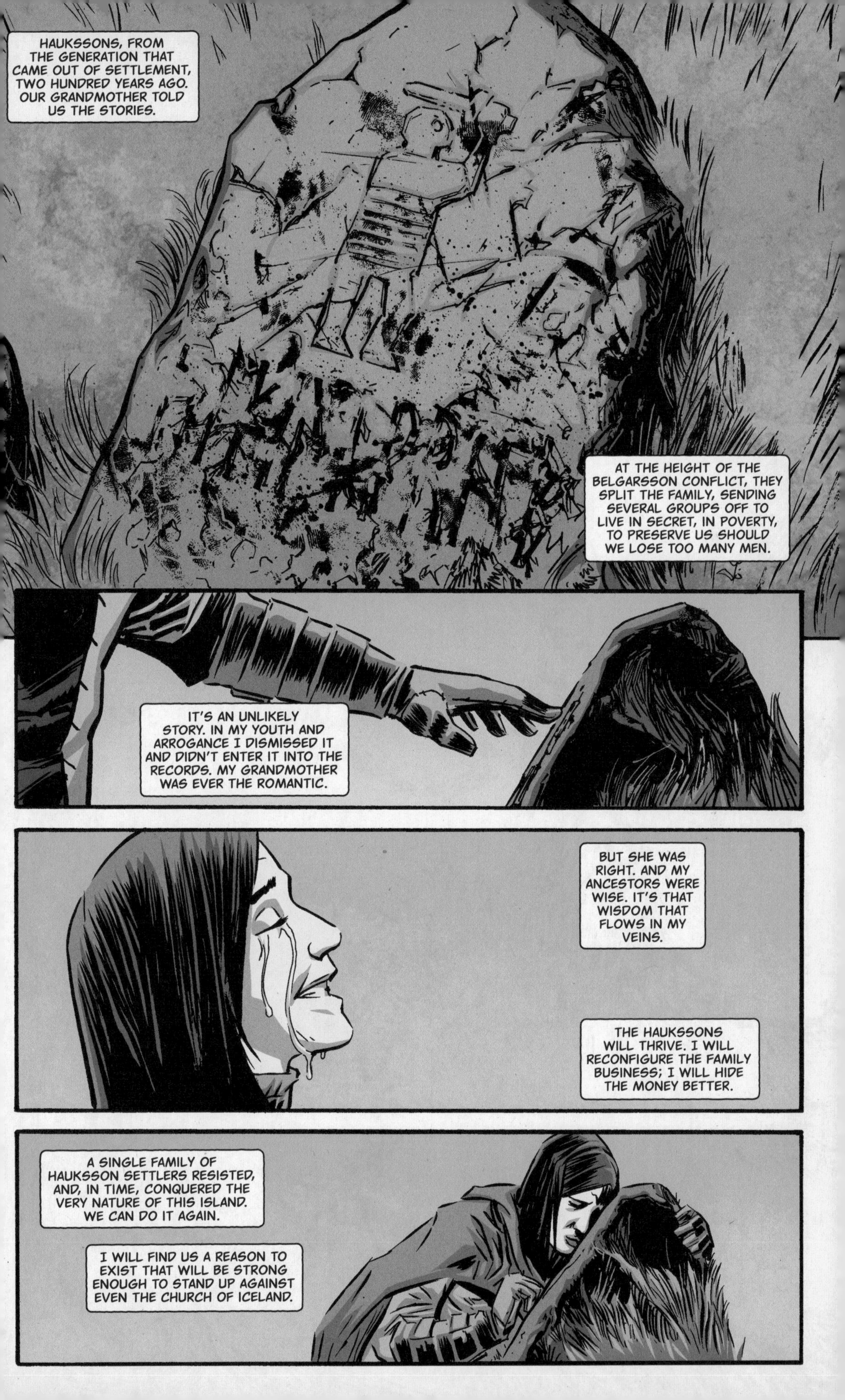
HAUKSSONS, FROM THE GENERATION THAT CAME OUT OF SETTLEMENT, TWO HUNDRED YEARS AGO. OUR GRANDMOTHER TOLD US THE STORIES.
AT THE HEIGHT OF THE BELGARSSON CONFLICT, THEY SPLIT THE FAMILY, SENDING SEVERAL GROUPS OFF TO LIVE IN SECRET, IN POVERTY, TO PRESERVE US SHOULD WE LOSE TOO MANY MEN.
IT'S AN UNLIKELY STORY. IN MY YOUTH AND ARROGANCE I DISMISSED IT AND DIDN'T ENTER IT INTO THE RECORDS. MY GRANDMOTHER WAS EVER THE ROMANTIC.
BUT SHE WAS RIGHT. AND MY ANCESTORS WERE WISE. IT'S THAT WISDOM THAT FLOWS IN MY VEINS.
THE HAUKSSONS WILL THRIVE. I WILL RECONFIGURE THE FAMILY BUSINESS; I WILL HIDE THE MONEY BETTER.
A SINGLE FAMILY OF HAUKSSON SETTLERS RESISTED, AND, IN TIME, CONQUERED THE VERY NATURE OF THIS ISLAND. WE CAN DO IT AGAIN.
I WILL FIND US A REASON TO EXIST THAT WILL BE STRONG ENOUGH TO STAND UP AGAINST EVEN THE CHURCH OF ICELAND.

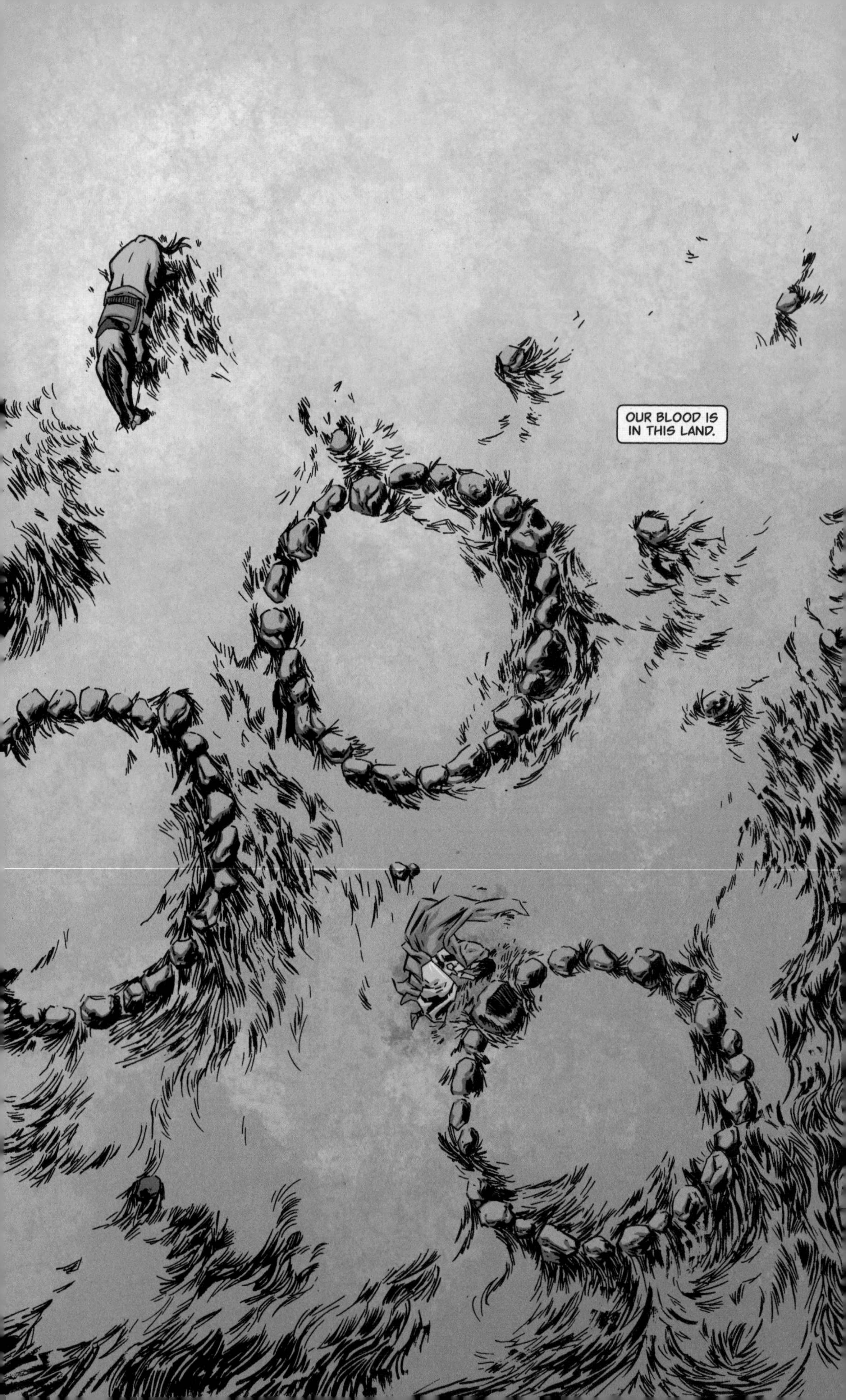
OUR BLOOD IS IN THIS LAND.

Part Seven: **War 1260**

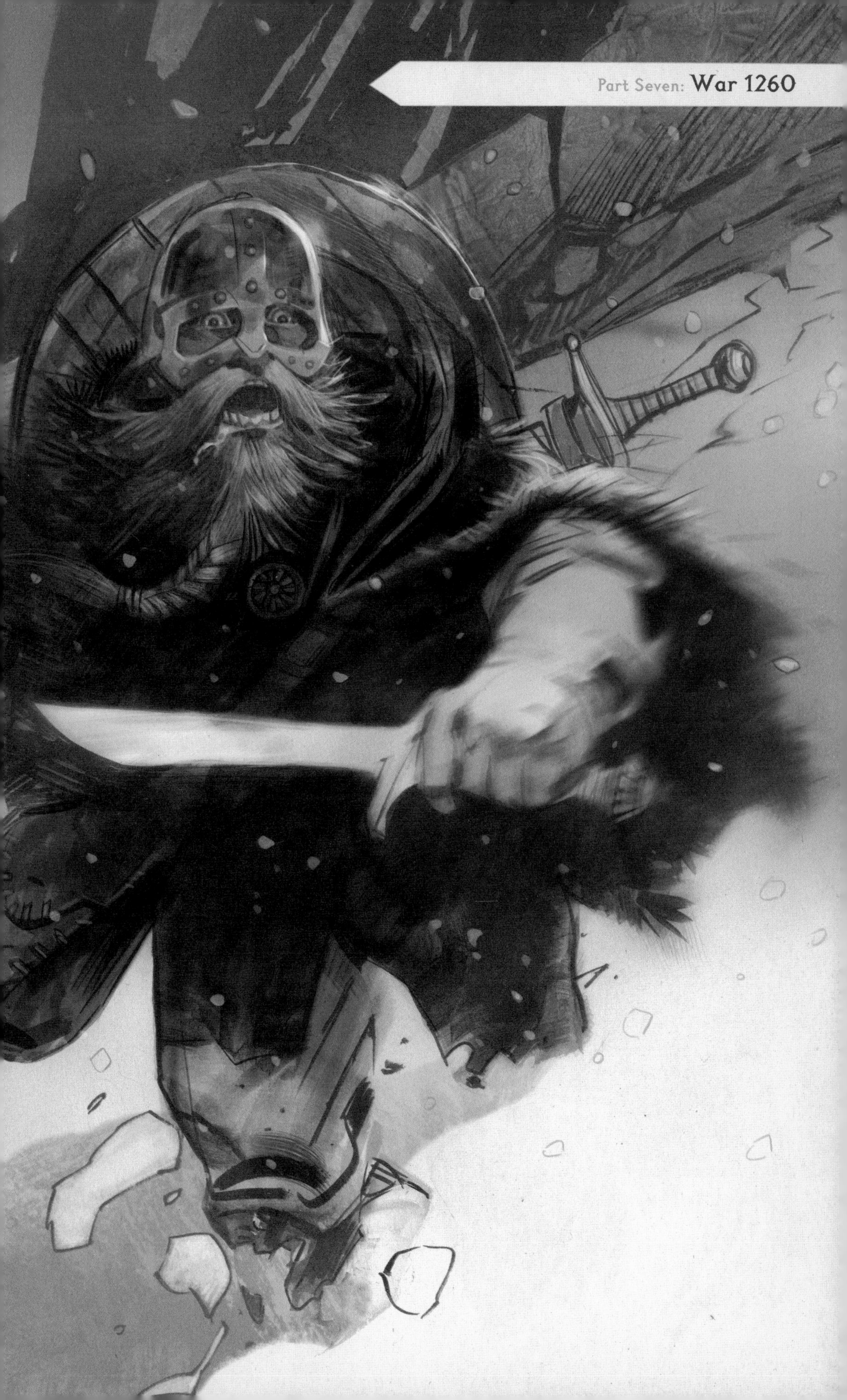

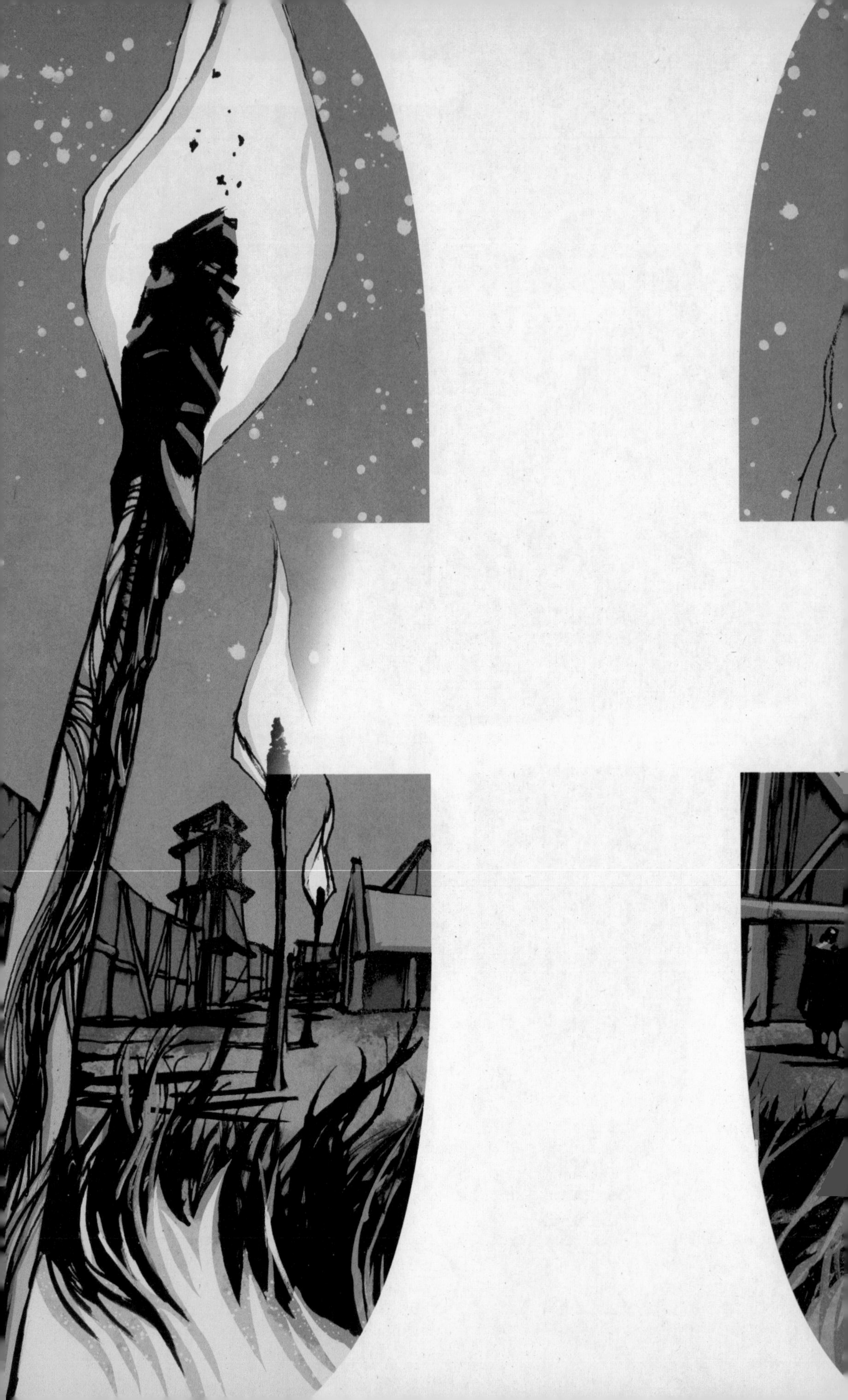

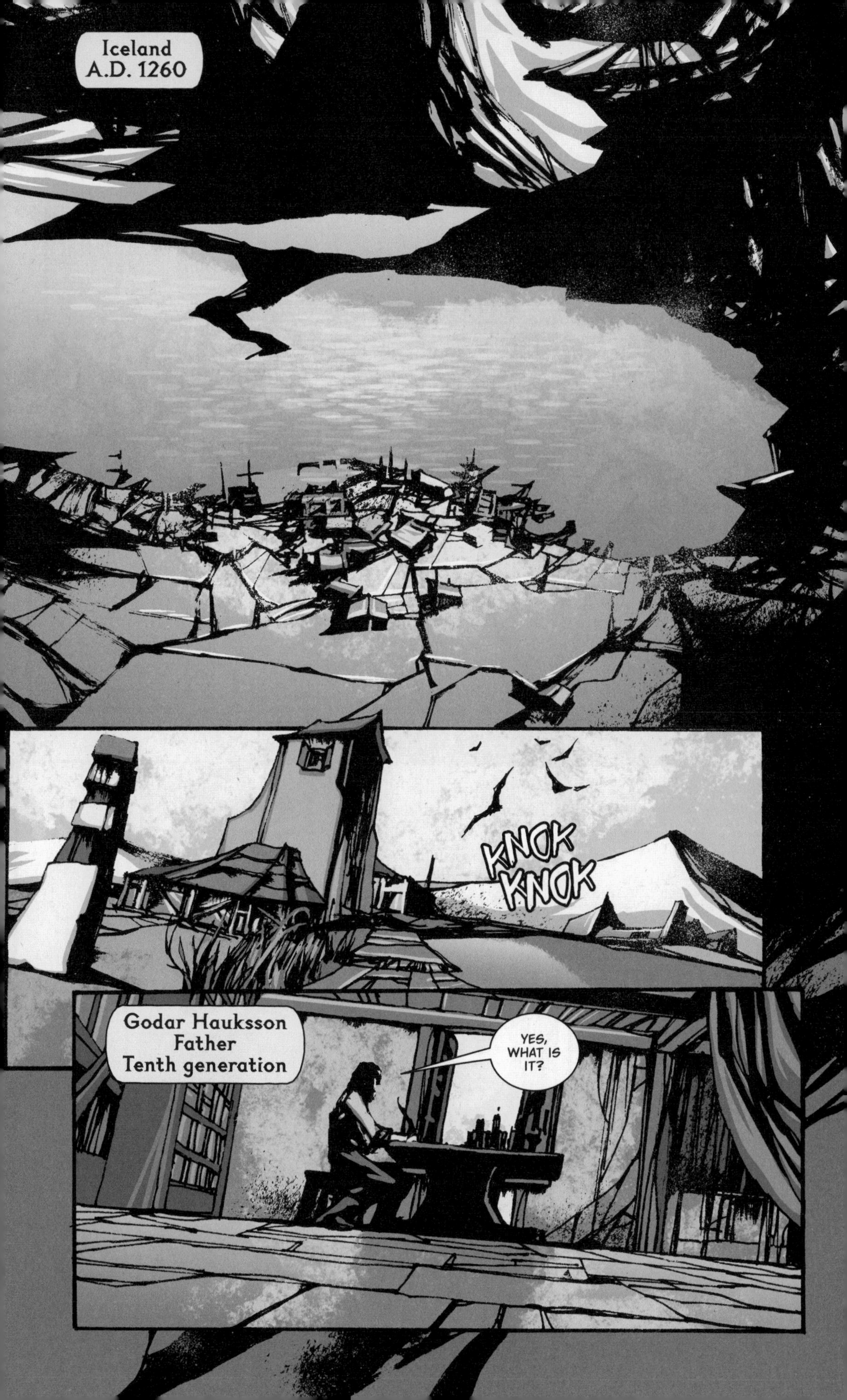
Iceland
A.D. 1260
KNOK KNOK
Godar Hauksson
Father
Tenth generation
YES, WHAT IS IT?

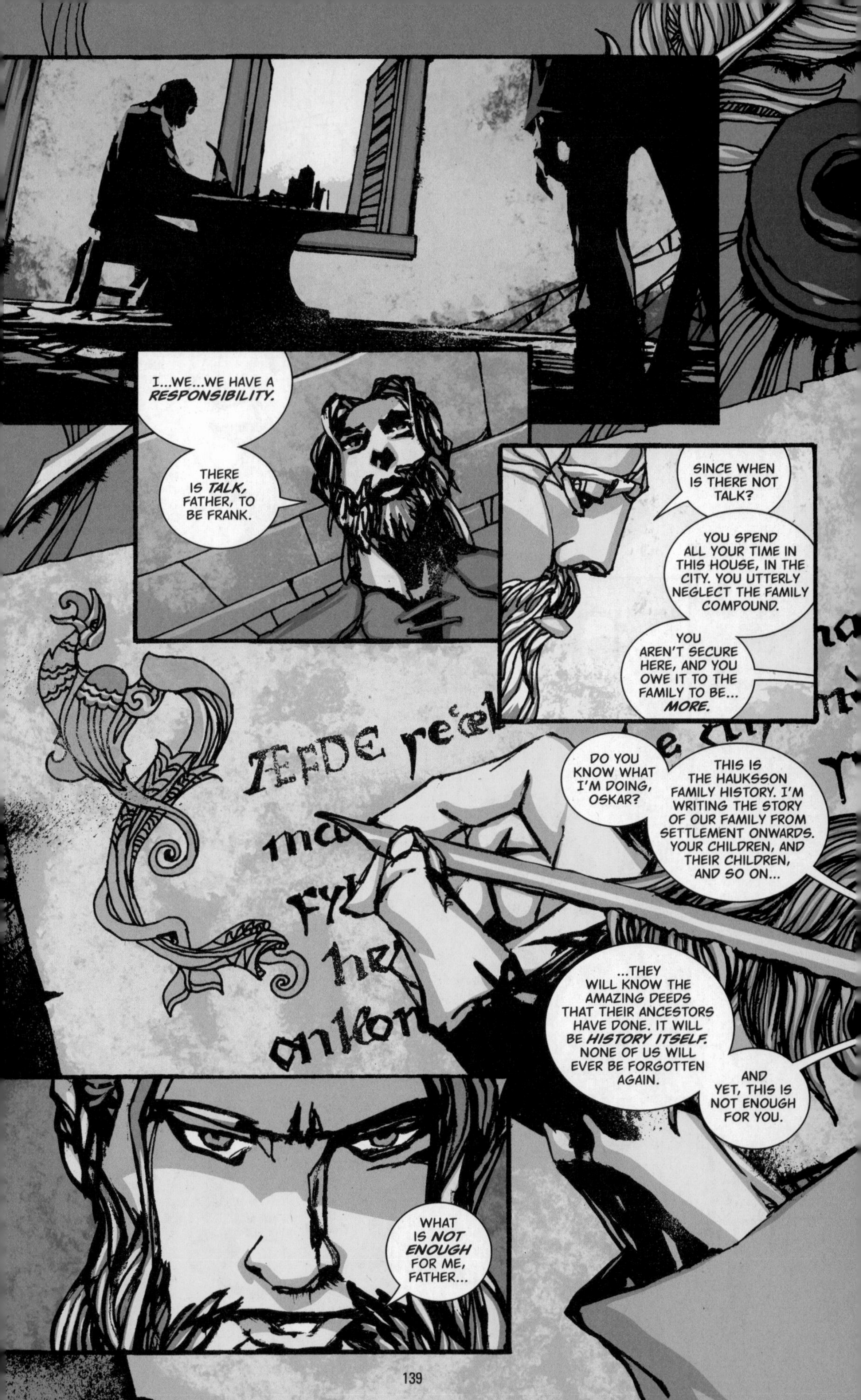
I...WE...WE HAVE A *RESPONSIBILITY.*
THERE IS *TALK,* FATHER, TO BE FRANK.
SINCE WHEN IS THERE NOT TALK?
YOU SPEND ALL YOUR TIME IN THIS HOUSE, IN THE CITY. YOU UTTERLY NEGLECT THE FAMILY COMPOUND.
YOU AREN'T SECURE HERE, AND YOU OWE IT TO THE FAMILY TO BE... *MORE.*
DO YOU KNOW WHAT I'M DOING, OSKAR?
THIS IS THE HAUKSSON FAMILY HISTORY. I'M WRITING THE STORY OF OUR FAMILY FROM SETTLEMENT ONWARDS. YOUR CHILDREN, AND THEIR CHILDREN, AND SO ON...
...THEY WILL KNOW THE AMAZING DEEDS THAT THEIR ANCESTORS HAVE DONE. IT WILL BE *HISTORY ITSELF.* NONE OF US WILL EVER BE FORGOTTEN AGAIN.
AND YET, THIS IS NOT ENOUGH FOR YOU.
WHAT IS *NOT ENOUGH* FOR ME, FATHER...

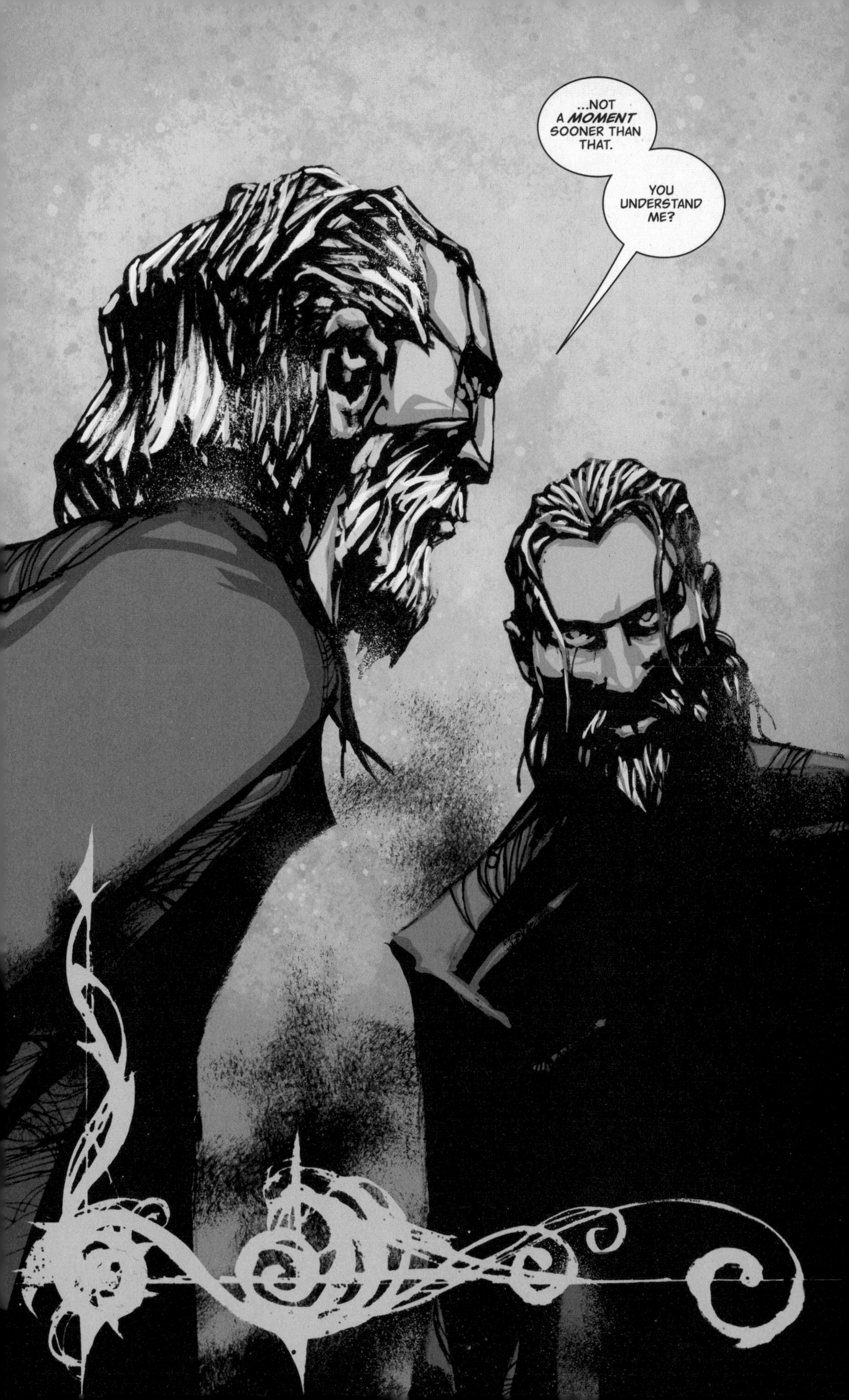
...NOT A MOMENT SOONER THAN THAT.
YOU UNDERSTAND ME?

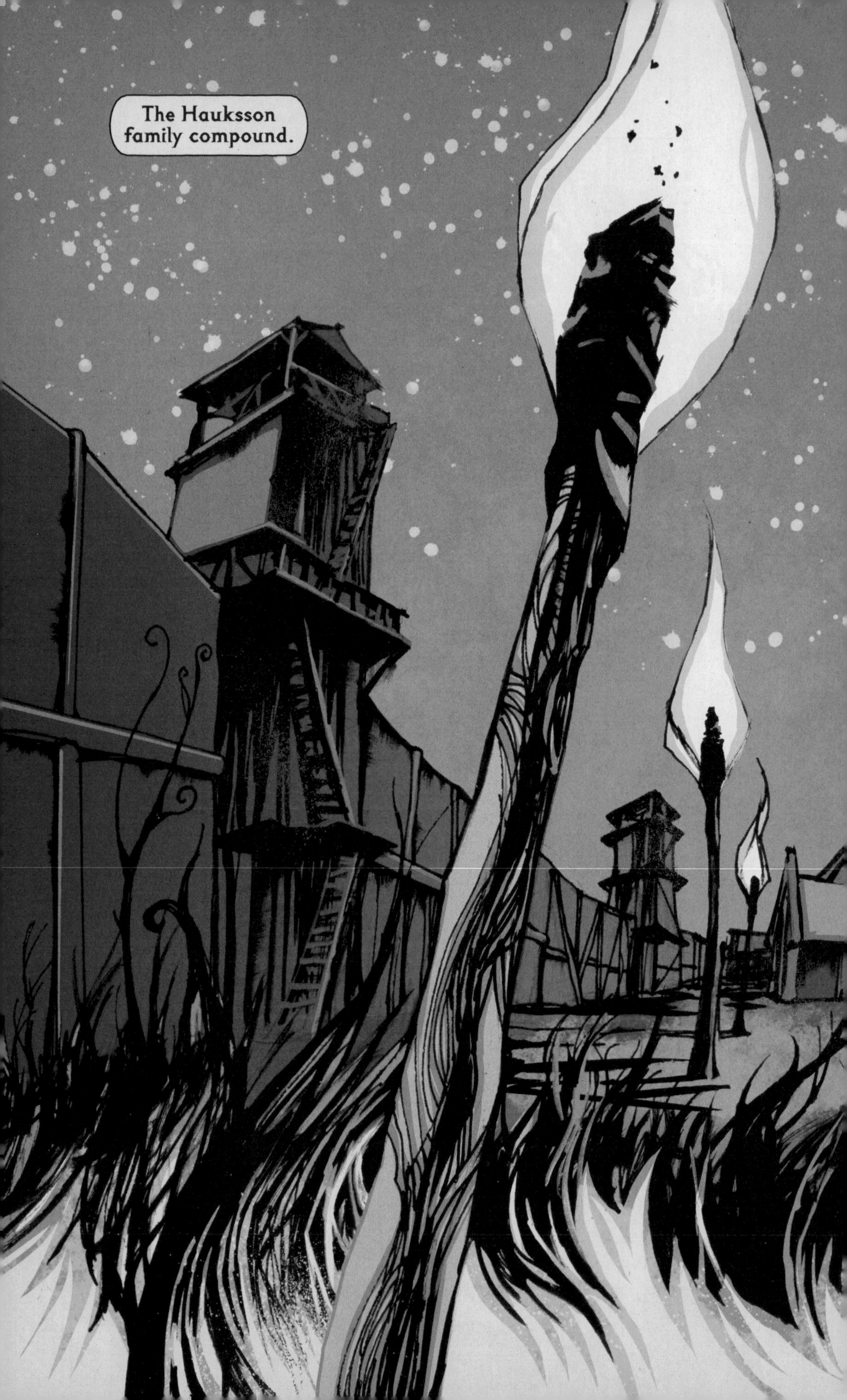
The Hauksson family compound.

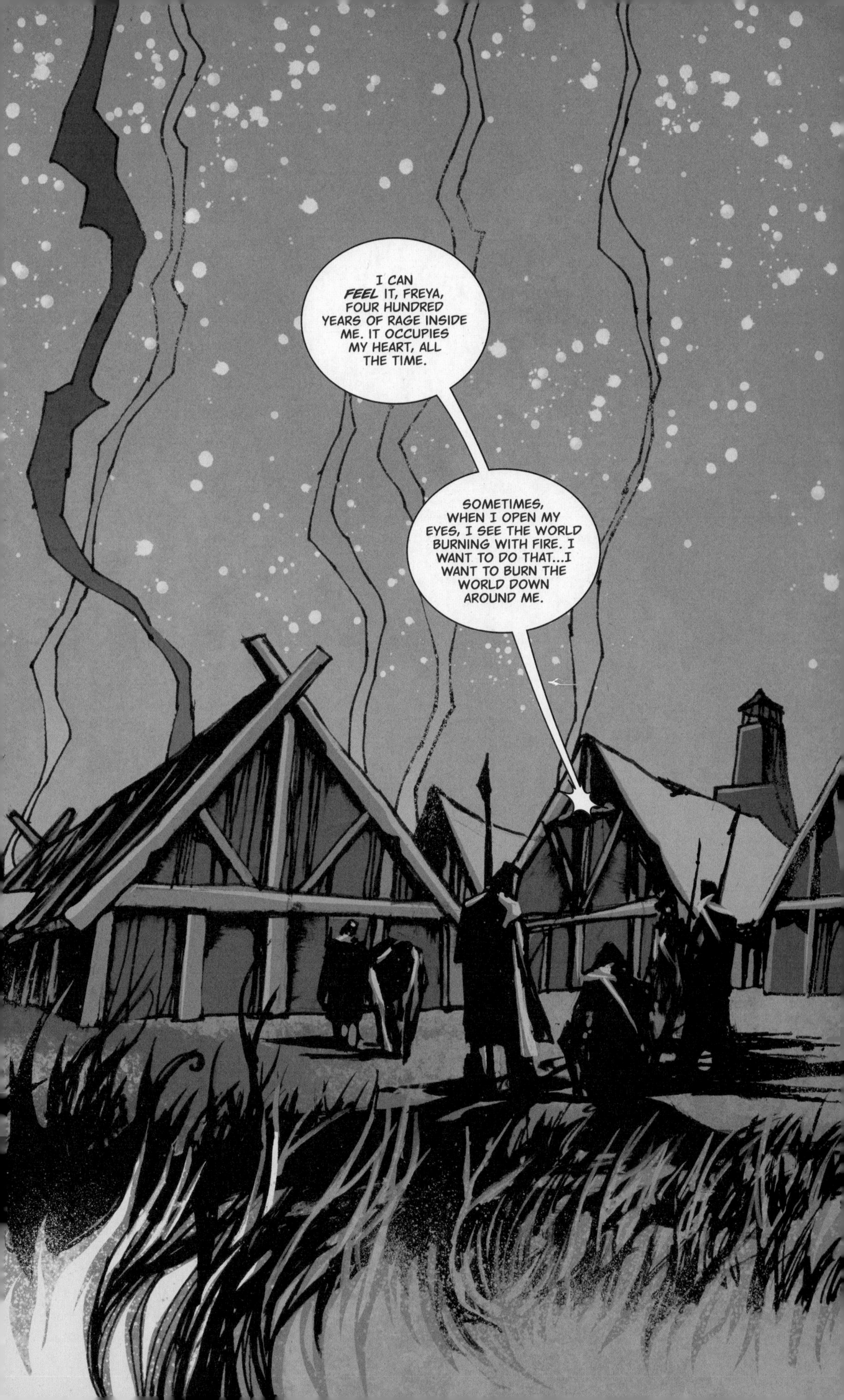
I CAN *FEEL* IT, FREYA, FOUR HUNDRED YEARS OF RAGE INSIDE ME. IT OCCUPIES MY HEART, ALL THE TIME.
SOMETIMES, WHEN I OPEN MY EYES, I SEE THE WORLD BURNING WITH FIRE. I WANT TO DO THAT...I WANT TO BURN THE WORLD DOWN AROUND ME.

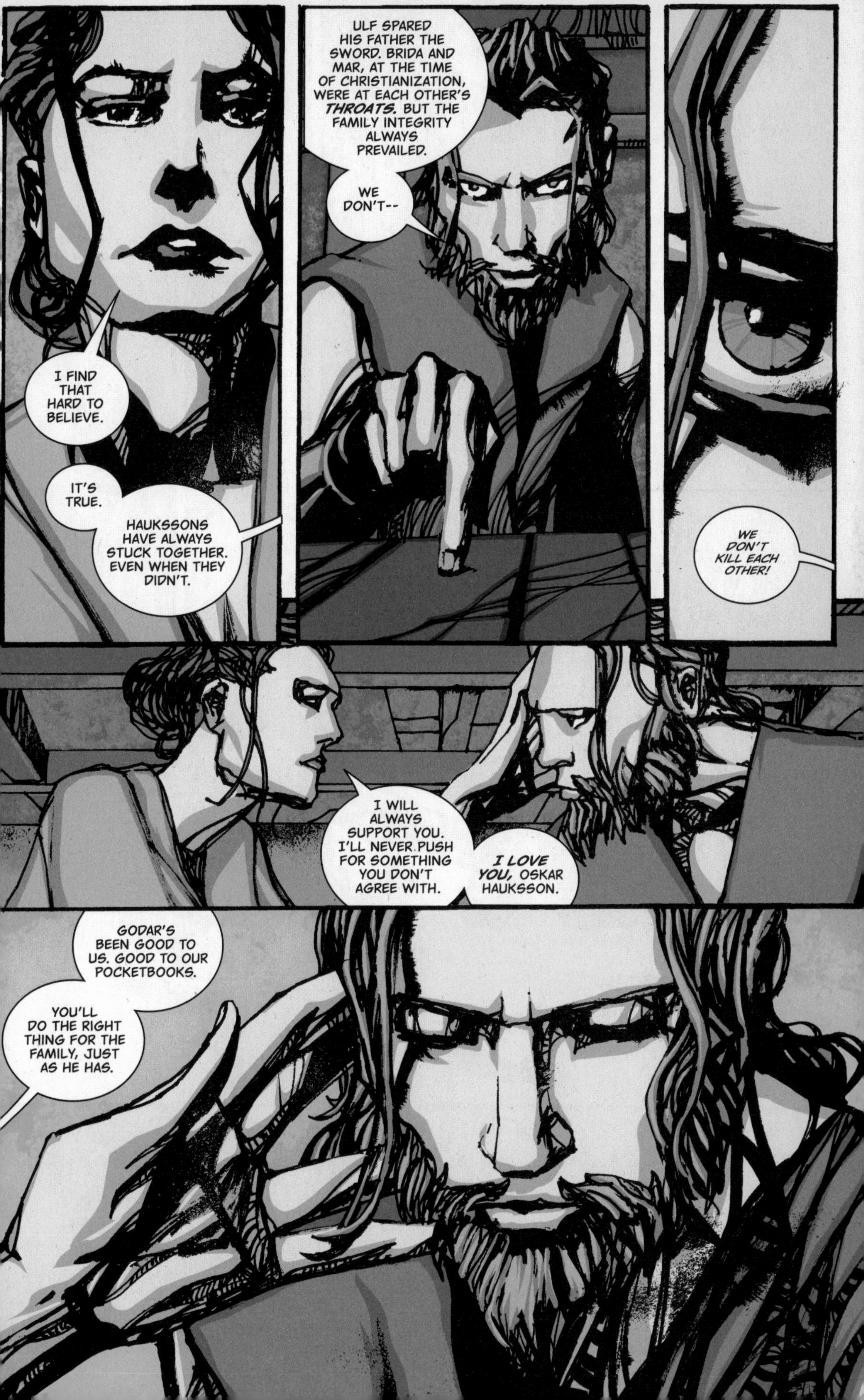
ULF SPARED HIS FATHER THE SWORD. BRIDA AND MAR, AT THE TIME OF CHRISTIANIZATION, WERE AT EACH OTHER'S *THROATS.* BUT THE FAMILY INTEGRITY ALWAYS PREVAILED.
I FIND THAT HARD TO BELIEVE.
IT'S TRUE.
HAUKSSONS HAVE ALWAYS STUCK TOGETHER. EVEN WHEN THEY DIDN'T.
WE DON'T--
WE DON'T KILL EACH OTHER!
I WILL ALWAYS SUPPORT YOU. I'LL NEVER PUSH FOR SOMETHING YOU DON'T AGREE WITH.
I LOVE YOU, OSKAR HAUKSSON.
GODAR'S BEEN GOOD TO US. GOOD TO OUR POCKETBOOKS.
YOU'LL DO THE RIGHT THING FOR THE FAMILY, JUST AS HE HAS.

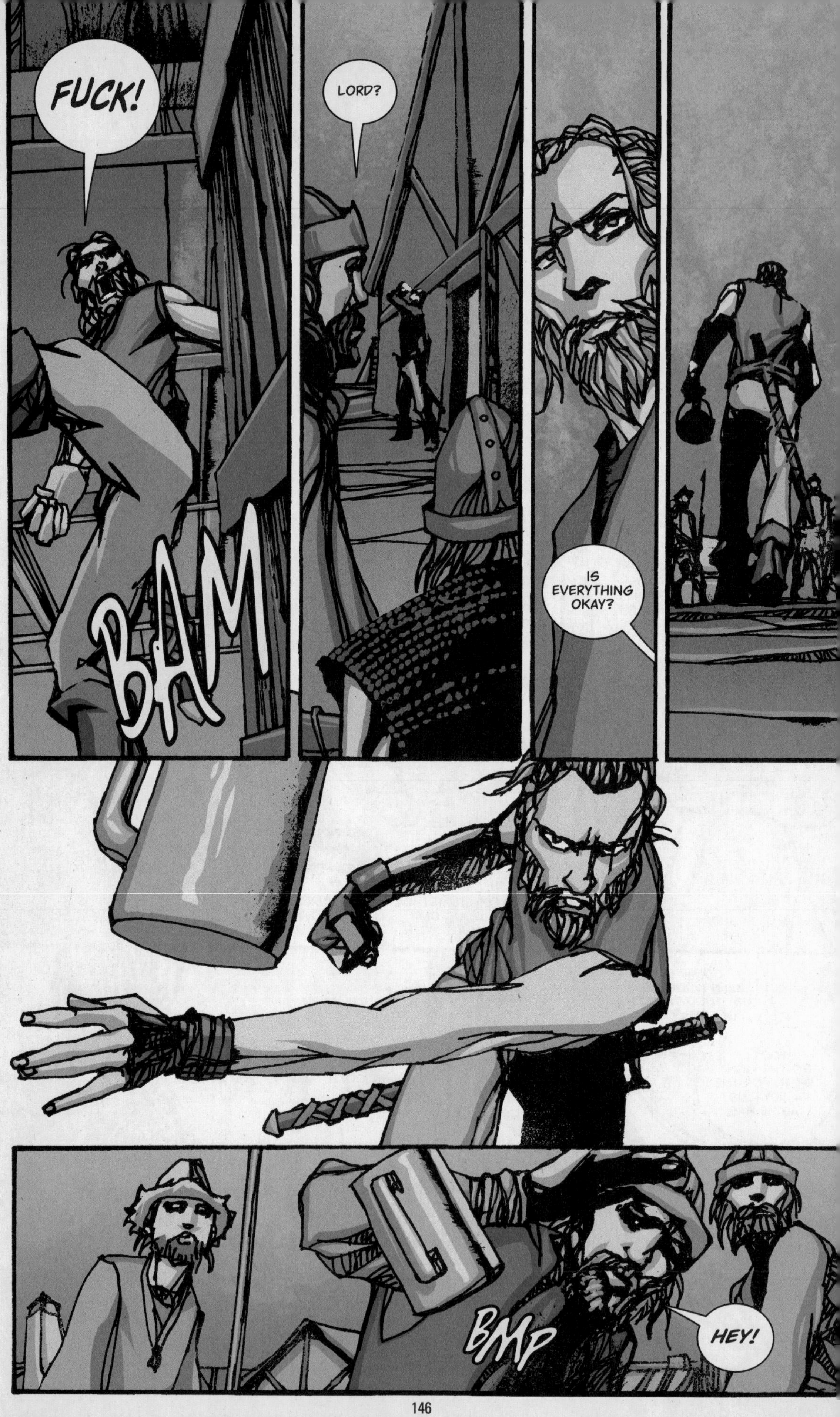
FUCK!
BAM
LORD?
IS EVERYTHING OKAY?
BMP
HEY!

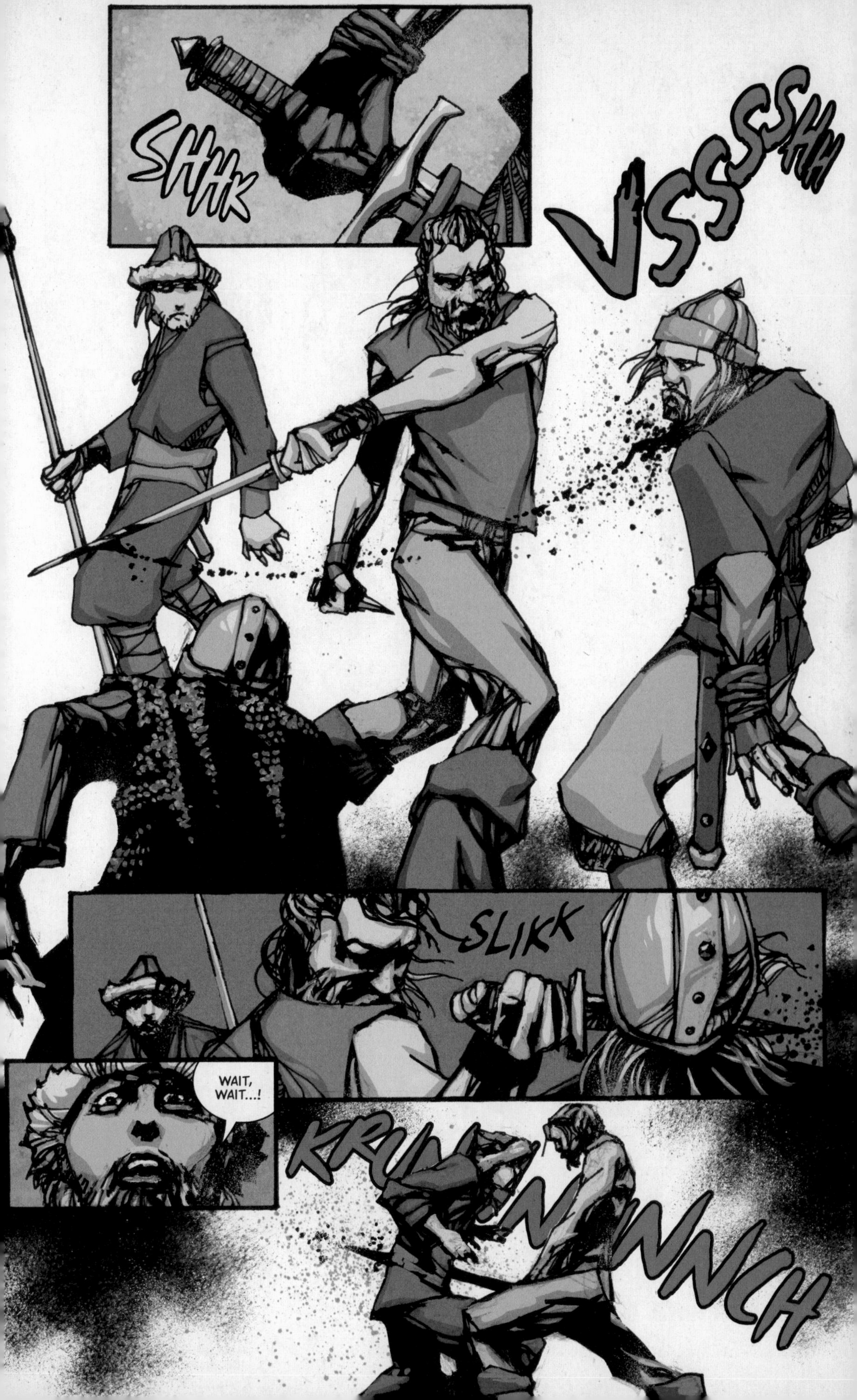
SHHK
VSSSSHH
SLIKK
WAIT, WAIT...!
KRUNNNNNCH

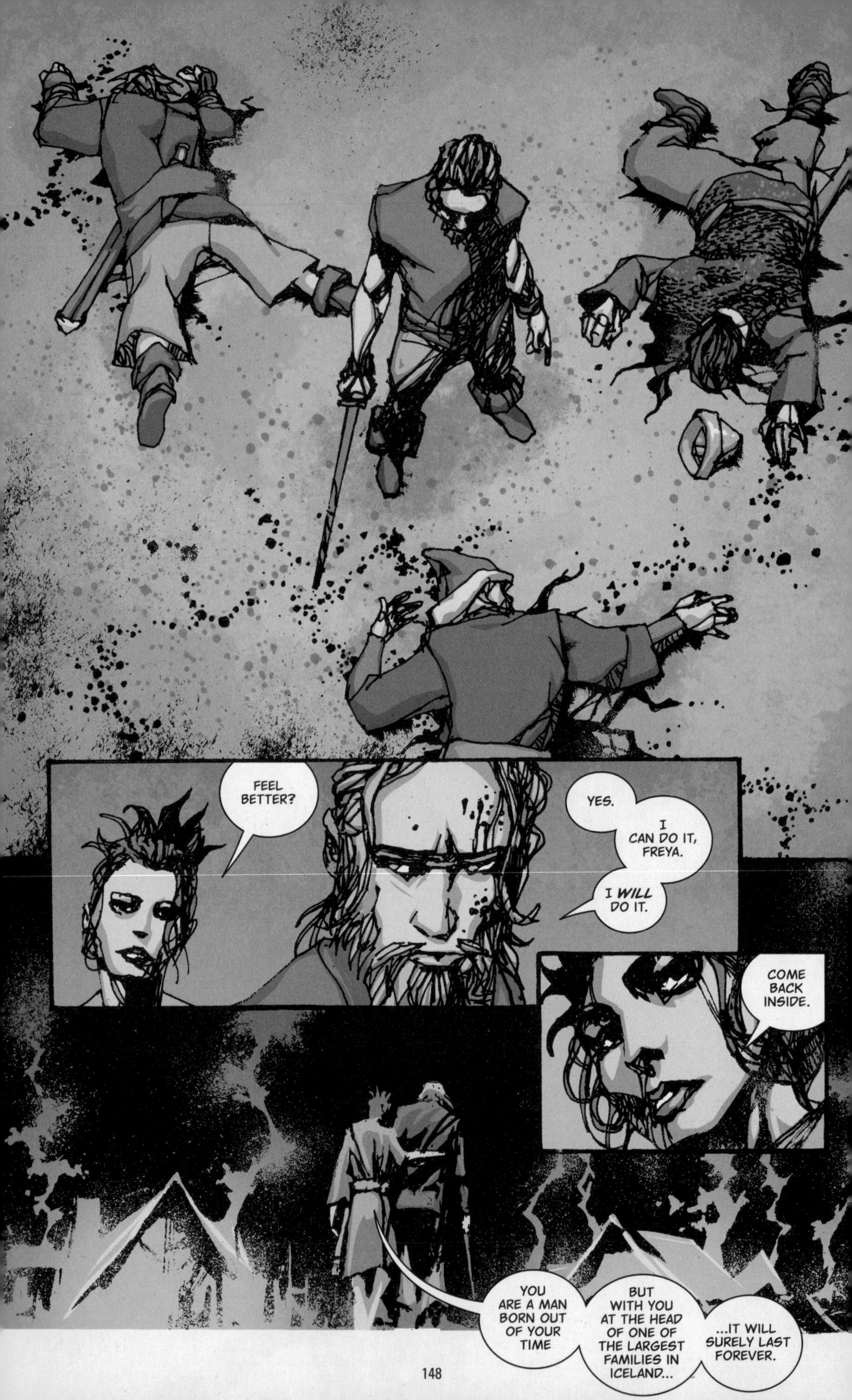
FEEL BETTER?
YES.
I CAN DO IT, FREYA.
I *WILL* DO IT.
COME BACK INSIDE.
YOU ARE A MAN BORN OUT OF YOUR TIME
BUT WITH YOU AT THE HEAD OF ONE OF THE LARGEST FAMILIES IN ICELAND...
...IT WILL SURELY LAST FOREVER.

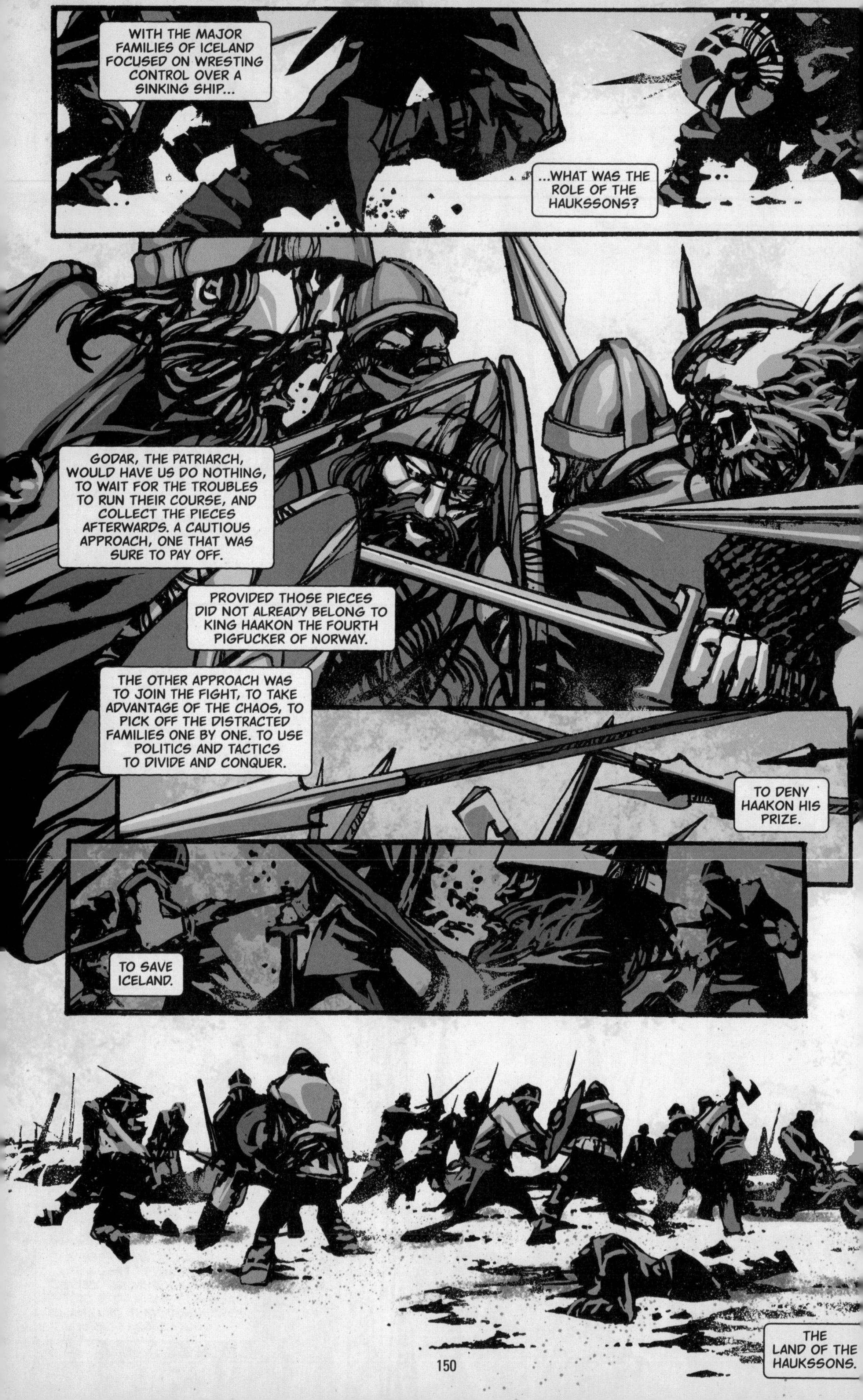

WITH THE MAJOR FAMILIES OF ICELAND FOCUSED ON WRESTING CONTROL OVER A SINKING SHIP...
...WHAT WAS THE ROLE OF THE HAUKSSONS?
GODAR, THE PATRIARCH, WOULD HAVE US DO NOTHING, TO WAIT FOR THE TROUBLES TO RUN THEIR COURSE, AND COLLECT THE PIECES AFTERWARDS. A CAUTIOUS APPROACH, ONE THAT WAS SURE TO PAY OFF.
PROVIDED THOSE PIECES DID NOT ALREADY BELONG TO KING HAAKON THE FOURTH PIGFUCKER OF NORWAY.
THE OTHER APPROACH WAS TO JOIN THE FIGHT, TO TAKE ADVANTAGE OF THE CHAOS, TO PICK OFF THE DISTRACTED FAMILIES ONE BY ONE. TO USE POLITICS AND TACTICS TO DIVIDE AND CONQUER.
TO DENY HAAKON HIS PRIZE.
TO SAVE ICELAND.
THE LAND OF THE HAUKSSONS.

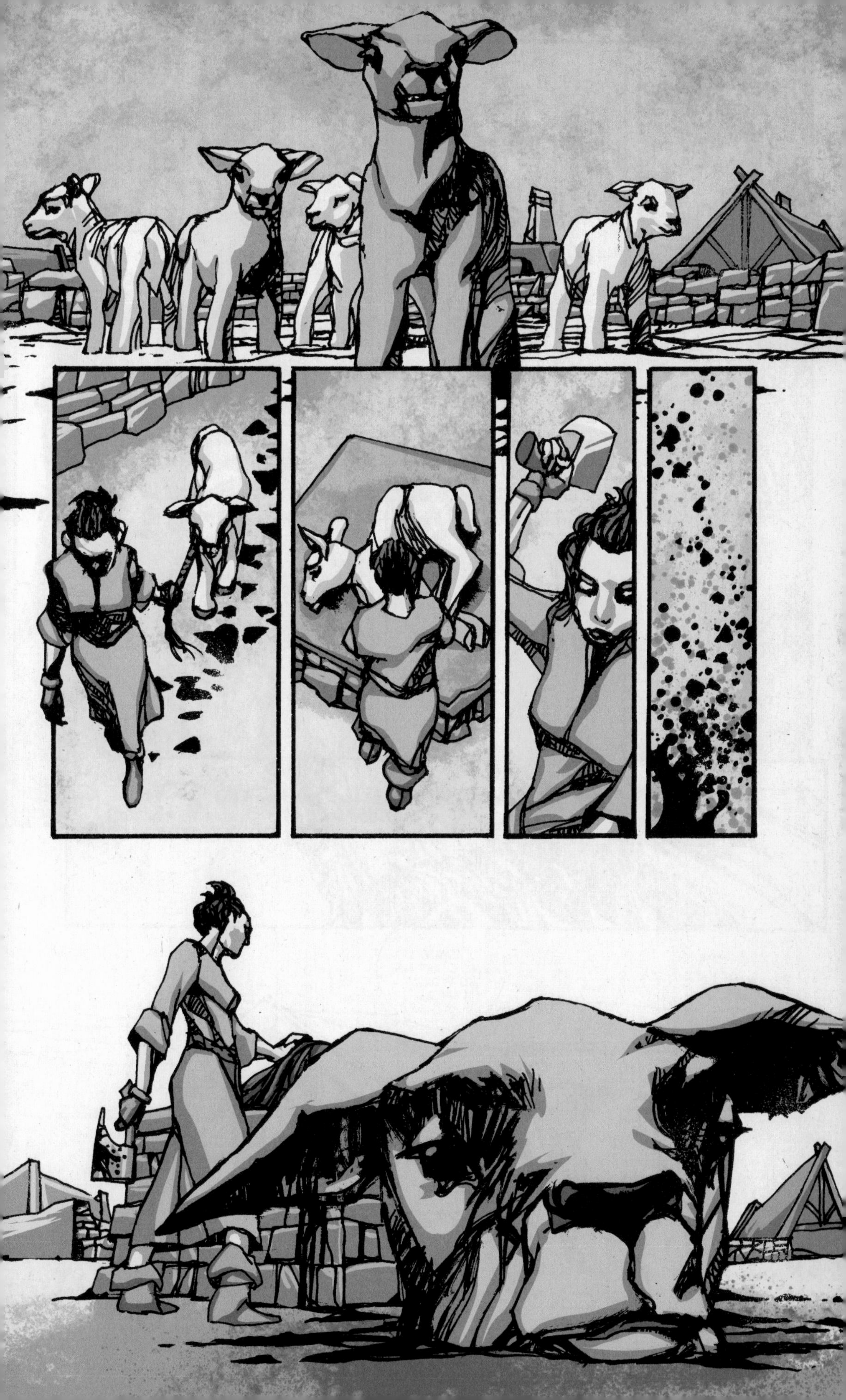

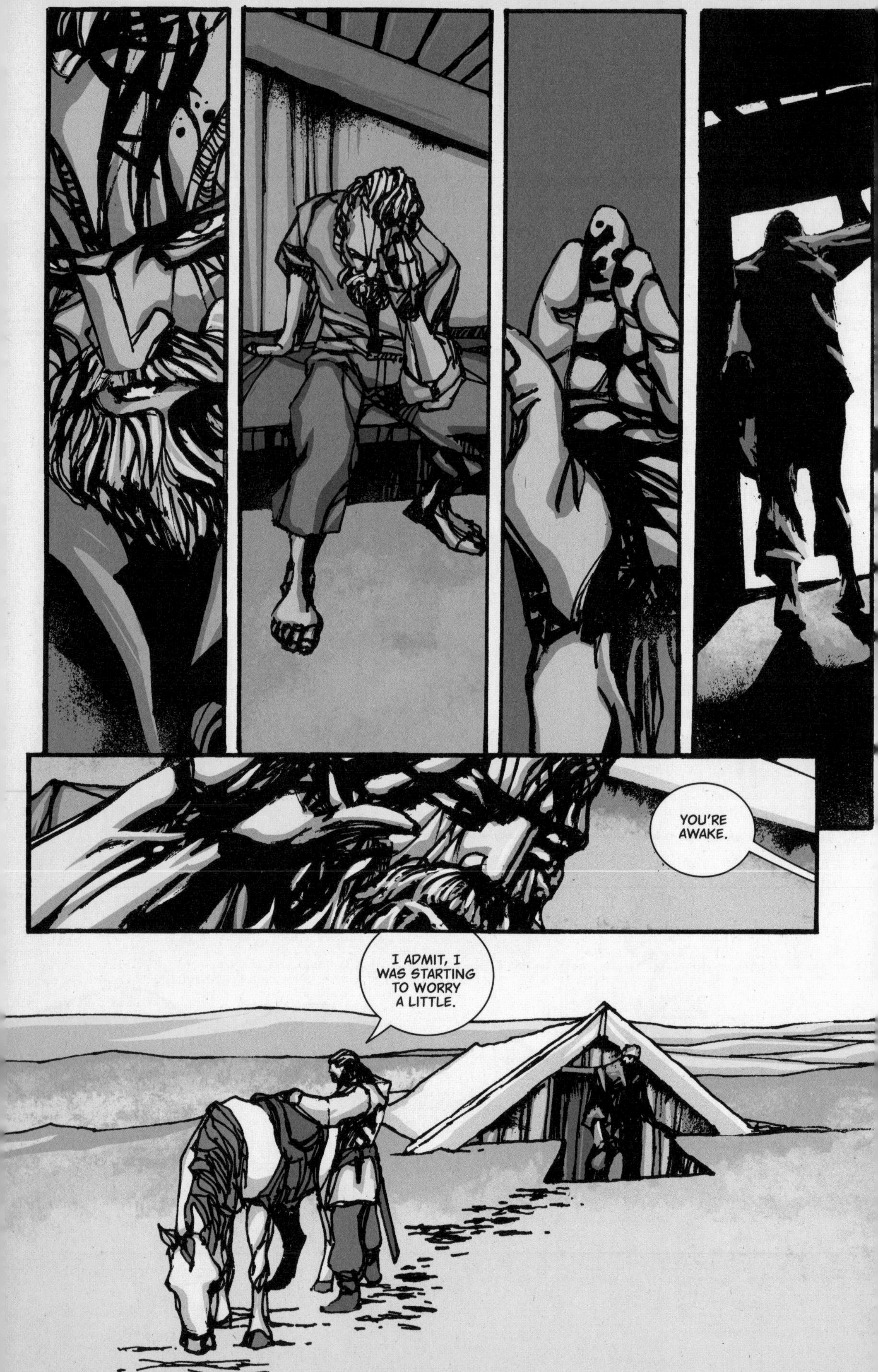
YOU'RE
AWAKE.
I ADMIT, I
WAS STARTING
TO WORRY
A LITTLE.

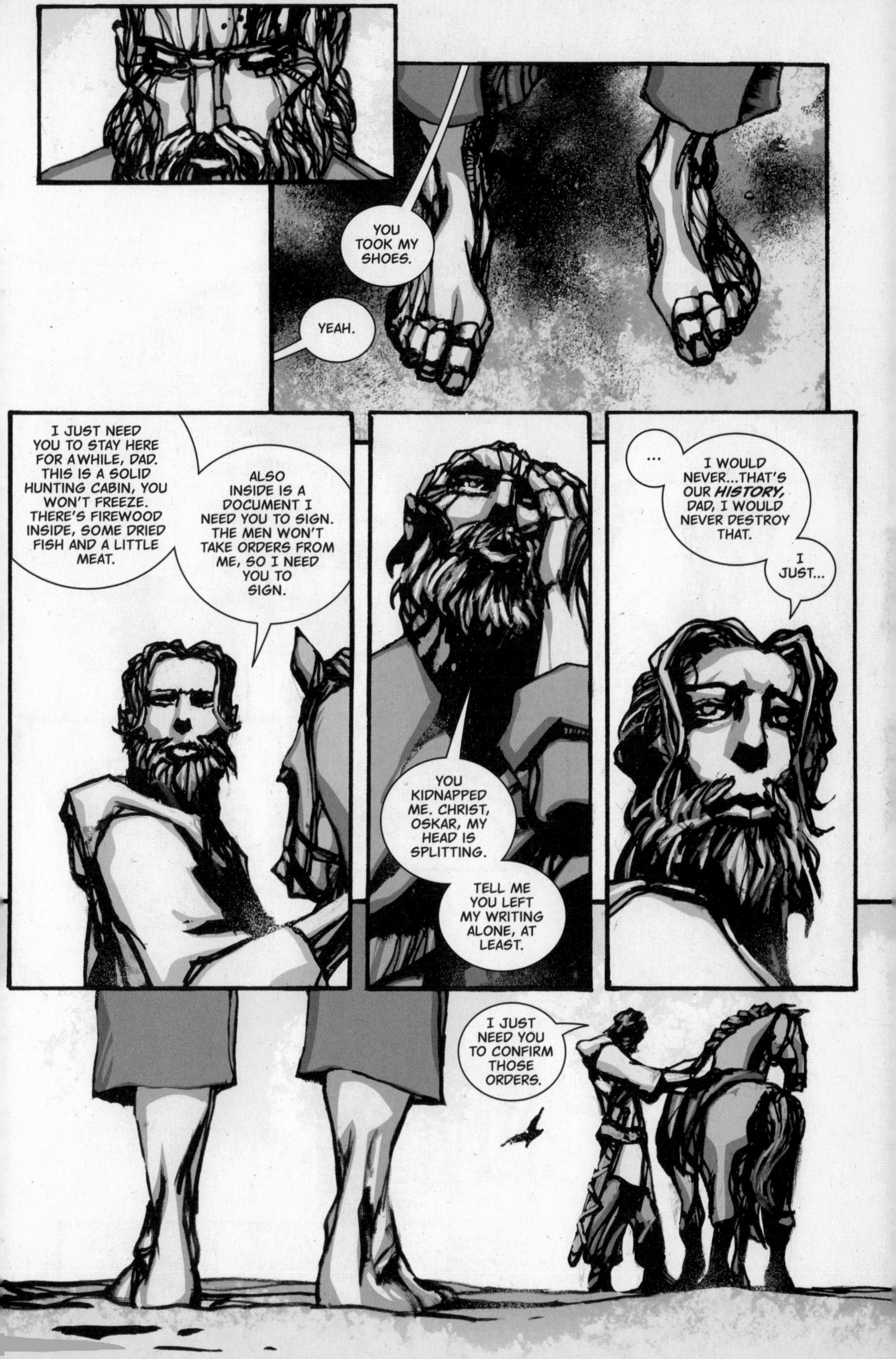
YOU TOOK MY SHOES.
YEAH.
I JUST NEED YOU TO STAY HERE FOR AWHILE, DAD. THIS IS A SOLID HUNTING CABIN, YOU WON'T FREEZE. THERE'S FIREWOOD INSIDE, SOME DRIED FISH AND A LITTLE MEAT.
ALSO INSIDE IS A DOCUMENT I NEED YOU TO SIGN. THE MEN WON'T TAKE ORDERS FROM ME, SO I NEED YOU TO SIGN.
YOU KIDNAPPED ME. CHRIST, OSKAR, MY HEAD IS SPLITTING.
TELL ME YOU LEFT MY WRITING ALONE, AT LEAST.
...
I WOULD NEVER...THAT'S OUR HISTORY, DAD, I WOULD NEVER DESTROY THAT.
I JUST...
I JUST NEED YOU TO CONFIRM THOSE ORDERS.

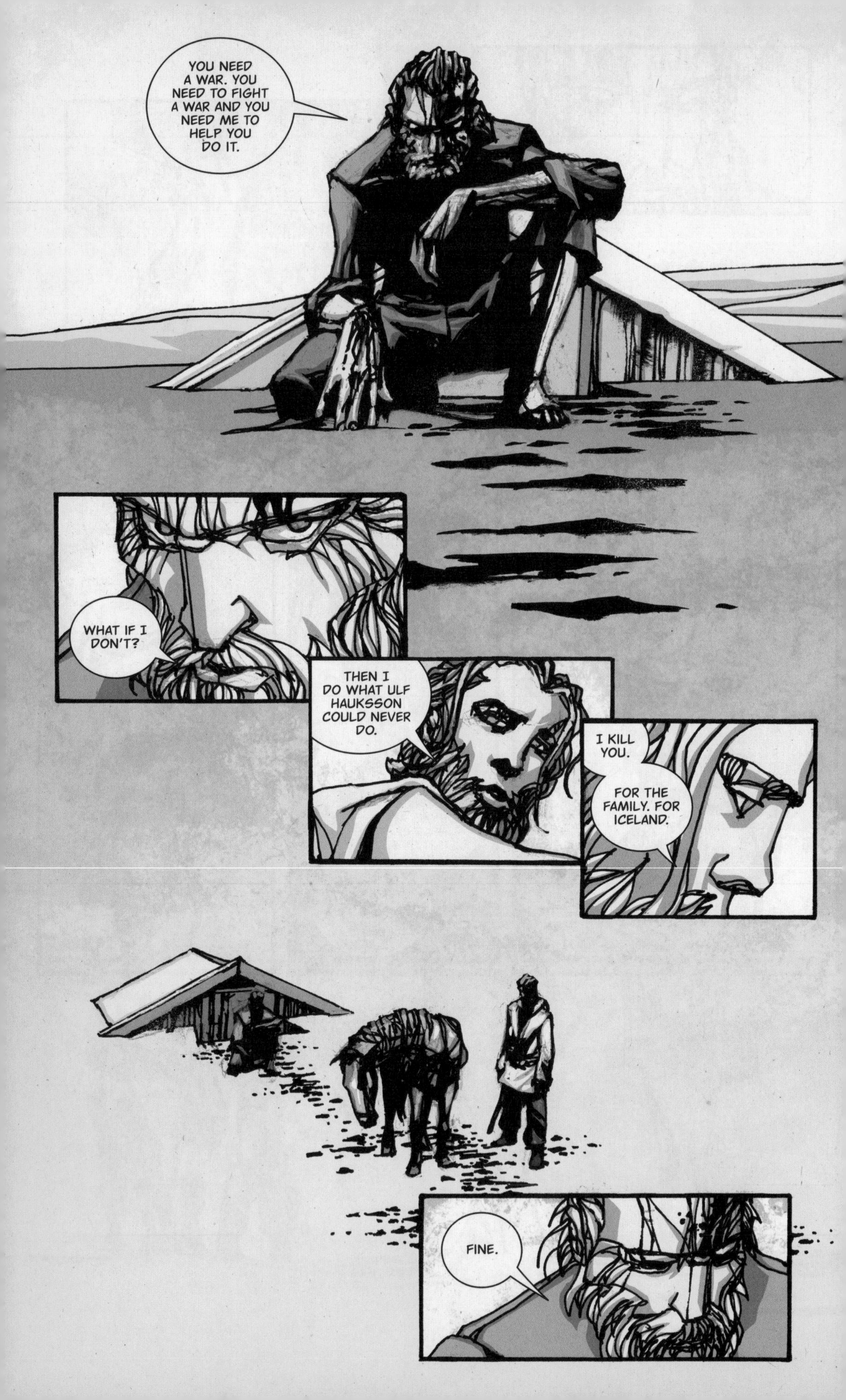
YOU NEED A WAR. YOU NEED TO FIGHT A WAR AND YOU NEED ME TO HELP YOU DO IT.
WHAT IF I DON'T?
THEN I DO WHAT ULF HAUKSSON COULD NEVER DO.
I KILL YOU.
FOR THE FAMILY. FOR ICELAND.
FINE.

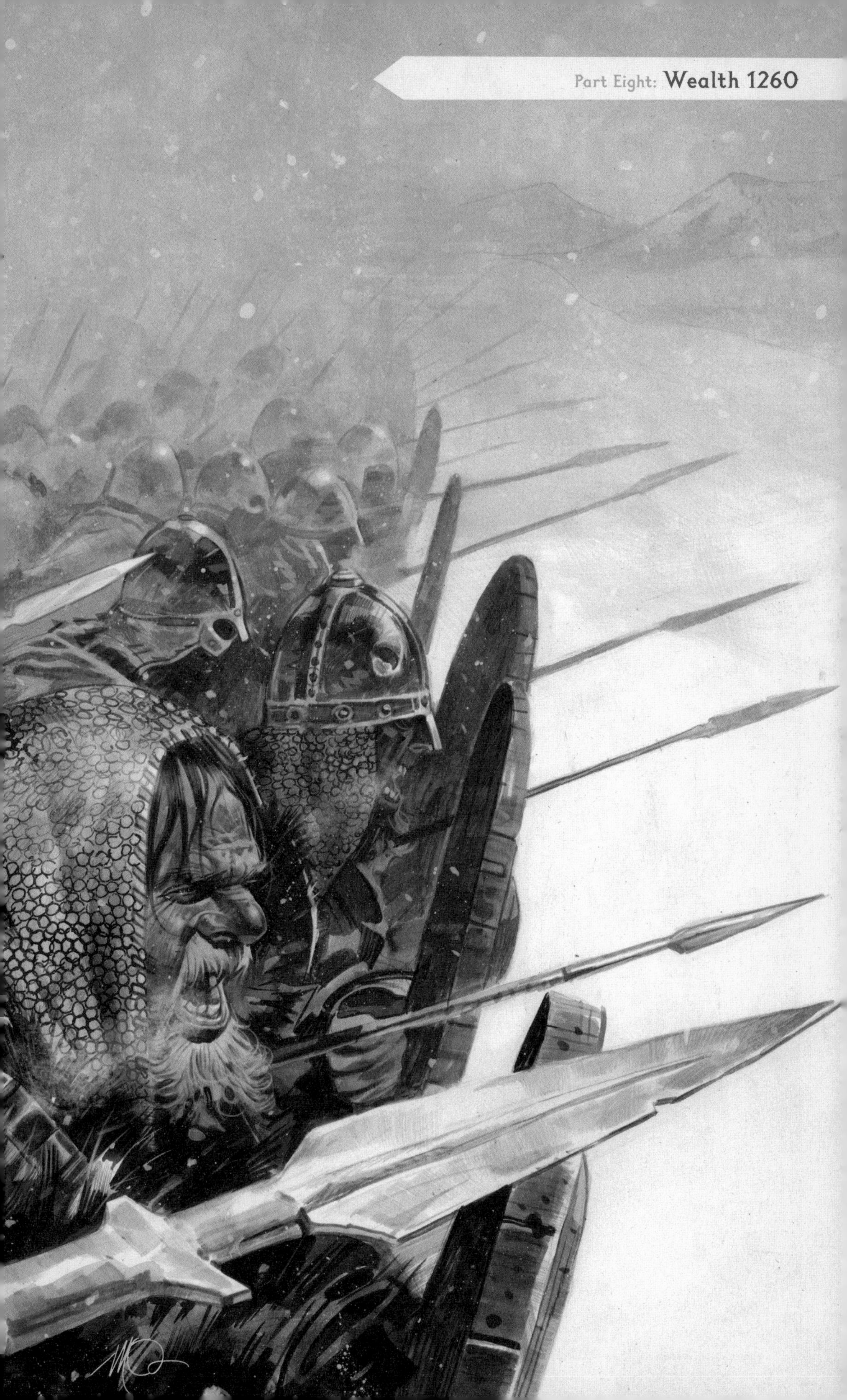

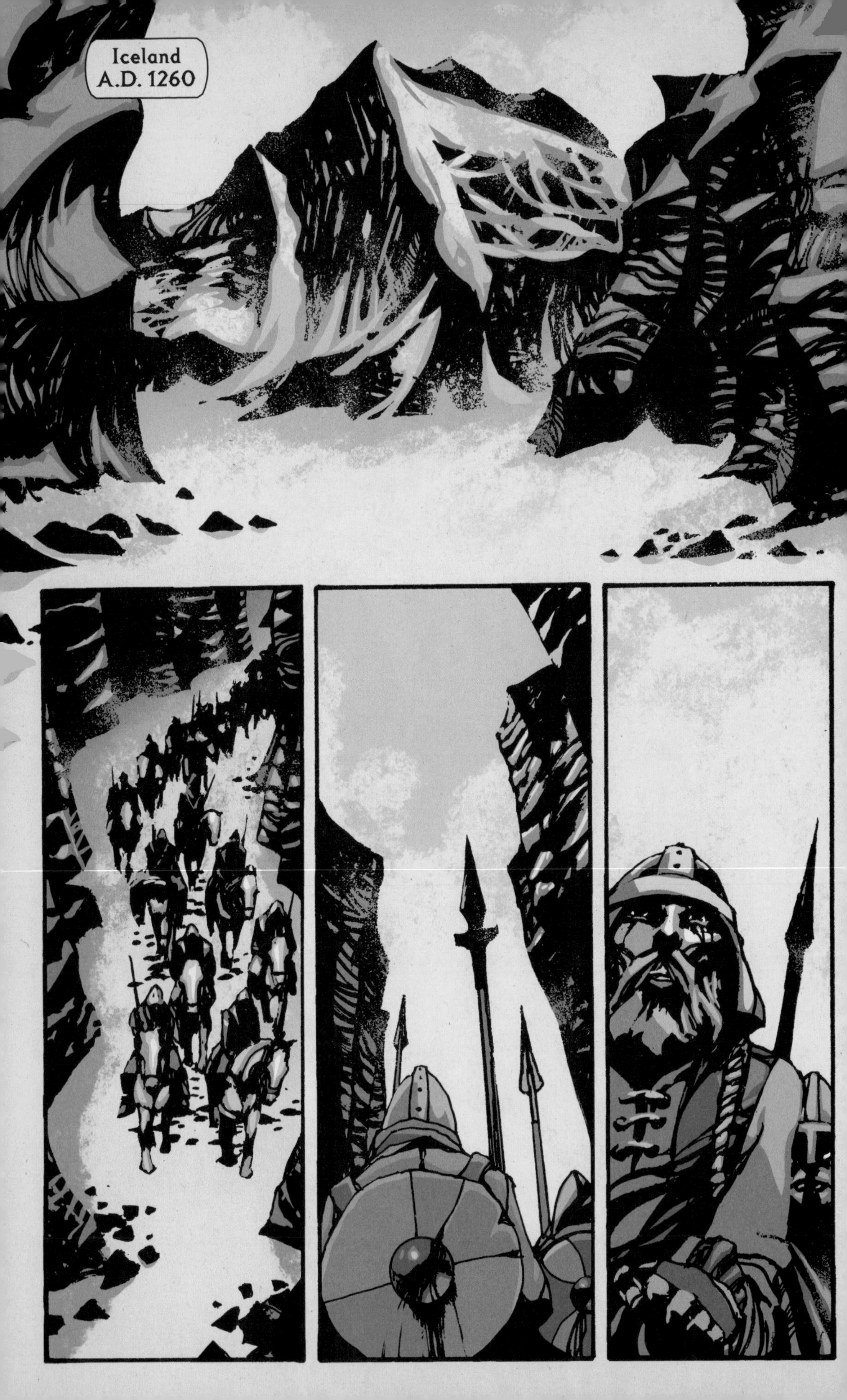
Iceland
A.D. 1260

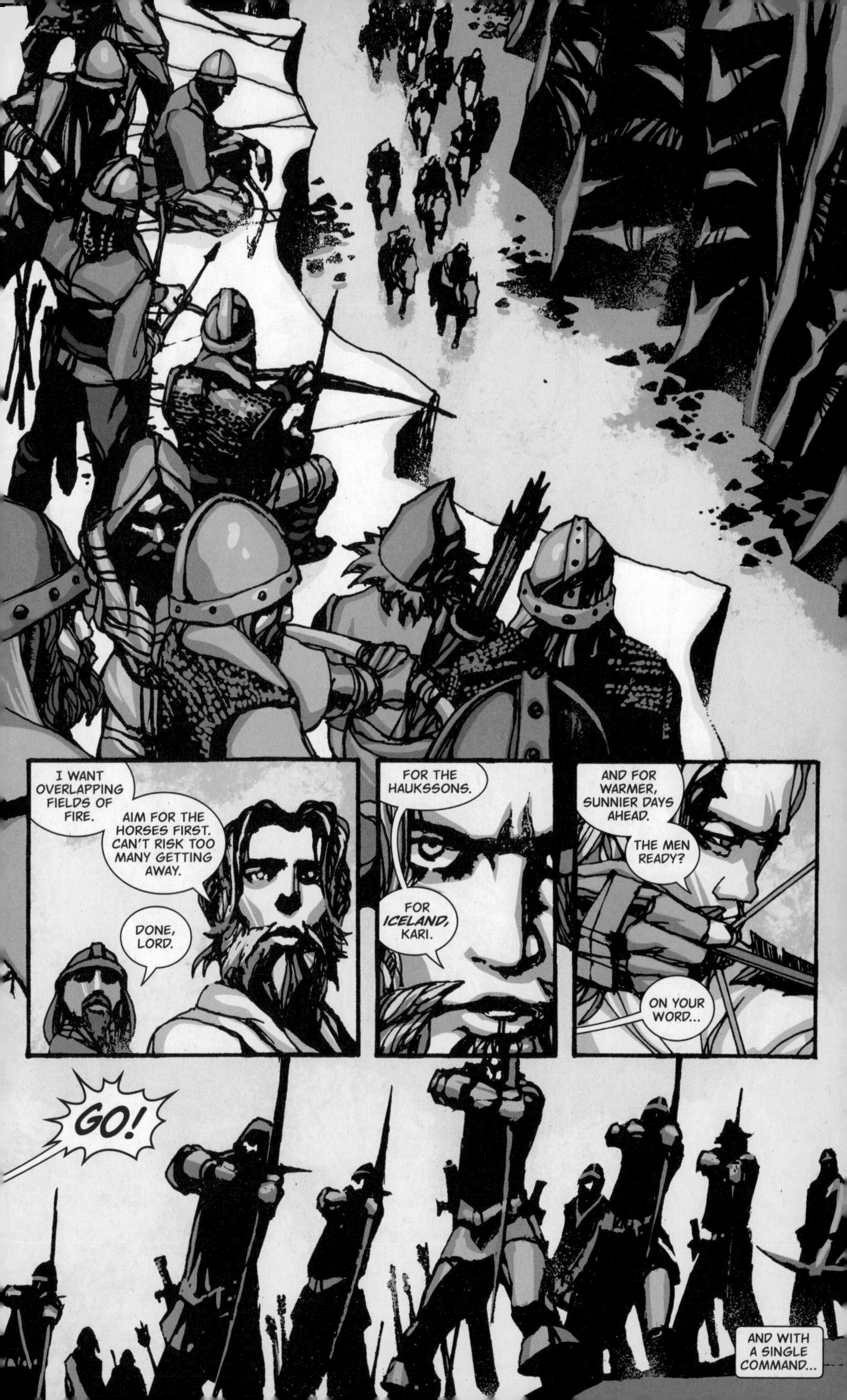
I WANT OVERLAPPING FIELDS OF FIRE.
AIM FOR THE HORSES FIRST. CAN'T RISK TOO MANY GETTING AWAY.
DONE, LORD.
FOR THE HAUKSSONS.
FOR *ICELAND,* KARI.
AND FOR WARMER, SUNNIER DAYS AHEAD.
THE MEN READY?
ON YOUR WORD...
GO!
AND WITH A SINGLE COMMAND...

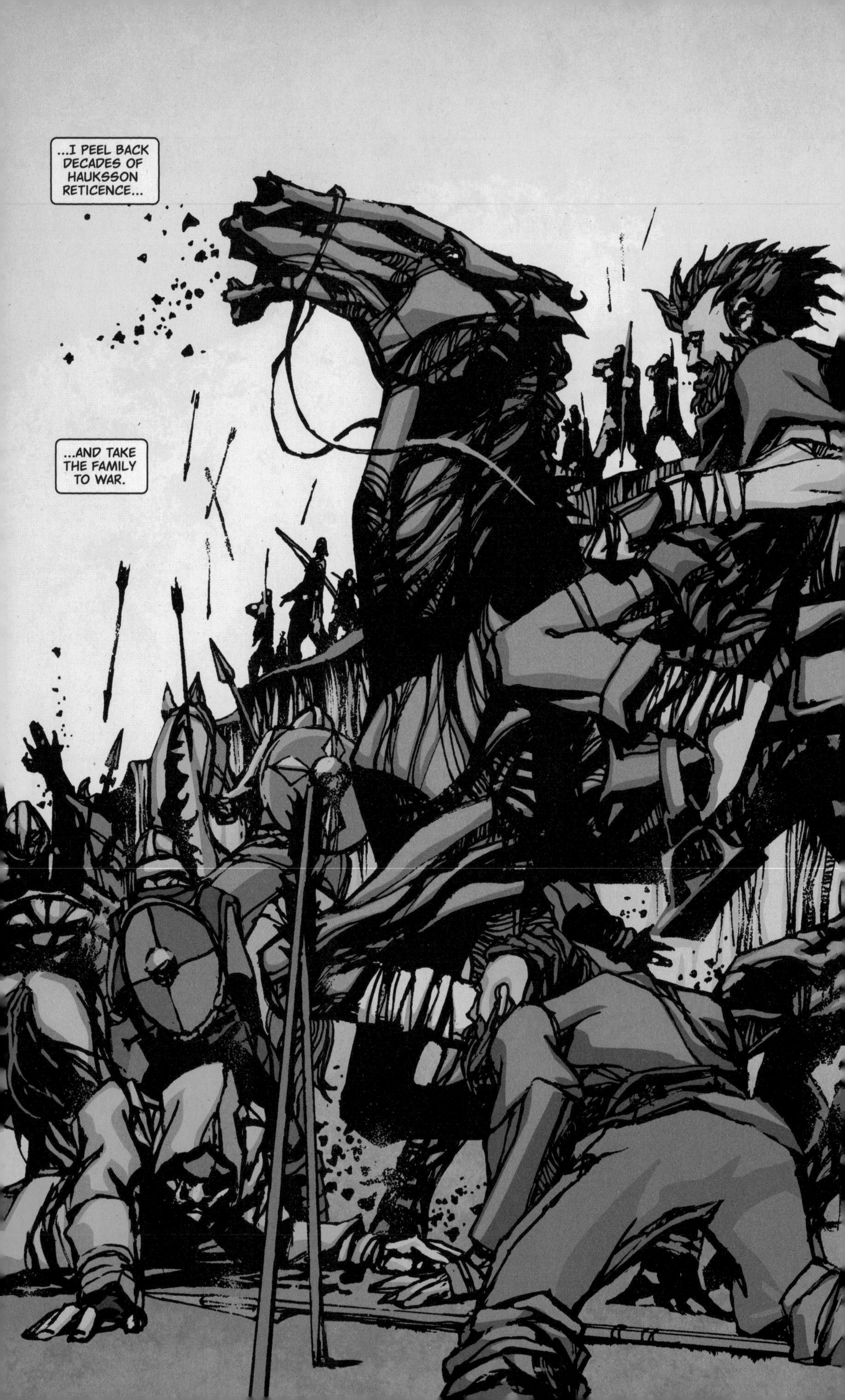
...I PEEL BACK DECADES OF HAUKSSON RETICENCE...
...AND TAKE THE FAMILY TO WAR.

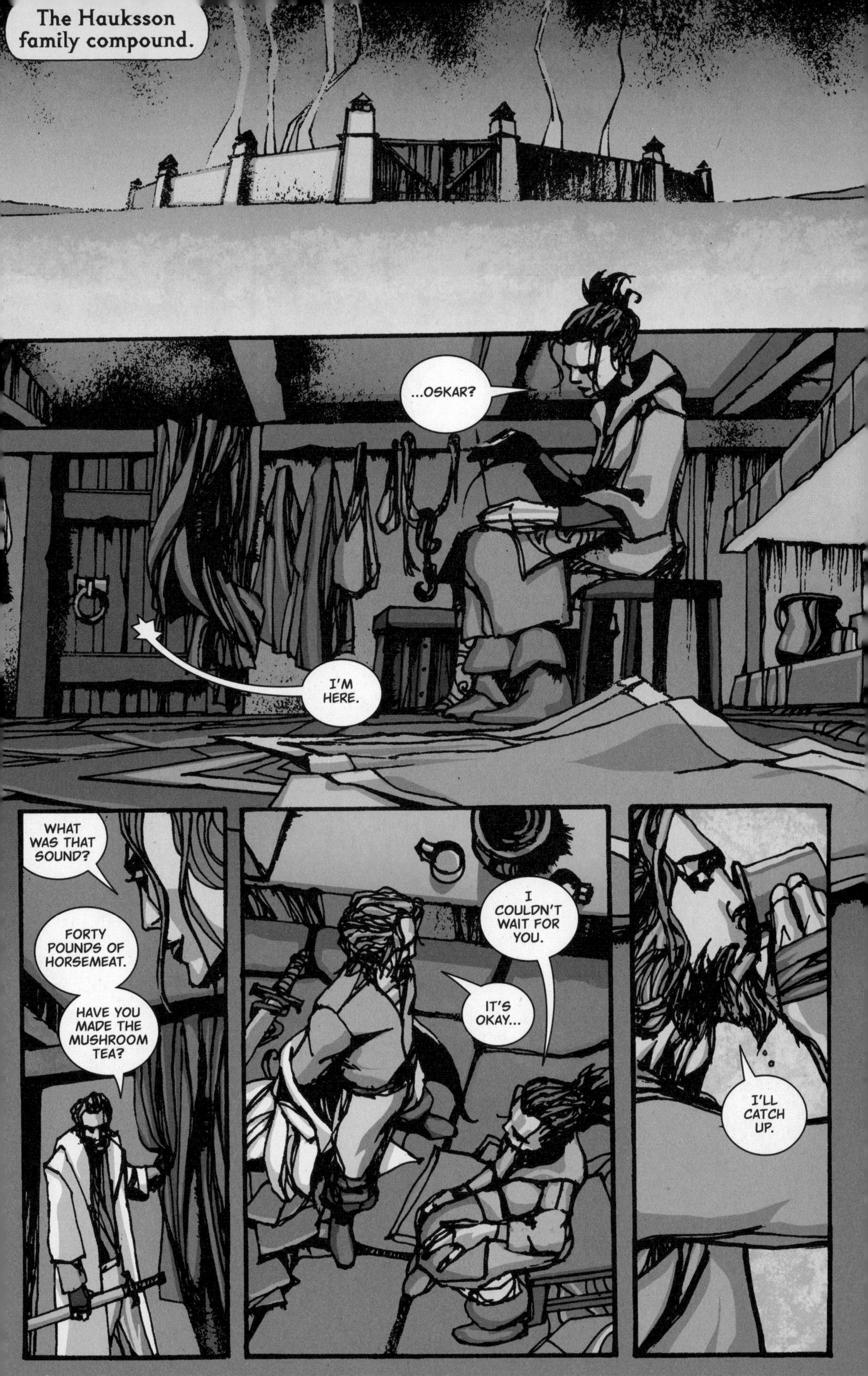
The Hauksson family compound.
...OSKAR?
I'M HERE.
WHAT WAS THAT SOUND?
FORTY POUNDS OF HORSEMEAT.
HAVE YOU MADE THE MUSHROOM TEA?
I COULDN'T WAIT FOR YOU.
IT'S OKAY...
I'LL CATCH UP.

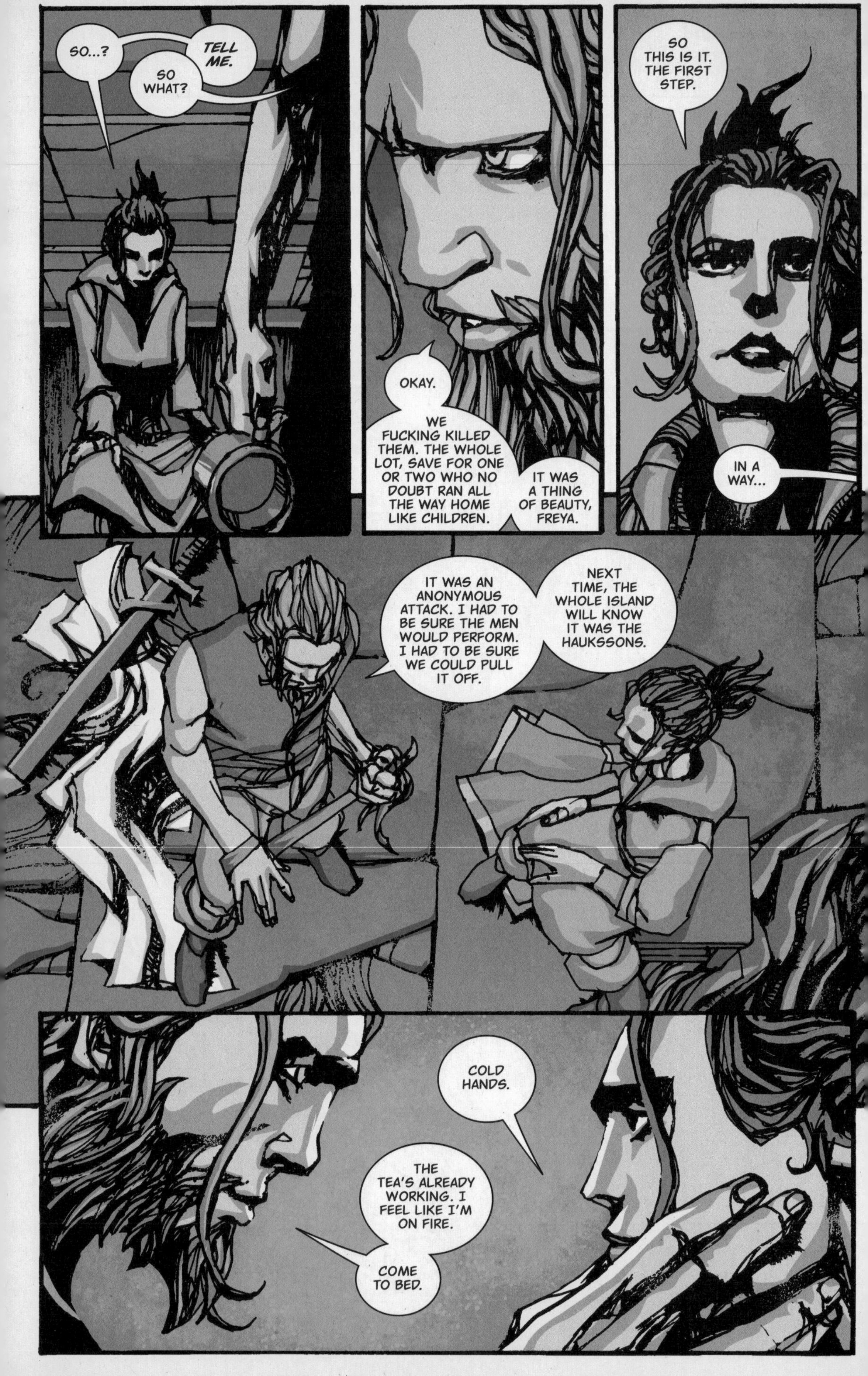
SO...?
TELL ME.
SO WHAT?
OKAY.
WE FUCKING KILLED THEM. THE WHOLE LOT, SAVE FOR ONE OR TWO WHO NO DOUBT RAN ALL THE WAY HOME LIKE CHILDREN.
IT WAS A THING OF BEAUTY, FREYA.
SO THIS IS IT. THE FIRST STEP.
IN A WAY...
IT WAS AN ANONYMOUS ATTACK. I HAD TO BE SURE THE MEN WOULD PERFORM. I HAD TO BE SURE WE COULD PULL IT OFF.
NEXT TIME, THE WHOLE ISLAND WILL KNOW IT WAS THE HAUKSSONS.
COLD HANDS.
THE TEA'S ALREADY WORKING. I FEEL LIKE I'M ON FIRE.
COME TO BED.

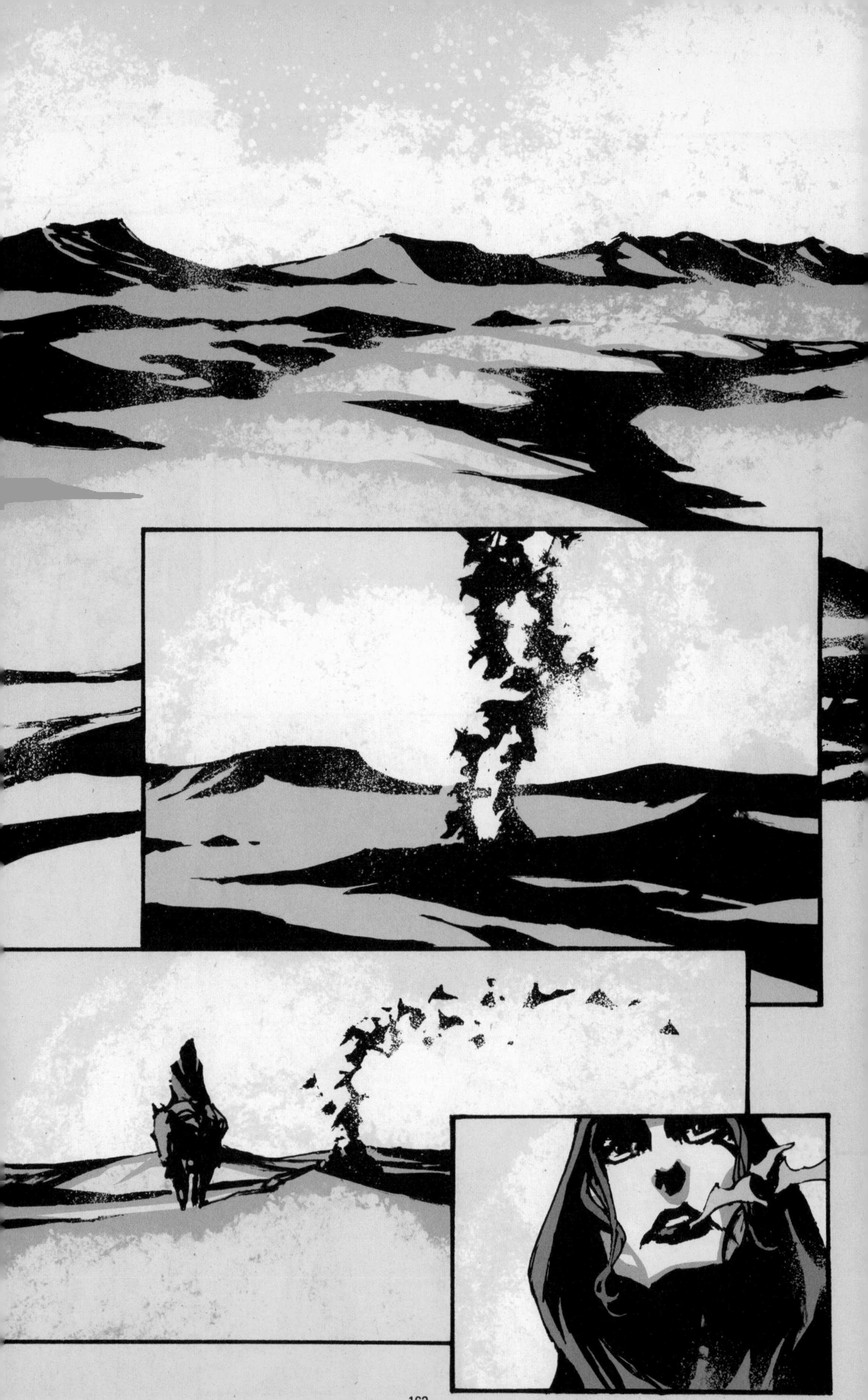

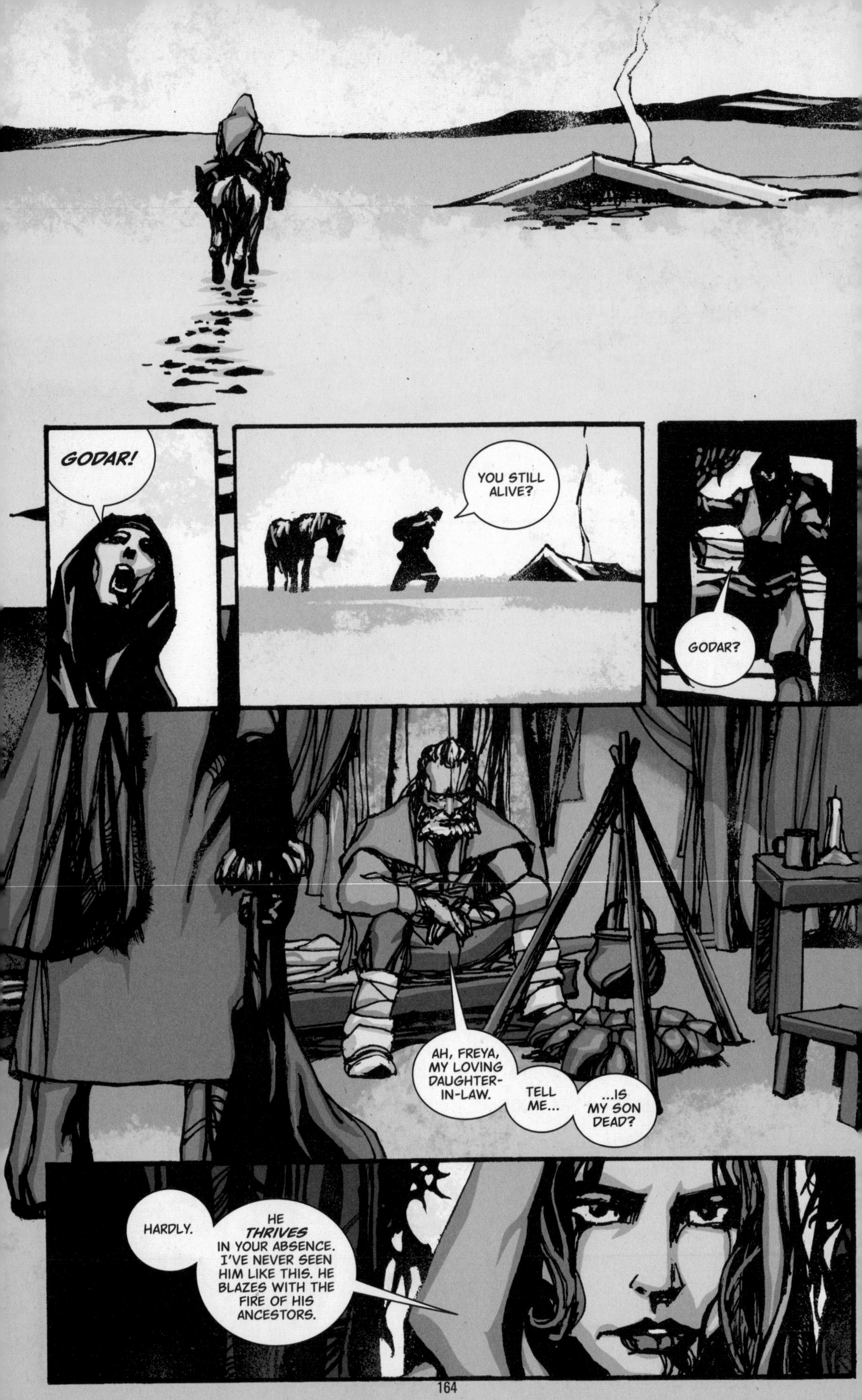
GODAR!
YOU STILL ALIVE?
GODAR?
AH, FREYA, MY LOVING DAUGHTER-IN-LAW.
TELL ME...
...IS MY SON DEAD?
HARDLY.
HE *THRIVES* IN YOUR ABSENCE. I'VE NEVER SEEN HIM LIKE THIS. HE BLAZES WITH THE FIRE OF HIS ANCESTORS.

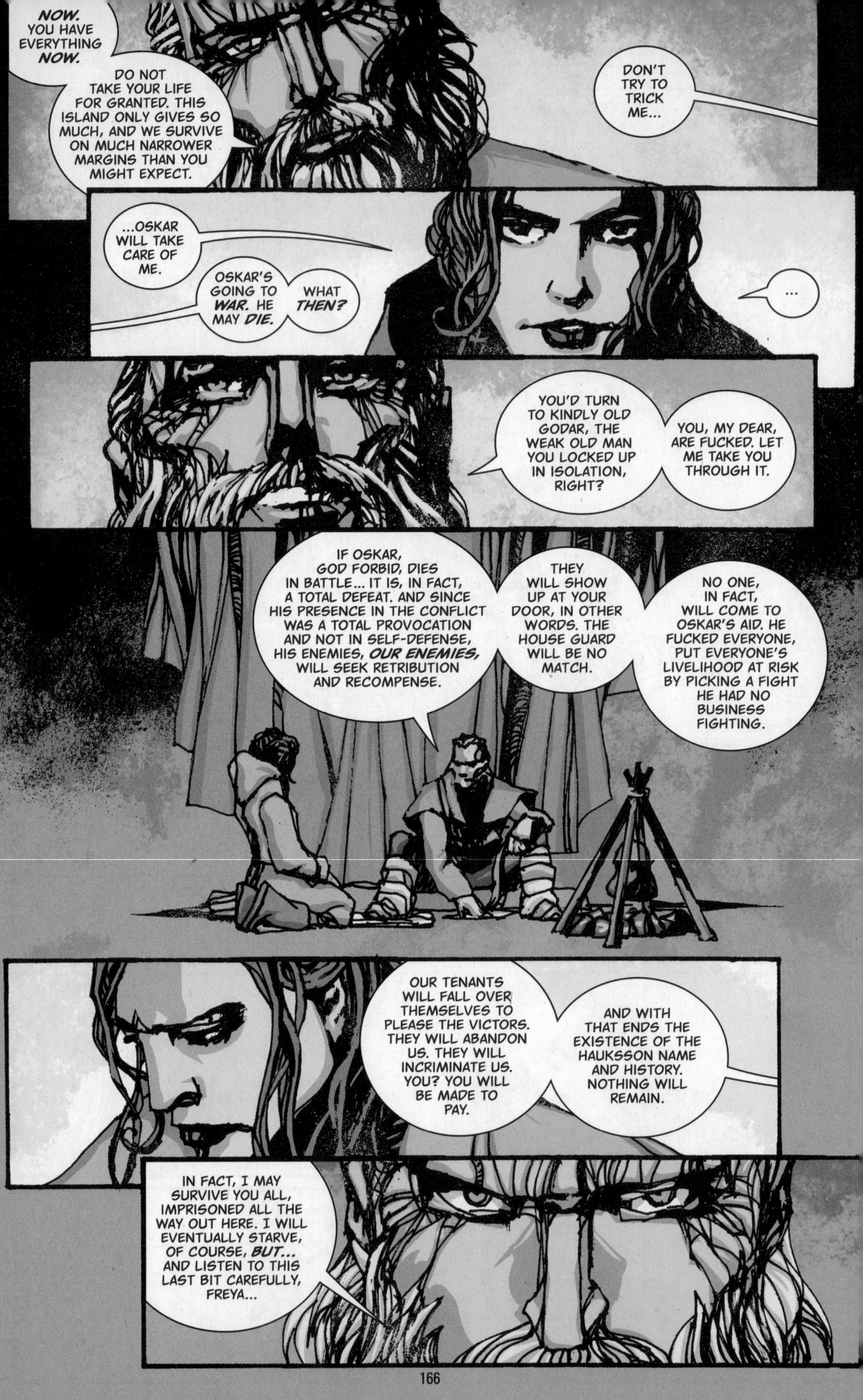

NOW. YOU HAVE EVERYTHING NOW.
DO NOT TAKE YOUR LIFE FOR GRANTED. THIS ISLAND ONLY GIVES SO MUCH, AND WE SURVIVE ON MUCH NARROWER MARGINS THAN YOU MIGHT EXPECT.
DON'T TRY TO TRICK ME...
...OSKAR WILL TAKE CARE OF ME.
OSKAR'S GOING TO WAR. HE MAY DIE.
WHAT THEN?
...
YOU'D TURN TO KINDLY OLD GODAR, THE WEAK OLD MAN YOU LOCKED UP IN ISOLATION, RIGHT?
YOU, MY DEAR, ARE FUCKED. LET ME TAKE YOU THROUGH IT.
IF OSKAR, GOD FORBID, DIES IN BATTLE... IT IS, IN FACT, A TOTAL DEFEAT. AND SINCE HIS PRESENCE IN THE CONFLICT WAS A TOTAL PROVOCATION AND NOT IN SELF-DEFENSE, HIS ENEMIES, OUR ENEMIES, WILL SEEK RETRIBUTION AND RECOMPENSE.
THEY WILL SHOW UP AT YOUR DOOR, IN OTHER WORDS. THE HOUSE GUARD WILL BE NO MATCH.
NO ONE, IN FACT, WILL COME TO OSKAR'S AID. HE FUCKED EVERYONE, PUT EVERYONE'S LIVELIHOOD AT RISK BY PICKING A FIGHT HE HAD NO BUSINESS FIGHTING.
OUR TENANTS WILL FALL OVER THEMSELVES TO PLEASE THE VICTORS. THEY WILL ABANDON US. THEY WILL INCRIMINATE US. YOU? YOU WILL BE MADE TO PAY.
AND WITH THAT ENDS THE EXISTENCE OF THE HAUKSSON NAME AND HISTORY. NOTHING WILL REMAIN.
IN FACT, I MAY SURVIVE YOU ALL, IMPRISONED ALL THE WAY OUT HERE. I WILL EVENTUALLY STARVE, OF COURSE, BUT... AND LISTEN TO THIS LAST BIT CAREFULLY, FREYA...

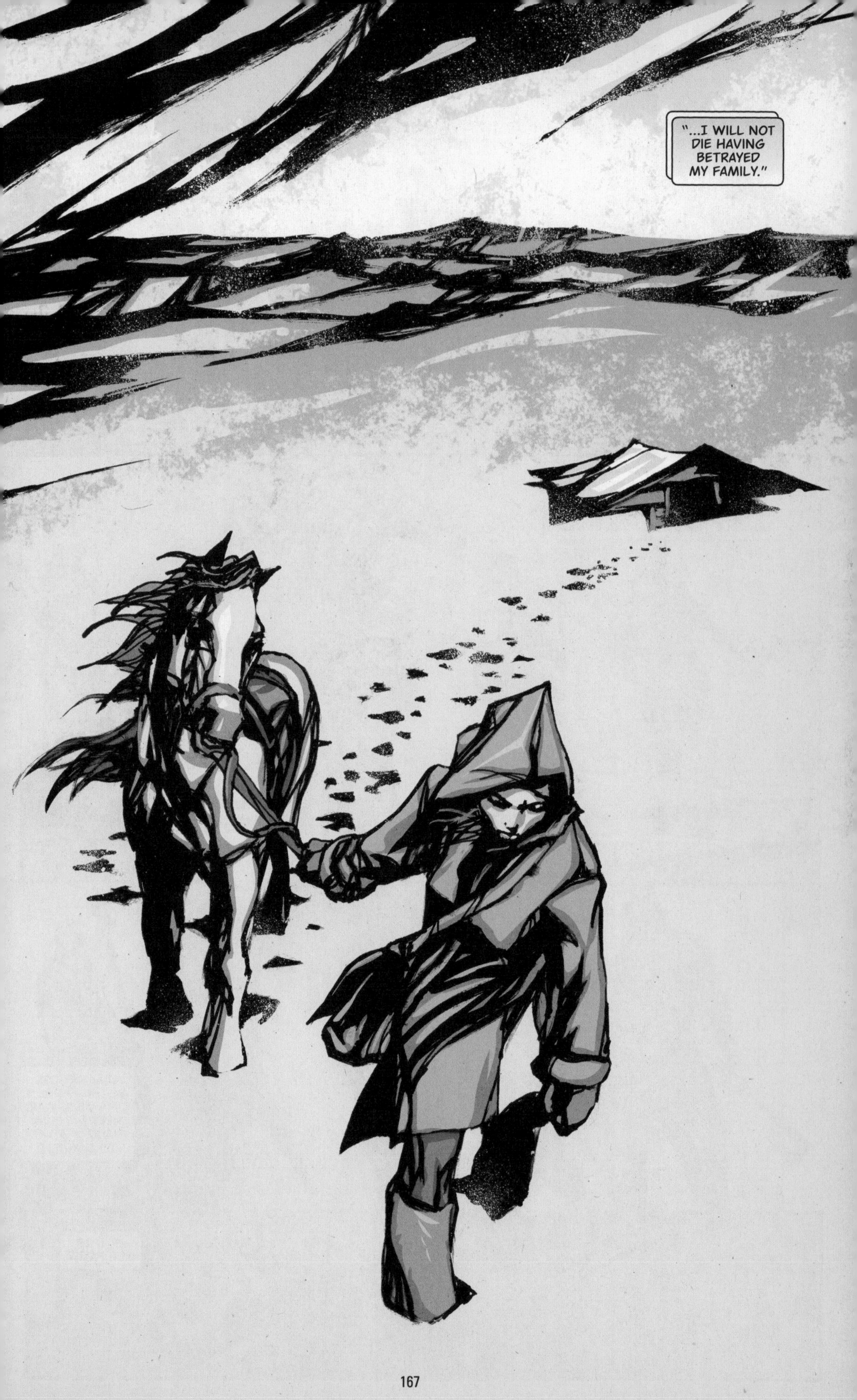
"...I WILL NOT DIE HAVING BETRAYED MY FAMILY."

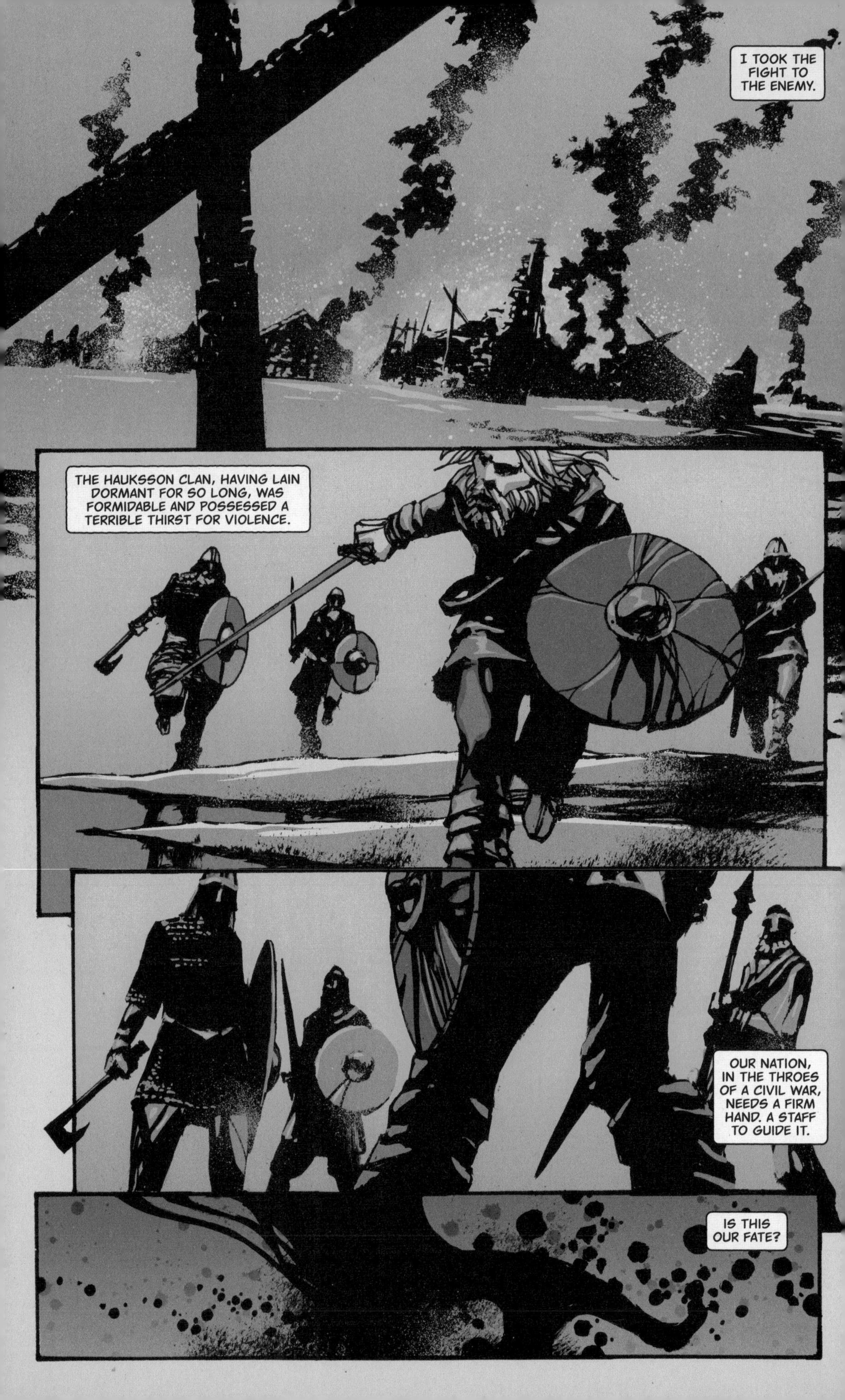
I TOOK THE FIGHT TO THE ENEMY.
THE HAUKSSON CLAN, HAVING LAIN DORMANT FOR SO LONG, WAS FORMIDABLE AND POSSESSED A TERRIBLE THIRST FOR VIOLENCE.
OUR NATION, IN THE THROES OF A CIVIL WAR, NEEDS A FIRM HAND. A STAFF TO GUIDE IT.
IS THIS OUR FATE?

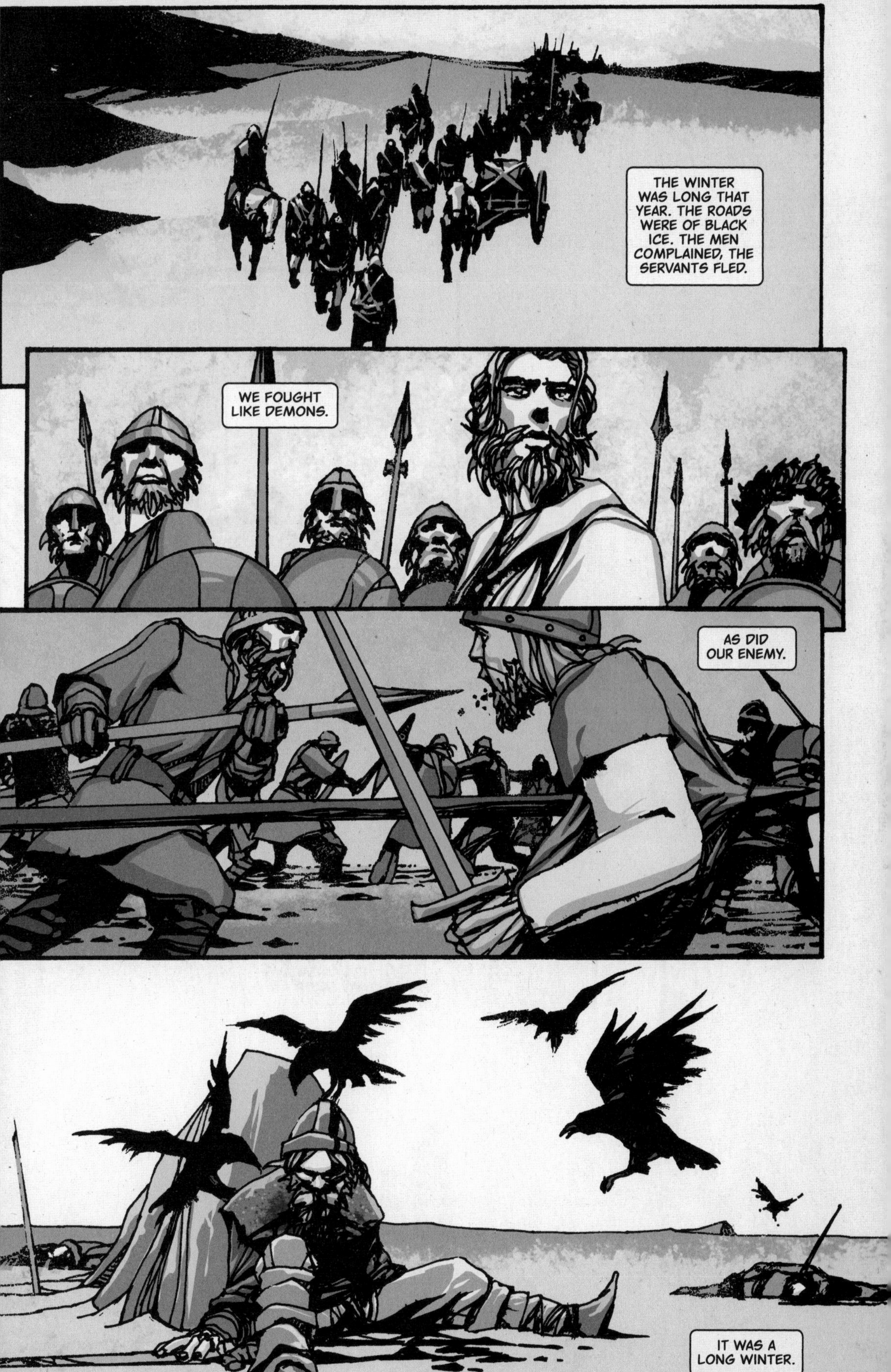
THE WINTER WAS LONG THAT YEAR. THE ROADS WERE OF BLACK ICE. THE MEN COMPLAINED, THE SERVANTS FLED.
WE FOUGHT LIKE DEMONS.
AS DID OUR ENEMY.
IT WAS A LONG WINTER.

FUCK!

OSKAR.

LIKE I WAS FUCKING *NOTHING,* THEY SPOKE TO ME. LIKE I WAS SOME PIECE OF *DOG SHIT,* THEY TURNED ME DOWN.

"LIFE IS GOOD." HOW DO THEY THINK IT *GOT* THAT WAY? BECAUSE HAUKSSONS LIKE ME GOT *DOWN* INTO THE *DIRT* AND *BLED.*

OSKAR, PLEASE.

THERE WILL BE ANOTHER WAY.

THERE *IS* NO OTHER WAY! I *NEED* THE *MEN!*

I SHOULD HAVE KILLED THE LOT OF THEM.

HEY!

COME HERE.

FREYA, LISTEN. THINGS ARE TRULY IN THE SHITTER NOW.

I HAVE NO POWER. MY ARMY, SUCH AS IT IS, IS LOSING MEN ON A DAILY BASIS. I HAVE MONEY, BUT THERE ARE NO MEN WILLING TO FIGHT FOR ME, FOR ANY PRICE! MY TRUSTED MEN SPEAK IN OPEN DEFIANCE OF MY ORDERS.

MEANWHILE, THE OTHER FAMILIES HOLD FAST. I DON'T KNOW HOW, BUT THEY SEEM TO *THRIVE.*

WHAT IS YOUR POINT?

WHAT DO I *DO?*

I SAW YOUR DAD THE OTHER DAY. COLD, BAREFOOT, AND ALONE IN A BOX IN THE MIDDLE OF NOWHERE...

...AND HE WASN'T *HALF* THE SNIVELING BASTARD YOU ARE RIGHT NOW. SO I SUGGEST YOU START FIGURING OUT WHAT MAKES A *HAUKSSON* A *HAUKSSON.*

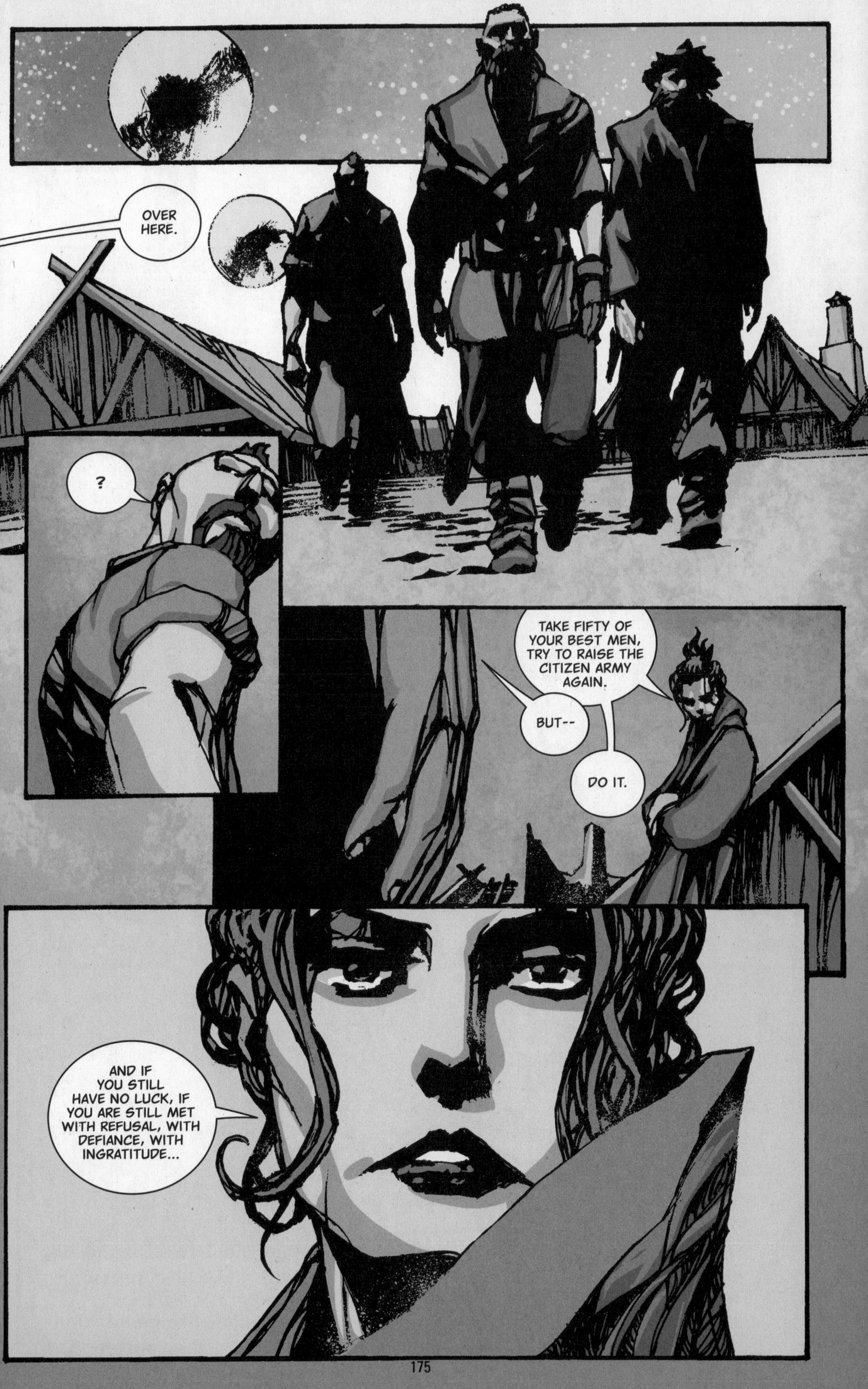
OVER HERE.
?
TAKE FIFTY OF YOUR BEST MEN, TRY TO RAISE THE CITIZEN ARMY AGAIN.
BUT--
DO IT.
AND IF YOU STILL HAVE NO LUCK, IF YOU ARE STILL MET WITH REFUSAL, WITH DEFIANCE, WITH INGRATITUDE...

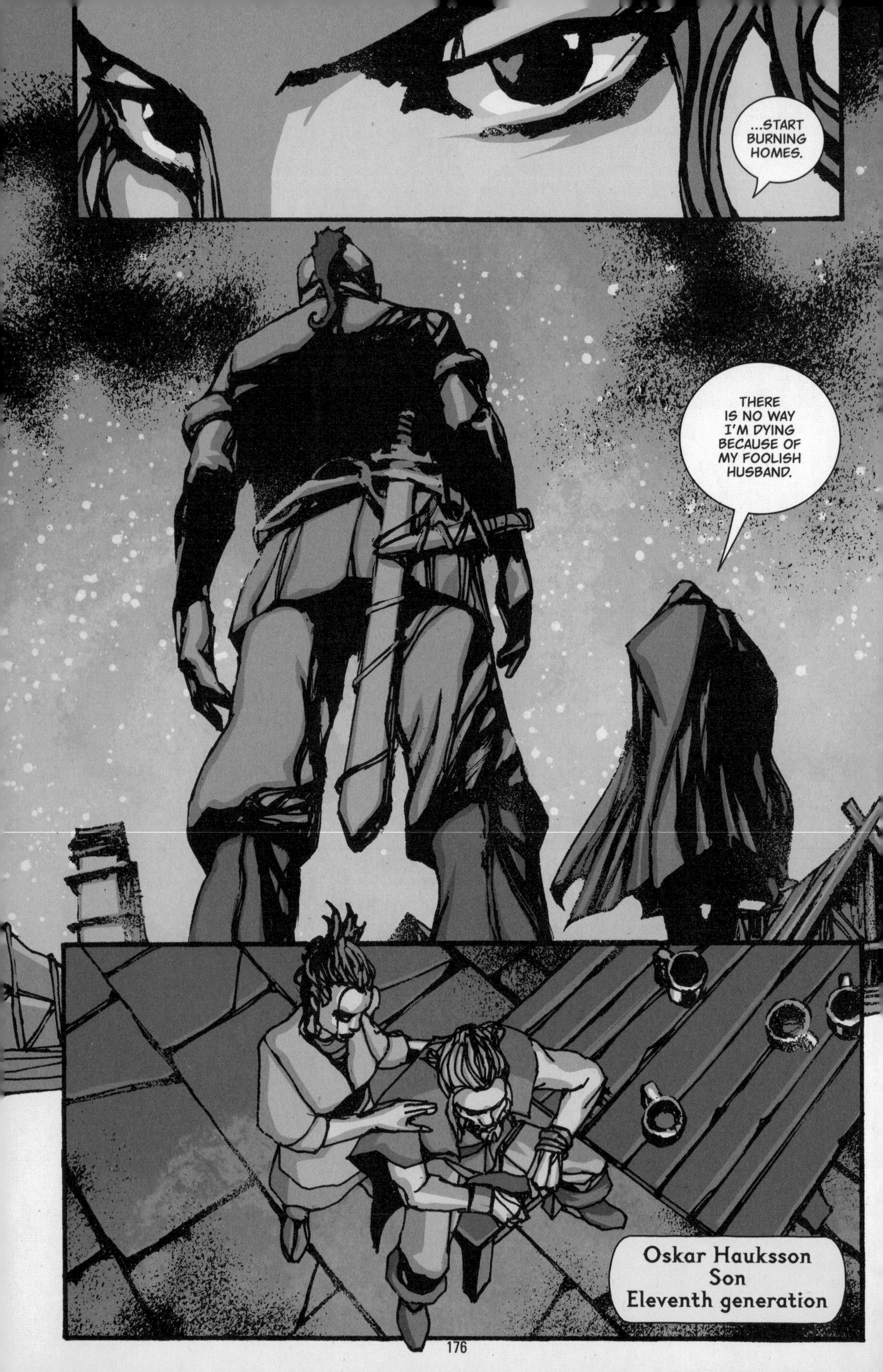
...START BURNING HOMES.
THERE IS NO WAY I'M DYING BECAUSE OF MY FOOLISH HUSBAND.
Oskar Hauksson
Son
Eleventh generation

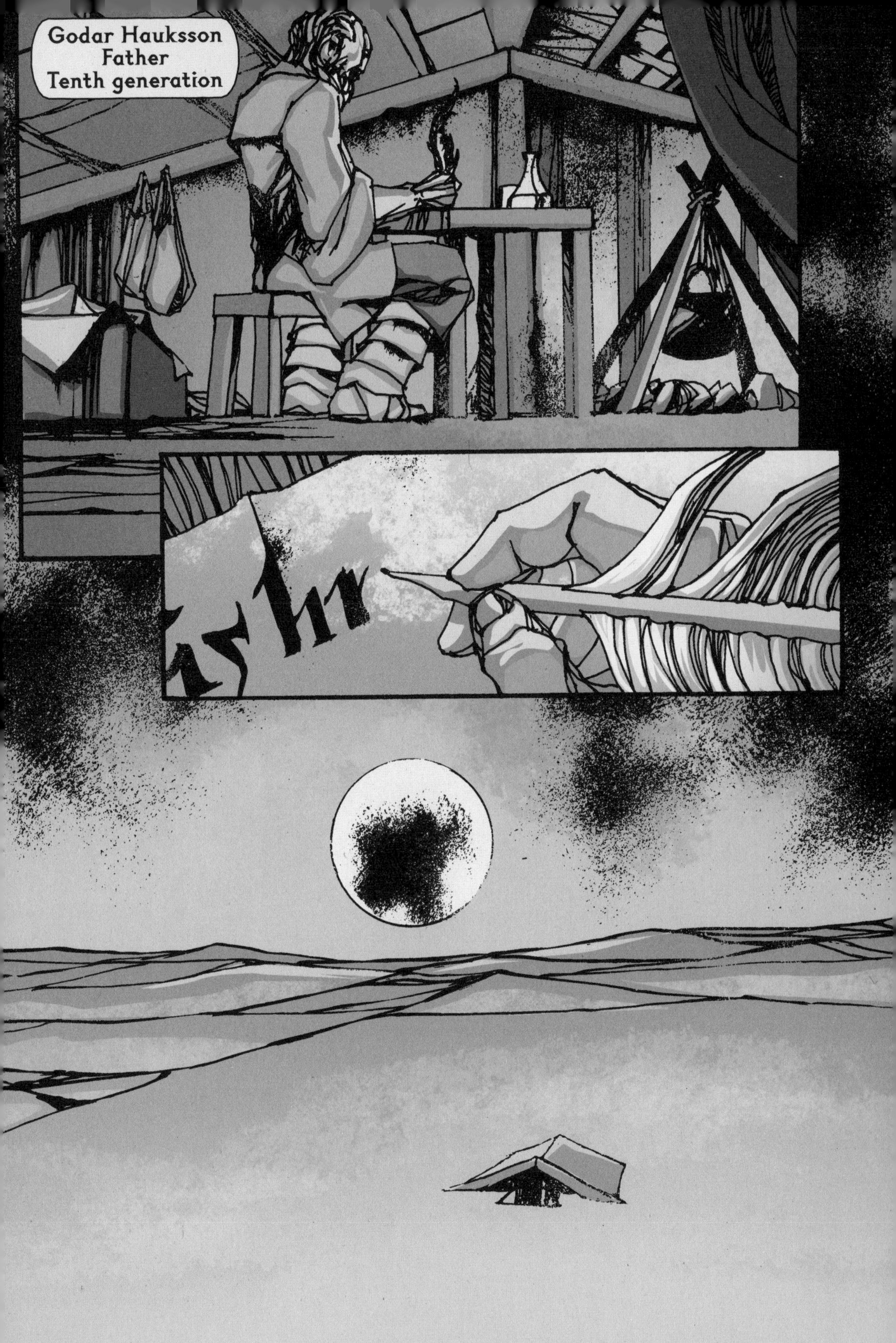
Godar Hauksson
Father
Tenth generation

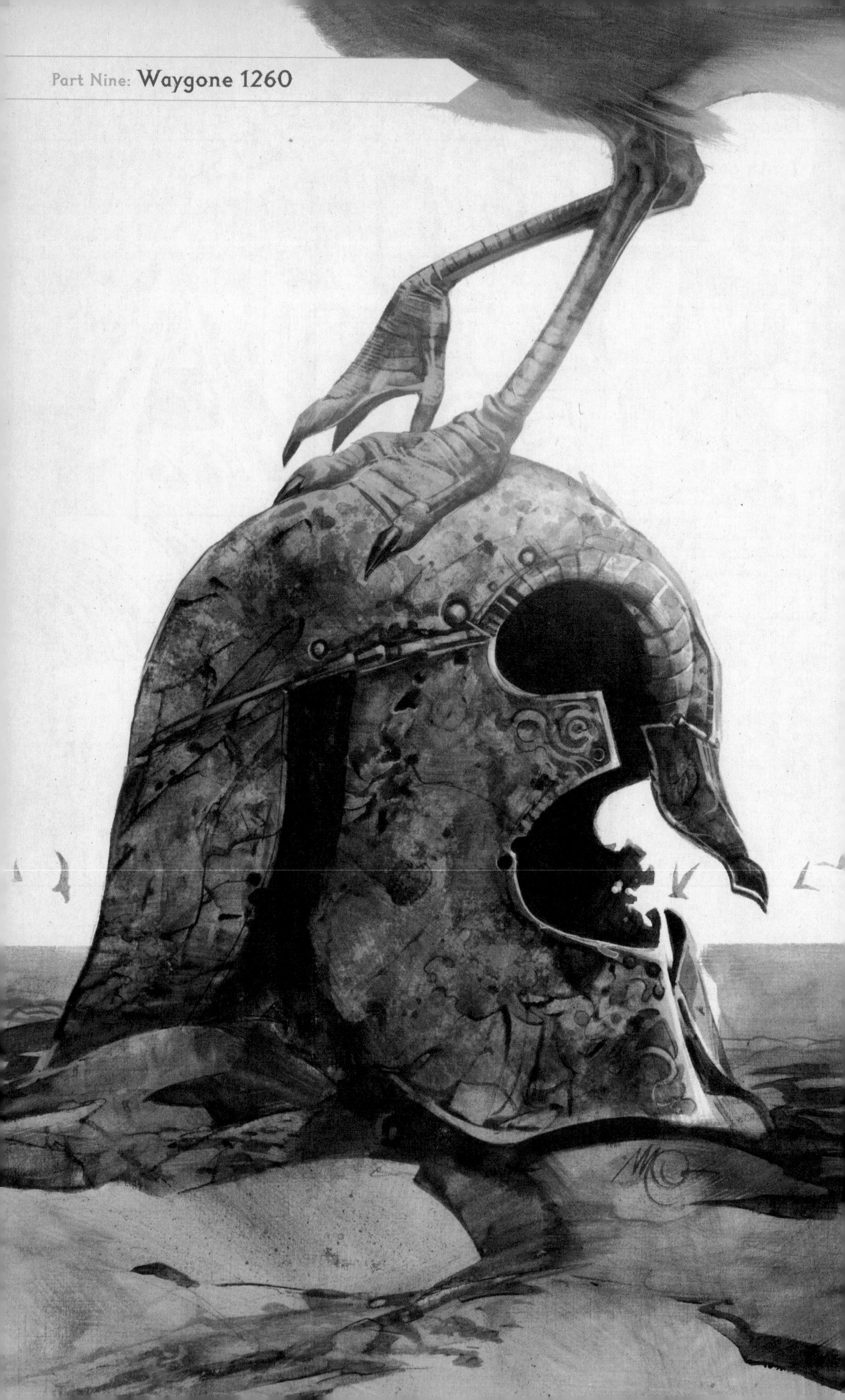

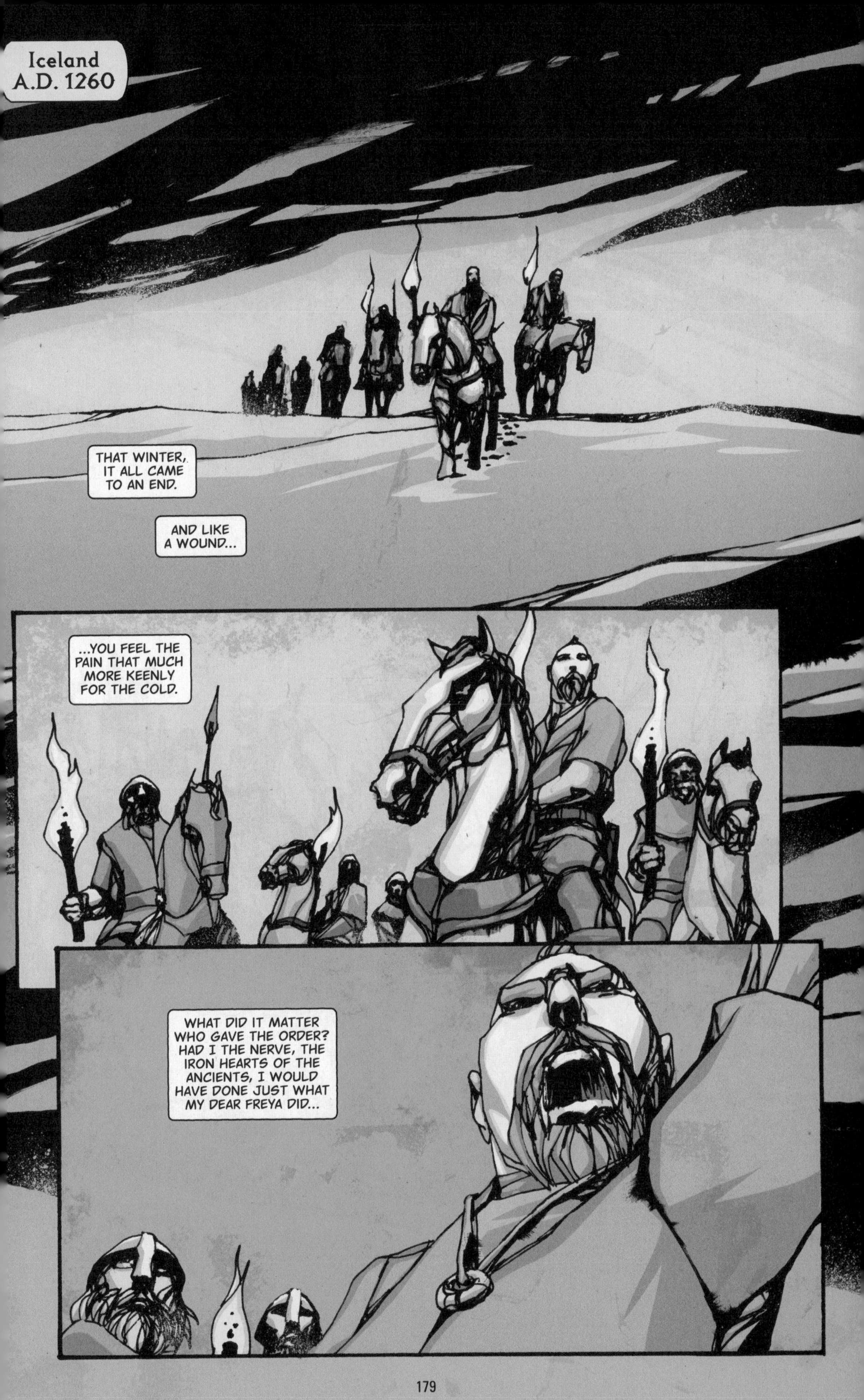
Iceland
A.D. 1260
THAT WINTER, IT ALL CAME TO AN END.
AND LIKE A WOUND...
...YOU FEEL THE PAIN THAT MUCH MORE KEENLY FOR THE COLD.
WHAT DID IT MATTER WHO GAVE THE ORDER? HAD I THE NERVE, THE IRON HEARTS OF THE ANCIENTS, I WOULD HAVE DONE JUST WHAT MY DEAR FREYA DID...

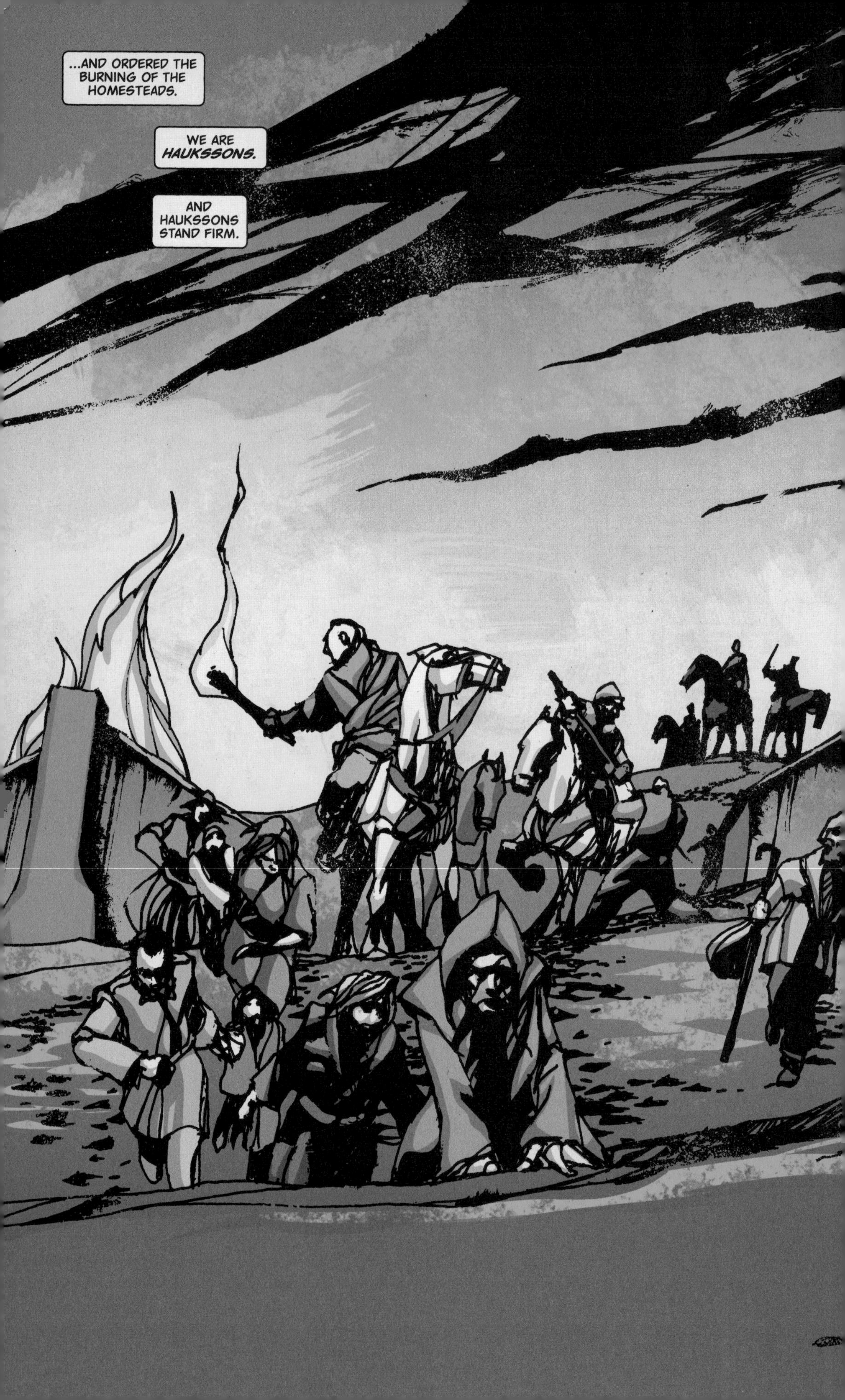
...AND ORDERED THE BURNING OF THE HOMESTEADS.
WE ARE *HAUKSSONS.*
AND HAUKSSONS STAND FIRM.

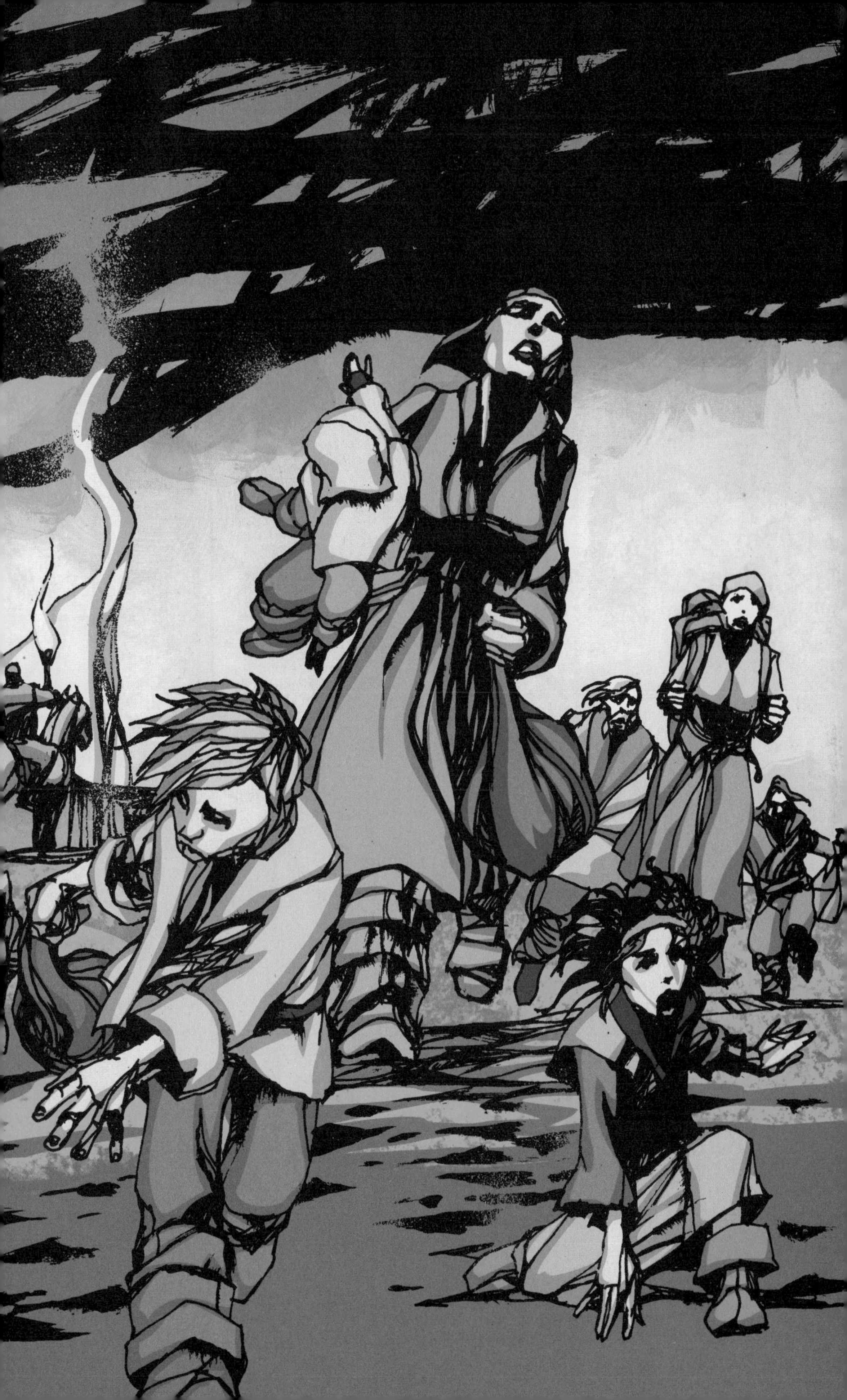

The Hauksson Family Compound

TO *OBEY* ORDERS.

YOU ASK THEM TO MAKE THEIR PARENTS AND GRANDPARENTS AND NEIGHBORS HOMELESS, LORD, AND BURN THEIR HOMES.

DISCUSSION IS IRRELEVANT, LORD. IT HAS HAPPENED. THE MEN HAVE CEASED THAT WORK AND ARE NOW OUTSIDE WITH THE REST OF THE GUARD, BUILDING DEFENSES.

YOU TALK LIKE A LOAD OF SHIT, MAN...

...I SHOULD CARVE THAT INSOLENT TONE OUT OF YOU WITH A *KNIFE*...

...THE MEN DID WHAT?

THEY REFUSED, LORD. YOU HAVE TO UNDERSTAND, THEY COME FROM THE HOMESTEADS...

...AND YOU ASK THEM TO--

LORD, NO NEED FOR ANY OF THAT.

IN THIS DIRE TIME, I FELT...

...I FELT *DIRECTNESS* WAS THE BEST WAY TO SERVE YOU.

YOU--

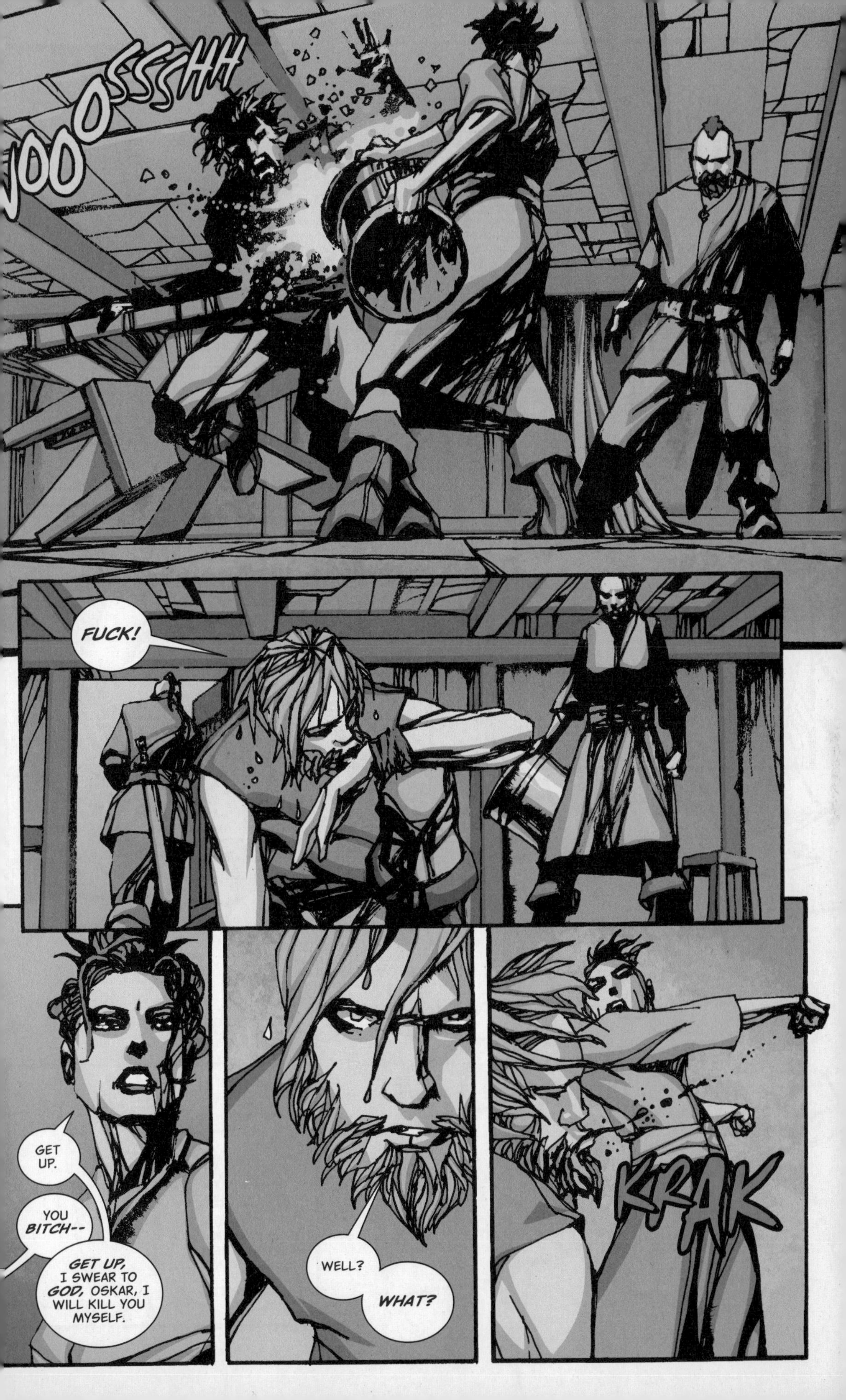
WOOOSSSHH
FUCK!
GET UP.
YOU BITCH--
GET UP, I SWEAR TO GOD, OSKAR, I WILL KILL YOU MYSELF.
WELL?
WHAT?
KRAK

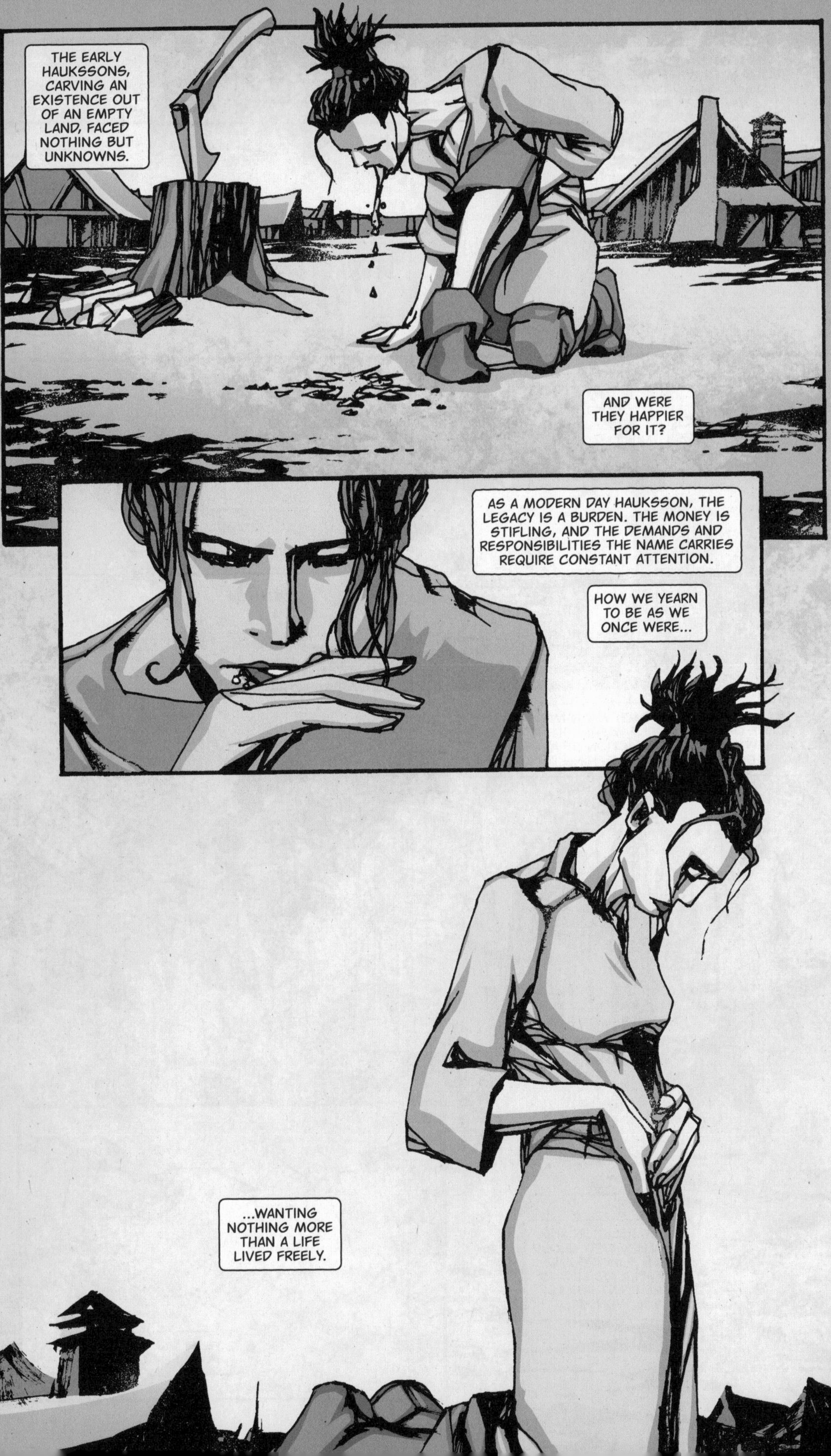
THE EARLY HAUKSSONS, CARVING AN EXISTENCE OUT OF AN EMPTY LAND, FACED NOTHING BUT UNKNOWNS.
AND WERE THEY HAPPIER FOR IT?
AS A MODERN DAY HAUKSSON, THE LEGACY IS A BURDEN. THE MONEY IS STIFLING, AND THE DEMANDS AND RESPONSIBILITIES THE NAME CARRIES REQUIRE CONSTANT ATTENTION.
HOW WE YEARN TO BE AS WE ONCE WERE...
...WANTING NOTHING MORE THAN A LIFE LIVED FREELY.

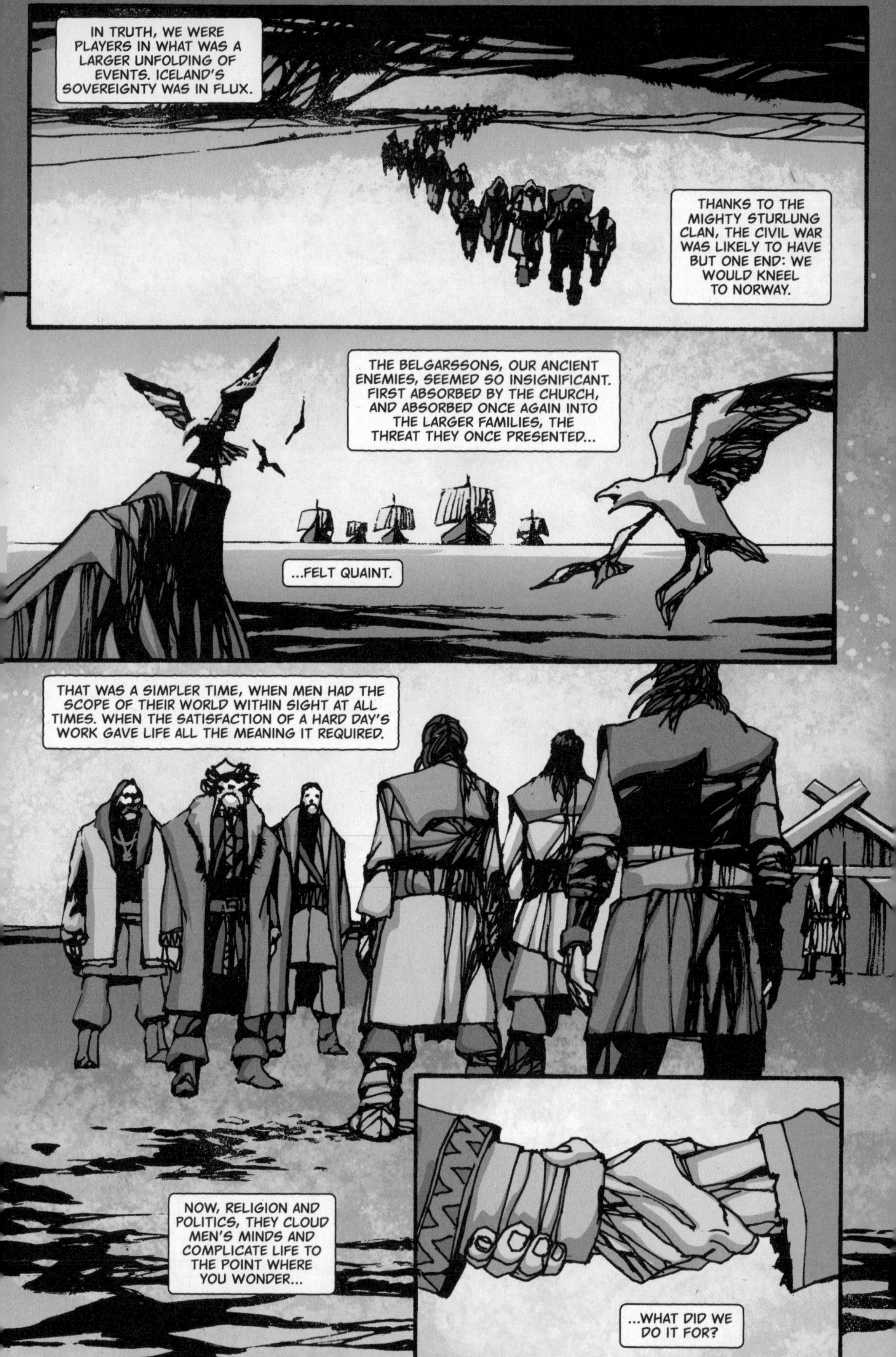
IN TRUTH, WE WERE PLAYERS IN WHAT WAS A LARGER UNFOLDING OF EVENTS. ICELAND'S SOVEREIGNTY WAS IN FLUX.
THANKS TO THE MIGHTY STURLUNG CLAN, THE CIVIL WAR WAS LIKELY TO HAVE BUT ONE END: WE WOULD KNEEL TO NORWAY.
THE BELGARSSONS, OUR ANCIENT ENEMIES, SEEMED SO INSIGNIFICANT. FIRST ABSORBED BY THE CHURCH, AND ABSORBED ONCE AGAIN INTO THE LARGER FAMILIES, THE THREAT THEY ONCE PRESENTED...
...FELT QUAINT.
THAT WAS A SIMPLER TIME, WHEN MEN HAD THE SCOPE OF THEIR WORLD WITHIN SIGHT AT ALL TIMES. WHEN THE SATISFACTION OF A HARD DAY'S WORK GAVE LIFE ALL THE MEANING IT REQUIRED.
NOW, RELIGION AND POLITICS, THEY CLOUD MEN'S MINDS AND COMPLICATE LIFE TO THE POINT WHERE YOU WONDER...
...WHAT DID WE DO IT FOR?

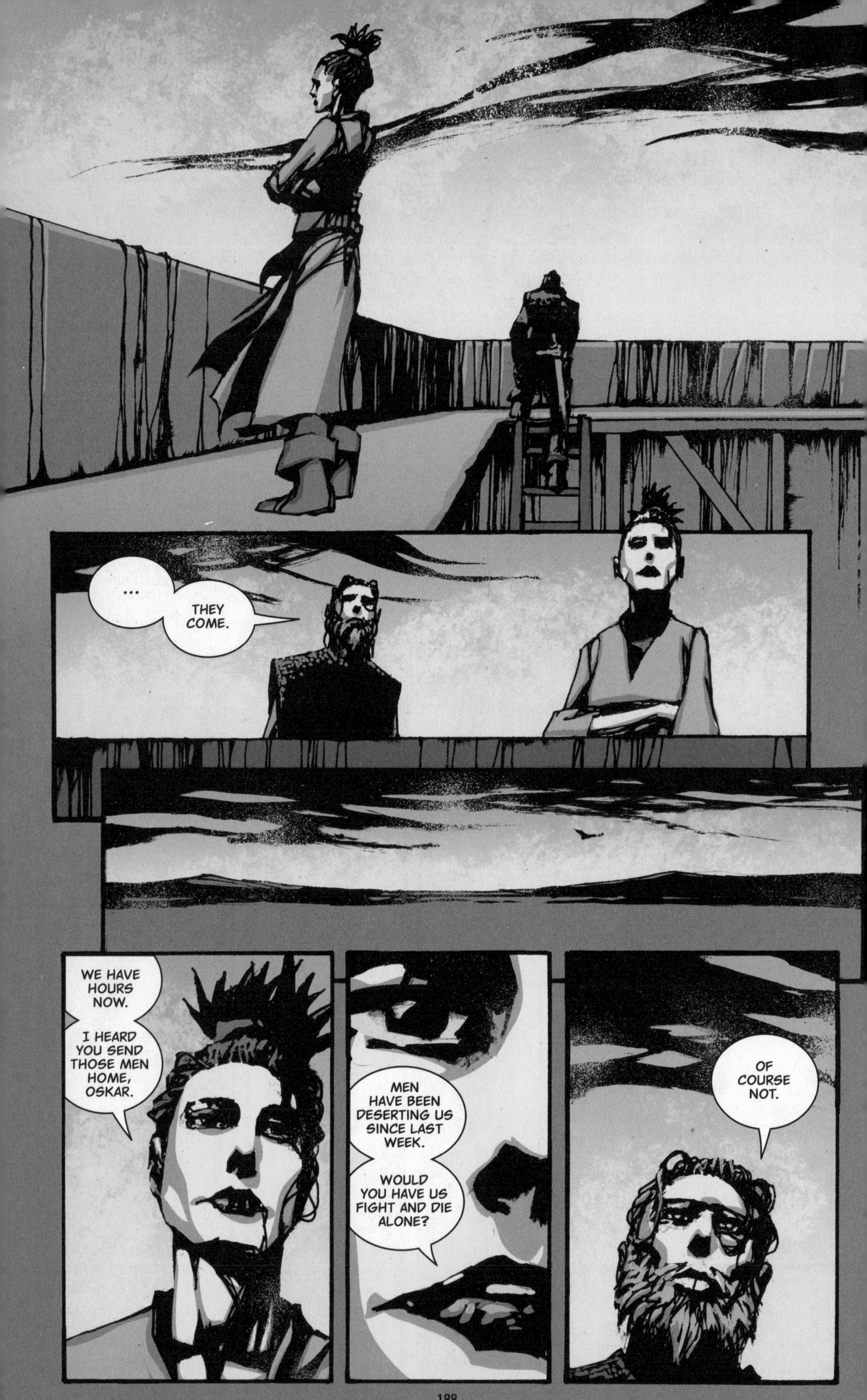
...
THEY COME.
WE HAVE HOURS NOW.
I HEARD YOU SEND THOSE MEN HOME, OSKAR.
MEN HAVE BEEN DESERTING US SINCE LAST WEEK.
WOULD YOU HAVE US FIGHT AND DIE ALONE?
OF COURSE NOT.

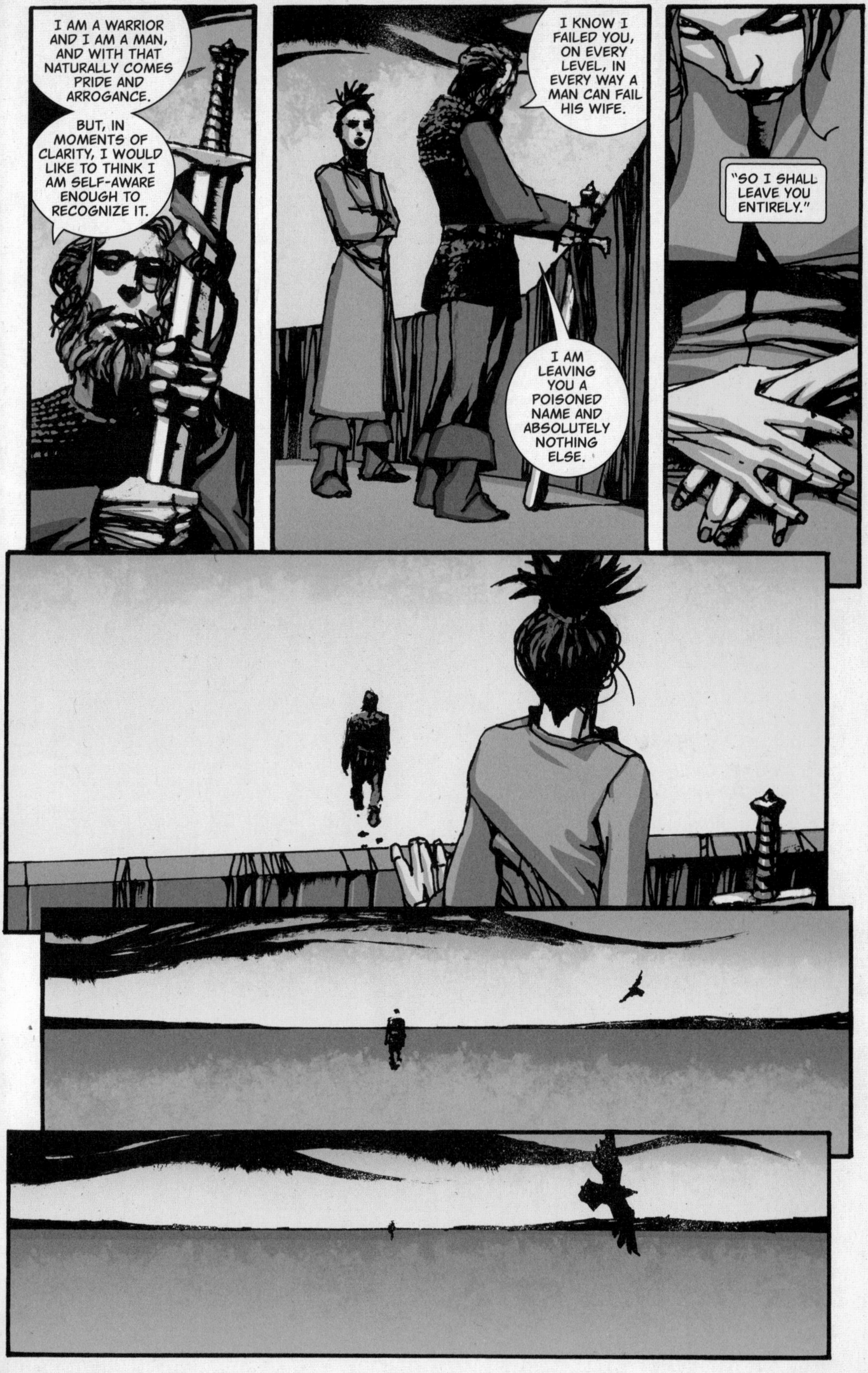
I AM A WARRIOR AND I AM A MAN, AND WITH THAT NATURALLY COMES PRIDE AND ARROGANCE.
BUT, IN MOMENTS OF CLARITY, I WOULD LIKE TO THINK I AM SELF-AWARE ENOUGH TO RECOGNIZE IT.
I KNOW I FAILED YOU, ON EVERY LEVEL, IN EVERY WAY A MAN CAN FAIL HIS WIFE.
I AM LEAVING YOU A POISONED NAME AND ABSOLUTELY NOTHING ELSE.
"SO I SHALL LEAVE YOU ENTIRELY."

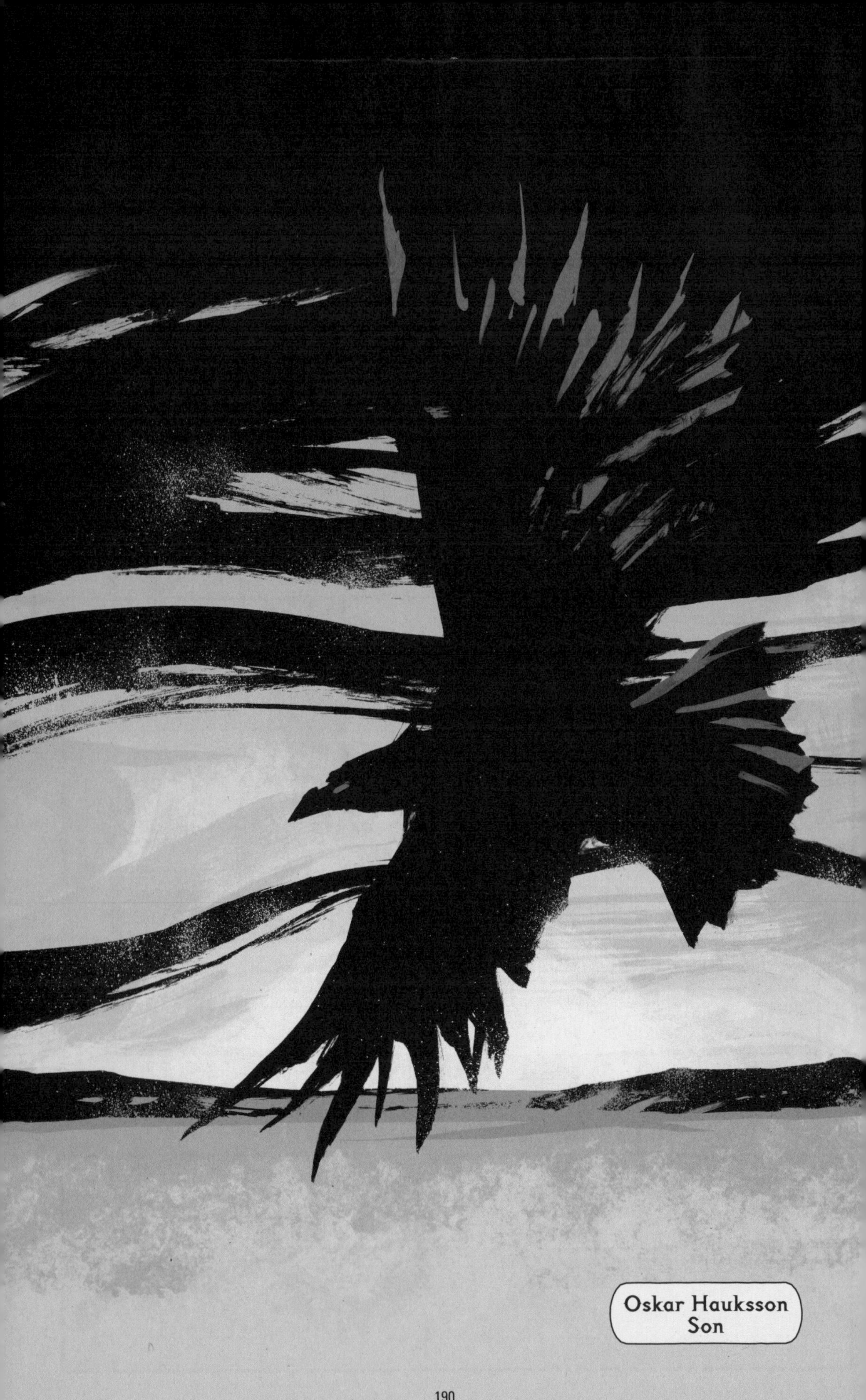
Oskar Hauksson
Son

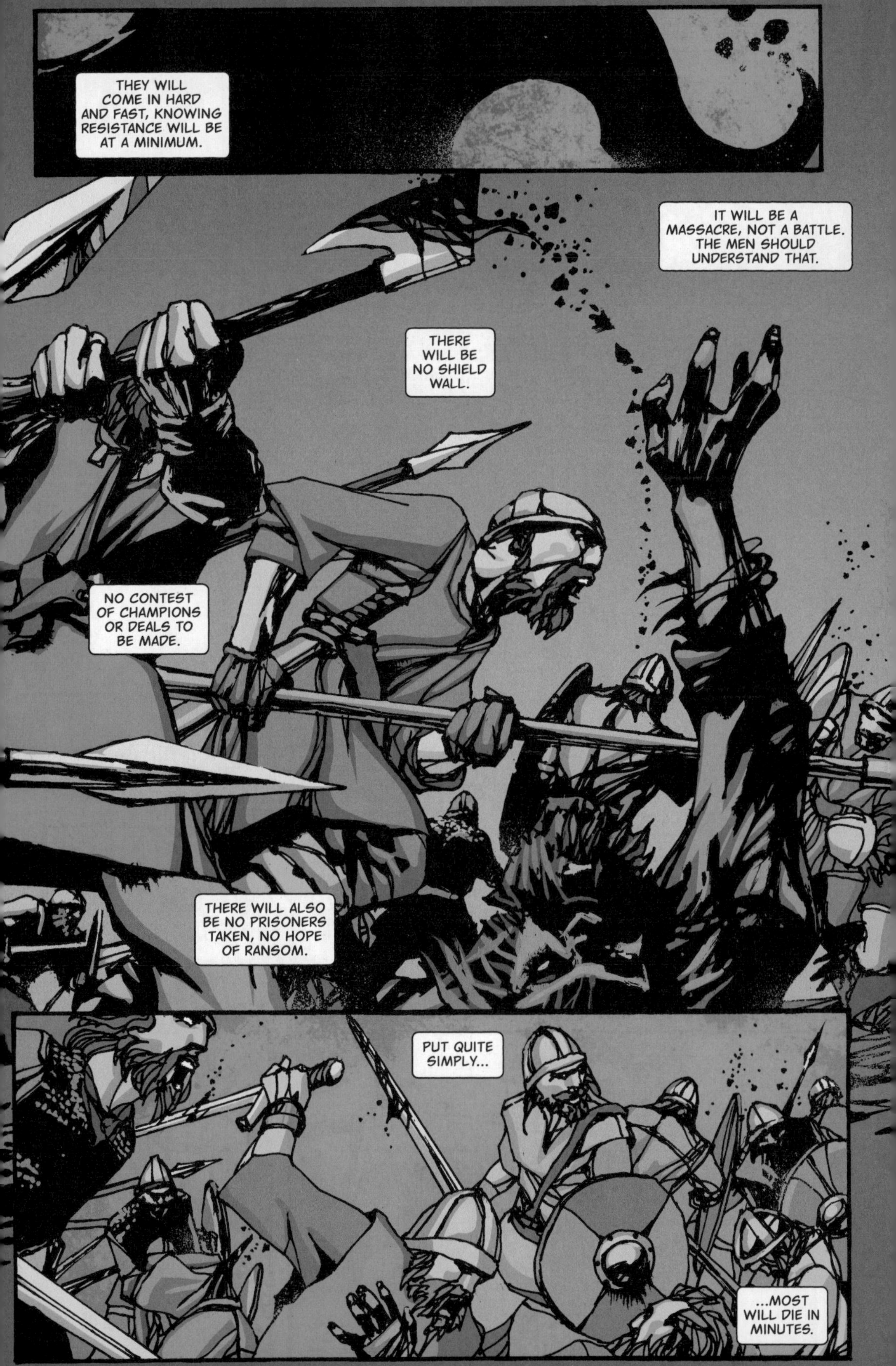
THEY WILL COME IN HARD AND FAST, KNOWING RESISTANCE WILL BE AT A MINIMUM.
IT WILL BE A MASSACRE, NOT A BATTLE. THE MEN SHOULD UNDERSTAND THAT.
THERE WILL BE NO SHIELD WALL.
NO CONTEST OF CHAMPIONS OR DEALS TO BE MADE.
THERE WILL ALSO BE NO PRISONERS TAKEN, NO HOPE OF RANSOM.
PUT QUITE SIMPLY...
...MOST WILL DIE IN MINUTES.

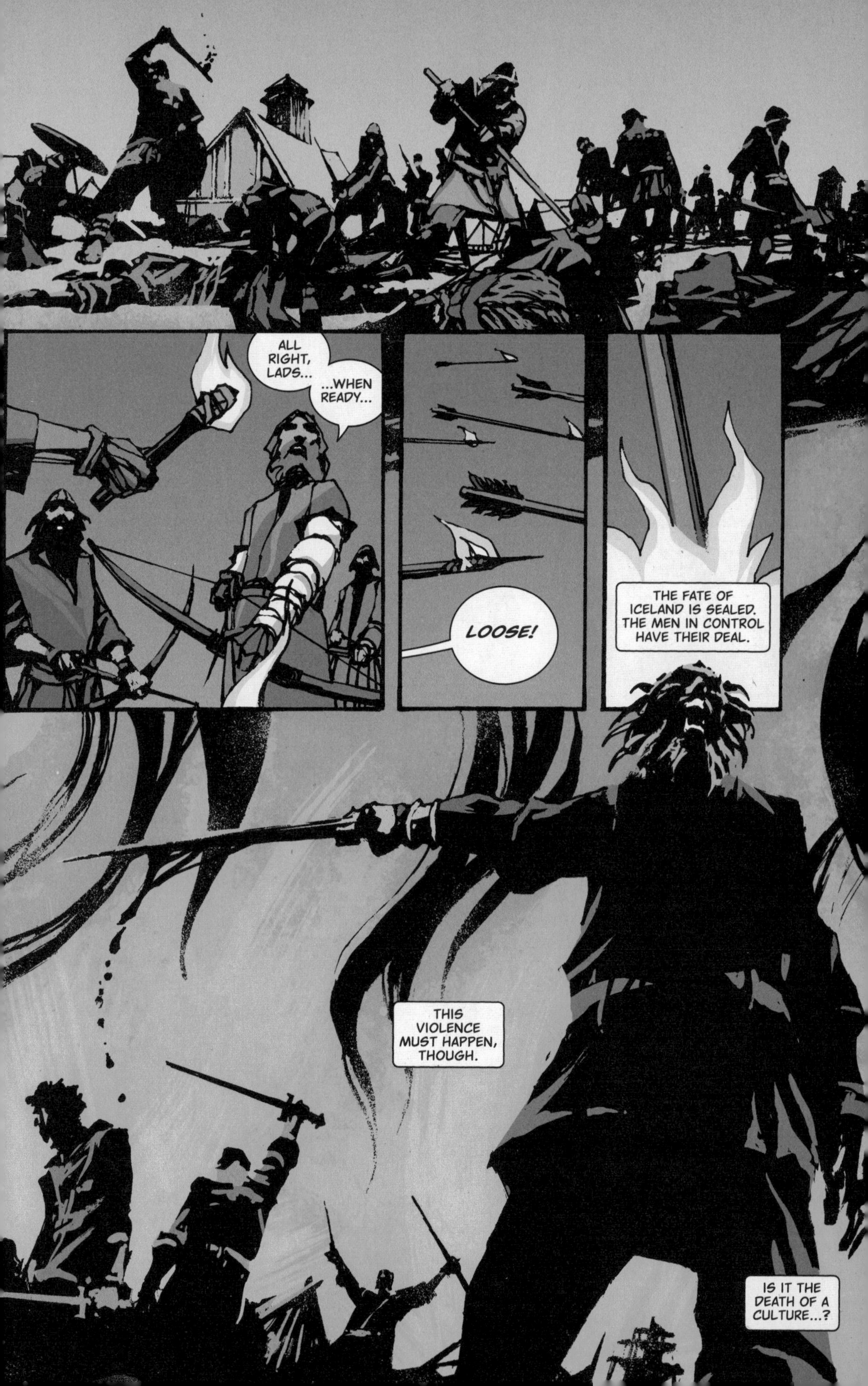
ALL RIGHT, LADS...
...WHEN READY...
LOOSE!
THE FATE OF ICELAND IS SEALED. THE MEN IN CONTROL HAVE THEIR DEAL.
THIS VIOLENCE MUST HAPPEN, THOUGH.
IS IT THE DEATH OF A CULTURE...?

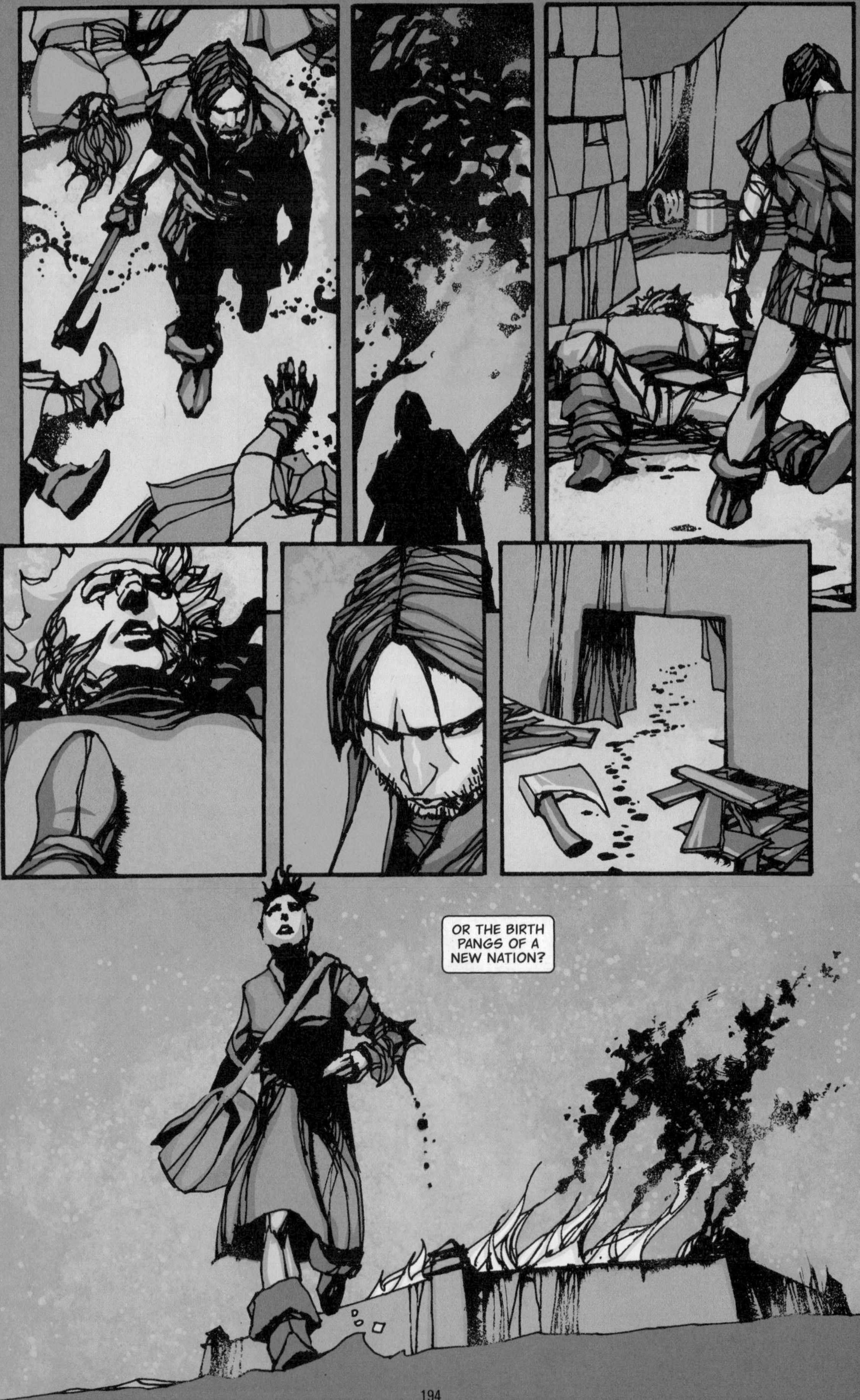
OR THE BIRTH PANGS OF A NEW NATION?

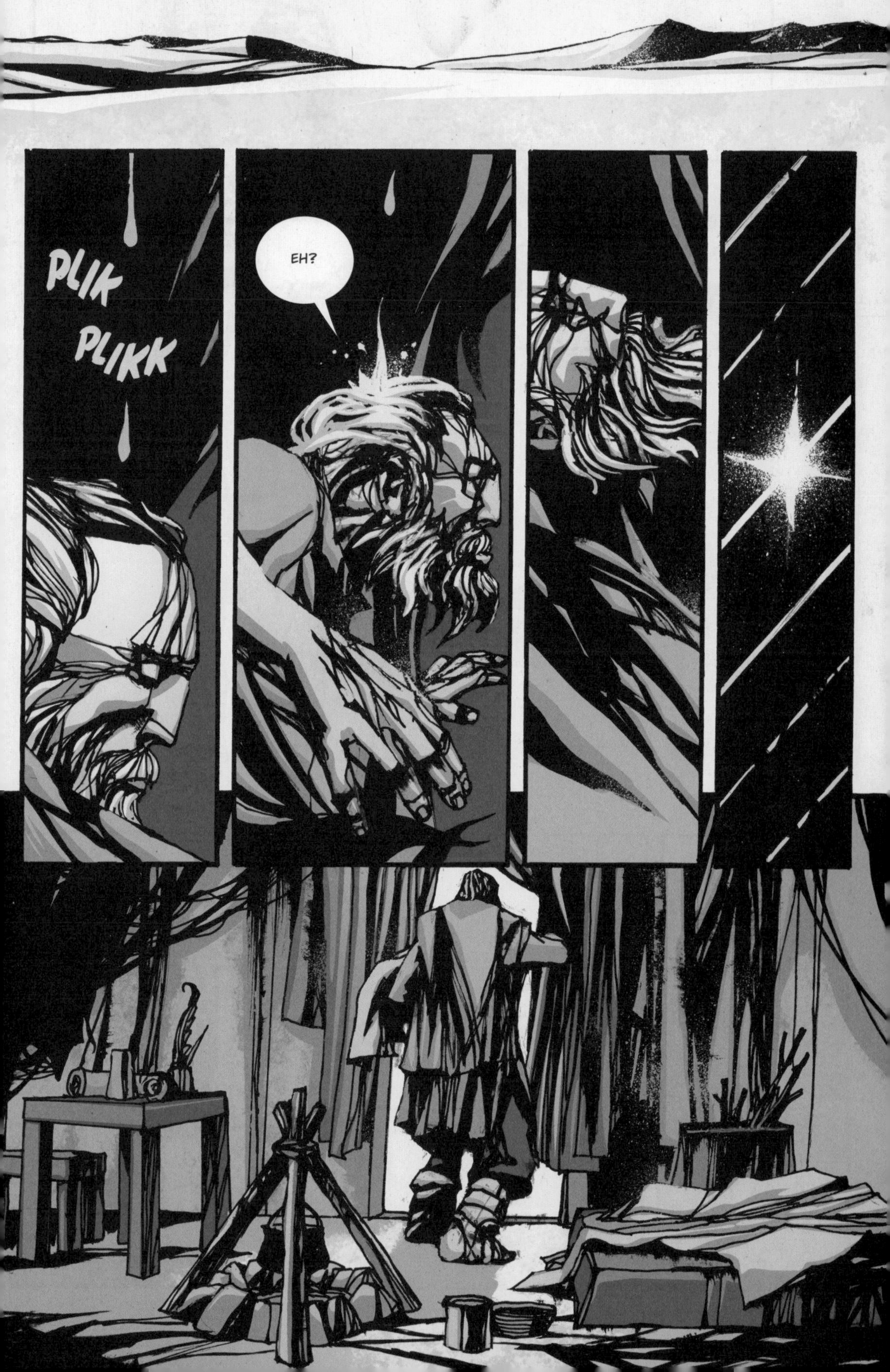
PLIK
PLIKK
EH?

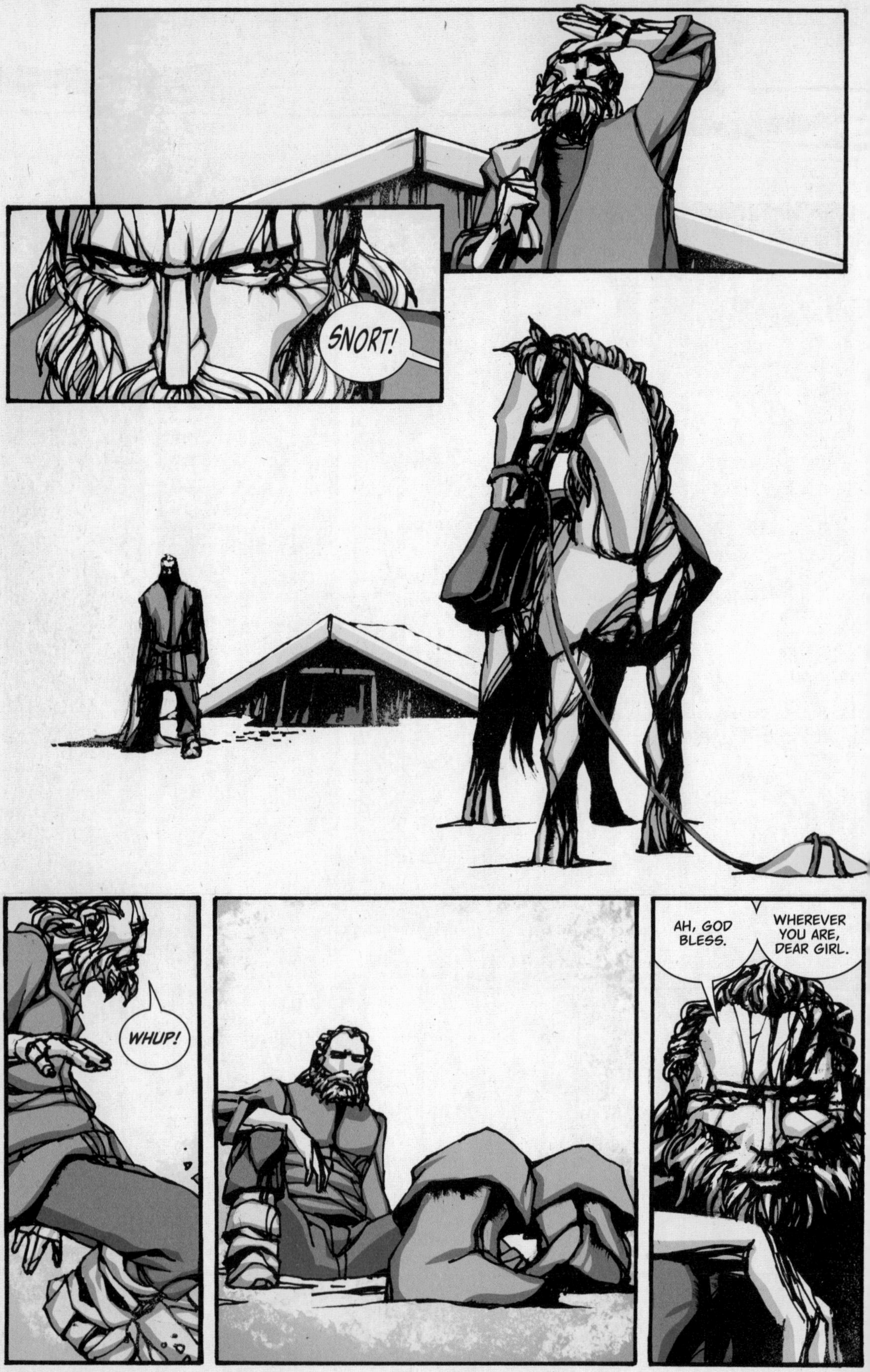
SNORT!
WHUP!
AH, GOD BLESS.
WHEREVER YOU ARE, DEAR GIRL.

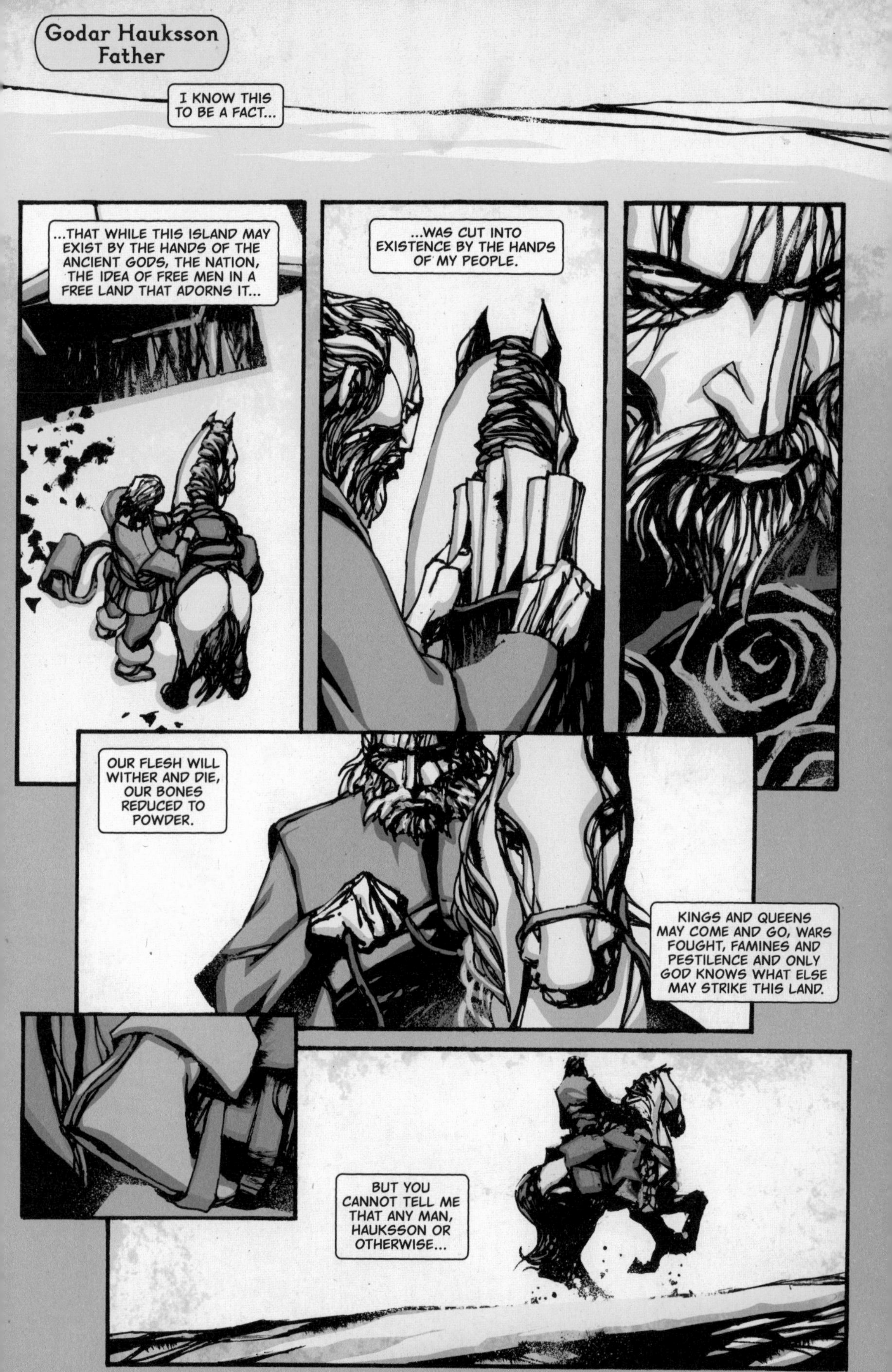
Godar Hauksson
Father
I KNOW THIS TO BE A FACT...
...THAT WHILE THIS ISLAND MAY EXIST BY THE HANDS OF THE ANCIENT GODS, THE NATION, THE IDEA OF FREE MEN IN A FREE LAND THAT ADORNS IT...
...WAS CUT INTO EXISTENCE BY THE HANDS OF MY PEOPLE.
OUR FLESH WILL WITHER AND DIE, OUR BONES REDUCED TO POWDER.
KINGS AND QUEENS MAY COME AND GO, WARS FOUGHT, FAMINES AND PESTILENCE AND ONLY GOD KNOWS WHAT ELSE MAY STRIKE THIS LAND.
BUT YOU CANNOT TELL ME THAT ANY MAN, HAUKSSON OR OTHERWISE...

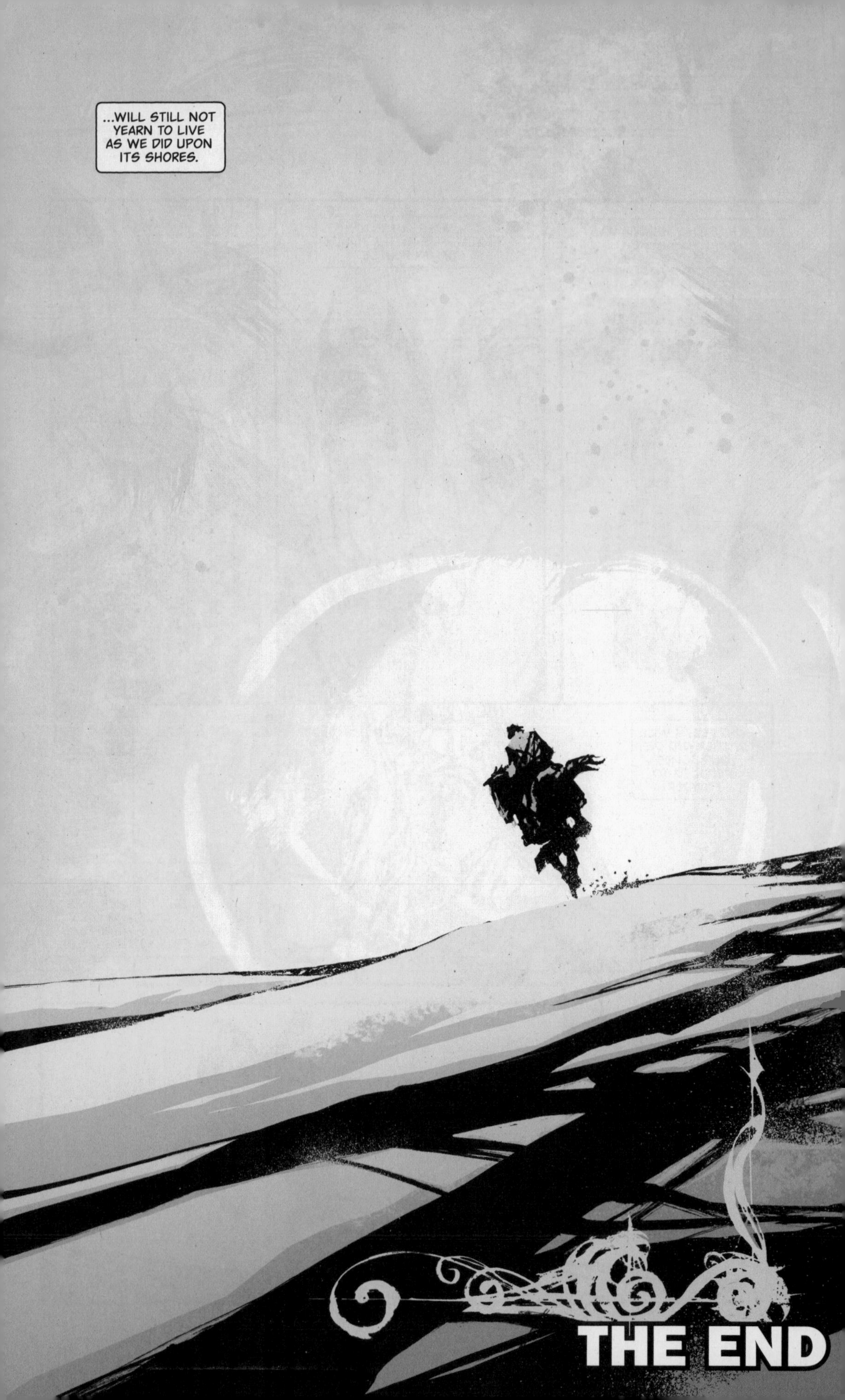
...WILL STILL NOT YEARN TO LIVE AS WE DID UPON ITS SHORES.
THE END

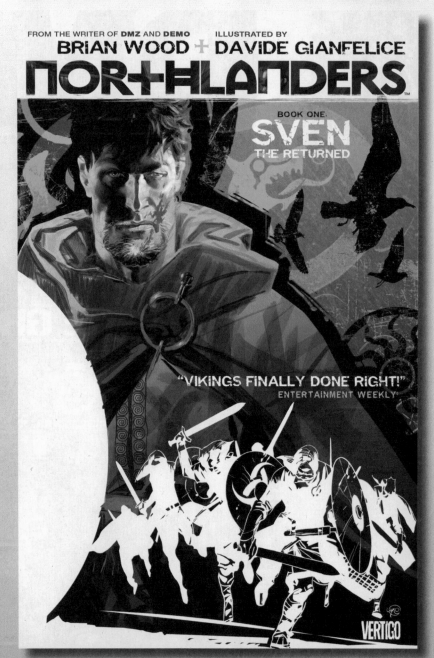

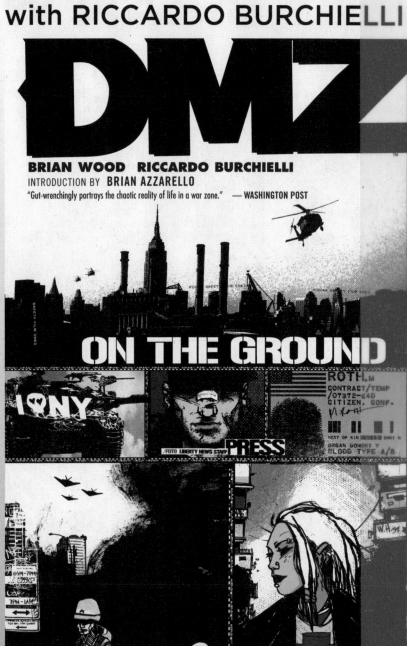